MEANING IN MOTION

Jane C. Desmond, editor

DUKE UNIVERSITY PRESS *Durham & London 1997*

in Motion

STUDIES of DANCE

Post-Contemporary Interventions *A series edited by Stanley Fish & Fredric Jameson*

Printed in the United States of America
on acid-free paper ∞
Typeset in Monotype Garamond by
Keystone Typsetting, Inc.
Library of Congress Cataloging-in-
Publication Data appear on the last
printed page of this book.

CONTENTS

ACKNOWLEDGMENTS

My thanks go first of all to the scholars who participated in this volume, and to the dancers who gave them so much to write about. My thanks also to Reynolds Smith, my editor at Duke University Press, who was enthusiastic about this project from the beginning and exhibited great patience in seeing it through its long development process. My research assistants at the University of Iowa, Ningping Yu, Hakan Dibel, Florence Tonk, and Sasha Su-Ling Welland, helped with the innumerable details it takes to get a manuscript to the publisher. I thank them for their persistence and gracious dispatch in everything from bibliographic searching to xeroxing. Thanks also to Charles Perrier, Nancy Stark Smith, and Urs Kaufmann for assistance in locating photographs.

The University of Iowa provided material support in the form of subvention funds and a developmental research leave with office space at the Obermann Center for Advance Studies, where I could work undisturbed, surrounded by cornfields. That work was immeasurably enriched by Virginia Domínguez's sustaining presence and intellectual stimulation. My gratitude goes to all those who over the years taught me to dance, to love dancing, and to think about it, and to all those who danced with me, on and off the stage.

This book is dedicated to my mother, Dorothy Ann Garfield Desmond, and to the memory of my father, Alton H. Desmond, both of whom always believed that dancers could think and thinkers could dance.

INTRODUCTION

The last decade has seen an explosion in critical dance scholarship. New work addresses issues of ideology, subjectivity, social categorization, representation, the production of "value" through aestheticized practices, and the disciplining of the body. This type of work represents a significant shift in the dance field. Up until the mid-1980s most dance scholarship consisted of historical narratives, aesthetic valuations, or auteur studies of great dancers or choreographers.[1] Many of these works are highly respected, indeed invaluable, contributions to dance history. But their main goals were to articulate aesthetic categories, to describe an ephemeral art form, or to provide a sense of the historical context in which certain forms flourished, not to investigate the operations of social power. Recent work, however, is beginning to foreground theoretical concerns which do focus on the ideological underpinnings of aesthetic practices. This work is engaged in dialogue with more established cultural studies scholarship on literature, popular culture, visual representation, and the media.

My immediate goal in bringing these essays together in one place is to facilitate and enhance the visibility of critical dance studies within the wider field of cultural studies. At the same time, I hope to make the increasingly influential cultural studies approaches within the dance field more easily available to dance scholars, thus encouraging further development of critically engaged scholarship.[2]

My longer-range goal is to put on the cultural studies agenda new questions and approaches regarding key concepts of embodiment, identity, and representation. Not only can the judicious adoption and adaptation of critical theory enable increasingly sophisticated and complex analyses of dance as a social practice; at the same time, the investigation of dance as an extremely underanalyzed bodily practice may challenge or extend dominant formulations of work on "the body." To date, some of the most influential of these formulations have focused on two- and three-dimensional visual representation (work on film, on visual arts) or on large-scale analyses of categories of subjectivity. In these works, the materiality of bodies and bodily movement can sometimes become paradoxically submerged. Dance, as an embodied social practice and highly visual aesthetic form, powerfully melds considerations of materiality and representation together. This is the productive interface of dance studies and cultural studies that this book seeks to make more visible and to encourage in the future.

In my essay "Embodying Difference: Issues in Dance and Cultural Studies," which opens this book and serves as a second introduction, I sketch out what I see as several productive arenas of investigation. I want to note briefly here some of those questions, along with several questions and concepts that arise in the other articles in this book and from the implicit conversations and productive critiques set up among them. These include: How does dance signal, enact, or rework social categories of identity? How do the meanings arising from the performance of various dance styles change as those styles migrate across national, racial, or class boundaries? Since dance takes the body as its primary medium, can it provide a potential utopian site for imagining what a feminist politics of the body might look like? How can dance analysis lead us toward a consideration of the vast range of social practices built on strictures of embodiment which form the tissue of everyday enactment, such as how we move in public, play sports, and communicate through an incredibly complex and undertheorized semiotics of the body? How are codified movement systems such as dance similar to or different from other forms of representation, such as language or visual representation? What is kinesthetic subjectivity? How does it shape and get shaped by other social formations of the self, and of communities? How and what do we come to know through kinesthesia as a historically particular register of meaning? How do we theorize it? How does it relate to visual perception and systems of visual representation?

Dance is both a product (particular dances as realized in production) and a process (dancing, and the historical conditions of possibility for the production and reception of such texts and processes, as well as their articulation in systems of value). How can we think about the relationships between processes and products—between when, where, and how we dance, with whom, under what conditions—and what gets danced, whether on the stage, in the street, or at a party? What are some of the relations between social dance practices and elite art products, for instance? How can such theorizations extend our understanding of the body in the production of pleasure in both elite and mass contexts? Obversely, what can such investigations tell us about the ways in which bodily meaning is constructed and enacted in other, supposedly separate, realms such as labor?

Looking at dance demands that we begin to find ways to talk about proprioception, sensation, emotion, and expressivity which lapse neither into the pretended objectivity of scientism nor the transcendent figurations of a unified "self." It demands that we theorize the relationships between the public display of bodily motion and the articulation of social categories of identity, of their transmission, transformation, perception, and enactment. These are some of the questions that dance studies can lead us into. They are based on the historical materiality of the body, and are thus questions which scholarship on visual representation in film or painting, or on narrative from literary studies, has not had to grapple with as consistently.[3] In addition, they call for an engagement with the tensions between the figurative and the abstract, and between the narrative and the nonnarrative. Taken together, all of these questions suggest an expanded agenda for dance studies and a significant contribution to the extension of cultural studies work on embodiment.

Before considering the contribution of each of the articles in detail, it is helpful to note how this particular conjuncture of cultural studies and dance studies has developed, and why it has taken so long to arrive.

The explosion of ideologically engaged dance studies began roughly in the mid-1980s as a group of scholars, many of them dancers, began to respond to the wave of influential transformations that had been reconfiguring the humanities during the preceding ten to fifteen years. The complexities of that epistemological history lie beyond the scope of these introductory remarks, but generally speaking during the postwar years one after another of the humanities disciplines (and to some extent social sciences) underwent a Kuhnian paradigm shift, buffeted and realigned in response to what became known variously as structuralism (building on the earlier work of Saussure) and then poststructuralism, sometimes referred to more generally as postmodern theory, or even simply as "Theory" with a capital "T." Under this rubric could be found various strains of feminist theories, of deconstruction, of Marxism as influenced by Gramsci, Althusser, and others, as well as the powerful discourse studies of Michel Foucault, and varieties of psychoanalytic-based analyses.

The excavatory practices of New Criticism, which sought to uncover meaning "in" the text itself, and the search for foundations promised by structuralism, gave way to intense engagement with the conditions of production and reception of cultural artifacts and practices. This emphasis was not just on social context, but on the historical contingency of forms, practices, and meanings, and their simultaneously formative and interrogatory relationship to the construction of subjectivity. The pervasive emphasis on the discursive aspects of texts and practices, on social construction and representation, meant that issues of ideology and of political economies of social distinctions came to the fore.

In the United States, literary studies emerged as the key player in this realm, enhancing its territory rapidly while expanding the notion of "text" and "textuality" to include hitherto devalued realms of popular culture, like comic books, science fiction, and various types of visual representations such as photographs. Film studies, propelled by the prominence of the British cultural studies group associated with the Birmingham School as well as the elaboration of psychoanalytic theory, facilitated the investigation of visual texts. Art history followed suit more slowly, as did portions of anthropology.[4] In general, the performing arts have come last to these debates, reflecting to different degrees the logocentrism of predominant paradigms and the differential histories of these departments within U.S. university hierarchies.[5] Performing arts scholarship that emphasizes aesthetic evaluation in transcendental terms, or confines its task to reconstructing what "really" happened in linear historical narrative is still often the norm. However, there is ample evidence that this is changing.[6] Recent collections published in the early 1990s chart the emergence in the mid-to-late eighties and early nineties of cultural studies in theater and, to a lesser degree, in musicology.[7] While dance rarely figures into those discussions, the scholarship paves the way for further expansion of critical studies in performance and provides an important interlocutory body of work for dance scholars.

Two key developments in cultural studies have prepared the way for these latest developments in dance scholarship. The current fascination with ideas of "performativity" and the rapidity with which such concepts have been embraced by some circles of cultural studies scholars (who follow the work of Judith Butler, Eve Sedgwick, and others)[8] is a boon to dance scholarship. It provides a new welcoming arena for entry into the debates, and an opportunity for the specificity of dance research and the tools already developed within dance scholarship to contribute to these debates in cultural studies. The last decade's emphasis on "the body" across many disciplines[9] similarly has provided not only interlocutory scholarship for dance scholars to work with but also a climate in which dance studies can now flourish as a part of wider and widely cross-disciplinary agendas for debate in the humanities.[10]

As the preceding brief tracing of intellectual developments shows, *cultural studies* is a loose term that indicates a shared community of scholarly endeavor across a multiplicity of fields, formats, and theoretical approaches.[11] In using the term here I mean to indicate both the (productive) lack of cohesion in this antidisciplinary discourse community and the shared sense of political engagement that the term connotes. As Stuart Hall reminds us, "Cultural studies is not one thing, it has never been one thing." Yet cultural studies scholars share, as Grossberg, Nelson, and Treichler have noted, "a commitment to examining cultural practices from the point of view of their intrication with, and within relations of power . . . to theorize and grasp the mutual determinations and interrelations of cultural forms and historical forces."[12] The range of methodologies and theoretical approaches used to perform this sort of analysis are wide ranging, at times even perceived as contradictory. For example, Marxists may criticize proponents of psychoanalysis for a perceived ahistoricity, while feminists criticize Marxists for ignoring the importance that gender plays in the operations of class. Each of these intellectual traditions, though, may offer something of use to dance scholars, and in turn may be reshaped by an encounter with dance as the object or social practice under investigation.

This volume does not attempt to provide a description of these "isms" (Marxism, deconstructionism, etc.) with sample analyses arrayed for each one. Instead, I hope to show the ways in which key concepts, debates, and problematics are emerging at the interface of cultural studies and dance studies in the United States. While this book makes no claims to be comprehensive, it does represent some of the most important issues animating contemporary writing on dance. Many of these essays appear in print for the first time. Others originally appeared in journals read primarily either by dance scholars or by cultural-studies/literary theorists, and they bear the traces of their origins in terms of style and tone of address. The readerships of these journals rarely overlap. On the whole, dance scholars rarely read *Social Text*, for instance, which first published Randy Martin's essay. Similarly, few subscribers to *Social Text* also get *Dance Chronicle*, the first home of Evan Alderson's piece. In each case, I felt the reprinted essays deserved a wider "cross-over" audience and the chance to comment upon each other.

The essays in this book are gathered into three parts: "Dance and Cultural Studies"; "Social Lives, Social Bodies"; and "Expanding Agendas for Critical Thinking." Within these loose groupings, they are also arranged by overlapping concerns. This arrangement provides readers with a sense of the resonance of neighboring essays. For instance, Susan Kozel's piece picks up on themes introduced by Janet Wolff in the preceding piece, and Amy Koritz's work is discussed by Susan Manning. But these linkings are by no means designed to be exclusionary. Many essays could have easily been placed in other pairings or another section altogether due to the complex social practices they investigate. The groupings are meant to function more like a lively exchange at a dinner table where small conversational subgroups emerge while continuing to maintain their part in the conversation as a whole. Readers are urged to make their own productive pairings and to insert themselves in these conversations at will, reading across sectional divisions.

In part I, "Dance and Cultural Studies," Norman Bryson and I each issue a call for increased engagement between cultural studies and dance scholarship and trace what we envision to be some of the intellectual payoffs. My essay primarily addresses cultural studies theorists and charts some of the disciplinary history sketched above but in greater detail. I then consider the theoretical challenges that arise when we look at cultural appropriation dialectically, charting the migration of bodily movement styles across class, racial, or national boundaries, and the resulting new economies of representation. I consider contemporary social, commercial, and theatrical dance styles, from ballet to hip hop to tango, drawing examples from the United States, Latin America, and China.

In a related piece, art historian Norman Bryson primarily addresses his remarks to dance historians and draws his examples from the court of Louis XIV and European modernism. In this subtle essay, Bryson makes a persuasive case for enlarging dance research to include potentially all forms of structured movement, the choreographic nature of daily life which functions as a "theater of power."[13] Previous work in dance ethnology has been one arena where such investigations have been pursued.[14] But here Bryson demonstrates the usefulness of approaches developed in art history, film, and comparative literature. To illustrate his claims, he offers two examples. The first uses the court of Versailles as a site to examine the way dancing and deportment were not peripheral to the operation of power but central to its announcement and maintenance. A second example considers nineteenth-century Paris and "the connections that dance history might make between forms of dance . . . and issues of spectatorship, modernity, and sexuality in the wider context of urban life." Arguing that the dancer "figured forth, in intense and specialized form, the essential social relation of observer to observed" during that modernist period, Bryson makes clear the value of such intertextual dance research not only to dance historians but also to scholars in other disciplines concerned with similar questions of cultural articulation and change.[15]

The nine pieces in part II, "Social Lives, Social Bodies," take on a number of the issues articulated in the opening essays. Each of these grapples with the complexities of an "aesthetic" practice which is at once social, historically specific, and grounded in the lived experiences of embodiment of both the performers and spectators. Each broadens the scope of dance history and dance analysis beyond formalist concerns or social contextualization to a deeper theorization of how social meanings emerge and are constituted and contested through dance practices and institutions.

The large number of these essays drawing heavily on feminist theories indicates the centrality of the display of the female body in dance practices. It is also indicative of the immense impact feminist work has had on new dance scholarship, having recently spawned the first books devoted solely to the subject of dance and gender[16] and providing the focus for a national conference.[17] Within feminist dance scholarship, the examination of Euro-American forms of ballet and modern dance has proliferated most rapidly. The first four articles in this section concentrate on those forms.

Just as feminist theories have moved in the last decade away from a unidimensional analytic frame to see gender in relation to many other salient social categories, so too do these discussions already lead us to considerations of nationality, race, sexuality, and class and their interaction. These intersections are activated not only via theatrical dance forms like ballet and modern dance, but also through popular forms of social dance and commercial dance, from country and western line dancing to MTV videos and Coke commercials. They inscribe, too, the writing of dance criticism and the act of choreography. A number of the essays in this section investigate these complex linkages of social lives and social bodies across a wide range of styles, practices, and time periods.

In the opening essay of "Social Lives, Social Bodies," Janet Wolff suggests that dance may help us imagine a feminist politics of the body for the future. Discussing feminist theories of Kristeva, Irigaray, Cixous, Gross, and others, she sketches the tensions between maintaining a politically effective sense of a category of "women" while skirting the quicksand of bodily essentialism. How, she asks, can we recognize and theorize the discursive construction of the body while simultaneously emphasizing its lived experience and materiality? As a way of moving forward from the potential impasse of essentialist/constructivist polarities, Wolff proposes dance as a "site for a radical cultural politics." The challenge for feminist theorists and artists, she argues, is how to "engage in a critical politics of the body, in a culture which so comprehensively codes and defines women's bodies as subordinate and passive, and as objects of the male gaze." Wolff suggests that postmodern dance, which takes the body as its primary medium and yet, at the same time, "disrupts and subverts existing regimes of representation," can provide a model of feminist art-making and theory-making as well.

Like Wolff, Susan Kozel looks to the dancing body as a potential site for the generation of new, radical representations of a feminist vision. Comparing the strategies of mimesis offered by feminist theorist Luce Irigaray and contemporary German choreographer Pina Bausch, Kozel argues that a reading of the work of each can illuminate that of the other. Irigaray and Bausch share a conception of mimesis not as simple imitation but as a principle of analogy which always yields an excess, something more than that which is re-presented. In this repetition, which is never complete, never exact, always distorted, lies the possibility of change, of revealing a representational frame while stepping outside it. This excess provides what Kozel terms "the hope for regeneration," for the emergence of new symbolic structures.

For both Bausch and Irigaray, notes Kozel, time, space, fluidity, and desire are significant elements in their mimetic strategy. For example, setting her works on a stageful of water or dirt, Bausch denaturalizes the category of "the natural" by putting it in a theatrical frame. Similarly, she blurs the distinction between "theatrical" and "everyday" gestures and uses filmic devices like montage and cross-fades to unsettle the time-space continuum of the performers and audience members. Kozel traces the links between Irigaray's concepts of mimesis and Bausch's staging of desire, physicality, and subjectivity, which functions not just to expose the "power relations between men and women, but the entire web of conventions and representations which shape us." Although some critics have charged Bausch with essentialism in her portrayal of a male/female binary, Kozel argues that, like Irigaray, Bausch is really participating in the creation of a new symbolic, a new "junction of body, psyche, and language."

And turning the relationship around, Kozel asserts that reading Irigaray through Bausch further illuminates the French theorist's work, revealing Irigaray's physical metaphors as both a strength and a limitation. Ultimately, Irigaray remains trapped within language, Kozel argues, and is "less concerned with the actual physical body than she is with the expansion of linguistic and symbolic structure which the movement of the body inspires." Kozel's work demonstrates the power of reading dance texts and feminist philosophical texts through each other, using their points of convergence around issues of the body to pry open our understanding of each while dissolving the false divide of "theory" and "practice."

The next two essays turn to ballet. Reprinted here, Ann Daly's "Classical Ballet: A Discourse of Difference" and Evan Alderson's "Ballet as Ideology: *Giselle*, Act 2" are pathbreaking pieces, among the first to foreground so clearly the centrality of notions of a "feminine" in classical ballets that remain immensely popular today. Succinctly yet persuasively Daly traces the "inscription of gender difference as an aesthetic virtue" throughout the course of ballet history, arguing that "these differences have been an unabashed hallmark of classical ballet at every level: costuming, body image, movement vocabulary, training, technique, narrative, and especially the pas de deux structure." Although the terms of valorization may shift from period to period, ballet from the eighteenth century through the twentieth remains heavily indebted for its production of pleasure to this bipolarity of difference.

Evan Alderson asks why we still find nineteenth-century ballets, with their ethereal dematerialization of the female body and an erotics of unattainable desire, so compelling. In other words, what can the continued programming of such a "classic" by ballet companies all over the world reveal about the ways in which its imaginary is still resonant? And for whom? Alderson relates his own moment of self-estrangement when he realized he "had been hooked on the point of [his] own desire" while watching the still popular 1841 ballet *Giselle*. His pleasure in the second act's alchemy of "longing, purity, beauty, and death" serves as a starting point for his theorizations. Alderson argues that such a "feeling of 'rightness' in a work of art also acts as a persuasion." By assenting to, and taking pleasure in, particular dominant notions of what is "beautiful," the individual spectator is situated in and supports an already existing social order.

Drawing on a Marxist framework, Alderson notes that ideological formations are projected in and through "aesthetic" value, and not apart from it, as proponents of timelessness would have it. *Giselle*'s presentation of a romantic ideal of femininity coincided with the rise of the bourgeoisie and as such bound up conceptions of beauty with ideals suitable to that social class. While such political analyses of canon formation are well under way in neighboring disciplines, historical dance studies often reproduce a "master works" and "masters" orientation that leaves such underlying issues untouched. Even though Alderson's emphasis here is on ideologies of gender, his Althusserian framing of the discussion in terms of the social production of the category "art" provides a useful invitation to those interested in class analysis as well. This area is not yet very developed in critical dance studies, but deserves a great deal more attention.

Like Alderson, Amy Koritz also investigates how the meanings of art practices and the pleasures they produce are shaped by dominant discourses in the time and place of their reception. She considers the enormous popularity in England of American dancer Maud Allan in the early 1900s and her notorious depiction of *The Vision of Salome*. Drawing on the work of Edward Said on Orientalism and Homi Bhabha on stereotypes, she analyzes the relationship of gender to the production of English nationalism at that time. She complexly situates this dance in a nexus of imperialism, nationalism, and resistance to a rising women's rights movement at a time when England was expanding its colonial base overseas. "By representing the English to themselves as vigorous, manly, direct, and so forth, the discourse of nationalism was couched in a vocabulary that explicitly excluded women," she writes. It similarly separated "the East" from "the West," assigning feminized traits to the latter. Maud Allan's representation of an "Oriental" princess brought "the dark continents of Western femininity and Orientalism" together in a vision of Salome that simultaneously seemed to embody and resolve the contradictions between these two discourses and that of rising English nationalism. Koritz's analysis reveals how concepts of nation are linked to those of race and gender, and how all three meet in bodily representation.

Susan Manning's "The Female Dancer and the Male Gaze: Feminist Critiques of Early Modern Dance" thinks with and through some of the significant debates as they have emerged in writings like Koritz's on modern dance of the first decades of this century. Her essay functions as something of a bookend with Wolff's opening call, considering the possibilities of a subversive dance practice, and our ways of theorizing such practices. Charting the limitations and liberations of this work, she offers in the end a new map for further excursions.

While critics have argued that Isadora Duncan, Maud Allan, Ruth St. Denis, and others (sometimes referred to as the "founding mothers of modern dance") were or were not producing work that subverted gender norms for their period, Manning says the real question lies in "how." She proposes that an overreliance on "gaze theory" (adapted from film theory and more recently from theater studies), has caused dance critics to downplay the role of kinesthetics for performers and spectators. This is one of the pitfalls in an overly enthusiastic adoption of theoretical paradigms from neighboring fields without adequate "refitting."

Manning ultimately argues that the kinesthetic and representational frames of early modern dance often worked at cross-purposes. Both liberatory and conservative, works by Duncan and others presented a new sense of individualized kinesthetic subjectivity in dynamic tension with hegemonic representational frames which depicted the sensuous, "natural" woman, or the exotic, orientalized other. Manning also opens up the possibility of discussing differential spectatorial experiences for men and women of the period owing to their divergent kinesthetic experiences. She makes the concept of a historically based kinesthesia central to her analysis of both the dance text and its reception.

Whereas the preceding essays address the complex social dimensions of dance forms, Brenda Dixon Gottschild addresses the social lives and social bodies of critics and scholars. In "Some Thoughts on Choreographing History," she draws on the work of Barthes and others to urge us to take a serious look at the "cultural, social, and pre-academic habits and predilections" that we bring to bear on our topics and in our methodologies. How, she asks, can we keep ourselves off center enough to avoid entrapment by naturalized conventions of valuation which have traditionally elevated some aesthetic criterion while devaluing others? "One of the easiest ways to disempower others," she cautions, "is to measure them by a standard which ignores their chosen aesthetic frame of reference and its particular criteria."

As an example, Gottschild dissects a recent review of Garth Fagan's Bottom of the Bucket dance company. The reviewer finds that the linear-oriented aesthetic of ballet is missing, and the abundant complexities of torso movement seem quirky and messy. Gottschild shows how such a misapplication of aesthetic criterion results in a hierarchical devaluation. Fagan's work is basically criticized as bad ballet, whereas the choreography utilizes Africanist-derived movement styles, styles that lie outside the cognizance of the reviewer. Regardless of color, class, or gender, Gottschild asserts, all of us educated in traditional, Europeanist institutions have a great deal to learn in order to practice responsible criticism.

To do this, she suggests a dance-inspired image, "keeping ourselves off center . . . in order to stay on target." Drawing on Roland Barthes's ideas of intertextuality, with every text made up of preexisting scraps of codes, formulas, and languages redistributed, reworked, and transformed by new contexts, Gottschild calls for an awareness of the relationship of one practice to another, and of the limitations of a linear, power-inflected narrative of performance history and criticism. This theoretical process-in-motion can be aided by what Gottschild calls "culture reversals," reversing the poles of a dichotomy to reveal their ultimately dialogic relationship. Taking African American presence as foreground, not background, for instance, reveals a strong Africanist intertextuality in all kinds of U.S. dance, she argues, even Balanchine ballets. The dominance of aesthetic hierarchies should be replaced by horizontal, context-specific intertextual studies which recognize the process of dance-making, not only its products.

In "Auto-Body Stories: Blondell Cummings and Autobiography in Dance," Ann Cooper Albright contributes just such a context-grounded consideration. She analyzes the complexities of dance production and reception when two of the dialogical poles Gottschild discusses are called into play. In the spirit of Wolff's call for a material feminist cultural studies, she considers the relationship among theories of autobiography, solo performance, and the socially prescribed categories of gender and race as they are read off the body. Thinking through concepts of identity, the "self," and community, she examines "the complex ways in which dancing can at once set up and upset the various frames of the self."

Like Manning, Albright concentrates on the bodily specificity of dance performance as contrasted with other modes of signification, in this case literary autobiography. In doing so, she connects her arguments with current notions of identity as a performative practice, and of "the self" as a postmodern decentered fiction, while at the same time opening those considerations to a further critique. She notes: "Although the act of performing . . . foregrounds the fact that the self is always performed, this constructed performative self is also always reinvented by a physical body which cannot be so easily or neatly fragmented. In the very act of performing, the dancing body splits itself to enact its own representation and simultaneously heals its own fissure in that enactment."

In a compelling discussion of the work of two powerful choreographers, Isadora Duncan in the early part of this century and Blondell Cummings today, Albright considers their solo performances, audience reception, and the choreographers' own words in describing their processes. Despite the many levels of representational complexity involved in staging the work, Albright cautions that "it is critical to realize that within the context of a dance performance, these different levels of representation are contained within one physical, racial, and gendered body." Our perception of bodies as always already racialized and gendered points out the powerful naturalizing function of the body in these discourses. The complexity of writing selves with and through the body is always framed by the social formations within which the work and its reception takes place.

Angela McRobbie's "Dance Narratives and Fantasies of Achievement" opens out these considerations of dancing and social formations to analyze the contradictory pleasures of social dancing and of the representation of dancing in the mass media. She discusses urban dance halls, the television series *Fame*, and the popular film *Flashdance*. McRobbie's work on popular culture and the special fantasies it can hold for girls and young women demonstrates the challenges of talking about dance as a social practice unlimited by the theatrical frame. She argues that such practices must be seen in a complex of youth culture involving intense engagement with music, fashion, the potential for romance, and the negotiation of adolescence within particular class and racial formations.

This important piece on dance fictions and popular culture still represents an anomaly among sociological studies. As McRobbie notes, "as a leisure practice, as a performance art, and as a textual and representational form, dance continues to escape analysis on anything like the scale on which other expressive forms have been considered." While there has been some shift since she first wrote these words, in general her statement is still true. Intensive work on social dance and on mass mediated forms is still to be done.[18]

McRobbie's essay provides a good model because it refuses a simplistic concept of popular culture as either subversive or disempowering. Instead, she fully engages with the multiple and often contradictory meanings generated by these practices. "Dance comes to us packaged in the messy social contexts of consumer capitalism, class culture, and gender and race relations," McRobbie reminds us. One of the key contributions of this essay is the centrality it gives to class analysis, a dimension strongly developed in British cultural studies but often muted in U.S. scholarship. Her discussions of *Fame* and *Flashdance*, for example, pay special attention to the ways class mobility is framed for non-dominant populations. In both of these texts, becoming a dancer is portrayed as the result of guts, talent, and hard work, open to anyone who is gifted, driven, and willing to persevere.

For young women these narratives provide a potential view of a life consumed by a career, without domesticity and child rearing. McRobbie argues that these dance fictions are so popular precisely because they provide fantasies of achievement for women and young girls, noting that "there are few other places in popular culture where girls will find such active role models and such incentives to achieve." But such progressive narratives often work in tension with romantic story lines and a visual subtext which presents women's bodies fetishistically, framed and caressed by cameras, as is the case in *Flashdance.* In that film, dance is used to provide moments of intense self-expression and kinesthetic release for the female protagonist, but it does so in opposition to visual and narrative strategies of containment. Here is another arena where kinesthesia pulls against other representational frames.

McRobbie's work makes us consider how the production of pleasure in these narratives is linked to the figure of the dancing body as a site of excess and to desires for class mobility. What are the cultural assumptions about movement and embodiment that produce this recurring trope? These popular representations of dance demand our attention as surely as the live theatrical forms like ballet and modern dance which have received more scrutiny thus far.

The essays in part III, "Expanding Agendas for Critical Thinking," move from the inside out. They start with the dancing body and delve into the theoretical implications of its materiality and the relation of that materiality to the construction of subjectivities and collectivities.

Susan Foster's "Dancing Bodies" is deeply informed by her own experience and training as a dancer. It draws on the author's substantial depth of experience as an "insider," one who has put in years of training, teaching, and performing in the studio and on the stage. Foster complements that ethnographic depth with a conceptual sophistication that allows her to analyze the training systems of dance techniques not as ends in themselves but as evidence of distinct conceptions of self and body, of materiality and social ideal. Addressing a tendency for much critical writing about the body to "treat it as a symbol for desire or sexuality [or] for a utopia," she calls for a "more meat-and-bones approach to the body based on an analysis of discourses or practices that *instruct* it." Foucault has led the way with his work on the historical construction of categories of madness, of sexuality, and of punishment and aberration. Echoing Bryson's call for scholars to consider socially structured human movement, Foster urges us to analyze the myriad other practices that cultivate the body, including "whole disciplines through which it is molded, shaped, transformed, and in essence created." Among these arenas are sports, etiquette and posture regulations, acting techniques, and of course, dance training regimes.

Foster's essay firmly anchors conceptual assessments and conclusions in a wealth of closely observed data, yet she does not stop at the level of description as so much dance writing in the past has done. Nor does she turn her energies to constructing a sort of teleological history of dance training techniques. Instead, she looks at the detailed processes through which conceptions of bodies and of selves are produced in five different training systems of theatrical dance: ballet technique, Duncan technique, Graham technique, Cunningham technique, and contact improvisation. With careful precision, Foster dissects exactly what goes on in the studio, how the classes are organized from beginning to end, the structures of authority posited in the relation between teacher and student, how bodily ideals are inculcated, and how they are related rhetorically to conceptions of an ideal self. She lays out "the formation of dancing bodily consciousness" and then "situates this bodily consciousness in a cultural and aesthetic moment."

Those who have trained in these forms will find her perspicacity satisfying, for she articulates assumptions that fill the air in the studio but that are rarely held up to self-reflexive examination. Nondancers will doubtless find the wealth of information illuminating. Rarely are these rigorous processes of building a dancing body discussed outside the studio walls. As Foster reminds us, "typically, a dancer spends anywhere from two to six hours per day, six to seven days per week for eight to ten years creating a dancing body." Critical writings on dance have barely begun to consider the wealth of information that such intensity of bodily training can provide. Hardly ever have we considered such process as labor, or used its examination to illuminate bodily practices in other spheres which are so designated. Indeed, the dance studio is perhaps one of the few arenas where such a literal configuring of social subjects is acted out. Dance, as Bryson reminds us, is "the most blatant and unarguable instance of the disciplined body." In Foster's writing, the studio joins the prison and the madhouse, analyzed by Foucault, as a privileged site of bodily inscription.

Anna Scott's essay, "Spectacle and Dancing Bodies That Matter: Or, If It Don't Fit, Don't Force It," also concerns the bodily politics involved in learning to dance. In this piece, written as a slice of a longer ethnographic study and related to her ongoing fieldwork in Bahia, Brazil, Scott's self-reflexive writing style clearly situates the "I" of the theorist in the middle of the social action. She describes and analyzes a *bloco afro* rehearsal in San Francisco, where fifty American dancers of various racial, ethnic, and national backgrounds had assembled to practice some Brazilian dances, like the *samba de galinha*, related to Carnival performances.

Subtexts of racial difference and desire surge through the space along with pulsing bodies as Scott describes the interactions among the students, musicians, and teacher, and her own experience as a participant-observer. "It was clear," Scott writes, "that [as an African American] in that space I was functioning as a measure or indicator or even regulator of [the] 'authentic' . . . I was a dangerous threat in this safe space for white transgression. . . . Spectacle, spectator, and specter, I precede myself as always and already racialized." Scott unpacks the social stakes in these dance practices and raises questions about who dances, in what way, and under what circumstances. Her arguments resonate with those raised earlier in "Embodying Difference" and "Auto-Body Stories." Arguing that dance is one of the "regulatory norms of spectacle [through which] race itself is materialized," Scott makes her argument with sharply etched observations and illuminating wit.

Like Foster and Scott, Cynthia Cohen Bull brings a depth of dancing experience to her essay, and the result is a similarly rewarding "meat and bones" engagement with her conceptual material. Writing from an anthropological perspective, Bull argues that "a close study of the physical, sensuous experience of dancing provides us with knowledge as unmistakable as that provided by the more conventional study and analysis of cultural beliefs and concepts." Not only is "the body" an object of knowledge and of discourse, it is also a lived entity whose practices and perceptions are culturally shaped and shaping. Therefore, a close examination of dance practices can reveal the dialogic process of enactment and constitution of social subjectivities.

Extending some of the concerns raised in Foster's essay, Bull looks not only at dance training but also at performance and audience perception in three different contemporary settings: ballet and contact improvisation in North America, and West African Ghanaian dance. Her goal is specifically to "compare the realms of the sensible and the intelligible," what we can feel and know. Bull argues that each form is differently organized around one of the senses: sight for ballet, touch for contact improvisation, and hearing for Ghanaian traditional dance styles. The foregrounding of these senses gives rise to different ways of learning and perceiving dance which are both reflective and constituent of social organization. Here Bull accomplishes two things simultaneously. First, she succeeds in discussing social formations while anchoring her analyses in ethnographic detail to support her generalizations. Then, like Foster, Manning, and others in this volume, she opens the parameters of analysis to include proprioception, kinesthesia, emotion, and concepts of expressivity without lapsing into scientism or transcendent conceptions of subjectivity.

As interesting as the particular conclusions of her argument are, the conceptual organization of Bull's approach and her methodology are even more important as another potential model for cultural studies of the body. These dancing bodies are performative in every sense of the word. They enact a conception of self and social community mediated by the particular historical aesthetic dimensions of the dance forms and their precise conditions of reception. They engage every sense of the body, and do so in socially meaningful ways which emphasize certain sensations over others. Such an analysis of nonverbal symbolic systems that are not only embedded in social contexts but also are formative of those contexts of lived experience can expand our understandings of ideologies and their discursive mobilization in realms that are often so overlooked as to be naturalized.

These realms specifically include kinesthetics, emotion, and concepts of bodily expressivity. They have been overlooked due to an overreliance on literary theory involved with verbal texts, or film theory derived primarily from studies of narrative films. Nonnarrative, nonverbal (even the naming of such in the negative underscores our reliance on verbal narrativity as the primary organizational paradigm for a great deal of cultural studies) moving "texts" and practices such as those Bull discusses can raise new parameters for analysis.

Mark Franko also delves into issues of emotion, repositioning the work of Yvonne Rainer in relation to the American tradition of radical performance to which she belongs. Drawing on recent reevaluations of modernism in art history, Franko dissects Rainer's famous and paradigmatic 1968 piece *Trio A*, a seamless solo of uninflected, pedestrian movements. Considering its simultaneous presentation and denial of subjectivity, agency, and bodily instrumentality, he asserts that "the originality of *Trio A* is precisely in the way it both preserves the subject but removes her from the narcissistic-voyeuristic relation." But Rainer found it impossible to retain/project this subjectivity while also dealing with emotion as "the body's social material." Her turn to nonnarrative filmmaking in the 1970s allowed "the possibility of a new synthesis which brings meaning and emotion to avant-garde practice." But as Franko notes, while Rainer "cuts the gordian knot of modernism" she also, "shortly thereafter, stops dancing, ceases to appear."

Franko's work unites critical theory in the visual arts with that on performance to refigure dance history. Where will such reconfigurations lead? Franko ends his essay by invoking the continuous loop between production/reception and between choreography/criticism. He asks: "What role will contemporary performance take in this critical breakthrough; what will dance look like in the aftermath of theory's performance?"

Critic and choreographer Marianne Goldberg grapples with this question by taking it one notch further and asking what if the page were a stage? Her highly playful yet deadly serious essay "Homogenized Ballerinas" is a reworking of a previous piece called "Ballerinas and Ball Passing."[19] Originally presented as a lecture accompanied by choreographed gestures, the work was later danced as a performance with lecture material inserted. Later still it was composed as a "performance piece for print," combining words and visuals choreographed on the page and presented in two-dimensional form. In its current incarnation, as a scholarly article, the work retains traces of its multifarious history, evoking images of movement in our heads as we read, the writing functioning almost like a filmscript. The issues Goldberg is dealing with—key questions about dance, history, representation, spectatorship, and gender—resonate with a number of the earlier essays in this book. She considers the authority of the word and the problematic pleasures of the body, of the "great luxuriousness" of movement and the always already gendered frames that shape its meaning. "The body," she says, "is a stage which must reinvent itself."

Here she reinvents her choreography for the page once again, turning our attention in this latest version not only to the issues cited above but also to the limitations of the scholarly book format, with its emphasis on reams of regulated text, a further disciplining of the body through its verbal/textual production. One way of expanding agendas for critical thinking about dance, she implies, may have to involve new scholarly strategies for visual and kinesthetic presentation.

Randy Martin considers Franko's question about the relationship of theories and practices from a different perspective. Starting from performance, he says, can suggest new paradigms for thinking about social formations. The relation of agency and history, Martin posits, is simulated in performance. Therefore, an examination of dance works "might reveal methodological insights into the tensions between agency and the representation of history lost to other analytic maneuvers." A dance audience is gathered at a particular time and place to actively, not passively, produce a reading/reception of the particularly ephemeral text, that is, the dance as it is realized in performance. The viewers form an unstable collective, soon to disperse, which is diverse in particulars yet unified in a desire to see/experience/produce the event. As such, the audience "suggests a mobilized critical presence such as that implicit in radical notions of 'history.'" The performance is the result of the exchange between audience and performers, informed by the text, and shaped by context. It is this complex of context and exchange that figures history as process.

It is also this complex of relationships that Martin finds missing in much of dance writing. Ethnography, he claims, is "the most appropriate procedure to explore [this] relation." Martin uses dance as a new site from which to think through wider issues of publics, agency, and the performative nature of "history" or histories. His work is an example of the type of intellectual extension possible through cultural studies of dance texts, practices, and institutions.

If Martin is concerned with using dance as a model for the performative nature of history, Kate Ramsey looks to history to see the generation of the state through its marshaling of performance. In "Vodou, Nationalism, and Performance: The Staging of Folklore in Mid-Twentieth-Century Haiti," she posits dance spectacle as a regulatory norm, as well as that which exceeds normatizing practices. Through ethnographic and archival research, Ramsey investigates the production of Haitian "folklore" performances during the 1940s and 1950s and their relation to a complex matrix of political conditions involving U.S. intervention, the search for a specifically "Haitian" national representation in the service of self-government, and of a burgeoning tourist industry based on U.S. stereotypes of sensationalized Vodou religious practices.

Ramsey's larger argument is especially important in suggesting new directions for dance and cultural studies. Her essay makes a compelling case that "the staging of folklore represents a critical focus for scholarly research and analysis" as it relates to the production of a national identity for postcolonial states. Just as dance has often been dismissed in political analyses as a peripheral entertainment, so too has the study of "folklore" been romanticized or marginalized. Ramsey shows how the development of a codified national folklore, heavily based in dance, was central to the production of a specifically postcolonial rendition of the "nation" in Haiti following the 1915–1934 U.S. occupation.

This process of production involved competing discourses of *indigénisme* (artistic movements focusing on the reclamation of "folk" cultures), "tradition," and "modernity," and it involved rural populations, the ruling elite, intellectuals, the Catholic church, and U.S. dancers and anthropologists working in Haiti. The complexity of this web illustrates the power of embodied practices to crystallize debates about identity and regimes of power. Ramsey demonstrates how the staging of folkloric dances, along with the very production of such a category by competing discourses, provides a prime locus for political analysis. As the essays throughout this book have revealed, we can extend such an assertion to include all types of dancing, whether categorized as theatrical, popular, social, mass-mediated, "folk," liturgical, or "avant-garde." Whether as practice or product, dance is an act of presentation and representation that literally embodies the political, historical, and epistemological conditions of its possibility.

I hope that these essays will be read in relation to each other and in conjunction with other recent cultural studies collections in related fields to stimulate new critical work in dance and new agendas in cultural studies. Page limitations and scholars' schedules made it impossible, of course, to include work by all those making significant interventions in these debates. Readers are urged to follow the notes in the essays to locate related work by other scholars, as well as additional works by those included here, in order to expand on these conversations.

Dance specialists who are unfamiliar with the leading debates in cultural studies as it has developed in the United States, or with some of the theoretical approaches drawn on here, such as Marxism or feminist theories, will find several key citations helpful. Extensive bibliographic references are contained in the notes to this Introduction.[20] Likewise, those unfamiliar with U.S. dance history will want to follow citations throughout the book which refer to historical works.[21]

A great deal of work still remains to be done. As the weighting of this collection suggests, some areas of investigation are already flourishing, such as feminist studies. However, many other critical dimensions, like studies of social class, for instance, or sexuality, are not nearly as well developed. In addition, much of the work so far has tended to concentrate on U.S. theatrical dance forms, often though not always on those derived from predominantly European sources. Nontheatrical dance and non-European-derived forms are considered to a lesser extent, but there is evidence that this is changing.[22] The international aspects of this dialogue also need to be expanded. This volume has focused on the work of scholars based in the United States, Canada, and Great Britain, but many active scholars in other countries are engaged in similar quests.

I am optimistic that these expansions will continue, and will shape the work of the future in ways we cannot fully imagine now.[23] We can expect this explosion to accelerate in the next few years as dance scholars continue to move into the wider intellectual arenas where concepts of embodiment, identity, and history are debated, and as scholars in other fields increasingly expand their knowledge of bodily "texts" and discourses to include the dancing body. I hope this book can serve as a benchmark for current cultural studies in dance and as a stimulus for a newly expanded agenda for cultural studies research—one which includes the dancing body, the site of meaning in motion.

Notes

My thanks to Kim Marra, Mark Franko, Norman Bryson, and Virginia Domínguez for their comments on earlier versions of this essay. I also appreciate the suggestions provided by two anonymous reviewers for Duke University Press.

1 Works by Marcia Siegel, Selma Jeanne Cohen, and Lynn Emery are among the most respected historical accounts. See, for example, Marcia Siegel, *The Shapes of Change* (Boston: Houghton Mifflin, 1979), and her collected essays in *The Tail of the Dragon: New Dance, 1976–1982* (Durham, N.C.: Duke University Press, 1991); Selma Jeanne Cohen, *Dance as a Theatre Art* (New York: Dodd, Mead, 1974); Lynne Fauley Emery, *Black Dance in the United States from 1619 to Today*, 2d ed. (Pennington, N.J.: Princeton Book Co., 1988). For an example of auteur studies, see Richard Buckle, *Nijinsky* (London: Weidenfeld and Nicolson, 1971). See also collections of dance criticism written for newspapers and magazines, such as Arlene Croce's *Afterimages* (New York: Knopf, 1977). These latter, while they rarely offer extended analyses, are often the only record of particular works or performers, since most dance is still not notated. The dance reviews by Deborah Jowitt, longtime dance critic with the *Village Voice*, excel in their kinesthetically evocative descriptions of contemporary dance, and in themselves provide a historical record of the New York dance scene for more than two decades. See her books *Dance Beat: Selected Views and Reviews, 1967–1976* (New York: Marcel Dekker, 1977) and *The Dance in Mind* (Boston: David R. Godine, 1985). Increasingly choreographers make their own archival videotapes, but these are not generally available to the public.

2 As I hope will become clear throughout the introduction, my use of the term *critical* here signals a reference to scholarly work that actively engages with and often foregrounds theoretical issues and their material consequences.

Not all dance scholars have welcomed these new theoretical approaches. Discussions at the 1992 interdisciplinary conference "Choreographing History" at the University of California–Riverside revealed some of these tensions. Some dance critics are distrustful of this new emphasis on "theory," fearing that the materiality of the dancing body, which they have struggled so hard to commit to the page, will get lost in the fray. In some instances, their fears may be justified. Theorists writing about dance from other disciplines sometimes approach dance merely as an exotic trope or metaphor. While these excursions may be useful in their own right, they may bear little relation to the sweaty bodily activity that many dance writers have come to know intimately. In addition, they may ignore previous dance scholarship. Ellen W. Goellner and Jacqueline Shea Murphy's introduction to their collection *Bodies of the Text: Dance as Theory, Literature as Dance* (New Brunswick, N.J.: Rutgers University Press, 1995) offers a clear and succinct discussion of this issue.

The marginal place of dance in the academy enhances the possibility that this will happen. A simple commutation test is revealing here. While some scholars in other disciplines may feel authorized to write about dance even if they have little familiarity with it, the reverse is rarely true. Both Norman Bryson and I address related politics of the academy in our articles in this collection. Clearly my argument in this book is that the new cultural studies of dance presented here represent exciting theoretical engagements anchored in a full acknowledgment of dance as an embodied social practice.

3 Some of the newer work in theater studies does consider the implication of the presence of the live body. See, for example, *Women in the American Theatre: Actresses and Audiences, 1790–1870* by Faye Dudden (New Haven: Yale University Press, 1994), especially her chapter on Charlotte Cushman and "the body problem." Although the categories "dance" and "theater" are certainly arbitrary, the importance of spoken words in so many theatrical productions presents a different relationship between the verbal and visual than does that which is most often termed "dance." Indeed, the presence or absence of spoken words, or their centrality to a production, is one of the markers invoked in categorizing dance and theater differently. The blurring of these boundaries operates differently at various historical moments. For additional work in theater studies, see also note 7.

4 See George Marcus and Michael Fischer, *Anthropology as Cultural Critique: An Experimental Moment in the Human Sciences* (Chicago: University of Chicago Press, 1986), and James Clifford and George Marcus, eds., *Writing Culture: The Poetics and Politics of Ethnography* (Berkeley: University of California Press, 1986), for examples of self-reflexive criticism in anthropology.

5 I discuss these developments more fully in my essay in this collection, "Embodying Difference: Issues in Dance and Cultural Studies."

6 Several institutional shifts mark the emergence of cultural-studies-oriented work in dance. The last few years have seen the establishment of the interdisciplinary University of California–Riverside Ph.D program in dance history, the first doctoral program of its kind in the country. Riverside has also initiated several important interdisciplinary symposia and conferences, such as the "Choreographing History" conference in 1992, at which two of these essays were first presented as shorter talks. Recent academic conferences hosted by the leading dance organizations such as the Congress on Research in Dance (C.O.R.D.), the Society of Dance History Scholars (S.D.H.S.), and the American Dance Guild have increasingly provided a welcoming space for debate about theoretical issues like those raised in this book. The 1994 C.O.R.D. annual conference, for example, had as its theme "Engendering Dance, Engendering Knowledge: Interdisciplinary Dialogues in the Arts." The 1994 S.D.H.S. conference was "Retooling the Discipline: Research and Teaching Strategies for the Twenty-first Century."

At the same time, dance scholarship is moving out from its previously marginalized position in the academy and into wider academic communities. For example, the 1994 national meetings of the American Studies Association featured, for the first time, several panels on dance issues. Theoretically oriented journals like *Culture Critique* and *Discourse* have recently published pieces of dance scholarship, and a number of book projects are currently in development, indicating the acceleration and extension of cultural studies of dance.

7 See, for example, Laurence Senelick, ed., *Gender in Performance: The Presentation of Difference in the Performing Arts* (Hanover: University Press of New England, 1992); Janelle G. Reinelt and Joseph R. Roach, eds., *Critical Theory and Performance* (Ann Arbor: University of Michigan Press, 1992); Lynda Hart and Peggy Phelan, eds., *Acting Out: Feminist Performances* (Ann Arbor: University of Michigan Press, 1993); Sue-Ellen Case, *Performing Feminisms: Feminist Critical Theory and Theater* (Baltimore: Johns Hopkins University Press, 1990); Philip Brett, Elizabeth Wood, and Gary Thomas, eds., *Queering the Pitch: The New Gay and Lesbian Musicology* (New York: Routledge, 1993); Ruth Solie, ed., *Musicology and Difference* (Berkeley: University of California Press, 1993). Case provides a narrative of the emergence of feminist scholarship in theater studies in her introduction to the book. Reinelt and Roach provide extensive references to theoretical texts as well as brief overviews of theoretical debates in Marxism, deconstruction, feminist theories, psychoanalysis, phenomenology, and other approaches.

8 See especially Judith Butler's *Gender Trouble: Feminism and the Subversion of Identity* (New York: Routledge, 1990). Butler has cautioned against a simplistic reading of her argument that genders are "constructed" through repeated acts and thus subject to liberatory reenactment. See her "Critically Queer," *GLQ: Gay and Lesbian Quarterly* 1, no. 1 (Spring 1993), pp. 17–32. Her latest book, *Bodies That Matter: On the Discursive Limits of "Sex"* (New York: Routledge, 1993), extends some of the arguments in *Gender Trouble.* See also Eve Sedgwick's "Queer Performativity" in the same *GLQ* issue.

9 A sample of these works drawn from the humanities and social sciences during the mid-1980s to mid-1990s follows: Susan Rubin Suleiman, ed., *The Female Body in Western Culture: Contemporary Perspectives* (Cambridge: Harvard University Press, 1985); Elaine Scarry, *The Body in Pain: The Making and Unmaking of the World* (New York: Oxford University Press, 1985); Catherine Gallagher and Thomas Laqueur, eds., *The Making of the Modern Body: Sexuality and Society in the Nineteenth Century* (Berkeley: University of California Press, 1987); Emily Martin, *The Woman in the Body: A Cultural Analysis of Reproduction* (Boston: Beacon Press, 1987); Jane Gallop, *Thinking through the Body* (New York: Columbia University Press, 1988); Alison Jaggar and Susan Bordo, eds., *Gender/Body/Knowledge: Feminist Reconstructions of Being and Knowing* (New Brunswick, N.J.: Rutgers University Press, 1989); Thomas Laqueur, *Making Sex: Body and Gender from the Greeks to Freud* (Cambridge: Harvard University Press, 1990); Robert R. Desjarlais, *Body and Emotion: The Aesthetics of Illness and Healing in the Nepal Himalayas* (Philadelphia: University of Pennsylvania Press, 1992); Peter Brooks, *Body Work: Objects of Desire in Modern Narrative* (Cambridge: Harvard University Press, 1993); Elizabeth Grosz, *Volatile Bodies: Toward a Corporeal Feminism* (Bloomington: Indiana University Press, 1994).

10 The range of potential disciplinary involvement is signaled by the wide variety of scholarly training represented in this volume. The contributing writers hold doctorates in art history, American studies, performance studies, literature, theater history, anthropology, sociology, philosophy, and political science, among others.

11 See the mammoth compendium *Cultural Studies*, edited by Lawrence Grossberg, Cary Nelson, and Paula Treichler (New York: Routledge, 1992) for a sense of the range of topics and theoretical debates that fall under the current usage of the term *cultural studies.* Their introduction sketches the development of the field, its domain, methodologies, objects, and debates, especially as they have developed in the United States and Britain. Also noted

is the instability of the term itself. The extensive bibliography that concludes the book provides an excellent introduction to the writings, theories, and problematics that animate debate in this international discourse community. For another overview of that history, as well as a call to integrate studies of the performing arts into cultural studies, see Sandra Kemp, "'Let's Watch a Little How He Dances'—Performing Cultural Studies," *Critical Quarterly* 34, no. 1 (Spring 1992), pp. 36–50. My article in this book also examines the historical contours of the development of cultural studies and some of the reasons dance in particular has been so marginalized in it.

12 *Cultural Studies*, p. 3.

13 The timeliness of Bryson's call is marked by the appearance of such new work in historical dance studies as Mark Franko's *The Dancing Body in Renaissance Choreography* (Birmingham, Ala.: Summa Publications, 1986) and his *Dance as Text: Ideologies of the Baroque Body* (New York: Cambridge University Press, 1993), as well as the forthcoming book by Skiles Howard, *The Politics of Courtly Social Dancing in Early Modern England*. For a very interesting analysis of bodily presentation, sexuality, and class in eighteenth-century England, see Thomas King, "Performing 'Akimbo': Queer Pride and Epistemological Prejudice," in Moe Meyer, ed., *The Politics and Poetics of Camp* (New York: Routledge, 1994). I thank Mark Franko for bringing some of these works to my attention.

14 For a good introduction to contemporary work being done in the anthropology of dance and human movement, see Brenda Farnell's *Human Action Signs in Cultural Context: The Visible and the Invisible in Movement and Dance* (Metuchen, N.J.: Scarecrow Press, 1995). Included are essays by well-known anthropologists such as Adrienne Kaeppler and Drid Williams. See also the *Journal for the Anthropological Study of Human Movement* and publications by the Ethnochoreology Study Group of the International Council for Traditional Music, as well as the journal *Dance Ethnology*, published by the UCLA department of dance ethnology. One of the most important contributions to dance studies in the United States has been a 1970 article by dance anthropologist Joann Kealiinohomoku, titled "An Anthropologist Looks at Ballet as a Form of Ethnic Dance," reprinted in Roger Copeland and Marshall Cohen, eds., *What Is Dance?* (New York: Oxford University Press, 1983). Its antiethnocentric argument continues to be widely influential.

15 For a related consideration of modernism, see Amy Koritz, *Gendering Bodies / Performing Art: Dance and Literature in Early-Twentieth-Century British Culture* (Ann Arbor: University of Michigan Press, 1995).

16 Two British authors are leading the way: Helen Thomas, ed., *Dance, Gender, and Culture* (New York: St. Martin's Press, 1993), and Christy Adair, *Women and Dance: Sylphs and Sirens* (London: Macmillan, 1992). Judith Lynne Hanna's earlier *Dance, Sex, and Gender: Signs of Identity, Dominance, Defiance, and Desire* (Chicago: University of Chicago Press, 1988) is one of the few other texts to consider issues of gender and dance, but does so more from a perspective based in sociology/anthropology than from a cultural studies point of view. Other books of note are Susan Manning's *Ecstasy and the Demon: Feminism and Nationalism in the Dances of Mary Wigman* (Berkeley: University of California Press, 1993); Jane Cowan's *Dance and the Body Politic in Northern Greece*; and Ann Daly's *Done into Dance: Isadora Duncan in America* (Bloomington: Indiana University Press, 1995). Ramsay Burt's *The Male Dancer: Bodies, Spectacle, Sexualities* (New York: Routledge, 1995) is the first to focus solely on the dancing male body.

17 The 1994 Congress on Research in Dance Annual Conference, "Engendering Dance / Engendering Knowledge," held at Texas Women's University, Denton, Texas.

18 While some excellent studies of social dance exist, they still remain relatively few in number. For example, see Katrina Hazzard Gordon's *Jookin': The Rise of Social Dance Formations in African American Culture* (Philadelphia: Temple University Press, 1990) for a sociological study of African American dance clubs; and see Kathy Peiss's *Cheap Amusements: Working Women and Leisure in Turn-of-the-century New York* (Philadelphia: Temple University Press, 1986), which includes a history of U.S. white urban dance halls. Lewis Erenberg's slightly earlier *Steppin' Out: New York Nightlife and the Transformation of American Culture, 1890–1930* (Chicago: University of Chicago Press, 1981) also includes a historical discussion of social dance spaces and practices. These excellent historical or sociological studies consider issues of race and class but do not delve deeply into ideologies of embodiment as they are played out in detail on the dance floor. For more recent works that move in that direction see: Carol Martin's *Dance Marathons: Performing American Culture in the 1920's and 1930's* (Jackson: University Press of Mississippi, 1994), which considers the theatrical staging of the social in marathons; and Tricia Rose, *Black Noise: Rap Music and Black Culture in Contemporary America* (Hanover, N.H.: Wesleyan University Press/University Press of New England, 1994). Although Rose's main focus is music, her book includes some discussion of hip hop dance. Jon Stratton provides an insightful analysis of dance and class in white Australian youth culture during the 1950s in chapter 5 of his *The Young Ones: Working Class Culture, Consumption, and the Category of Youth* (Perth, Australia: Black Swan Press, Curtin University of Technology, 1992). Two excellent ethnographic studies analyze practices that cross the boundaries of "theatrical" and "social" dance, and thus reveal the historical contingency of such divisions. See Sally Ness, *Body, Movement, and Culture: Kinesthetic and Visual Symbolism in a Philippine Community* (Philadelphia: University of Pennsylvania Press, 1992), and Cynthia Cohen Bull [Novack], *Sharing the Dance: Contact Improvisation and American Culture* (Madison: University of Wisconsin Press, 1990). Marta Savigliano's *Tango and the Political Economy of Passion* (Boulder, Colo.: Westview Press, 1995) also breaks new ground in her politically astute analysis of the shifting class and national dimensions in the history of this social dance form.

Works on mass-mediated dance texts are even rarer, and come mainly from film scholars. See, for example, writings by Jane Feuer, Jerome Delamater, and Rick Altman on the Hollywood musical.

19 "Ballerinas and Ball Passing" was published in *Women and Performance: A Journal of Feminist Theory* 3, no. 2.6 (1987/1988), pp. 7–31. "Homogenized Ballerinas" operates intertextually with that earlier piece, and the reader is invited to compare the two.

20 See the collections *Cultural Studies* and *Critical Theory and Performance* cited above both for their overview of theoretical issues and their bibliographic references. In addition, the following introductions are recommended: Terry Eagleton, *Literary Theory: An Introduction* (Minneapolis: University of Minnesota Press, 1983), provides a very clear introduction to phenomenology, hermeneutics, reception theory, structuralism and semiotics, poststructuralism, and psychoanalysis as they have influenced literary criticism. Toril Moi's *Sexual/Textual Politics: Feminist Literary Theory* (New York: Methuen, 1985) introduces the work of leading Anglo-American and French feminist theorists. In *Yearning: Race, Gender, and Cultural Politics* (Boston: South End Press, 1990), bell hooks discusses black feminist theory, and in *Feminist Practice and Post-Structuralist Theory* (Oxford: Basil Blackwell, 1987) Chris Weedon considers the implications of feminism for several of the approaches discussed by Eagleton, above.

See also: Jonathan Culler, *On Deconstruction: Theory and Criticism after Structuralism* (Ithaca:

Cornell University Press, 1982); Goran Therborn, *The Ideology of Power and the Power of Ideology* (London: Verso, 1982) for a discussion of Marxist-derived concepts of ideology; and Raymond Williams, *The Sociology of Culture* (New York: Schocken Books, 1981), for a discussion of the arts as forms of cultural production. Two recent collections in art history explore the intersections of cultural studies with that discipline and develop new critical approaches to a history of visual representation. See *Visual Culture: Images and Interpretations*, edited by Norman Bryson, Michael Ann Holly, and Keith Moxey (Hanover, N.H.: Wesleyan University Press, 1994), and, by the same group, *Visual Theory: Painting and Interpretation* (1990).

21 In addition, readers may want to consult Susan Foster's *Reading Dancing: Bodies and Subjects in Contemporary American Dance* (Berkeley: University of California Press, 1986). Foster draws on the historiography of Hayden White to propose a new model for a poetics of dance history. *The Dictionary Catalogue of the New York Public Library Dance Collection*, available in many libraries in book form or on CD ROM, is an exceptional resource for finding dance scholarship catalogued by specific historical period, dance style, country, performer, choreographer, etc. For those unfamiliar with U.S. dance history, the following books provide canonical overviews of key events and participants: Richard A. Long, *The Black Tradition in American Dance* (New York: Rizzoli International Publications, 1989), focuses on concert dance forms; Lynn Fauley Emery, *Black Dance in the United States from 1619 to Today*, rev. ed. (Pennington, N.J.: Princeton Book Company, 1988), discusses both theatrical and social dance forms; and Susan Au, *Ballet and Modern Dance* (London: Thames and Hudson, 1991), emphasizes European and Euro-American concert dance history.

22 Several authors in this volume, including Dixon-Gottschild, Albright, Scott, Ramsey, and myself, consider non-European-based forms as well as the complexities of cultural crossings of racial and national boundaries, thereby problematizing the notion of a European/non-European binary (itself a Eurocentric construction) to focus on concepts of hybridity. Other authors with works in progress engaging related issues include Veta Goler, John Perpener, and VèVè Clark, who write from a performance studies or literary studies point of view, as well as a number of dance ethnologists. See also the forthcoming collection *Looking Out: Perspectives on Dance and Criticism in a Multicultural World*, ed. David Gere, Lewis Segal, Patrice Koelsch, and Elizabeth Zimmer. New work engaging the political importance of social dance forms includes Marta Savigliano's *Tango and the Political Economy of Passion*, cited earlier.

23 The number of new works just published or in progress indicates an exciting surge in dance studies that engage the theoretical issues under discussion here. They will create a critical mass of texts and readers which should sustain and extend these conversations in stimulating directions. For a new collection that focuses on the relationship of dance and literature, see *Bodies of the Text: Dance as Theory, Literature as Dance*, ed. Ellen W. Goellner and Jacqueline Shea Murphy, cited earlier. Also newly published is *Choreographing History*, ed. Susan Foster (Bloomington: Indiana University Press, 1995), which involves scholars from a number of disciplines, and her *Corporealities* (1996). See also *Moving Words: Re-writing Dance* (1996), edited by dance critic Gay Morris.

I DANCE AND CULTURAL STUDIES

1 EMBODYING DIFFERENCE: ISSUES IN DANCE AND CULTURAL STUDIES

Jane C. Desmond

A man and a woman embrace. Each stands poised, contained. They look past each other, eyes focused on distant points in the space. Like mirror images, their legs strike out, first forward, then back. As one, they glide across the floor, bodies melded at the hips, timing perfectly in unison. They stop expectantly. The woman jabs the balls of her feet sharply into the floor, each time swiveling her hips toward the leading foot. The man holds her lightly, steering her motion with the palm of his hand at her back. This is tango . . .

Most readers of this passage probably have some image of the tango in their minds, whether from dancing, watching others dance, or seeing representations of the tango in Hollywood films. Most, if pressed, could even get up in their living rooms and demonstrate some recognizable if hyperbolic rendition of the tango. Few of us, however, have given more than passing thought to such an activity or have chosen to include it in our scholarly work. Dance remains a greatly undervalued and undertheorized arena of bodily discourse. Its practice and its scholarship are, with rare exception, marginalized within the academy.

But much is to be gained by opening up cultural studies to questions of kinesthetic semiotics and by placing dance research (and by extension, human movement studies) on the agenda of cultural studies. By enlarging our studies of bodily "texts" to include dance in all its forms—among them social dance, theatrical performance, and ritualized movement—we can further our understandings of how social identities are signaled, formed, and negotiated through bodily movement. We can analyze how social identities are codified in performance styles and how the use of the body in dance is related to, duplicates, contests, amplifies, or exceeds norms of nondance bodily expression within specific historical contexts. We can trace historical and geographic changes in complex kinesthetic systems and can study comparatively symbolic systems based on language, visual representation, and movement. We can move away from the bias for verbal texts and visual-object–based investigations that currently form the core of ideological analysis in British and North American cultural studies.

Cultural studies remains largely text-based or object-based, with literary texts still predominating, followed by studies of film texts and art historical objects.[1] Even excursions into popular culture are concerned largely with verbal or visual cultural products, not kinesthetic actions. Much current work on rap music, for instance, focuses primarily on the spoken text or legal and economic aspects of the music industry. Even the now popular subfield of critical work on "the body" is focused more on representations of the body and/or its discursive policing than with its actions/movements as a "text" themselves.[2] In part this omission reflects the historical contours of disciplinary development within the academy.[3] In addition, the academy's aversion to the material body, as well as its fictive separation of mental and physical production, has rendered humanities scholarship that investigates the mute dancing body nearly invisible. That dancing—in a Euro-American context at least—is regarded as a pastime (social dancing) or as entertainment (Broadway shows), or, when elevated to the status of an "art form," is often performed mainly by women (ballet) or by "folk" dancers or nonwhites (often dubbed "native" dances, etc.) also surely contributes to the position of dance scholarship. However, these omissions signal reasons why such investigation is important. They mark clearly the continuing rhetorical association of bodily expressivity with nondominant groups.[4]

The rhetorical linkage of nondominant races, classes, gender, and nationalities with "the body," to physicality instead of mentality, has been well established in scholarship on race and gender.[5] But the implications of those linkages, their continuance or reworking within the context of daily bodily usage or within dance systems per se, have yet to be investigated fully. Nor have the complex effects of the commodification of movement styles, their migration, modification, quotation, adoption, or rejection as part of the larger production of social identities through physical enactment, been rigorously theorized.

Such analysis will be responsive to many of the tools already developed in literary theory, film theory, Marxist analysis, and feminist scholarship, as well as ongoing theoretical debates about hierarchies based on racial, ethnic, and national identities. Pierre Bourdieu (*Outline*), for example, refers to the physical embodiment of social structures in his concept of "the habitus," but this idea has not been greatly elaborated. But it will also require the acquisition or development of new tools as well—tools for the close analysis of movement and movement styles (already well developed in the dance field itself), just as such tools have been developed for detailed analyses of specific books and objects in literature and art history.

Dance scholarship, with a few notable exceptions, has until recently remained outside the influence of the poststructuralist shifts that have reshaped the humanities during the last twenty or so years. And conversely, cultural analysts have evidenced little interest in dance,[6] although literary, filmic, and art historical texts have garnered great attention. But there is evidence that this is changing, both within the dance field itself and with isolated excursions into dance by literary critics and philosophers in the recent past.[7]

Movement Style and Meaning

Of the many broad areas of movement investigation sketched out above, I specifically want to discuss dance as a performance of cultural identity and the shifting meanings involved in the transmission of dance styles from one group to another.

Like Bourdieu's concept of "taste" (*Distinction*), movement style is an important mode of distinction between social groups and is usually actively learned or passively absorbed in the home and community. So ubiquitous, so "naturalized" as to be nearly unnoticed as a symbolic system, movement is a primary not secondary social "text"—complex, polysemous, always already meaningful, yet continuously changing. Its articulation signals group affiliation and group differences, whether consciously performed or not. Movement serves as a marker for the production of gender, racial, ethnic, class, and national identities. It can also be read as a signal of sexual identity, age, and illness or health, as well as various other types of distinctions/descriptions that are applied to individuals or groups, such as "sexy." Given the amount of information that public display of movement provides, its scholarly isolation in the realms of technical studies in kinesics, aesthetics, sports medicine, and some cross-cultural communications studies is both remarkable and lamentable.

"Dance," whether social, theatrical, or ritually based, forms one subset of the larger field of movement study. And although we tend to think of dances, like the tango, lambada, or waltz, as distinctive aggregations of steps, every dance exists in a complex network of relationships to other dances and other nondance ways of using the body and can be analyzed along these two concurrent axes.[8] Its meaning is situated both in the context of other socially prescribed and socially meaningful ways of moving and in the context of the history of dance forms in specific societies.

When movement is codified as "dance," it may be learned informally in the home or community, like everyday codes of movement, or studied in special schools for social dance forms (like the Arthur Murray Studios) and for theatrical dance forms (like the School of American Ballet). In either case—formal or informal instruction, quotidian or "dance" movement—the parameters of acceptable/intelligible movement within specific contexts are highly controlled, produced in a Foucauldian sense by specific discursive practices and productive limitations.

To get at what the "stakes" are in movement, to uncover the ideological work it entails, we can ask what movements are considered "appropriate" or even "necessary" within a specific historical and geographical context, and by whom and for whom such necessities obtain. We can ask who dances, when and where, in what ways, with whom, and to what end? And just as importantly, who does *not* dance, in what ways, under what conditions and why? Why are some dances, some ways of moving the body, considered forbidden for members of certain social classes, "races," sexes? By looking at dance we can see enacted on a broad scale, and in codified fashion, socially constituted and historically specific attitudes toward the body in general, toward specific social groups' usage of the body in particular, and about the relationships among variously marked bodies, as well as social attitudes toward the use of space and time.

Were we to complete a really detailed analysis of social dance and its gender implications, for example, it could provide us with a baseline from which to pursue further questions that are much larger in scale. We might ask, for instance, how the concept of pleasure is played out in this kinesthetic realm. Who moves and who is moved? In what ways do the poses display one body more than another? What skills are demanded of each dancer, and what do they imply about desired attributes ascribed to men or to women? What would a "bad" rendition of a particular dance, like the tango for instance, consist of? An "un-Latin" or "un-American" version? An "improper" one?

These questions are useful for historical as well as contemporary analysis. For example, the waltz was regarded as too sexually dangerous for "respectable" women in Europe and North America when it was first introduced in the nineteenth century. The combination of intoxicating fast whirling and a "close" embrace was thought to be enough to make women take leave of their senses. Some advice books for women even claimed waltzing could lead to prostitution.[9] Nineteenth-century dance manuals included drawings showing "proper" and "improper" ways to embrace while dancing, specifying the position of the head, arms, and upper body, and the required distance that should be maintained between male and female torsos. In manuals directed toward the middle and upper classes, bodies that pressed close, spines that relaxed, and clutching arms were all denigrated as signs of lower-class dance style. The postural and gestural maintenance of class distinction was a necessary skill to be learned, one that could even be represented with precision in "yes" and "no" illustrations of dancing couples.[10]

Such detailed bodily analysis of the linkage of gender and class provides another discursive field through which to understand the shifting constitution of class relations and gender attributes during the nineteenth century. Changing attitudes toward the body as evidenced in the "physical culture" movement, changes in dress such as the introduction of "bloomers," and new patterns of leisure activities and their genderedness provide part of the wider context through which such dance activities gain their meaning. Similarly, the rapid industrialization and class realignments that took place during the latter half of the century, giving rise to new ideas about the division between leisure and work, between men and women, and toward time and physicality, are played out in the dance halls. As "dance," conventions of bodily activity represent a highly codified and highly mediated representation of social distinctions. Like other forms of art or of cultural practice, their relation to the economic "base" is not one of mere reflection but rather one of dialogic constitution. Social relations are both enacted and produced through the body, and not merely inscribed upon it.

Appropriation / Transmission / Migration of Dance Styles

Obviously, ways of holding the body, gesturing, moving in relation to time, and using space (taking a lot, using a little, moving with large sweeping motions, or small contained ones, and so forth) all differ radically across various social and cultural groups and through time. If dance styles and performance practices are both symptomatic and constitutive of social relations, then tracing the history of dance styles and their spread from one group or area to another, along with the changes that occur in this transmission, can help uncover shifting ideologies attached to bodily discourse.

The history of the tango, for example, traces the development of movement styles from the dockside neighborhoods of Buenos Aires to the salons of Paris before returning, newly "respectable," from across the Atlantic to the drawing rooms of the upper-class portions of the Argentine population during the first decades of the twentieth century. As Deborah Jakubs has noted, the taste of the upper classes for "a fundamentally taboo cultural form is a recurrent phenomenon," as evidenced by the passion for Harlem jazz exhibited by many wealthy white New Yorkers in the 1920s and 1930s.

A whole history of dance forms could be written in terms of such appropriations and reworkings occurring in both North and South America for at least the last two centuries and continuing today. Such practices and the discourse that surrounds them reveal the important part bodily discourse plays in the continuing social construction and negotiation of race, gender, class, and nationality, and their hierarchical arrangements. In most cases we will find that dance forms originating in lower-class or nondominant populations present a trajectory of "upward mobility" in which the dances are "refined," "polished," and often desexualized. Similarly, improvisatory forms become codified to be more easily transmitted across class and racial lines, especially when the forms themselves become commodified and sold through special brokers, or dance teachers.

In studying the transmission of a form, it is not only the pathway of that transmission but also the form's reinscription in a new community/social context and resultant change in its signification that it is important to analyze. An analysis of appropriation must include not only the transmission pathway and the mediating effects of the media, immigration patterns, and the like, but also an analysis *at the level of the body* of what changes in the transmission. Often in the so-called desexualization of a form as it crosses class or racial boundaries, we can see a clear change in body usage, especially (at least in Europe and North and South America) as it involves the usage of the pelvis (less percussive thrusting, undulation, or rotation for instance), and in the specific configurations of male and female partnering. For example, the closeness of the embrace may be loosened, or the opening of the legs may be lessened. In analyzing some of these changes we can see specifically what aspects of movement are tagged as too "sexy" or "Latin" or "low class" by the appropriating group.[11] Of course, the same meaning may not at all be attached to the original movements by dancers in the community that developed the style.

Looking back to the early years of this century in North America, for instance, the case of the professional dance team of Vernon and Irene Castle provides a good example. The husband and wife duo became well known among the middle and upper classes through their exhibition ballroom dancing and their popular movies. They were so popular that Irene Castle set the standard for fashion and hairstyle and appeared in many magazines. Performing in elegant dance clubs, and running their own dance school in New York City, they built their reputations on popularizing (among the middle and upper classes) social dances that originated in the lower classes, especially within the black population. They "toned down," "tamed," and "whitened" such popular social dances as the Turkey Trot and the Charleston. Such revisions tended to make the dances more upright, taking the bend out of the legs and bringing the buttocks and chest into vertical alignment. Such "brokering" of black cultural products increased the circulation of money in the white community which paid white teachers to learn white versions of black dances.

But it would be a mistake to consider that such appropriations, while they seem to recuperate the potential contestatory power of cultural production by subordinate groups, do so monolithically. While markers of social "difference" can be to some extent reduced to "style" and repositioned from a contestatory marginality to more mainstream fashionable practice, both the specific practices themselves and their meanings shift in the process. Indeed, even in those instances where the recuperation seems very "successful," there is some change in the dominant population's cultural production.

And, of course, appropriation does not always take the form of the hegemonic groups' "borrowing" from subordinated groups. The borrowing and consequent refashioning goes both ways. To take just one example, the "Cakewalk," a strutting couples dance performed by African Americans during the slavery era, is thought to have been based on a mimicry of European social dance forms, where (heterosexual) coupled dancing was prevalent, as opposed to the separate-sex dance traditions of West Africa. The meanings of the movement lexicons change when transported into the adopting group. While the notion of "appropriation" may signal the transfer of source material from one group to another, it doesn't account for the changes in performance style and ideological meaning that accompany the transfer. Concepts of hybridity or syncretism more adequately describe the complex interactions among ideology, cultural forms, and power differentials that are manifest in such transfers.

Dialectics of Cultural Transmission

In their work on African American cultures in the Americas, Sidney Mintz and Richard Price have argued persuasively for this more dialectical conception of cultural transmission.[13] They emphasize the strong influence that slavery, as an institution, exerted on both African- and European-derived cultural practices. They argue against a simplistic back-writing of history, which would unproblematically trace African American practices to origins in Africa. While they acknowledge that some specific practices as well as very large epistemological orientations toward causality and cosmology may have survived the violence of enslavement, they emphasize instead the particularity of African American cultures—their distinctiveness from African cultural institutions and practices.

New practices necessarily arose within the new historical context of slavery, which mixed Africans from many distinctive linguistic and social groups and resituated these "crowds" (their term) within the parameters of the subjugating relationship of slavery. New religious practices, male and female relationships, reworkings of kinship patterns and their meanings, as well as artistic practices arose from these new conditions of prohibitions and possibilities. And while the balance of power remained ultimately and overwhelmingly among the slave owners, this too was negotiated at the micropolitical scale and varied from country to country, region to region, and even plantation to plantation. White cultural practices, including notions of paternity, cooking, language, and so forth, were also reformed by the relationships of the plantation.

Mintz and Price state it succinctly: "the points of contact between persons of differing status, or different group membership, did not automatically determine the direction of flow of cultural materials according to the statuses of the participants" (p. 16). Quoting C. Vann Woodward, they note that "so far as their culture is concerned, all Americans are part Negro." And following Melville Herskovits, they quote, "Whether Negroes borrowed from whites or whites from Negroes, in this or any other aspect of culture, it must always be remembered that the borrowing was never achieved without resultant change in whatever was borrowed, and, in addition, without incorporating elements which originated in the new habitat that, as much as anything else, give the new form its distinctive quality." Mintz and Price go on to say that "borrowing" may not best express the reality at all—"creating" or "remodelling" may make it clearer (pp. 43–44).

I have quoted at length on this point because the emphasis in some cultural studies work on appropriation, which helpfully situates these exchanges in the unequal power economies in which they take place, also serves to dampen the transactional, relational aspects of the process. When tied with political assertions of cultural specificity (as in the liberal version of "multiculturalism" or in versions of "identity politics" on the left), this can ultimately slide into what Paul Gilroy has termed "ethnic absolutism."[13]

Identity, Style, and the Politics of Aesthetics

Mintz and Price are right about the complexities of cultural transmission and exchange. But in counterpoint to that complexity (i.e., what "really" happens) is a more two-dimensional public discourse that marks some cultural products as "X" and others as "Y," as "black" dance or "white" dance, for instance. Sometimes these designations are used in the service of celebrating a particular cultural heritage, and an emphasis on uniqueness is one way to do so. Within these ideologies of difference, the historical realities of cultural production and change are muted. Dance, as a discourse of the body, may in fact be especially vulnerable to interpretations in terms of essentialized identities associated with biological difference. These identities include race and gender and the sexualized associations attached to bodies marked in those terms, as well as national or ethnic identities when these are associated with racial notions, as they so often are.[14]

In the United States, the dominant structuring trope of racialized difference remains white/nonwhite. Within this horizon, black/white and Latin/white dyads of difference reinforce essentialized notions of cultural production. In reality, a much more complicated matrix of racial/cultural identities is played out with the specifics of the relationships among and between various groups shifting in response to changing events, demographics, economics, and so on. But while these dyads may be misleading and historically inaccurate, such distinctions function powerfully in popular discourse both within communities (serving as a positive marker of cultural identity) and across communities.

In cases where a cultural form migrates from a subordinate to a dominant group, the meanings attached to that adoption (and remodeling) are generated within the parameters of the current and historical relations between the two groups, and their constitution of each as "other" and as different in particular ways. For example, the linkage in North American white culture of blacks with sexuality, sensuality, and an alternately celebrated or denigrated presumedly "natural" propensity for physical ability, expressivity, or bodily excess tinges the adoption of black dances. On one level, it allows middle- and upper-class whites to move in what are deemed slightly risqué ways, to perform, in a sense, a measure of "blackness" without paying the social penalty of "being" black. An analogue might be "slumming"—a temporary excursion across lines dividing social classes in the search for pleasure.

The submerged class dimension in this metaphor is an important one that is often missed when we concentrate solely on discussions of cultural transmission and modification across racial lines. For the process is ultimately more complicated than that. The meaning of moving in a style associated with "blacks" is different for various classes of whites, and different for various classes of blacks, and for people who affiliate with other categories of race, such as Asians. And such categories of "othering" vary significantly geographically, in the Caribbean, for instance, or in Latin America, where the strongly bipolar white/black discourse, which until recently at least has been a structuring trope for difference in the United States, is too simplistic.

Furthermore, in the process of "whitening" as the dance form migrates across social lines, it is no longer the same form as in the community of origin. Rather, the dance retains traces of that origin, now refashioned both through changes in movement style and through its performance by different dancers in different contexts. While there is in all this a containment and subduing of the difference or particularity of the originating group, there is also a shift in the bodily lexicon of the dominant group. Rather than "black" movement styles or "white," a gray scale may give a more accurate metaphor. Even ballet, the most highly codified, highly funded, and perhaps most elite symbol of European-derived theatrical dance in the United States,[15] has undergone changes that some scholars associate with African American aesthetic values, including rhythmic syncopation and accented pelvic articulations. Brenda Dixon Gottschild makes this argument specifically with regard to Balanchine's ballets when she proposes looking at an African American "blues aesthetic" as a Barthesian intertext for ballet.

To take a contemporary example drawn from North American popular culture, we can consider the enormous influence that black rap music and its accompanying dance style ("hip hop") has had over the last few years. "Hip hop" dance classes can now be found in predominantly white neighborhoods at the local aerobics studio. The dance style and the music are featured in the mass media in commercials and on MTV.

Such popular black groups as Public Enemy have developed a very percussive style. Their music videos emphasize the sharp repeated thrusting of the pelvis as well as complex stepping or hopping patterns that clearly mark out and punctuate the beat of the music. Pelvic grinds (slow or fast circlings) also feature prominently, often with the knees well bent and legs spread. Both women and men perform these movements. In addition, in some videos the male dancers (and more rarely the female) grab their crotches and jerk them forward. In the upper body we see strong, isolated movements of the head, hands, and arms, often in complex counterpoint to the pumping movements of the lower body and legs. In the dance style we can see striking similarities to some forms of West African dance, where pelvic articulation features prominently along with polyrhythmic relationships between stepping patterns in the feet and concurrent arm gestures.

In dance traditions originating in Europe, both popular and theatrical, such as ballet, the torso tends toward quietude and verticality, and the pelvis rarely functions as an expressive bodily unit of its own. In a "white" version of hip hop, represented by the enormously popular and financially successful group New Kids on the Block, we can see a similar toning down of the movement. The emphasis on vigorous, patterned stepping and hopping remains, as do the punctuating arm gestures, but the pelvic thrusting, rotating, and crotch grabbing are much attenuated, as is the explicit sexuality of some of the lyrics. Even the name of the group, while asserting a sort of cocky arrival, evokes more the "boy next door" image, kids rather than men, and a far different image than the outlaw and outsider designation of "Public Enemy."

In this "whitewashing" of the hip hop style we can see several factors at work. Members of the hegemonic group reap economic success built on the exhibition of a black-derived movement and song style. They do so by transposing the sexuality of the original into a more acceptable form. In this case, the stereotypical image of the aggressively sexual young black male is defused and transposed to an image of adolescent heartthrobs, suitable for consumption by white teenage girls and less threatening to white, male sexuality. But at the same time, a sort of reverse sexualizing and aggressivity, deriving from the vigor of the tightly patterned movement as well as from the words of the songs, accrues to these "new kids" from a working-class background. Class and gender remain the submerged elements in this analysis of transmission and popularity. The explosion of rap into the middle-class youth market, facilitated by the mass-mediated commodification of rap music and its accompanying dance styles via radio, MTV, and national commercials and movies, has shifted the context of consumption and thus the meaning of participating as listener/viewers or dancers. What was once a "black" music and dance style has now become more of a marker of "youth" than only a marker of racial identification.[16] In addition, most rap singers are male, although there is a visible contingent of black female singers. Rap remains a male-dominated and to some extent male-identified form.

To talk about the circulation of rap music and associated dance styles from the lower classes of urban black populations to the predominantly white middle-class suburbs is to map one part of the trajectory and would result in a reading that emphasizes the appropriation theme again. But it would also ignore the change in the forms as they travel, their shifting meanings, now standing more for "youth" than just for "black" culture, as well as the complexities of class involved in the successful mass marketing of such a cultural product. For rap can be found in white working-class neighborhoods and in black middle-class neighborhoods too. And for each of these groups the meanings attached to this type of music and dance must be different. Detailed studies of patterns of consumption and the particularities of movement style in each community would be necessary to really trace the changes and similarities associated with the style and its usage as social dividing lines are crossed.

As noted above, issues of class and of locality (urban/nonurban, for example) are often played out through changing lexicons of movement. Sometimes this differential marking out comes not in the form of transmission and remodeling, as I have discussed above, but rather in a form of bodily bilingualism. To take one striking example from North America, we can consider the use of movement on the *Bill Cosby Show.* Cosby often inserts African American movement markers into his otherwise white-identified upper-middle-class professional demeanor. Slapping high fives or adding a street-style knee dipping walk, Cosby signals "blackness" to his audience. Here, interestingly, class and racial identification collide, with North American middle-class body codes being derived from Anglo and northern European styles, and "black" body language being associated not with the black middle class, but rather the lower economic class. Cosby and his successful family represent a form of bodily bilingualism rather than hybrid movement forms. Each way of speaking with the body is used in specific instances, depending on whether class or racial codes are semantically overriding.

At an outdoor nightclub in Dakar, Senegal, I observed a different case of bilingualism a few years ago. To the music of a very popular band that played electronic music mixing Euro–North American and West African instruments, rhythms, and harmonies, the Africans on the dance floor, dressed in shirts, slacks, and dresses, executed a version of popular dancing similar to that seen in the United States. With vertical postures, each member of a couple stepped softly in place while bending the knees slightly and gesturing close to the body with relaxed arms. However, as the night went on and the dancers warmed up, traces of the Senegalese rural dance styles I had seen earlier in the week bled through. Knees bent more and opened wider, arms swung more forcefully, feet stepped more sharply, and hands grabbed garments to hold them slightly out from the body as was done with more traditional dress. Here, in the movement of social dance forms, we saw the rural/urban tensions being acted out. The adoption of a more European style verticality, for instance, formed part of a whole complex of behaviors, including dress, that differentiated the urban population from rural ones. The "urbanization"-"modernization"-"Westernization" ideology was being carried on here, acted out as a bodily trope which gradually slipped away as the night went on.

"Hot and Sexy" Latin Dances

The emphasis on pelvic motion and syncopated rhythms that characterize hip hop is found, in a very different way, in "Latin" dances imported from South to North America. While the specific characterizations and stereotypes associated with "Latins" and with "blacks" in dominant public discourse in the United States vary, there is significant overlap.

In such cases, a discourse of racialism that ties nonwhites to the body and to sexuality expands to include Latin American populations of European origin. Racial, cultural, and national identity are blurred, yielding a stereotype of "Latin" along the lines of Carmen Miranda crossed with Ricardo Montalban. The ascription of sexuality (or dangerous, potentially overwhelming sexuality) to subordinate classes and "races" or to groups of specific national origin (blacks, "Latins," and other such lumped together terms to denote non-Anglo-European ancestry) yields such descriptions as "fiery," "hot," "sultry," "passionate." All of these terms have been used to describe the tango, for instance, or the lambada, or in marketing recent movies using those dances, such as *The Gypsy Kings.*

In North America, it is no accident that both "blacks" and "Latins" are said to "have rhythm."[17] This lumping together of "race," "national origin," and supposed genetic propensity for rhythmic movement rests on an implicit division between moving and thinking, mind and body. Even the upper classes of Latin America do not escape this stereotyping, since their "Latinness" can be said to override their class distanciation from the realm of the supposedly "naturally" expressive body.

So what does it mean for an upper-middle-class Anglo suburban couple in Indiana to dance the tango, or samba, or lambada? On one level, by dancing "Latin" or "black" dance styles, the dominant class and/or racial group can experience a frisson of "illicit" sexuality in a safe, socially protected and proscribed way, one that is clearly delimited in time and space. Once the dance is over, the act of sexualizing oneself through a performance of a "hot" Latin style, of temporarily becoming or playing at being a "hot Latin" oneself, ceases. The dance then becomes a socially sanctioned way of expressing or experiencing sexuality, especially sexuality associated with subtle, sensuous rotations of the pelvis. But in doing so the meaning of the dance and of the act of dancing undergoes a change. It is no longer "Latin" but now "Anglo-Latin" and its meaning arises from and contributes to the larger dialectic between these two social and political entities and their current political and economic relations. Within the United States, these relations vary distinctly from region to region and city to city.[18]

The history of social dance in the United States is strongly marked by these periodic importations of styles from Latin America, and more recently by the popularization of styles developed within Latin American or Caribbean communities within the United States. But in almost every case the spread of the dance craze to the non-Latin population is represented and promoted in terms of the dance's sexual allure. Over time, these dances become more and more codified and stylized and often pass into the category of "sophisticated," marked as sensual rather than sexual. The tango, rhumba, and samba all now fall into this category, as evidenced by their canonical inclusion in social dance classes and in national ballroom dance competitions. With this passing often comes a generational change in the avid performers as well. Older dancers tend to perform the more "sophisticated" versions.

Sometimes the symbolism of the dance becomes detached even from its performance and permeates different nooks of popular culture. The Carmen Miranda figure, perhaps the most enduring and potent stereotype of the Latin bombshell, recently reappeared on the stage of the Brooklyn Academy of Music. Arto Lindsay, Brazilian pop musician, calls her "a foreigner reduced to the foreign."[19] His tribute to Miranda featured Brazilian performers such as Bebel Gilberto, Miranda's sister Aurora, and Laurie Anderson, pop icon of the U.S. avant-garde, in an attempt to rescue Miranda from her "every-Latina" stereotype.

Miranda's own story reveals the complexities of translation and transportation. A singer and a dancer, her bodily display was significant in her rise to stardom in North America, where her flirtatious charm ("Look at me and tell me if I don't have Brazil in every curve of my body") and style of florid excess made her the premier symbol of Latinness during her heyday. Showcased by Hollywood in films like *That Night in Rio* (1941), *Weekend in Havana* (1941), *Springtime in the Rockies* (1942), and Busby Berkeley's extravaganza, *The Gang's All Here* (1943), Miranda was by 1945 the ninth-highest-paid person in the United States. Her Brazilianness was soon turned into a generic "Latin" stereotype.

What remained unnoticed in this United States translation was the source of her character and trademark costume (frilly dress with bare shoulders, oversized jewelry, and fruit-topped turban). To the Brazilian audience that first saw this costume when it debuted in the film musical *Banana da Terra* in 1938, the stylization of the black *baiana* woman, often seen selling food on the streets of the northern city of Bahia and associated with the practice of the *candomble* religion, would have been immediately apparent. As Julian Dibbell has noted, Miranda's "racial cross-dressing" occurred in a Brazilian climate of increasing racial fluidity, but the origins and meanings attached to such recreations were lost on the middle-class United States populations who flocked to her movies and sambaed the night away. For most North Americans, Miranda came to symbolize "Latin" music and dance. Within Brazil, a different type of genericization took place. The samba, which developed in the African-Brazilian community and which Miranda helped popularize in the United States, soon spread to all sectors of the Brazilian population and came to be a marker of "Brazilian" culture.

Back home in Brazil, Miranda's increasing genericization did little to endear her to her Brazilian audiences. Eventually, years after her death in 1955, her image resurfaced in Brazil, reclaimed within the "tropicalismo" movement within the arts. In the United States, her image recirculates in the male "drag queen" pantheon of characters, her manufactured sexual excess providing a ready-made performance persona. And it greets us in the supermarket in those little Chiquita banana stickers, each marked with a flirty Miranda figure.

The Miranda case points out several aspects of the transportation of music and dance styles. The importance of the mass media in facilitating such spread during the last fifty years has been exceptional. Such mediated images flatten the complexities of the dance style (as a social practice) into a "dance" (transported as a series of steps to music) removed from its context of origin and its community of performance. Such representations are a key factor in the reworking of the meanings of these movements as they travel. Further, the identities once attached to certain styles of moving (associated with "black" or "white" or "mestizo" populations in Brazil, for instance) become genericized in the transportation, standing now for an undifferentiated "Latinness," with original markers of class, racial identity, and national specificity all but erased.[20]

The effect of such generalization is often to reinforce U.S. stereotypes of Latin Americans as overly emotional, inefficient, unorganized, and pleasure-seeking. The very same qualities that may be valued in the movement—characterized in the United States as sensuous, romantic, expressive, emotional, heteroerotic, and passionate—reinforce these stereotypes even while they contribute to the perception of the dance in those same terms. (The unstated equation is that Latins are how they dance, and they dance how they are.) The fact that dancing is a bodily discourse only enhances the perception of these characteristics as "true" or truly expressive. The pleasure aspect of social dancing often obscures our awareness of it as a symbolic system, so that dances are often seen as "authentic" unmediated expressions of psychic or emotional inferiority. They are often taken as evidence of a "character," sometimes of a "national character," and often of "racial character." This is where the nonverbal aspect of dance and our general ignoring of movement as a meaningful system of communication reinforce popular beliefs about the supposed transparency of expressivity.

Theatrical Dance

The preceding discussion has focused on aspects of identity, transmission, and perception relating to the performance of social dance forms. Similar issues arise when considering the more highly codified dance forms of the professional theatrical world. These forms are less likely to be disseminated through the mass media and rely more on the physical transportation or migration of performers, students, teachers, and choreographers from one locale to another, especially when national boundaries are involved. There are differences, too, in this category between professional performance forms that are more or less popular. For instance, the dynamics are slightly different in the categories of show dancing, like jazz or Broadway-style dance, than they are in the modern dance world. I want to close by giving two brief examples of the migration of dance styles across national boundaries, the first looking at ballet in China, the latter at selected aspects of Latin American modern dance.

Even though we might be tempted to dismiss the importation of ballet to China as just one more example of Western cultural imperialism, the complexities of the transmission belie such a simple explanation. Ballet in China represents a striking case of a creolized form still very much emerging. It exhibits a combination of movements from the Soviet ballet tradition and the theatrical dance, folk dance, and operatic traditions of China.[21] In some cases, this mixture results in arresting moments where half the body looks "Chinese" in its lexicon of movement, and the other half looks "European."[22] In these cases, we might see the legs poised *en pointe* in arabesque, while the upper torso, arms, and head are molded into a dramatic pose drawn from the Chinese tradition, especially the Chinese opera, where dramatic pantomime played a large role.

The Chinese example is particularly interesting because it represents a case in which the change in a form of cultural production occurred largely from the top down, that is, as a state-level government decision. All the complexities of the migration of various forms from one community to the next at the local level, or even among regions or countries when facilitated by the mass media, are somewhat streamlined here, yet the particularities of the Chinese experience remain distinct. Chinese ballet is different from its counterparts in Europe and America not only at the level of movement vocabulary and syntax (i.e., what movements are done and the ways movement sequences are put together), but also in terms of choreographic method (where collective projects of choreography are not uncommon) and in terms of audience (ballet in China is conceived of as a popular entertainment). In addition, the narrative or storytelling aspect of ballet, which has dropped in prominence in European and American ballet forms since the mid–nineteenth century as more abstract styles have emerged, is a strong component of the Chinese repertory. Thus, far from representing merely the appropriation of a "Western" form, the Chinese ballet produces a whole complex of meanings as well as formalistic innovations specific to its function in China.

Gloria Strauss has written about the history of dance in China and has speculated on the reasons why ballet might have been actively imported by the state during the Cultural Revolution.[23] The arts were considered integral to the ideological functioning of the new China, and dance received much attention at the state level. The choice to import Soviet ballet forms revealed more than the Soviet economic and political influence of the time period. Strauss speculates that the government was actively seeking the creation of art forms that would make visible the need for rapid and radical change that the revolution called forth.

Theatrical dance in China had, with the exception of the dramatic forms in the Chinese Opera, fallen into a decline among the Han (the Chinese majority population) after the Sung period (A.D. 959–1278). A contributing factor in this decline, argues Strauss, may have been the widespread practice of foot binding, which severely reduced female movement especially, but not exclusively, among the upper classes.[24] Acrobatic and folk dance forms survived, but they did not bring with them narrative traditions. (In addition, the folk forms were heavily marked with ethnic associations, and the government wanted to play down ethnic enmities while celebrating the nation as a whole.) The narrative possibilities of ballet may have been one factor in its adoption, as the leaders sought the creation of art that would reinforce the tenets of the revolution and appeal to the masses. Furthermore, it offered visions of action and strength, through a combination of Chinese acrobatic traditions (also found in the opera) with the leaps and turns of the ballet vocabulary. Strauss notes that "highly extended postures such as attitudes and arabesques and a variety of flying leaps such as *grand jeté en avant* are given great prominence" in Chinese choreography (43). Similarly, the female dance vocabulary could be extended to showcase women who were as strong and active as men, literalizing the emphasis on equal legal rights for women that the government supported. In the well-known *Red Detachment of Women*, gun-toting ballerinas fight for the revolution while leaping across the stage in *grand jetés*.

This in itself represents a shift from the earlier history of European ballet, through a particular emphasis on some of its characteristics along with a downplaying of others (the soft, light movement style of female roles in the traditional nineteenth-century ballets that continued to be performed in the Soviet Union, for example, such as *Swan Lake*). But it would be misleading to posit a simple correspondence between the new status for women in cultural revolution and the martial movements of ballerinas in these works. There is also a strong tradition of female warrior characters in Chinese opera, and historically popular entertainments often featured women dancing with swords. The gun-toting ballerina, while unusual in European or American ballets, becomes meaningful in *The Red Detachment of Women* through a complex nexus of old and new forms of both Chinese and non-Chinese origin.

In the more recent past, the ballet repertoires have expanded. The dramatic, narrative ballet remains a staple, but it now exists side by side with nonnarrative ballets as well as modern dance works. Little of the U.S. modern dance repertory has been seen in China yet, although a few companies have toured and some teachers have done guest residencies. But some of the younger dancers copy poses found in dance magazines, making up their own versions of "modern dance."

In China, a state policy that would seem at first to foster imitation of industrialized nations' art forms instead results in new, hybrid forms. The wider geopolitical relations between China and the industrialized nations, from whence certain cultural forms are originally borrowed, may ultimately form a horizon circumscribing the meanings that can possibly circulate with those forms. But it does not determine either the use, ultimate shape, or socially constructed aesthetic valuation of the resultant hybrid.

Owing to a greater flow of professional dancers between countries in North and South America and to different governmental policies about the arts, the situation in Latin America is different. But here too we can see the process of hybridization and recontextualization, influenced but not determined by the dance institutions in the various countries, as well as international arts exchange and funding policies.[25] Without trying to generalize about the wide range of Latin American theatrical dance, let me close with brief examples that demonstrate something of the variety of forms and situations encompassed.[26]

The range of contemporary dance in Latin America is very wide, and while the United States tendency may be to think of Latin American dance in terms of the popular and well-known social dances, in fact a full range of traditional and contemporary styles coexist on the stage. The case of DanceBrazil is interesting. Although based in New York, this contemporary company is composed mainly of dancers born and trained in Brazil. Their repertory consists of what appear to be stagings of ritual ceremonies based on the Afro-Brazilian *candomble* religion, traditional *capoeira* (a martial arts–dance form), the samba, and, to some extent, dance vocabulary derived from American modern dance styles.

DanceBrazil foregrounds its "Brazilness." That in fact may be what it is selling to both its Euro-American and Latin American audiences in New York. In live and televised appearances, this is a company that "stages" tradition. A televised performance presented on United States public television in 1989 was particularly interesting. Shown as part of the Alive from Off Center series, DanceBrazil was contextualized as part of a contemporary avant-garde showcase. Each week the series presents dance and performance works featuring (mainly United States) artists outside of the mainstream. Susan Stamberg, the announcer, introduces the night's offerings with brief comments about artists who are reinterpreting traditional dances through "modern sensibilities," the evidence of cultural contact. In fact, the words "culture contact" float by on the screen. On the show with DanceBrazil, interestingly, are a solo by Raul Trujillo, who reinterprets his American Indian heritage in "The Shaman," and a duet by the Japanese-born, United States–based duo of Eiko and Koma, whose excruciatingly slow movement underlines the sculptural qualities of their nearly nude bodies in what Stamberg terms a melding of Japanese Butoh and American avant-garde techniques.

It is interesting that of these three examples of "culture contact" only the Japanese piece is not based on religious rituals and "traditional" costuming. Japanese Butoh is a relatively recent stylistic development, and it may be that essentializing the Japanese through a discourse of traditionalism is more difficult in the United States due to Japan's new position as our primary economic competitor on the world financial scene. On the other hand, American Indians and Latin Americans may more easily be situated within such a traditionalizing/primitivizing discourse of preindustrialism.

Trujillo's piece, which is first, sets the stage for the DanceBrazil piece that follows. In fact, both feature large circles drawn in the earth (literally, truckloads full of dirt dumped in the television studio). Trujillo dons traditional American Indian dress, complete with feathers, and enacts a ceremonial type of dance that concludes with his vanishing in a hazy light. By the time DanceBrazil appears, their stage set of dark earth, white chalk circle, and flowing white curtains around the perimeter comes as no surprise. We are already placed firmly in the "primitive" aesthetic, with people enacting magical ceremonies in village clearings on rich, dark earth.

The set effectively shuts the dancers and the "ceremony" off from any historical time or place. These rituals are presented as "timeless," but this "outside of time" quality refers to the past and somehow fails to index the present. If the dances cannot be contemporary, then neither, we are to assume, are the people who perform them. In an odd category of "avant-garde folklore," PBS has produced another hybrid form, one reflecting the dominance of the United States, with economic and political power played out in the staging decisions of a television series, the framing of its discourse, and the composition of its audience, self-selected connoisseurs of the "avant-garde."

This is not at all to imply that theatrical dance companies in or from Brazil always work in traditionally based styles. The Grupo Corpo of Brazil, which appeared in New York City during the fall of 1991, presented an evening of works nearly indistinguishable in movement vocabulary from that of many U.S. companies based in New York. Also during the same season in New York, Hercilia López, director of the Venezuelan troupe Contradanza, and Luis

Viana, founding member of the Venezuelan Acción Colectiva Dance Company, presented solo works. In both cases the movement vocabularies and presentation of these works showed strong affiliation with contemporary U.S. modern dance production. Of course, we could say that this merely reflects the dominance of U.S. modern dance on the worldwide dance scene, and indeed many of these performers have trained in the United States. But this would be to overlook the specific meanings that arise in the performance of such works in their home cities in Latin America, as well as in the United States where they are framed and marketed specifically as "Latin American" artists.

On the same program with López and Viana, marketed as Latin night at Movement Research in downtown New York, was a piece by Arthur Aviles, a spectacular dancer with the New York–based Bill T. Jones company, here presenting his own work. Titled *Maeva (A New York–Ricans Ensalada)*, the piece featured as the main character an irrepressible woman, squeezed into a too-small frilly gown, regaling the audience with a nonstop monologue in Spanish and English. Creating a whirlwind of energy with her breathless talking and exuberant posing, she recalled the larger-than-life Carmen Miranda, here both reasserted and caricatured at the same time. She introduces herself with a skein of fifty names, marking the maternity and paternity of past generations, and talks about her fifteen "childrens" as four other dancers crawl around and through her legs to the pulse of Tito Puente music. Periodically, someone offstage yells out "Spic!," but she continues, unflappable, picking up the monologue where she left off, addressing the audience directly, with "so, as I was telling you. . . ." Dancers samba around her like back-up singers as she jokes about lazy "caballeros." At times, the dancers climb on top of her, holding her down, but she always emerges, still talking and gesturing, claiming, in heavily accented English, "What do you mean you won't hire me, I don't have an accent!"

Although obvious and somewhat heavy-handed in its attempt at political critique, this piece was effective in its mix of Spanish and English, of abstract modern dance movements with the ethnically coded gestural language of the Latin caricature. It simultaneously genericized and particularized, placing the 1940s' "every-Latina" stereotype in the contemporary struggle to find work and to create community within the heavily accented hybrid space of New York. Its placement on a program of "Latin dances" in a small loft downtown, part of the "avant-garde" circuit, also signaled the complex mix of identities being played out on that stage. Somewhere between Carmen Miranda and the successful avant-gardism of the Bill T. Jones company, Aviles staged his own bilingual modern dance, articulating through its bodily enunciation the complexities of his own position and the permeability of movement lexicons always in transition.

Concluding Thoughts

I have argued throughout this piece for an emphasis on the continually changing relational constitution of cultural forms. Concepts of cultural resistance, appropriation, and cultural imperialism are important for the light they shed on the unequal distribution of power and goods that shape social relations. And indeed these inequities may form a kind of limit or substrata that ultimately determines the topography of cultural production. But an overemphasis on such concepts can obscure the more complex dialectics of cultural transmission. Such concepts can overemphasize formal properties that circulate or are "lost" in the process of moving from one group to another, thus resulting in an inattention to the contextual specificity of meanings attached to or arising from the usage of formal properties, and obscuring as well the hybridization of such forms.

I have also argued for increased attention to movement as a primary, not a secondary, social text, one of immense importance and tremendous challenge. If we are to expand the humanities now to include "the body" as text, surely we should include in that new sense of textuality bodies in motion, of which dance represents one of the most highly codified, widespread, and intensely affective dimensions. And because so many of our most explosive and most tenacious categories of identity are mapped onto bodily difference, including race and gender, but expanding through a continual slippage of categories to include ethnicity and nationality and even sexuality as well, we should not ignore the ways in which dance signals and enacts social identities in all their continually changing configurations.

But to do so will require special tools. Although I have been emphasizing the larger theoretical level of analysis of the transmission and hybridization of cultural production in this essay, extended treatment of specific cases, both historic and contemporary, is clearly necessary. Such research will allow us to test the validity of these frameworks and to provide the data necessary for detailed accounts of exchange, change, and circulation and the ways in which those are attached to the social production of identity. But if we are to talk about dancing in anything other than the broadest terms, we must be able to do close analysis of dance forms, just as we might of literary texts. While most scholars have spent years developing analytic skills for reading and understanding verbal forms of communication, rarely have we worked equally hard to develop an ability to analyze visual, rhythmic, or gestural forms. As cultural critics, we must become movement literate. Here is where skills drawn from the dance field become indispensable.

Systems of movement analysis developed in dance, such as Laban's Effort/Shape system, provide a good starting point. Effort/Shape methodologies employ abstract concepts of continuums in the use of the weight of the body (ranging from "strong" to "light"), in the body's attitude toward space (ranging from "direct" to "indirect"), and in the use of time (ranging from "quick" to "sustained"). In so doing, they can provide an analytical system as well as a language with which to speak about the body moving in time and space.

Consider, for example, the pioneering work of Irmgard Bartenieff. In the 1960s and 1970s, she explored the efficacy of Effort/Shape for describing and comparing movement patterns in particular communities. Such work provides one model for cross-cultural comparisons of movement lexicons. I think it can also provide a model of the changes that take place in movement style among populations undergoing cultural contact of either a voluntary (immigration, for example) or involuntary (colonial occupation or slavery) sort. We could, for example, relate this to Homi Bhabha's work on mimicry, although he does not develop this line of argument directly himself. Bhabha discusses the slippage that occurs when colonial behaviors, such as military ritual, are performed (always he says "imperfectly" or overly "perfectly") by the colonized. His concept of mimicry could, when combined with a detailed system of movement analysis, provide us with a useful way to chart some of the changes that occur in the semantics of movement as a result of cultural contact and/or domination. The key in cases such as he refers to would be to look closely at what constitutes "imperfection" or "over"-perfection in movement performance.

Although the Effort/Shape system does not code movements in terms of gender or cultural affinities, all analytical systems reflect the contours of their historical etiology and of their objects of analysis. The Effort/Shape system, for example, developed out of Rudolph von Laban's analysis of twentieth-century European movement patterns. Given the demands of cross-cultural and intracultural research, no one system will be sufficient. To keep our broader levels of analysis anchored in the materiality and kinesthesia of the dancing body, we need to generate more tools for close readings, and more sophisticated methodologies for shuttling back and forth between the micro (physical) and macro (historical, ideological) levels of movement investigation.[27] The difficulty of this research will repay us well, expanding understanding of the ways in which the body serves both as a ground for the inscription of meaning, a tool for its enactment, and a medium for its continual creation and re-creation.

Notes

An early version of this essay was presented at the conference "Politics in Motion: Dance and Culture in Latin America" held at Duke University in the winter of 1991. I thank the organizers Celeste Frazier and José Muñoz for inviting me to speak. My thanks also to Jennifer Wicke, Cathy Davidson, Bryan Wolf, and Jane Gaines for their helpful critiques on this material, and especially to Virginia Domínguez for bringing the Mintz and Price material to my attention.

1 The debates about what "cultural studies" is, should be, and should not be have intensified during the last ten years as the term has gained greater circulation and as its practitioners have gained increasing institutional power in the academy. I use this term in the sense of a group of self-nominated scholars who affiliate themselves and their work with such a term. Implicit in its usage is usually a concept of critique, antidisciplinarity, and the importance of investigating the linkages between social/economic/political power and cultural production. See Richard Johnson, "What Is Cultural Studies Anyway?" *Social Text* 16 (1986–87), pp. 38–80, and the massive collection *Cultural Studies*, edited by Lawrence Grossberg, Cary Nelson, and Paula Treichler (New York: Routledge, 1992) for discussions about the scope of cultural studies. The American version of cultural studies is greatly influenced by the pioneering work of Stuart Hall and the Birmingham Centre for Contemporary Cultural Studies in Britain. See Stuart Hall's essay in *Cultural Studies* for a discussion of this relationship ("Cultural Studies and Its Theoretical Legacies," pp. 277–86). Some important work investigating British subcultural groups has focused on bodily practice associated with music and fashion, but rarely has movement figured centrally in these analyses. See, for example, Dick Hebdige's *Subculture: The Meaning of Style* (London: Methuen, 1979).

2 For example, see Thomas Laqueur's *Making Sex: Body and Gender from the Greeks to Freud* (Cambridge: Harvard University Press, 1990) and Emily Martin's *The Woman in the Body: A Cultural Analysis of Reproduction* (Boston: Beacon, 1987). Foucault's work remains a standard.

3 The humanities disciplines' emphasis on words is exemplified in the histories of the disciplines. The prestige of literature is followed by that of art history, which discusses art historical objects. Usually the making of those objects is segregated into a separate "art" department. Funding distributions reflect the different valuations placed on the act of making "art" versus the act of writing about it. Music history and theory have attained a higher status in the academy than dance history due in part to their more extensive written history, both in terms of criticism and in terms of the musical scores that stand in for live performance and permit extensive, reflective study. Dramatic literature holds an analogous position, thanks to its written texts and extensive critical history. Until recently, dance has remained the most ephemeral of the arts, its "texts" existing primarily in the moment of viewing and leaving little in the way of material residue. This is one reason why its historical and theoretical analysis represents a relatively tiny body of work. (I am always reminded of the attitude toward dance scholarship when I go to the library and search for books that are invariably filed in the section bounded by "games and cards" and "magic tricks and the

circus"). Although some movement analysis systems do and have existed, they are often schematic at best or, if very complex like Labanotation, very difficult to read except by those specifically trained as professional notators and reconstructors. In any event, only a minute portion of dance practice is notated in any way. The field remains predominantly an "oral" tradition, passed on from person to person in both formal and informal settings. Video has mitigated this problem to some extent, but all video records are partial, showing usually one visual angle and recording only one specific performance of a dance.

4 Here I am referring specifically to the post-Enlightenment scholarly tradition developing from European sources.

5 See, for example, articles in Henry Louis Gates, ed., *"Race," Writing, and Difference* (Chicago: University of Chicago Press, 1986).

6 Interestingly, as Janet Wolff has pointed out to me, metaphors of dance figure prominently in the work of several critics such as Derrida and Annette Kolodny. However, this metaphoric invocation contrasts sharply and provocatively with a distinct absence of interest in the material and social practice of dance.

7 Within the dance field, an excellent work by Susan Foster, *Reading Dancing: Bodies and Subjects in Contemporary American Dance* (Berkeley: University of California Press, 1986), marks the first full-length study situated within a structuralist/poststructuralist position, and increasingly articles and new books evidence a familiarity and willingness to engage ideological issues. See, for example, Mark Franko, *Dance as Text: Ideologies of the Baroque Body* (Cambridge: Cambridge University Press, 1993). The recent important conference "Choreographing History" at University of California–Riverside, in February 1992 brought together dance scholars and nondance scholars who write about bodily discourse. Among those participating were Randy Martin, Susan Manning, Thomas Laqueur, Elaine Scarry, Norman Bryson, Peggy Phelan, and Lena Hammergren. *Choreographing History* (1995), ed. Susan Foster, presents many of those essays. And critical journals like *Discourse* have recently published articles on dance. This still remains the exception rather than the rule, but does indicate a growing conversation between dance scholarship and cultural studies.

8 This is not to imply that the division between "dance" and "nondance" is always clear, nor that it is always of primary importance in formulating research. Such a designation is subject to change historically and geographically. What may be particularly useful to note is what movements and what spatial sites are associated with "dancing" when that concept is used, and what are not. By asking what constitutes "dance" within a particular context, we can find out more about what values are associated with dance, whether as entertainment, social activity, ritual, or "art." For example, debates over "pornography" include arguments over what constitutes "lewd" movement, with no "redeeming" artistic value. By recontextualizing such movements as dance, or by relocating them to a so-called legitimate theatrical venue, an argument could be made that such movements are artistic, and therefore not subject to censure. The shifting dividing line between dance and nondance activities and the moments of such an invocation are part of a political history of bodies and movement.

9 I thank Cathy Davidson for bringing the information about advice books to my attention.

10 On women and dance halls in the nineteenth century, see Kathy Peiss, *Cheap Amusements: Working Women and Leisure in Turn-of-the-century New York* (Philadelphia: Temple University Press, 1986), especially "Dance Madness," pp. 88–114.

11 In asking what an "un-Latin" rendition of a particular dance would be, for instance, we can begin to identify the movement parameters deemed necessary to identify it as such both within and outside of "Latin" communities. See also Lewis A. Erenberg, *Steppin' Out: New*

York Nightlife and the Transformation of American Culture, 1890–1930 (Chicago: University of Chicago Press, 1981).

12 Sidney Mintz and Richard Price, *An Anthropological Approach to the Afro-American Past*, ISHI Occasional Papers in Social Change, 2 (Philadelphia: Institute for the Study of Human Issues, 1976).

13 See Paul Gilroy, "Ethnic Absolutism," in *Cultural Studies*, ed. Grossberg, Nelson, and Treichler, pp. 187–98, whose argument focuses on the need to reconceive black culture in terms of an Atlantic diaspora. He argues that "much of the precious political, cultural, and intellectual legacy claimed by Afro-American intellectuals is in fact only partly their 'ethnic' property. There are other claims to it which can be based on the structure of the Atlantic diaspora itself" (p. 192). My argument similarly calls for a historical examination of the movement of people and their cultural products; although drawing on Mintz and Price, I have accented the difficulty in applying concepts of absolutism to Euro-American and African American populations which have developed an intense relationship to each other.

14 In the United States, for example, see the rise of a new category "Hispanic" as a racial identity in federal census forms during the last two decades. Countries of origin and language are ignored in the categorization.

15 With rare exceptions, African American dancers were not welcome in U.S. ballet companies until recently. Even today, their numbers remain small, for reasons related to class as well as race. Early arguments against their participation were based on racialist assumptions that their bodily configurations were incompatible with the aesthetics of line for European form. The Dance Theater of Harlem, pioneered by Balanchine dancer Arthur Mitchell, has not only provided a forum for African American dancers to perform the traditional "white" ballets but has also developed a number of ballets based on African American themes or African-style movement resources.

16 This is not to imply that patterns of consumption are the same within predominantly black urban communities, for example, as they are in predominantly white suburban communities.

17 Remember that the character Ricky Ricardo, Lucy's husband on the *I Love Lucy* show, was a band leader. Even all these years after the show, his character still represents the longest-running and best-known Cuban character on American television. While most film scholars have concentrated on the Lucy character, Ana Lopez, in a paper delivered at the 1992 Society for Cinema Studies Conference, points out the importance of the Lucy-Ricky marriage and of his Cuban descent (paper, Society for Cinema Studies conference, Pittsburgh, Penn., 1992).

18 Due to mass media, dance styles, like music styles, can migrate separately from the groups of people who develop them. In New York, with large Latin American and Caribbean populations, dancing the lambada in Scarsdale is likely to mean something different than it does in suburban Indiana, where the ratio of Latin Americans to Anglo-Americans is much smaller than in the New York metropolitan area.

19 Julian Dibbell, "Notes on Carmen: Carmen Miranda, Seriously," *The Village Voice* 36, no. 44 (October 29, 1991), pp. 43–45.

20 Jazz dance, like jazz music, represents an analogous creolized form of cultural production in the United States, with body usage and rhythmic elements drawn from African American and Euro-American sources. Now no longer identifiable as "black" or "white," jazz has, like the case of the Brazilian samba, become "nationalized" or genericized into an American product, often regarded as quintessentially so in other countries. However, its

history, both in the United States and abroad, is deeply imbricated with issues of racial identification. In the early decades of this century, for example, during the rise of modernism with its reliance on "the primitive," the Parisian passion for jazz coincided with an appetite for African American performers like Josephine Baker, known for her "banana dance" in a skimpy bikini of those fruits. The national versus racial identification of jazz is a tension that still exists today.

21 These comments are based primarily on personal observation in a number of state training schools in China during 1990.

22 The European reference is schematic at best, meant to imply the ballet tradition as it developed in Europe and the former Soviet Union and then was transplanted to the United States, where it has since taken on its own particularity.

23 Gloria Strauss, "Dance and Ideology in China, Past and Present: A Study of Ballet in the People's Republic," *Asian and Pacific Dance: Selected Papers for the 1974 C.O.R.D.–S.E.M. Conference*, ed. Adrienne L. Kaeppler, Judy Van Zile, and Carl Wolz, Dance Research Annual 8 (1977), pp. 19–54.

24 Strauss notes that this explanation is certainly not fully adequate. Bound feet would not prevent women from performing kneeling dances, for instance, nor would it have any influence on male dancing. However, she notes that the binding practice was very widespread, especially in areas where the Han population predominated. Some estimates argue that in areas like Tinghsien, more than 99 percent of all females born before 1890 had bound feet. The most severe practices were reserved for upper-class women. Although both the Manchus and reformers after the 1911 revolution tried to outlaw the tradition, footbinding was not fully extinguished until after 1940. See Strauss, pp. 28–30.

25 Whereas the transmission and transportation of social dance forms is effected by mass media marketing and population migrations, in the professional art world (although population demographics have some influence) equally important are the internal politics of each country (multiculturalism as a current funding paradigm in the United States, for example) and the circuit of exchange set up among departments of state in various countries, as well as the international avant-garde circuit. A study of State Department funding of leading artists and companies would reveal an interesting profile of what is promoted as "U.S. art," for example.

26 Live performances cited: DanceBrazil at the Alliance Francaise Theater, New York City, December 1991; Grupo Corpo at the Joyce Theater, New York City, November 1991; Hercilia López, Luis Viana, and Arthur Aviles at Ethnic Arts Theater, December 1991.

27 In the last few years, three new works have appeared which exemplify this approach of moving with assurance between the micro and macro levels of analysis. All three were written by scholars with extensive dance experience and/or with training in movement analysis in addition to their disciplinary training in the social sciences. See Sally Ness, *Body, Movement, and Culture: Kinesthetic and Visual Symbolism in a Philippine Community* (Philadelphia: University of Pennsylvania Press, 1992); Cynthia Novack, *Sharing the Dance: Contact Improvisation and American Culture* (Madison: University of Wisconsin Press, 1990); and Marta Savigliano, *Tango and the Political Economy of Passion* (Boulder, Colo.: Westview Press, 1995).

2 CULTURAL STUDIES AND DANCE HISTORY

Norman Bryson

It is an exciting moment for dance history, which may explain the breathlessness of the remarks that follow. The feeling of the pent-up and its release also comes from a personal context that I am hoping may be more generally shared. Briefly stated: I have never been able to understand why it is that dance, as an object of inquiry, seems to belong in a different disciplinary universe from the fields in the humanities that as a scholar I am drawn to—comparative literature, critical theory, cultural studies, art history, and film studies. In none of the departments where I have worked has dance history featured even remotely in the curriculum. Graduate students hoping to work on dance in the context of two of these departments have, in my experience, been discouraged from doing so in ways both subtle and not so subtle, ranging from head-shaking about employment to queries about the viability and vitality of the field. In the 1970s I counted dance history as one of a number of institutionally oppressed fields whose time nonetheless would one day come. For instance, if the history of art moved far enough away from its canon, if it widened its scope from "masterpieces" to "visual culture," then surely dance, as a key component of visual culture, would inevitably swing into view in art history departments.[1] In the same way, if cultural theory moved far enough away from models of base and superstructure and from economic determinism, if it was truly gearing up to embrace the idea of cultural representation as productive of its own specific range of social and political effects, then forms of art that had hitherto been consigned to the margins of the superstructure would surely move back toward center stage.

In the 1980s two developments in particular made me hope that dance historians would soon be joining my colleagues in the fields then emerging as critical theory and cultural studies. The first was the impact of Foucault. It now became possible to think of the body itself as a key component in cultural history; and since the disciplines that historically defined and organized the body (in the clinic, the anatomy theater, the barracks, the penitentiary, the school, the workplace) were now being explored on all sides, it could not be long before dance—the most blatant and unarguable instance of the disciplined body—would appear high on scholarship's Foucauldian agenda.[2] The second development that fanned my hopes for dance history was the rapid evolution of gender studies, including gay and lesbian studies. If this epochal change now made it hard to go to the movies with an innocent eye, without thinking of the ideas emanating from *Screen* or *Camera Obscura*, or from Laura Mulvey, Teresa de Lauretis, Mary Ann Doane, or Kaja Silverman, by the same token it was hard to keep those ideas entirely out of one's mind when seeing dance performances.

One afternoon in New York, watching the Joffrey reconstruction of *The Rite of Spring*, I realized something had snapped. I had grown up loving every bar of the score, in much the same way I had grown up believing eagerly in all the tales of modernism: that modernist painting was a progress from depth to flatness, from mimesis to "abstraction," from Manet to Picasso to Jackson Pollock; that modernist music was a progress from tonality to seriality, from the first to the second Vienna school, from Wagner to Webern to Boulez. *The Rite of Spring* was a work one approached with reverence, in the same awed way one approached Picasso's *Demoiselles d'Avignon* at the Museum of Modern Art: great harbinger of modernity, shatterer of the classical peace, source of unimagined freedoms. Yet one after another those tales of modernism began to lose their power to convince. Now what I tended to see in Manet's *Olympia* was not so much the flatness as the voyeurism. What first embarrassed and later offended me about MOMA's dramatic placing of *Les Demoiselles d'Avignon* at the monumental threshold of its collection was its equation of modernity with virility and domination.[3] Reading what Mondrian painted in the light of what Mondrian actually wrote about it—his loopy notions of fallen feminine matter versus masculine spiritual vision, "male" verticals and "female" horizontals[4]—the pristine grids and lozenges underwent something of a sea-change, or at least they were put on hold until I could figure out more about the implications.

Watching the culminating dance of the virgin of the tribe who in jerks and spasms ritually dances herself to death before the gaze of the tribal elders, I felt my slow, male, bearlike brain begin to make a connection. Hadn't I seen this sort of thing somewhere before? this furious announcement of modernity, that was at the same time an investigation of the sexuality of the female body and a massive punishment for that sexuality inflicted from within the male imaginary? this theater of cruelty in which the spectacle of the female body, with its capacity to provoke dread and awe in the normatively masculine spectator, is dealt with through sadism, voyeurism, and a fetishism that deflects the charge of that body into protective substitutes and shields (the "abstract" choreography, the modernist aesthetics of movement)?

I am deliberately presenting my responses as a kind of lowest common denominator of postmodern taste. Even so, I wasn't sure whether I had any allies. Looking round the audience at the Joffrey *Rite of Spring*, rapturous in their applause, I wondered how many others there might be for whom the masterpiece we had just seen might be beginning to slide off the Olympian pedestal of works of art one is not supposed to question. Did the population that followed *Screen* or *Camera Obscura*, or Laura Mulvey or Linda Nochlin, have *no* overlap with the population that stood up to applaud a sacrificial virgin dancing herself to death in front of tribal potentates in ludicrous headgear? Did the fans of *The History of Sexuality* ever coincide with the fans of *Coppelia* or *L'Après-midi d'un faune* or *Clytemnestra*? Did the cultural historians who work on fantasies of the mechanical body ever go to see Nijinska, or Josephine Baker—or Busby Berkeley? Did they only read books?

My hopes for the "Choreographing History" conference held at Riverside in 1992 were, then, at least twofold. First, if it were true that despite all the institutional efforts to keep dance history away from the center of humanities funding and research, and well away from poststructuralism, postmodernism, and cultural studies, nevertheless there were dance historians who were surreptitiously absorbing the same intellectual influences that were having such an impact on their colleagues in comparative literature or art history, then such a conference might perhaps have a role in reconnecting that beleaguered underground with those lucky enough to be working in fields better established in terms of grants, jobs, journals, and university recognition. Second, my hope was that institutions with names like Humanities Research Center, Center for Literary and Cultural Studies, Ph.D. Program in Visual Representation and Cultural Theory, and the like would be inspired by the conference to go out of their way to encourage their own colleagues and graduate students to work on the history of dance with some of the same intellectual tools and the same formats (seminars, lecture courses, qualifying papers, articles) used in the domain still called art history, literary criticism, comparative literature. Less and less are those domains able to point to an agreed disciplinary center, a canon, a circumscribed object of knowledge; and this being so, the subject that was most profoundly hit by the previous division of the humanities, in being marginalized and underfunded, might now be in a position with the most to gain by the loosening or breakup of the old dispensation.

In such a context, the object of dance history can no longer be assumed as a given. It may no longer be "dance." If by dance one understands the ballet of the nineteenth and twentieth centuries, or even of the court, then the definition of dance that those very particular and local forms of dance historically forged for themselves is inevitably reimposed upon the discipline of dance history itself, so that a historically parochial definition is made over into a general framework for all dance, universally. Since, oddly enough, dance thus defined turns out to coincide only with the forms of dance recognized and patronized by modern Western elites, by a methodological slide the terms proposed *by the object* are repeated as the terms for *investigating* the object. One corrective move here would be resolutely anticanonical, following the direction pursued by much recent art history and literary criticism: to put the canon and its values into brackets (which is not necessarily to discount or negate those values), and to ask why it was that particular historical societies ascribed value to certain distinct forms of movement, segregating such "high" forms from other vernacular forms. And to ask, why the segregation? why *those* values? which were *whose* values?

A noncanonical definition of dance deliberately avoids using the same proscenium frame that European ballet produced in the course of its own development; instead of accepting the proscenium as the discipline's own viewfinder, it detaches itself from that frame and opens itself to wider angles of vision. The question is, how wide? In an anthropological perspective, for instance, there is no guarantee that what would count as "dance" would necessarily be recognized by most dance historians as what *they* mean by dance. Applying the wide-angle lens of anthropology to our own milieux, it could not be ruled out that the investigation would turn out to include forms of socially structured movement one would not normally think of as dance at all: the coded movements of a cocktail party, a wedding, a funeral, a parade; the opening of parliament, a lecture hall, an office block, a community center; a bar, a mall, an aerobics class, a graduation ball, "commencement exercises."

Opening the viewfinder to maximum and moving the definition of dance from "ballet" to "socially structured human movement" may be vertiginous as an opening move, but it has heuristic advantages in showing how local and limited our sense of dance tends to be. Furthermore, the maximally capacious definition is typically found to lose its amorphous character the moment it is actually put into practice, and the potentially infinite space of analysis it opens up (the study of *any* human movement?) fills with remarkably finite objects. In a famous exchange between the Roland Barthes of *Critique et vérité* and its opponents, Barthes was accused (in moving away from then standard definitions of criticism and literature) of opening the gates of literary study to *any* text at all, and of destroying the basis for the disciplinary study of meaning—now "anyone could say anything about anything."[5] Barthes' rejoinder is worth recalling in this particular situation, where an anticanonical or postcanonical definition of dance would seem to risk taking in both everything and nothing. Barthes' observation was that although meaning arises through mobility, that mobility operates under close constraints: the ways a reader reads a text is precisely shaped by the conventions and institutions that regulate and authorize the fields of meaning. In practice, discourse is not at the disposal of the individual subject; it is configured in precise ways, activating only a fraction of the field of possibilities. In the same way, what would count as significant, organized, socially structured movement is in practice decided by social values (intellectual, ethical, political) and by institutional conventions: one could perhaps study any old set of movements, but in practice the decision as to what one chooses to study is discursively and historically constrained. And constrained twice over: by what the society that one studies proposed as *its* definition of significant human movement; and by what in our own contexts of scholarship are thought to be the areas in which larger cultural patterns and values may be found and thought about.

An example—though my discussion must be brief. A dance historian working on Versailles might choose to concentrate on reconstructing what the court itself proposed as its highest level of aesthetically charged movement, court ballet and social dancing; and perhaps this is dance history's classic trajectory. Another possibility, however, would be to place dance as one among many in the larger context of all those disciplines that centered on the body at the court of Versailles.

What emerges at once is the choreographic nature of daily life and of the body's vernacular self-presentation, most evident in the ubiquity of the bow. The bow was part of daily movement through space; it was difficult to execute correctly, and manuals were profuse in the pages and diagrams they devoted to its graceful execution. At the same time the bow was the first movement of social dancing: one bowed to one's partner or audience before the first steps. The continuum between the skills of dance and vernacular movement is clear also in the promenade, with its strict rules of carriage and demeanor, and its closely observed protocols of recognition, introduction, and leave-taking. The body that performed these movements was the site of constant injunctions and prescriptions concerning social spectacle; it was expert in making a show. Moreover, the performance of both men and women in equestrian activities demanded detailed training and a mastery of posture and movement which the court coded in its values as the rider's *bonne allure*. The importance of equestrian culture at the court was acknowledged in the layout of Versailles (originally a hunting lodge, a function it retained and elaborated), in the dramatic siting of equestrian sculpture on its grounds, and in energetic debates concerning old versus new styles of riding. To be at court entailed that one already had full control over the base bodily functions which, from Erasmus on, filled the conduct manuals with advice concerning the sneeze, the yawn, the laugh; on this basic foundation of polite behavior the culture of Versailles built a whole further edifice of refinements and complications, so that while all could play the game, only a few might excel (and some might be disgraced), where excellence itself was figured in its most radiant form by the figure of the king.

One could reconstruct in detail the behavioral codes that governed the court, together with their evolution decade by decade: the rules concerning religious and secular ceremony, the king's *lever* and *coucher*, the etiquette of eating, the regimens of diet and bleeding, the complex codes surrounding an individual's birth, death, and sexuality. Yet such reconstruction remains antiquarian unless the historian looks for the global functioning of the bodily disciplines in the systems of prestige and power by which court life was regulated. The advantage of Versailles as a methodological test case is that a good deal of recent research has stressed the importance of the intersections at Versailles between real and symbolic capital. Daniel Dessert's *Argent, pouvoir et société au Grand Siècle* has shown that, given the bankruptcy of the royal coffers during the fronde and the long-term disadvantages of the sale of state offices, the funds that the monarchy required could best be obtained by negotiating loans from the landed aristocracy, in a trade-off that exchanged cash for prestige at court.[6]

The extravagance of Vaux-le-Vicomte and later of Versailles had as its hard-currency rationale the king's need to produce a system that would generate, at court, forms of prestige so dazzling that to acquire them those willing to lend to the king were prepared to pay out fortunes. A double system, then: symbolic capital in exchange for money, the convertibility of prestige and cash. The base-and-superstructure model, in which the king's absolute power is expressed through the *ancillary* elaborations of prestige, misses the point of this convertibility altogether; it would regard the court's prestige system as functionally inert, an ornamental by-product of absolutist power. But for Dessert, as for Louis Marin in *Le Portrait du Roi*, the king's function as arbiter and pinnacle of the court's system of spectacle and bodily display is not the reflection of a power located elsewhere, but power's actual locus.[7] It is in the production of Versailles as an integrated system of social display that the political effects of absolutism are to be situated. The king's image is where the king generates his personal authority, and in relation to that image all the lesser levels of the court hierarchy are measured: the king as solar center of personal spectacle, round which all the lesser satellites of power revolve.

The work of Dessert and Marin is of importance to dance history in that the model of explanation they use, which locates power in spectacle and the capacity of spectacle to produce hierarchical effects, immediately gives central importance to "socially structured movement" as the main theater of power; like Clifford Geertz's Bali, Versailles was a "theater state."[8] Where Foucault's emphasis on the body as site of discipline shows how subjects of the court drilled, rehearsed, and perfected their bodily movements, Dessert and Marin show why such discipline was politically and economically necessary and effective. The social dancing of Versailles is not a minor, ornamental affair somewhere at distance from the actual processes of the court's power: the system of which it is a part stands at the very center. If Louis XIV has himself represented in painting (by Hyacinthe Rigaud) as one who dances, it is because his dance, in its widest sense, orchestrates the entire milieu, from its mode of dress down to its actual revenues. Instead of gold as the infrastructure subtending court culture, the infrastructure becomes the king's manipulation of spectacle and prestige, and his orchestration of the courtiers' bodies into a kind of permanent dance of power.

I mention the case of Versailles to indicate a number of theoretical possibilities of general relevance to dance history. First, that by widening the angle of vision to "socially structured movement," the designation does not, in fact, cause the classic object of dance history (dance at the court) to evaporate (if that were a concern). Rather the opposite: in placing dance in the larger context that would embrace all the acts of discipline that the courtly body performs, dance does not disappear, it reemerges as the cultural form that deals with the most central processes of its society, its primary economy of spectacle, discipline, and prestige. Second, the example shows how it is possible not to be intimidated in the face of the economic or political historian who, relegating dance to some distant periphery of the cultural "background," concentrates on the supposedly serious and determining business of power, economics, gold, class, taxation, land. If, as Marin and Dessert both argue, spectacle is at the heart of Versailles' political and economic systems, then the image of the king as dancer becomes absolutely central to economic and political, as well as to "cultural" history. Dance is no longer an adornment, a decoration, an epiphenomenon of power; bodily orchestration, discipline, and spectacle are the heart of the state apparatus (by the same token, dance history is no longer the adornment, decoration, or epiphenomenon of the academy).

A second example—though, again, my comments must be brief. It concerns the culture of dance in nineteenth-century Paris, the connections that dance history might make between forms of dance on stage in the theaters and café-concerts, and issues of spectatorship, modernity, and sexuality in the wider context of urban life.

The nature of dance spectacle here stands in stark contrast to its earlier manifestations in the seventeenth and eighteenth centuries. Dance at Versailles was essentially a heightened and dramatized form of the diverse bodily disciplines and training that all members of the court shared; it figured that discipline in a distilled and concentrated way, creating an idealized image of the controlled and coordinated body that formed the basis of courtly self-presentation (figure 1). In Enlightenment theorizations of dance, the repeated claim is that dance is a universal medium, able to bypass the arbitrary conventions of speech by communicating at a level of natural expression deeper than the lexicons and symbols of "artificial" languages. For Diderot, the most efficient forms of human communication are the tableau and the pantomime; for Rousseau, while the danger of theater is that it falsifies human nature, by the same token the free and improvised movement of citizens at a festival enables them to attain a condition of ideal mutual transparency in which human nature, uncorrupted by artifice, reveals itself directly through the natural movements of the body. In the dance culture of the nineteenth-century metropolis, all this has gone: the continuum between dancer and observer is broken at the proscenium arch, with the two camps, performers and spectators, separated by an enormous theatrical, social, and economic interval. The movements of the dancer are professional skills that the audience could not match if it tried. One paid to see them. Dance is one spectacular diversion among many in a metropolis increasingly organized according to spectacle, consumption, and social distance.

T. J. Clark has written wonderful chapters on spectacle and nineteenth-century Paris (in *Paris in the Art of Manet and His Followers*), and all I would wish to do here is indicate how relevant that work is to the history of dance.[9] Haussmann's designs for the layout of the city provided the architectural foundation, where instead of being addressed as the subject of feudal authority, with urban space clustered round the ancient sites of power (the royal palaces, cathedrals, churches, law courts), those who live and work in the city are addressed as citizens, Parisians, diverse in their classes and occupations yet unified as subjects of the city itself. With increasing money and leisure at their disposal, the new social groups formed by intensive urbanization are in a position to afford diversion, and an array of new amenities comes to animate the urban landscape: parks, expositions, arcades, department stores, plays, the races, restaurants, cafés. In all of these, urban life takes on the characteristic modern form of spectacle: the urban subject is an observer, of the boulevards,

1. Hyacinthe Rigaud,
Portrait of Louis XIV, King of France, in Royal Costume. Louvre, Paris.
Photo: Erich Lessing/Art Resource, N.Y.

2. Edouard Manet, *Bar at the Folies-Bergère.*
Courtauld Institute Galleries, London. Photo: Foto Marburg/Art Resource, N.Y.
3. Edgar Degas, *Two Dancers on the Stage.* Courtauld Institute Galleries, London.
Photo: Giraudon/Art Resource, N.Y.

4. Georges Seurat, *La Grande Jatte*. Art Institute, Chicago.
5. Georges Seurat, *Le Chahut*.
Rijksmuseum Kroeller-Mueller, Otterlo, The Netherlands.
Photo: Erich Lessing/Art Resource, N.Y.

the theaters, the races, the shops, the crowds. It is spectacle driven by the market, and all available for a price.

As Griselda Pollock and others have pointed out, the spectacle of the metropolis is also structured according to a principle of strict sexual division: the flâneur, watcher-hero of the boulevards, is male, and mastery of the urban prospect is essentially a masculine prerogative.[10] Urban subjectivity is increasingly organized by a split between the male as bearer of the look and the female as object for that looking.[11] At the same time, the double standard with regard to men and women increasingly consigns respectable women to domestic space, leaving the urban landscape as a place of encounter between the flâneur who can afford to pay for his pleasures, and those women whose bodies are, or might be, available to cater to them. Manet's *Olympia* makes plain the equation between modern life, male visual pleasure, and female objectification. *The Bar at the Folies-Bergère* (figure 2) sounds the same theme in another key: in the new epicenters of urban entertainment, the classes are thrown together in illegible confusion, as an anonymous public; social rank grows indistinct, especially at night, and the man with the top hat might be a banker, a lawyer, or a haberdasher.[12] Yet the blurring of rank is matched and counterbalanced by the discourses of masculinity, and however much or little a man may earn by day, in the nocturnal economy class differences reconfigure as sexual identity and privilege conferred upon all. What all flâneurs share is the right to view and the right to pleasure; in the metropolis female glamour acquires a new social function, as the great equalizer in a society still starkly divided along lines of class and livelihood.

Hovering over the barmaid in Manet's *A Bar* stands, or rather floats, a dancer-acrobat. From here, at the bar, one does not see the acrobat clearly—but the figure's act is the current draw of the house, and enough is glimpsed for the painting to imply a parallel between acrobat and barmaid: both are there to cater to the male gaze, and both occupy the same position of object of entertainment for the paying customer. Manet's painting *The Masked Ball at the Opera* is even more explicit about the connections between spectacle, dance, and the role of cash in encounters between the sexes.[13] The men are evidently well-heeled, and the women evidently nonrespectable; what is significant is that, again, the context is that of dance, both in the setting of the opera house and in the occasion, the ball that seems to be of interest mostly for the open displays of sexual behavior it sanctions and provides for. In late-nineteenth-century Paris, dancers and dancing became crucial subjects for representation because the figure of the female dancer, in particular, came to embody social and sexual processes at the heart of the modern city. Since modernity involved the expansion of spectacle and the generalization of the relation seer/seen to an increasing number of social domains, the female dancer could stand for modernity as a whole; the dancer figured forth, in intense and specialized form, the essential social relation of observer to observed now to be found in all aspects of metropolitan life. If urban culture distributed power in the visual field between those flâneur-subjects who possessed the keys to the city and those who featured only as the objects for the flâneur's gaze, the female dancer iconized the system, standing for the truth of the visual (and sexual) economy as a whole.

Yet the representation of women dancers is not uniform, and staying only with the most obvious imagery it is evident that the range of attitudes toward dance and dancers was complex and conflicted. In Degas' pictures of dancers rehearsing and performing, the way in which the women are so completely absorbed into the conditions of spectacle makes them, from one point of view, ultimate objects of the masculine gaze (figure 3). They appear to have no other destiny than to serve as creatures there to be seen; all signs of individuality, of an inwardness that might complicate the role of visual object, are effaced. The dancers rarely communicate with one another outside the terms of the dance itself, so that while the movements of one may echo or pair with the movements of another, the groupings remain formal rather than psychological, as though female interaction and solidarity—with one another, away from the requirements of the masculine gaze—were nonexistent, were simply not there as a possibility for the male psyche to contemplate and reckon with. Furthermore, if in these paintings Degas uses the dancers as elements in a meditation on the art of painting, the dancers' conversion and disappearance into metaphors for Degas' own craft is facilitated by, and may require, the dancers' own apparent self-evacuation as alternative centers of subjectivity. Should we take these works as being, on some level, Degas' dramatization of his own goals as a painter (perfection of technique, a grace and ease possible only through strict training and self-control), what enables this to happen is Degas' ruthless overriding of the dancers as independent agents; they become essentially extras, staffage in pictures whose emotional center is not dance at all but painting, and what Degas imagines is meant by the idea of himself as master-painter—a conception whose consequence is that the dancers are made over into the art of painting's handmaids or attendants.

And yet this is still not all there is to the paintings. Degas' own self-projection as the great technician, in the service of an impersonal muse, also elevates and ennobles the dancers: they, too, are utterly absorbed in their exercise of technique; their absence of self-expression is proof of their seriousness in art, at least as Degas defines art. Though the sense of visual objectification is so strong in these pictures, they are also the professional homage of one art to another; there is no question that painting regards dance in patronizing or condescending fashion.

Comparable degrees of complexity are to be found everywhere in Impressionist paintings of dance and social movement. In Seurat, the uncanny rigidity of the strollers in *La Grande Jatte* points to something profoundly wrong in their world—they cannot move with grace (figure 4). They have the leisure and the means, they have an idyllic setting, they have been set free, at least for as long as Sunday lasts, from the routines and confinements of the world of work. Yet the fact that the strollers *should* at last be experiencing the freedom of their bodies and the pleasures of improvised, untrammeled movement only makes more painful their wooden-doll gait and puppetlike movements, as though in the industrial society to which they belong the rhythms set by the factory and office had been internalized into a perpetual prison-house. Where earlier Impressionist landscape scenes had found something utopian about the free range of movement that modern life seemed to release,[14] Seurat sees that freedom as thoroughly inhabited by mechanical control: even his brushwork, with its renunciation of any kind of self-expressiveness, enacts the triumph of the mechanical in its repeated dots that mime the technology of the late century's mass-reproduced imagery.[15]

In terms of what Foucault called the "repressive hypothesis" (the nineteenth- and twentieth-century notion that modern civilization represses the natural body and especially its sexuality), Seurat's handling of bodily movement could be described as a battle between a natural, spontaneous body that should now be appearing in the new world of leisure and affluence, and the relentless forces of repression that clamp down on that body and reimpose upon it forms of control all the stronger and more insidious for being internalized. Yet it may be more interesting to follow Foucault's own critique of the repressive hypothesis, which suggests that it is in the name of liberating the "natural" body's buried energies and drives that social control in fact achieves its deepest purchase on the body; and to view Seurat as exactly capturing that double process which Foucault describes, whereby techniques of discipline move forward into the body by always positing, just beyond their line of advance, a body wholly free of repression and restraint. That, at any rate, would explain the continuity between *La Grande Jatte* and Seurat's vision of the circus performer in *La Chahut.* Both works suggest that modernity gives a glimpse of a body freed at last from inhibition, a body released from the prison-house of workaday existence. Both view freedom in terms of the body's capacities for movement: *La Grande Jatte* by negation, through the strollers' lack of grace, and *Le Chahut* through excess, as a release of bodily energies in a wild and dangerous defiance of the law (figure 5).

Yet in both works that liberated, energetic body is viewed as instantly returned to order by mechanical forces, its dynamism subordinated to geometric recoding and its energies trivialized and objectified by the society of spectacle. That double aspect, of increased freedom and increased subjection to the negative conditions of modernity, is equally present in Toulouse-Lautrec's analysis of the dance culture of such establishments as the Moulin Rouge. The new dances of the late nineteenth century break free of the armature of respectability that had imprisoned the body in a cage of bourgeois repression; they reveal and liberate a new level of public sexuality; the police are called in. But even without the police, the cancan—like its later offshoots in Busby Berkeley—marks a new advance of mechanized order into the body's movements. Though erotic, the dance is entirely impersonal, dehumanized, and repetitious; though it reveals the anatomical body with unprecedented frankness, this is accompanied by an extraordinary objectification of the body by its owner, who in order to perform the dance successfully (pulling one leg straight up to the head while hopping on the other) must treat her body absolutely as a thing, as a puppet or marionette. In the cancan, to its most acute observers, at least three forces were at work: modernity, presented in its latest, most outrageous and chic form; sexual vitality; and the display of female sexuality before a masculine gaze that not only objectifies but persuades the owner of the body on display to concur with the objectification and to heighten it by treating the body as its own object or instrument, through conspicuous self-manipulation and contortion.

I have touched on nineteenth-century dance in order to sketch, in however crude a fashion, some more general possibilities that dance history might choose to explore. The first I want to stress is that dance history stands to gain a good deal by taking on board some of the findings of nineteenth-century art history, especially those concerning such key social processes as urbanization, the proliferation of spectacle, and the development of commodified leisure. The second is that no history of nineteenth-century dance is likely to be complete unless its framework includes analysis of the structures of sexual difference at work in performance and spectatorship, whether in ballet or in popular culture. The third concerns the scope of evidence for dance history, which should not be unduly constrained by the demands of dance reconstruction. Degas, Seurat, and Toulouse-Lautrec may not tell us much about nineteenth-century choreography, but they are good places to start from in gauging the complexity of cultural attitudes toward the body in motion, the degrees of idealization and abjection associated with dance in the cultural imaginary, and the paradoxical interplay between liberation and regulation at work in modern dance.

Earlier I mentioned a problem of circularity in dance history, that the ways in which dance historically came to frame itself in relation to its own audiences and its surrounding culture can come to be repeated in the ways that the history of dance approaches its object—a methodological slippage whereby the terms proposed by the object are transferred to the mode of investigating that object. Nowhere is the process of circularity more pronounced than in the case of modernism, and in all domains—painting, sculpture, dance, literature, music. With painting, the result of the circularity or methodological slide is that the nonrepresentational image, the image that breaks with the classical functions of mimesis and presents itself as pure form, comes to be seen through a formalist criticism organized around an art historical narrative of progress from classical mimesis to formal purity, from illusionistic depth to the flat space of the picture plane, from paint subordinated to the task of transcribing the surfaces of the world to paint freed to express its own autonomy as a medium. With dance, a similar or parallel narrative describes the progressive liberation of dance movement from narrative function and setting and even narratively expressive gesture; movement is freed from illustrative or mimetic reference, and in later stages from subservience to the musical score.

When, in the grand narratives of modernity, the nature of the object being described (the emergence of pure form) comes to converge with the critical framework through which it is approached (formalism), the results can be both highly persuasive and at the same time severe in the limitations imposed upon criticism. Certainly a history of modern dance can be written that depends centrally on formal analysis of the changes in structured movement over time, and the approach can impose itself as authoritative in the literal sense that the nature of the object authorizes what criticism does with it. The analysis can claim to bear the closest possible relation to its object, to be true to that object as nothing else can, since its eyes need never lift from the object or wander from the central quadrature of the stage into other areas of the social formation to which dance might be related—or reduced.

The formalist narrative has the further virtue of its heroic or triumphalist aspect, in that modern dance fought long and hard to achieve its liberation into pure movement, and criticism that bases itself on the success of that historical endeavor participates vicariously yet nobly in the struggle itself, now from the perspective of victory. Yet there is at least one major limitation: that the "abstraction" of dance movement from reference and illustration can be taken as criticism's own internal horizon. Abstraction becomes the end-point of the historical narrative (from Manet to Picasso to Jackson Pollock: from Petipa to Nijinsky to Merce Cunningham), and at the same time the irreducible core of criticism: any number of developments and details in dance may be referred to and subsumed under abstraction, but abstraction itself may not be subsumed into anything else; to postulate a further or higher term would be to threaten the modernist paradigm itself.

One way to move beyond the framework of modernist criticism is to look for meanings in the term *abstraction* that refer to other domains of movement than dance, to other social regions where motion is analyzed and represented, and to larger social processes that turn on the redesigning and stylization of action and gesture. And in the West it is no exaggeration to say that the analysis of movement into abstract fields of force has played a central cultural role since at least the time of the Industrial Revolution. Already in the plates of the *Encyclopédie* are found detailed descriptions of mechanical processes and their human operations, in which the movements to be performed by the machine and the movements to be performed by human agency unfold, without differentiation, within the same framework of applied kinetics and mechanics. Industrialization requires the coming together of at least two great systems of abstraction. First, an economic system in which the contribution supplied by human labor can be homogeneously quantified as material cost. In Marx's analysis of proto-industrialization, capital cannot engage with productive forces until labor itself can come to be represented as a uniform substance, withdrawn from the local, specific, nonconvertible instances of use-value and entered into a system where labor becomes one commodity among others in a universal market of exchange. Second, a technical system is required in which tasks to be performed can be broken down through scientific mechanics into abstract units of force (weights, vectors, horsepower, ergs); building a machine of any kind assumes that all of its motions, internally and externally, obey a kinetic calculus. The meshing together of economic and kinetic abstraction in industrialization represents, in anthropological terms, an epochal change in the history of socially structured movement and in the human object world; over a course of three centuries the Western vision of industrial movement gradually imposes itself on a global scale.

What inevitably changed in the course of this historical transformation was the classical conception of the body's relation to its material environment and to itself. In the sphere of production, the artisanal harmony between maker, craft, and product was broken. Based on the conception of the object as formed by the skill and touch of the craftsman's body, the harmony could not survive in a dispensation predicated on the object as the product of mechanical forces. The industrial object comes into being by a fundamental *withdrawal* of craft and touch from the object world. It entails a deep severance of the body from the world. In the sphere of consumption, expansion of the industrial economy brought in its wake a mechanically generated abundance, a plethora of goods, that nevertheless no longer speak from one body to another, from artisan to user. On its surface the new form of object bears no traces of its making, and as industrial objects proliferate and gradually fill the environment to saturation, a milieu is created in which the human subject can no longer find itself *reflected* in the surrounding world. The material environment comes from labor that no longer follows any kind of organic process, unified by the maker's body, since labor itself is now a fractional process, broken into stages, each of which is only one discontinuous fragment of engineered motion. Looking at the world built by abstraction, the subject sees reflected back not the rhythms of the body but the rhythms of the machine, and above all the three great, hammering rhythms of the first machine age: fragmentation (in bursts, spasms, jerks, pulses); repetition (the first precise repetitions, since the body repeats only approximately); and velocity (the trio of trains, cars, planes).

Fascination with the idea of the body/machine appears in many cultures, and not only in the West. Yet before the twentieth century its European associations still seem to be with the magic of sorcery, the doll that comes to life, and with evil, the turning of Odette into Odile. In the era of mechanization this conception begins to shade into its opposite: concerned less with transgressions of the categories of animate and inanimate than with the instability of the distinction between them. In the traditional idea of the automaton, there is no relation between the automaton and the environment: the automaton's fascination is exactly that it walks by itself, without input from the outside. But in the emergent conceptions of automation within modernism, the whole environment resembles the automaton; between the figure whose movements are automatic and its surrounding world no precise line or boundary can be found. These movements are something new in the world; behind them there stands no controlling image, only the conditions of modernity. The movements most expressive of modernity incarnate fragmentation, repetition, and velocity into the human figure, but the figure is only a synecdoche, a part for the whole. On stage, it will have no bounded outline; it will not play with the shapes formed by its own enclosedness and boundary, as in the arabesque. Rather its body is rethought as an assemblage of parts: the angle formed at a joint (elbow, wrist, knee, ankle) stays in place in its own zone, and is not accompanied by the instant adjustments throughout the body as a whole that occur in classical dance.

It would be a wonderful project to trace the interplay between residual and emergent senses of movement which, in early modernism, polarize as the traditional or folkloric figure of the automaton, looking to Coppelia and Odile, and the futurist repertoire of movement, figured in distilled form in constructivism and *ballet mécanique.* Nijinsky's own performances seem divided between both worlds. In *Petrouchka* the folkloric conception officially governs the plot, and the line between real and simulated movement is sharply drawn in the difference between the bustlingly "real" movements of the crowd at the fairground and the automatic movements of the Blackamoor and the Trumpet Girl. Yet the central figure is also ambiguous: at the end, when Petrouchka "dies," he seems far more engaging and sympathetic than his puppet-companions, who really are marionettes. And, to judge from reconstruction, the role of Petrouchka is not simply an exploration of the limited range of mechanical movements associated with toys: its pathos comes from Petrouchka's existing in some ungraspable blur or transition between organic and inorganic, which he is both at once. In the *Rite* the vocabulary of movement is far more aggressively modernist: every movement on stage is governed by jerks, spasms, pounding repetitions, and the amazing absence of the classical trope of the body as a unified whole bounded by the enclosure of the arabesque: morcelization of the body and fragmentation of movement rule the stage.

There are alternatives to a history of modernist dance as the discovery of a language of pure movement; one might well begin by viewing the term *abstraction* with some suspicion, refusing to take it at face value, and rethinking abstraction as in some sense providing a "literal" representation of new and emergent conditions in the industrialized West. One need not be arguing along base-and-superstructure lines, that changes in the means of production are reflected in dance passively and remotely, as though at last hearing the distant rumble of history. Rather, modernist dance can be taken as a reflection *upon* the undeniable changes of modernity, as these affected the body and the sense of the body's relation to its historically new environment. For me, at least, this makes for a far more persuasive account of the impact of modern dance on its first audiences than the formalist narrative of the discovery of pure movement; what a dance like the *Rite* could draw on and speak to, like futurist painting and sculpture, was exactly the sense of extended reference, beyond the enclosed world of romantic plots and movement, into contemporary perceptions of how it felt to live in a body and an environment subject to such rapid social and technological change.

Such reflection is not only a matter of dance's *registering* the conditions of modernity, presenting them for the first time through dramatic performance. Dance deals with modernity also through the operations of fantasy, and it is the activity of fantasy round the machine and the body's relation to the machine that might provide some of the richest materials for the dance historian to investigate.[16] As an example one might choose the ways in which the fantasy image of the mechanized environment or of the machine/body is mapped in modernism on to the fantasy image of the primitive environment and the primitive body. Between the body as imagined in a primal state and the body as figured forth by the machine a structure of linkage or engagement is formed that seems, in early modernism especially, to possess an extraordinary cultural charge. Elements from one fantasy migrate to the other and back, as though the images that were involved performed closely related functions in the cultural imaginary. Behind the fantasy of the primitive body lies the whole evolution, from the mid-nineteenth century onwards, of the idea that beneath the civilized exterior the individual harbors a secret life that consistently disobeys or cuts across the formal arrangements of society, a core of energies that finds outlet in dreams, obsessions, perversions; the seat of this secret life is the body, and above all the body's sexual desires and drives (psychoanalysis, *scientia sexualis*). In European societies this secret body, with its lava of libido, is theorized as governed by repression, and if we wish to see—and control—its operations we have to look to modern Europe's others: to prehistory (*Totem and Taboo*, the primal horde), Africa (for Freud the unconscious is always the "dark continent"), the Middle East (Orientalism in all its forms), the Pacific (Gauguin), central Asia (Nijinsky), Oceania or Meso-America (as invented by Surrealism). In the fantasy of the mechanized body or machine/body a related conception or structure is apparent: that the machine is the human body's Other, its negative or anti-type; machines are slaves, meant to serve humanity; nevertheless, there is the risk that these slaves might rise up against their masters, take over the environment, and seek to govern on their own (*Robot*, *Metropolis*). The core of each fantasy is the danger—and the fascination—of dissolution: that the body's primitive energies may erupt and overturn the rule of civilization; that mechanization will take command and make the world over in its own image.

In dance, the mapping of the machine/body on to the primitive body takes a variety of forms, all crucial to early modernism, and in both high culture and low. One point of convergence is the *Rite* itself, with its double or superimposed temporal structure: the distant prehistory of the primal horde, which is at the same moment the ultramodern present of the avant-garde. Another is the convergence of the "primitive" with the mechanized body in jazz dance, with its reference to African movement and music and its fascination with the body of the black dancer, though the reference is fused with the velocities, syncopations, and élan of the modern metropolis (Paris, New York). Since both fantasies seek to come close to energies that are also configured as threatening, they are ultimately fantasies of control (like Freud's own fantasy of the savage band of brothers who nevertheless originate the social contract and found the patriarchy). The dangerous energies of the primitive body and the machine/body, though released by the *Rite*'s music and choreography, are in the end subdued, and exorcized, through the virgin of the tribe who dances herself to death before the tribal elders: feminized, the primitive body is thus securely placed under patriarchal rule, while at the same time the whole mise-en-scène is presented as ethnically alien to its audience (non-European, Asiatic, aboriginal). Following a similar logic of negation and displacement, the release of energy in the dance of Josephine Baker is controlled by presenting Baker as the object of an insistent voyeurism, and at the same time as ethnically other: the fascinations and threats posed by her "primitive" movements, which nevertheless are also the quintessential movements of the machine age, are contained by reimposing upon them the combined authority of the masculine, colonial gaze.

I have attempted to sketch, as rapidly as possible, the kind of issues that seem to have some of the greatest interest and potential for further development, as these appear at the intersection between dance history and cultural studies. My conclusions can be simply stated. First, the decline of the base/superstructure model of the social formation is a highly auspicious event, so far as dance history is concerned at least, since for as long as that model held sway dance could be represented as the most superstructural adornment of the superstructure, light years away from the real motors of historical power and change. Second, dance history has everything to gain by opening up to the wider terrain of the history of structured social movement; a discipline not yet born, "social kinetics" or the anthropology of movement would nevertheless embrace crucial cultural territory, including the complex histories of spectacle and industrialization. Third, dance historians could find eminently useful working concepts by transferring to their own domain procedures and approaches already well elaborated in art history, film theory, and comparative literature. That dance historians have tended not to participate in the debates of these subjects says more, I think, about the quirkiness of academic institutions than it does about any fundamental incompatibility between the study of dance and of literature or film or painting. The possibility of a paradigm shift in dance history opens up some of the most interesting vistas for the humanities at the present time; I for one am keeping my fingers crossed.

Notes

I am grateful to Henry Zerner, Hal Foster, Mark Franko, Farès el-Dahdah, Judith Gelernter, and Branden Joseph for the conversations that prompted this essay; with apology to them all for the mere sketch that resulted.

1 On art history's tendency away from "visual masterpieces" toward "visual culture," see *Visual Culture: Images and Interpretations*, ed. Norman Bryson, Michael Ann Holly, and Keith Moxey (Hanover, N.H.: Wesleyan University Press, 1994).

2 See Michel Foucault, *Surveiller et Punir: Naissance de la prison* (Paris: Editions Gallimard, 1975); translated by Alan Sheridan as *Discipline and Punish: The Birth of the Prison* (New York: Vintage Books, 1979).

3 See Carol Duncan, "Virility and Domination in Early Twentieth-Century Vanguard Painting," in *The Aesthetics of Power: Essays in Critical Art History* (Cambridge: Cambridge University Press, 1993), pp. 81–108.

4 On the place of sexual difference in Mondrian's abstraction, see Mark A. Cheetham, *The Rhetoric of Purity: Essentialist Theory and the Advent of Abstract Painting* (Cambridge: Cambridge University Press, 1991), pp. 121–29.

5 Roland Barthes, *Critique et vérité* (Paris: Seuil, 1966); translated and edited by K. P. Keuneman (London: Athlone Press, 1977).

6 See Daniel Dessert, *Argent, pouvoir, et société au Grand Siècle* (Paris: Fayard, 1984).

7 See Louis Marin, *Le Portrait du Roi* (Paris: Minuit, 1981); *Portrait of the King*, translated by Martin Houle (Minneapolis: University of Minnesota Press, 1988).

8 See Clifford Geertz, *Negara: The Theater State in Nineteenth-Century Bali* (Princeton: Princeton University Press, 1980).

9 See T. J. Clark, *The Painting of Modern Life: Paris in the Art of Manet and His Followers* (New York: Alfred A. Knopf, 1985).

10 See Griselda Pollock, "Modernity and the Spaces of Femininity," in *Vision and Difference: Femininity, Feminism, and the Histories of Art* (London: Routledge, 1988), pp. 50–90.

11 For the first sustained elaboration of the idea of women as objects of the male gaze, see Laura Mulvey, "Visual Pleasure and Narrative Cinema," *Screen* 16, no. 3 (1975), pp. 8–18. Mulvey's thesis has been explored in a variety of arguments within film criticism: see, for example, Linda Williams, "Film Body: An Implantation of Perversions," *Ciné-Tracts* 3, no. 4 (1981), pp. 19–35; Lucy Fisher, "The Image of Woman as Image: The Optical Politics of *Dames*," in *Genre: The Musical*, ed. Rick Altman (London: Routledge and Kegan Paul, 1981), pp. 70–84; Sandy Flitterman, "Woman, Desire, and the Look: Feminism and the Enunciative Apparatus in Cinema," *Ciné-Tracts* 2, no. 1 (1978), pp. 63–68; and Kaja Silverman, "Fassbinder and Lacan: A Reconsideration of Gaze, Look, and Image," in *Visual Culture*, ed. Bryson, Holly, and Moxey, pp. 272–301.

12 See Clark, *The Painting of Modern Life*, pp. 205–58.

13 See Linda Nochlin, "Manet's *Masked Ball at the Opera*," in *The Politics of Vision: Essays on Nineteenth-Century Art and Society* (London: Thames and Hudson, 1991), pp. 75–94.

14 On Impressionist painting as the expression of new kinds of personal freedom and release, see Meyer Schapiro, "The Nature of Abstract Art," *Marxist Quarterly*, January–March 1937,

p. 83; and T. J. Clark's discussion of Schapiro's point of view, in *The Painting of Modern Life*, pp. 3–22.

15 See Linda Nochlin, "Seurat's *La Grande Jatte*: An Anti-Utopian Allegory," in *The Politics of Vision*, pp. 170–93.

16 See, for example, Andreas Huyssen's "The Vamp and the Machine: Fritz Lang's *Metropolis*," in *After the Great Divide: Modernism, Mass Culture, Postmodernism* (Bloomington: Indiana University Press, 1986), pp. 65–81.

II SOCIAL LIVES, SOCIAL BODIES

3 REINSTATING CORPOREALITY: FEMINISM AND BODY POLITICS

Janet Wolff

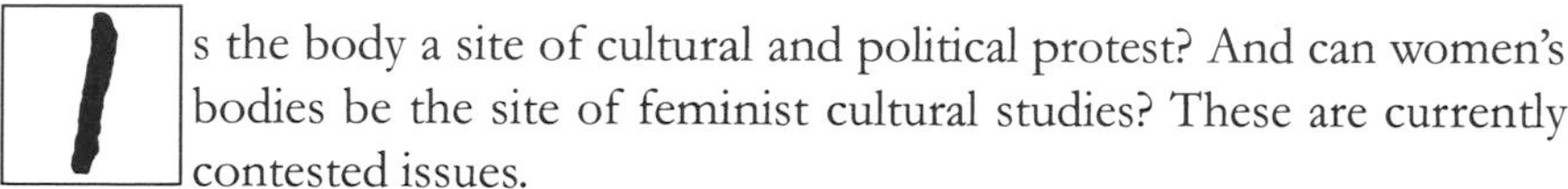

Is the body a site of cultural and political protest? And can women's bodies be the site of feminist cultural studies? These are currently contested issues.

> I do not see how . . . there is any possibility of using the image of a naked woman . . . other than in an absolutely sexist and politically repressive patriarchal way in this conjuncture.[1]

> To use the body of the woman, her image or person is not impossible but problematic for feminism.[2]

Crucial to the debate about the political potential of the body is the more fundamental question of whether there *is* any body outside discourse—another matter of dispute.

> Experience of the body even at the simplest level is mediated by a presentation of the body, the body-image.[3]

> The positing of a body *is* a condition of discursive practices.[4]

In this essay I will argue for a cultural politics of the body, based on a recognition of the social and discursive construction of the body, while emphasizing its lived experience and materiality.

The Dangers of Body Politics

On 17 July 1989, a group of women staged a protest against the sole use by men of a bathing area at Sandycove, Dublin. The men often swam naked in this area, an artificial harbor on the seafront called Forty Foot Pool. The women's protest was to invade the area and to remove their own swimming suits. The reporting of this event makes clear the ambiguities and ultimate failure of such body politics. The *Guardian* carried a short note, as a caption to a photograph. The photo depicts one of the women, facing the camera and walking out of the water, wearing only a small pair of briefs. Behind her men and boys in small boats stare. She walks past a line of young boys, who gawp at her body and laugh at her. It is not an attractive scene. Without having been at the event, one can only assume that female nudity achieved nothing more than male lechery. Moreover, the photograph in the press the next morning renders the liberal (and generally pro-feminist) paper the *Guardian* little different from the tabloids, with their Page Three topless pinups. The political gesture is neutralized and doubly canceled—first by the look of those at the scene, and second by its representation in the press for the reader's gaze. The lesson (or one of them) is that there are problems with using the female body for feminist ends. Its preexisting meanings, as sex object, as object of the male gaze, can always prevail and reappropriate the body, despite the intentions of the woman herself.

This can also occur with less naive interventions, which incorporate a critical understanding of the meanings and uses of the female body in our culture. The movie *Not a Love Story* is a documentary about the pornography industry, made by women and presenting a clearly feminist and critical view of pornography. When it arrived in Leeds, England, in the early 1980s, however, it was for some reason shown in one of the rather sleazy city-center cinemas. Its audience consisted of a few groups of women (the film had not had much advance publicity, and this, together with the rather peculiar venue, meant that large numbers of local feminists did not turn up) and a considerable contingent from the raincoat brigade. Individual men were scattered throughout the cinema. And the point is that they would not have been disappointed, for, as sympathetic critics have pointed out, in order to discuss the pornography industry, the movie spent a good deal of time showing pornographic images and sequences.[5] Again, this raises the question of whether, or how, women can engage in a critical politics of the body in a culture which so comprehensively codes and defines women's bodies as subordinate and passive, and as objects of the male gaze. Peter Gidal's pessimism, in the first quotation with which I began this essay, is a well-founded one.

Yet I want to argue that a feminist cultural politics of the body *is* a possibility. As Mary Kelly says, this may be problematic but it is not impossible. There is every reason, too, to propose the body as a privileged site of political intervention, precisely because it is the site of repression and possession. The body has been systematically repressed and marginalized in Western culture, with specific practices, ideologies, and discourses controlling and defining the female body. What is repressed, though, may threaten to erupt and challenge the established order. It is on such grounds that some have argued for a body politics, and some feminists have urged a cultural and political intervention which is grounded in, and which employs, the body. I shall review these arguments, in order to draw some conclusions about the prospects for a feminist body politics in contemporary culture.

Repression and Marginalization of the Body in Western Culture

As Mary Douglas has shown, the body operates as a symbol of society across cultures, and the rituals, rules, and boundaries concerning bodily behavior can be understood as the functioning of social rules and hierarchies.[6] In some cultures, bodily refuse (excreta, blood, tears, hair, nail clippings) has magical, and dangerous, qualities. In its marginality, in the way in which it traverses the boundaries of the body, it comes to represent particular threats and powers, which ultimately symbolize social boundaries, transgressions, and threats. What counts as pollution varies from society to society, but in all cases, according to Douglas, it is a "symbolic system, based on the image of the body, whose primary concern is the ordering of a social hierarchy."[7]

There is a wonderful scene in Buñuel's film *The Phantom of Liberty* in which a bourgeois couple arrives for a dinner party. With the usual social pleasantries and exchanges, they are led by the hosts to join the others. The guests are all seated round a large dining table, but the table is not laid for a meal. Instead, it is covered by magazines. The guests leaf through these casually, while exchanging remarks. Each guest is sitting on a toilet. After a while, one of the guests discreetly excuses himself, stands up, adjusts his dress, flushes the toilet, and leaves the room. He goes to a small closet, locks the door behind him, and sits down. Then he pulls down a tray of food from the wall, and eats this in privacy, before going back to join the others.

This scene, of course, illustrates graphically the arbitrary nature of our social customs—specifically those that deal with appropriate and acceptable bodily behavior. We might rush to argue that there are *objective* reasons, of health, hygiene, cleanliness, for eating in public and defecating in private. But Mary Douglas's work clearly shows that these are only rationalizations. In this, "civilized" customs are no different from "primitive" customs. The discourse is one of cleanliness and hygiene, but in all cases the hidden meanings are those of social order and social hierarchy. This crucial anthropological perspective helps us to make sense of the particular, and peculiar, development of regimes of the body in Western culture.

Norbert Elias's pioneering study *The Civilizing Process* analyzes the development and sophistication of manners in relation to social transformations in Europe in the sixteenth century and since. In particular he perceives the growth of notions of *intimacy* as part of the rise and consolidation of an intellectual class, which was able to distance itself from other classes, including the ruling strata. Manners thus serve as differentiating characteristics. Erasmus's *De civilatate morum puerilium* of 1530 was a key text, a turning point in the literature of manners and civilized behavior. Elias makes his point most clearly by straightforward quotation from earlier and later handbooks on manners. Examples from the Middle Ages include: "A man who clears his throat when he eats and one who blows his nose in the tablecloth are both ill-bred, I assure you." And "If a man snorts like a seal when he eats, as some people do, and smacks his chops like a Bavarian yokel, he has given up all good breeding."[8]

In Erasmus, we already have a much greater refinement of behavior, though not yet one that we would recognize as "civilized" by our own contemporary standards.

> Your goblet and knife, duly cleansed, should be on the right, your bread on the left.
>
> Some people put their hands in the dishes the moment they have sat down. Wolves do that . . .
>
> To dip the fingers in the sauce is rustic. You should take what you want with your knife and fork. . . .
>
> To lick greasy fingers or to wipe them on your coat is impolite. It is better to use the tablecloth or the serviette.[9]

And, with regard to behavior in the bedroom, Erasmus recommends: "If you share a bed with a comrade, lie quietly; do not toss with your body, for this can lay yourself bare or inconvenience your companion by pulling away the blankets. . . . If you share a bed with another man, keep still."[10] By 1729, a couple of centuries later, the rules of the bedroom were stricter. "You ought neither to undress nor go to bed in the presence of any other person. Above all, unless you are married, you should not go to bed in the presence of anyone of the other sex. . . . When you get up you should not leave the bed uncovered, nor put your nightcap on a chair or anywhere else where it can be seen."[11]

In the civilizing process, the body is increasingly patrolled, the range of acceptable behavior increasingly carefully and narrowly defined. Emerging from this process of gradual exclusion and privatization of areas of bodily functions is what Bakhtin called the "classical body." The classical body has no orifices and engages in no base bodily functions. It is like a classical statue. It is opposed to the "grotesque body," which has orifices, genitals, protuberances.[12] Francis Barker's fascinating study of seventeenth-century Europe documents the developing idea of the separation of the body from the soul, showing in relation to selected key texts (a Marvell poem, a Rembrandt painting, Pepys's diary) how the body was increasingly redefined and privatized, its sexual and other needs and appetites denied.[13] Like Elias, Barker analyzes these transformations of discourse in relation to changes in class structure, labor demands, and the reconstitution of subjectivity. The "positive body," founded on the exclusion of desires and appetites, which now constitute the "absent body," is the ideal and necessary subject and object of rational science and bourgeois society.

Barker's analysis is indebted in turn to the work of Michel Foucault, particularly on the history of madness and the birth of the prison. From Foucault's detailed examination of the institutions of confinement, we have come to understand the construction in bourgeois society of the docile body[14] and the new forms of discipline (factories, schools, prisons, asylums) in which the most comprehensive surveillance has come to be exercised. The body is increasingly brought into discourse, and supervised, observed, and controlled by a variety of disciplines. In this process, and with the disappearance of older forms of bodily control such as torture, public spectacle, and so on, control operates through internalization, and becomes, to a large extent, *self*-surveillance. At the same time, large areas of bodily experience, such as sexuality and illness, are delimited and redefined. As is well known, however, Foucault argues *against* the thesis that the nineteenth century witnessed a severe repression of sexuality. Rather, sexuality came increasingly into discourse, with the proliferation of disciplines and practices that spoke of it: medicine, psychiatry, sexology, and so on.[15] These processes have continued into the late twentieth century, where new forms of discipline in consumer society operate through advertising, fashion, popular culture, and the market.[16]

Finally, the recognition that the body has been systematically denied and marginalized in Western culture, and that this development is closely related to the needs and ideologies of bourgeois capitalism (its construction of a particular notion of subjectivity, its requirement for a reliable, docile, regular work force, its dependence on the self-regulation of its subjects), is confirmed by social historians, who have documented the control and elimination of working-class sports and popular recreations during and after the Industrial Revolution.[17] Blood sports, such as bullbaiting and cockfighting, were criminalized in England in the first half of the nineteenth century (though upper-class pursuits like the hunt were not). Fairs were controlled, and football transformed from a game of the streets to an organized spectator sport by the end of the century. Licensing laws were intended to contain drinking habits. Behind these measures lay a mixture of concern to retain a reliable working population, fears about the political dangers of working-class gatherings, and ideological concerns linked to the class and domestic morality of the bourgeoisie.

If the body has thus been repressed since the seventeenth century, does it follow that the irruption of the "grotesque" body, the explosion into visibility of its suppressed features (sex, laughter, excretion, and so on) constitutes a political revolution as well as a moral transgression? Stallybrass and White are rightly cautious about any blanket endorsement of bodily transgression as inherently radical.

> It would be wrong to associate the exhilarating sense of freedom which transgression affords with any necessary or automatic political progressiveness. . . . Often it is a powerful ritual or symbolic practice whereby the dominant squanders its symbolic capital so as to get in touch with the fields of desire which it denied itself as the price paid for its political power. Not a repressive desublimation (for just as transgression is not intrinsically progressive, nor is it intrinsically conservative), it is a counter-sublimation, a delirious expenditure of the symbolic capital accrued (through the regulation of the body and the decathexis of habitus) in the successful struggle of bourgeois hegemony.[18]

Indeed, the transgressions of the carnivalesque and of the grotesque body can in many cases, as they also point out, operate in reactionary ways, particularly with regard to gender. This is something I shall return to.

The Female Body in Western Culture

Despite Foucault's radical argument that the nineteenth century saw an incitement to sex, not a repression of it, there is no question about the oppression of women through the discourses of the body. One collection of essays, largely inspired by Foucault's work, demonstrates the many ways in which contemporary discourses and practices rendered women inferior, put control of women's bodies into men's hands, and produced new sciences which redefined women and femininity centrally in terms of reproductive function, denying female sexuality while perceiving women as somehow closer to nature than men.[19] This equation of woman with the body, for the most part a product of eighteenth- and nineteenth-century debates and ideologies,[20] has a pre-history in classical thought. Elizabeth Spelman has shown that Plato, despite an apparent commitment to the equality of the sexes (in *The Republic*, for example), believed that women exemplified the failure to value the soul above the body.[21] His somatophobia and his misogyny, she suggests, are closely linked. Here, then, we already have the notion that women are closer (too close) to the body compared with men. When we recognize the great value put on the soul or the mind as against the body (which is a central aspect of the process discussed by Barker, in which the "positive body" of rational science excludes and obscures the "absent body" of desires and appetites), the significance of the identification of women with the body is clear.

It is through the body, too, that women in our culture learn their own particular form of self-surveillance. Sandra Bartky identifies the "panoptical male connoisseur" in women's consciousness.[22] The discursive practices that produce "femininity" are in the culture and within women. Thus they diet, dress for certain effect, monitor their movement and gestures. Unlike Bartky, I do not conclude that radical social change will come about as a result of a refusal of particular definitions and demands of "femininity" and the substitution of an "as yet unimagined transformation of the female body,"[23] for this addresses only the *effects* of gender inequalities. It is likely that any *new* definitions of "femininity" would equally provide the basis for control and self-surveillance. But the perception is accurate, that it is through the body that women collude in their own oppression, and the specifically feminist slant on Foucault's analysis of the effects of discourse is an invaluable one.

Women learn as girls to monitor their appearance, and to conform to what is presented in the culture as some ideal of femininity. A group of German women explored in discussion the ways in which this policing (and self-policing) works, and how early it begins.

> Every Thursday afternoon, the park was open to me for free; I had a special pass to let me in for my gym lesson. My mother had put my name down for the class so I could do something about my weak stomach muscles. She said the only way I could get rid of my tummy at my age was by strengthening the muscles with exercise. In a few years' time, when I was grown up, I'd then be able to deal with it by pulling it in.[24]

Advertising and the fashion industry show us the perfect body for women, though, as Rosalind Coward has said, this ideal shifts slightly from one season to the next,[25] as shown in this text from *Cosmopolitan.*

> If you just *love* being a girl (and really look like one), this is *your* time! After decades of "You can never be too rich or too thin," the all-girl girl has reemerged to be celebrated and adored. Curves à la Monroe (if she'd worked out a bit more!) are what's red-hot right now. So if you've been disguising all those luscious lines under industrial-strength bras and baggy sweaters, stop! Here are a few suggestions for really showing *off* this shapely, gorgeous girl.[26]

(It is noticeable, however, that the all-girl girl still has a small waist and perfectly flat stomach. There are apparently limits to the revolution in body ideal.)

Cultural theory, particularly in the visual arts and film studies, has explored for a decade and a half the representation of women's bodies in patriarchal culture, informed first by John Berger's early perception that paintings of the nude in Western art imply a male spectator and are constructed for the male gaze, and then by Laura Mulvey's influential article of 1975, which analyzed the operation of the male gaze and the representation of the female body in film in terms of psychoanalytic theory.[27] The issue of women's viewing positions and possible identifications has been one much discussed (and disputed) in recent years, though this is not something I shall consider here. The devastating implication of this work in general appears to be that women's bodies (particularly the nude, though not just that) *cannot* be portrayed other than through the regimes of representation which produce them as objects for the male gaze, and as the projection of male desires. The failure of the Dublin intervention should have been predicted, in the light of this. We have to ask what this means for feminist art practice (can women paint women's bodies? are there ways of subverting or circumventing the dominant modes of representation?) and for body politics (*can* the body, after all, be a site of cultural critique?).

Transgression and the Female Body

What happens when the female body is affirmed and displayed, in defiance of the dominant ideals of the "perfect body," acknowledging the reality of actual women, the diversities of shape and size, the functions of corporeal existence (eating, excreting, menstruation, sex, pregnancy, aging, illness)? The "grotesque body," at least, should be immune from incorporation into the objectifying gaze. (The question of hard-core pornography, which depends on a particular deviation from the classical to the grotesque body, is an interesting one, requiring a more complex analysis of such imagery in relation to sexuality and representation in patriarchal society. It is something I shall have to leave to one side, however.)

Mary Russo considers the female grotesques of carnival. The examples she discusses are unruly women (including men cross-dressing as women, in this role) in popular uprisings in seventeenth-century England, terracotta figurines of "senile, pregnant hags" (discussed by Bakhtin), and Charcot's famous photographs of women hysterics.[28] She concludes that these figures are deeply ambivalent. As she says, "women and their bodies, certain bodies, in certain public framings, in certain public spaces, are always already transgressive—

dangerous and in danger."[29] These cases and images of women "in excess" of the idealized feminine may operate as threat (as well as example to other women). However, there are always reactionary connotations. The unruly woman is pilloried as a scold, henpecking her husband. Cross-dressing men are as likely to be portraying women with contempt as with respect. The image of the pregnant hag is "loaded with all of the connotations of fear and loathing associated with the biological processes of reproduction and of aging."[30] Female hysterics have a history of being locked up and contained. And at fairs and carnival festivities women were frequently abused and raped.

In any case, the excesses and reversals of the carnivalesque often operate to reaffirm the status quo, providing licensed but limited occasions for transgressions which are guaranteed to be neutralized. Whether or not there is any leakage into the culture in general from such occasions is an important question, though it is not one to which we can assume a positive answer. What I think we *can* safely affirm is the importance of the appearance itself of such transgressive images, practices, and ideas, for they render visible the suppressed. As Mary Russo says, how the category of the grotesque "might be used affirmatively to destabilize the idealizations of female beauty or to realign the mechanisms of desire" is the subject of another study.[31] Like her, at this stage I simply note the potential value of the existence of spaces for the female grotesque body for the daunting project of the subversion of its dominant construction and portrayal.

Related to the notion of the female grotesque is Julia Kristeva's concept of the "monstrous-feminine." In her psychoanalytic account, the maternal body is the object of horror, a feeling based in the fear of reincorporation into the mother, as well as in the fear of the mother's generative power. In becoming a subject, with defined boundaries, the child is separating from the body of the mother. As a result the maternal body becomes "abject"—an object of horror and threat.[32] Although Kristeva does not discuss this as a specifically gendered process, other recent work in psychoanalytic theory suggests that it is particularly the *male* child who confronts the trauma of separation, and who retains into adulthood the fear of reincorporation (and, hence, loss of masculinity and self).[33] This psychic process, undergone in a culture where it is women who do the mothering, explains the barely concealed level of violent fantasy men often manifest against women, the well-known construction of the virgin/whore dichotomy which counterposes the "pure" woman (the classical body?) to the slut (the grotesque?). As Barbara Ehrenreich has put it, in a foreword to Klaus Theweleit's shocking study of male fantasies about women:

> It seems to me that as long as women care what we are in this world—at best, "social inferiors," and at worst, a form of filth—then the male ego will be formed by, and bounded by, hideous dread. For that which they loved first—woman and mother—is that which they must learn to despise in others and suppress within themselves. Under these conditions, which are all we know, so far, as the human condition, men will continue to see the world as divided into "them" and "us," male and female, hard and soft, solid and liquid—and they will, in every way possible, fight and flee the threat of submersion. They will build dykes against the "streaming" of their own desire. . . . They will confuse, in some mad revery, love and death, sex and murder.[34]

Discussions about the female body in terms of abjection, or the monstrous-feminine, tend to operate on different levels and to refer to rather different aspects of psychic processes. Sometimes they concern the Oedipal drama and the fear of castration. Sometimes they are based in a theory of fetishism (the phallic woman). At other times they rely on a psychoanalytic account that stresses the pre-Oedipal moment, and deal with the need for separation and consequent fear of reengulfment which I have been discussing. A more Lacanian version is based on the threat to the man's place in the Symbolic, which produces a resistance to the pre-Symbolic (and the mother). Yet another version rests on the fear of maternal authority, or of the power of the "archaic" mother. All these accounts can be found in current film studies and cultural theory, and it is not my intention to assess or compare them. The general question raised by the notion of the "monstrous-feminine," whatever its presumed origins, is whether it renders the (abject) body a potential site of transgression and feminist intervention. And I think our answer must be in terms of the same guarded optimism with which I considered the female grotesque: namely that the operative word is *potential*, for the dominant culture of patriarchy has already defined and situated the body, and the prospects for reappropriation are, to say the least, fraught with hazards and contradictions.

A third area of feminist body politics is what has been called "*l'écriture féminine.*" A concept originating in what is generally referred to as French feminism, this notion has a number of slightly different manifestations, of which I shall briefly discuss two.[35] In *La Révolution de langage poétique*, Julia Kristeva contrasts the realm and language of the Symbolic (the law of the Father, identified with and coincident with the coming into language of the child) with what she calls the "semiotic." The semiotic is the prelinguistic, the bodily drives, rhythms, and "pulsions" experienced by the child in the infantile fusion with the mother. These pleasures and feelings are repressed on entry into the

Symbolic, but, according to Kristeva, since they remain in the unconscious, they may emerge at a later stage. In the writing of Lautréamont and Mallarmé, as well as Joyce and Artaud, the experience of the semiotic is articulated. (The term *l'écriture féminine* is not Kristeva's, and of course her examples of this kind of writing here are all of men. However, the "feminine" nature of the writing consists of its supposed origins in the pre-Symbolic, prepatriarchal moment of the child-mother relationship.)

Kristeva is well aware that it makes no sense to propose the semiotic as somehow outside of language. In the first place, she is talking about writing, which is necessarily linguistic. And in the second place, the writers she discusses are, like everyone else, in the Symbolic—an essential condition of human development. "The semiotic that 'precedes' symbolization is only a *theoretical supposition* justified by the need for description. It exists in practice only within the symbolic and requires the symbolic break to obtain the complex articulation we associate with it in musical and poetic practices."[36]

Nevertheless, her argument is that there is possible a particular kind of writing that originates in the prelinguistic, bodily experiences of infancy that have persisted in the unconscious into adulthood. Inasmuch as such writing subverts the Symbolic, it can therefore be seen (and has been so, by some feminists) as "feminine"—both in the sense that its origins are in the pre-Oedipal child-mother relationship, and in the sense that it escapes the rule of the Father and the dominance of patriarchal language and thought.

Luce Irigaray and Hélène Cixous have proposed a more direct relationship between women, writing, and the body, one in which men could not be the agents of "feminine writing." Both begin from the specificity of woman's body—for Irigaray, a plural, multiple, diffuse sexuality, for Cixous, similarly multiple libidinal impulses (oral, anal, vocal, the pleasures of pregnancy). Woman, says Cixous, must "write from the body". "Her libido is cosmic, just as her unconscious is worldwide. Her writing can only keep going, without ever inscribing or discerning contours. . . . She alone dares and wishes to know from within, where she, the outcast, has never ceased to hear the resonance of fore-language."[37] *L'écriture féminine* is writing grounded in women's experience of the body and sexuality, an experience which is not mediated by men and by patriarchy. This has been found to be an exceptionally liberating and suggestive notion by many feminists, who perceive in it the prospect of a cultural practice which is not compromised and contained by patriarchal discourses. The painter Nancy Spero has referred to her work as *la peinture féminine*, on the model of "feminine writing," which, as Lisa Tickner says, commenting on Spero's work, is "a form of writing marked by the pulsions of a female sexual body . . . and effecting various kinds of displacement on the western phallogocentric tradition of writing and the subject."[38] In the next section of this essay, I will look at some of the problems involved in the notion of "writing from the body" as feminist practice.

Discourse and the Body

One objection to the kind of body politics just discussed is that identifying women with their bodies is perilously close to those reactionary arguments in sociobiology and other disciplines, as well as in conservative common sense, which justify women's oppression in terms of their biology—size, hormones, lack of strength, child-bearing functions, lactation, monthly cycles, and so on. So, for example, Judy Chicago's famous art work *The Dinner Party*, which celebrates the hidden history of women, and, among other things, employs vaginal imagery to represent selected women from the past, has been criticized by other feminists for this equation of women with their biology (and specifically their genitals).[39] This is a complex issue, for there is also every reason to want to affirm that which is denied or denigrated, and to assert the specificity and experience of the female body.

Related to this is the objection that *what* the female body is varies by culture, by century, and by social group. It is a social, historical, and ideological construct. (As I argued earlier, it is clear that, for example, medical science has "made" the female body into a new entity in the modern age.) Biology is always overlaid and mediated by culture, and the ways in which women experience their own bodies is largely a product of social and political processes. The charge of "essentialism" is a serious one—that is, the criticism that concepts like *l'écriture féminine* often depend on an assumed basic, unchanging identity of "woman" and women's bodies which ignores the realities of historical change, social production, and ideological construction. Elizabeth Gross has produced a carefully judged assessment of this debate, which I think is worth adopting, and which leaves us with the insights of Kristeva and Irigaray without the problems of an unacceptable essentialism: "Both these feminists have shown that *some* concept of the body is essential to understanding social production, oppression, and resistance; and that the body need not, indeed must not be considered merely a biological entity, but can be seen as a socially inscribed, historically marked, psychically and interpersonally significant product."[40] The female body is seen as psychically and socially produced and inscribed. At the same time, it is experienced by women—primarily as lacking or incomplete. The feminist project of Irigaray, "to speak about a positive model or series of representations of femininity by which the female body may be positively marked,"[41] is endorsed by Gross.

The more radical version of this critique of essentialism argues that *there is no body outside discourse.* Parveen Adams's argument, indicated in the third quotation at the beginning of this essay, is the psychoanalytic one that we never have an unmediated experience of a pre-given body, but rather that perceptions of the body are "represented from the start as agreeable or disagreeable."[42] The experience of the body is always mediated by libidinal energy. To this we may add the parallel argument that the body is never experienced except as mediated through language and discourse. As I have already shown, the "body" is a product of social histories, social relations, and discourses, all of which define it, identify its key features (ignoring others), prescribe and proscribe its behavior. With regard to women's bodies, Denise Riley follows through this perception to conclude that whether and when bodies are *gendered* "is a function of historical categorisations as well as of an individual daily phenomenology."[43] The body is not always lived or treated as sexed. For, as she points out in relation to the politics of maternity:

> If women did not have the capacity of childbearing they could not be arrayed by natalist or anti-natalist plans into populations to be cajoled or managed. But the point is that irrespective of natural capacities, only some prior lens which intends to focus on 'women's bodies' is going to set them in such a light. The body becomes visible *as* a body, and *as* a female body, only under some particular gaze—including that of politics.[44]

There can, therefore, be no "direct" experience of the body, and we cannot talk about, or even conceive of, the body as some pre-given entity. This is as true for men as it is for women, but the particular implication here is that we need to be very careful in talking about a feminist body politics, whether one of *l'écriture féminine* or one of celebration of the female body. What constitutes the body, and what constitutes the female body and its experience, is already implicated in language and discourse. But this does not mean we must abandon the project. Recent developments in linguistics, psychoanalysis, and cultural theory have achieved the important task of challenging essentialism and naive realism, and of deconstructing the category of "woman," demonstrating its construction in psychic processes, social and historical relations, ideological struggles, and discursive formations. But there are pragmatic, political, and philosophical reasons for resisting a total agnosticism of the body. As Denise Riley puts it, "it is compatible to suggest that 'women' don't exist—while maintaining a politics of 'as if they existed'—since the world behaves as if they unambiguously did."[45]

In the first place, then, the instability of the category "woman" and the specific objection to identifying women with the female body (itself seen to be ill-defined and not a constant), need not lead to the conclusion that the subject is irrevocably dispersed. There is some agreement among feminists that deconstruction, poststructuralism, and postmodernist theory are valuable allies in feminist analysis, critique, and political action, since they operate to destabilize patriarchal orthodoxies and also to oppose mistaken notions of uniform female identity.[46] At the same time, politically and experientially, it makes sense for women to mobilize around the social construct of "woman," for, as Riley says, modern feminism "is landed with the identity of women as an achieved fact of history and epistemology."[47] To that extent, too, the female body, as discursively and socially constructed, and as currently experienced by women, may form the basis of a political and cultural critique—so long as it is one which eschews a naive essentialism and incorporates the self-reflexivity of a recognition of the body as an effect of practices, ideologies, and discourses.

Finally, inconsistencies of the more radical anti-essentialist position have been pointed out. In the context of feminist film theory, Mary Ann Doane sees essentialism and anti-essentialism as opposite but equivalent mistakes.

> Both the proposal of a pure access to a natural female body and the rejection of attempts to conceptualize the female body based on their contamination by ideas of "nature" are inhibiting and misleading. Both positions deny the necessity of posing a complex relation between the body and psychic-signifying processes, of using the body, in effect, as a "prop." For Kristeva is right—the positing of the body *is* a condition of discursive practices. It is crucial that feminism move beyond the opposition between essentialism and anti-essentialism.[48]

As she says, the question about the relation between the female body and language, raised by deconstructionists and discourse theorists, is a question about a relation between two terms.[49] In other words, the critique of essentialism does *not* amount to a proof that there *is* no body.

In the following section, I will draw some preliminary conclusions from this discussion about the prospects of a feminist cultural politics of the body, which need not be doomed to negation or reincorporation by the male gaze and by a patriarchal culture.

Gender, Dance, and Body Politics

Since the body is clearly marginalized in Western culture, it might appear that dance is an inherently subversive activity. Indeed, the marginality of dance itself as an art form in the West suggests that this is so; compared with orchestral music, opera, film, and literature, dance has had minority appeal.

But we must beware of making the easy assumption that use of the body is itself transgressive, in a culture which allows only the "classical body." Here, from a key text on dance, is an accredited discussion of the ballet.

> The bearing of the classical dancer . . . is characterized by compactness. The thigh muscles are drawn up, the torso rests upon the legs like a bust upon its base. This bust swivels and bends but, in most *adagio* movements at any rate, the shoulders remain parallel to the pelvis bone. Every bend, every jump is accomplished with an effect of ease and of lightness. . . . In all such convolutions of the *adagio* the ballerina is showing the many gradual planes of her body in terms of harmonious lines. While her arms and one leg are extended, her partner turns her slowly round upon the pivot of her straight point. She is shown to the world with utmost love and grace. She will then integrate herself afresh, raise herself on the points, her arms close together, the one slightly in front of the other. It is the alighting of the insect, the shutting of the wings, the straightening into the perpendicular of feelers and of legs. Soon she will take flight and extend herself again. Meanwhile she shows us on the points what we have not seen in the *arabesque* or *développé*, two unbroken lines from toes to thighs.[50]

The classical ballet has colluded in the preservation of the classical body, emphasizing in its commitment to line, weightlessness, lift, and extension an ethereal presence rather than a real corporeality. In addition, the strict limits on body size and shape for girls and women dancers reinforce a denial of the female body in favor of an ideal of boyish petiteness. (It is no surprise that the incidence of eating disorders among ballerinas and would-be ballerinas is far higher than that among the general population.[51]) The roles created for women in the classical repertoire—fairies, swans, innocent peasant girls—collude in a discourse which constructs, in a medium which employs the body for its expression, a strangely disembodied female.

Modern dance, from its beginnings early in the twentieth century, has usually been seen as an important breakthrough for women. For one thing, many of the major innovators and choreographers in modern dance have been women, whereas the classical ballet has always been dominated by men. Isadora Duncan, Martha Graham, Doris Humphrey, and Mary Wigman are among the key figures here. The modern repertoire also consists of many pieces which deal with strong women, and with myths and stories from women's point of view. Most important, modern dance has totally transformed the types of movement seen on the stage, abandoning the purity of line and denial of weight of the classical ballet and introducing angularity, pelvic movement, emphasis on the body's weight and its relationship to the ground. A notion of the "natural body" has been employed in this development, particularly by Duncan and Graham and their followers. This particular combination, of a conception of the natural body and a commitment to women's stories and lives, has led many practitioners and critics to conclude that modern dance *is* a medium for political as well as aesthetic transgression.

But, as the critique of essentialism has shown, we must be wary of a cultural politics which is based on any notion of women's natural body, or women's universal essence—the kind of conception, for example, which lies behind many of Martha Graham's representations of Greek myths. What this means is that dance can only be subversive when it questions and exposes the construction of the body in culture. In doing so, it necessarily draws attention to itself *as* dance—a version of the Brechtian device of laying bare the medium. Postmodern dance has begun to achieve this, and thus to use the body for the first time in a truly political way. This development is discussed by Elizabeth Dempster, who stresses that the key focus of postmodern dance (going back to Merce Cunningham in the 1940s, but for the most part emerging in the 1960s and 1970s) has been the body itself.[52] It is not uncommon for a postmodern choreographer to use untrained bodies in a work, alongside trained dancers. (Michael Clark's work is a British example of this practice.) Dance itself is thus deconstructed, and the operations and actions of the body made clear. The body itself may be the theme of the dance, and a good deal of postmodern dance is concerned with gender and sexual politics (Yvonne Rainer in the United States, DV8 in Britain). The repertoire, the style, the ideologies, and the illusion of transparency of the medium of both classical and modern dance have been overturned by postmodern dance. In such a practice, the body can indeed provide a site for a radical cultural politics.

The implications for a feminist politics of the body are clear, not just for dance, which is necessarily founded on the body as its medium of expression, but also for visual representation, performance art, and other arts disciplines. A straightforward celebratory art of the female body may have the welcome effect of producing positive images for women, in defiance of the dominant constructions of femininity in our culture. At the same time, it runs two kinds of risk: first, that these images can be reappropriated by the dominant culture and read against the grain of their intended meaning (as in the Dublin demonstration); and second, that they may collude with a kind of sexist thinking which identifies woman with the body and assumes an unchanging, pre-given essence of the female. Any body politics, therefore, must speak *about* the body, stressing its materiality and its social and discursive construction, at the same time as disrupting and subverting existing regimes of representation. Feminist artists and critics have suggested strategies for this kind of intervention, including ironic quotation of works by men, juxtapositions of text and image which challenge representation, addressing the construction of femininity in the work itself, incorporating the self-reflexive commentary on the mode of representation employed, and what Mary Kelly has called the "depropriation" of the image.[53]

Body politics need not depend on an uncritical, ahistorical notion of the (female) body. Beginning from the lived experience of women in their currently constituted bodily identities—identities which are *real* at the same time as being socially inscribed and discursively produced—feminist artists and cultural workers can engage in the challenging and exhilarating task of simultaneously affirming those identities, questioning their origins and ideological functions, and working toward a nonpatriarchal expression of gender and the body.

Notes

1 Peter Gidal, quoted by Mary Ann Doane, "Woman's Stake: Filming the Female Body," in Constance Penley, ed., *Feminism and Film Theory* (New York: Routledge, 1988), p. 217.

2 Mary Kelly, quoted by Rosemary Betterton, "New Images for Old: The Iconography of the Body," in *Looking On: Images of Femininity in the Visual Arts and Media* (London: Pandora, 1987), p. 206.

3 Parveen Adams, "Versions of the Body," *m/f* 11/12 (1986), p. 29.

4 Doane, "Woman's Stake," p. 226.

5 See, for example, Susan Barrowclough, "Not a Love Story," *Screen* 23, no. 5 (1982).

6 Mary Douglas, *Purity and Danger: An Analysis of the Concepts of Pollution and Taboo* (1966; London: Routledge and Kegan Paul, 1984).

7 Ibid., p. 123.

8 Norbert Elias, *The Civilizing Process*, vol. 1 of *The History of Manners* (Oxford: Blackwell, 1978), p. [illegible].

9 Ibid., pp. [illegible]

10 Ibid., pp. 161, 162.

11 Ibid., p. 162.

12 See Peter Stallybrass and Allon White, *The Politics and Poetics of Transgression* (London: Methuen, 1986), for an analysis of body imagery and social change in Europe from the seventeenth century, based on Bakhtin's division.

13 Francis Barker, *The Tremulous Private Body: Essays on Subjection* (London: Methuen, 1984).

14 Michel Foucault, *Discipline and Punish: The Birth of the Prison* (Harmondsworth: Penguin, 1979), pp. 135–69.

15 Michel Foucault, *The History of Sexuality*, vol. 1, *An Introduction* (London: Allen Lane, 1979).

16 See Mike Featherstone, "The Body in Consumer Culture," *Theory, Culture, and Society* 1, no. 2 (September 1982).

17 See, for example, Robert Malcolmson, "Popular Recreations under Attack," in Bernard Waites et al., eds., *Popular Culture: Past and Present* (London: Croom Helm, 1982).

18 Stallybrass and White, *The Politics and Poetics of Transgression*, p. 201.

19 Catherine Gallagher and Thomas Laqueur, eds., *The Making of the Modern Body: Sexuality and Society in the Nineteenth Century* (Berkeley: University of California Press, 1987).

20 See L. J. Jordanova, "Natural Facts: A Historical Perspective on Science and Sexuality," in Carol MacCormack and Marilyn Strathern, eds., *Nature, Culture, and Gender* (Cambridge: Cambridge University Press, 1980).

21 Elizabeth V. Spelman, "Woman as Body: Ancient and Contemporary Views," *Feminist Studies* 8, no. 1 (Spring 1982).

22 Sandra Lee Bartky, "Foucault, Femininity, and the Modernization of Patriarchal Power," in Irene Diamond and Lee Quinby, eds., *Feminism and Foucault: Reflections on Resistance* (Boston: Northeastern University Press, 1988), p. 72.

23 Ibid., p. 79.

24 From Frigga Haug, ed., *Female Sexualization: A Collective Work of Memory* (London: Verso, 1987), p. 126.

25 Rosalind Coward, *Female Desire* (London: Paladin, 1984), p. 39.

26 *Cosmopolitan* (U.S.) (August 1989), p. 186.

27 John Berger, *Ways of Seeing* (Harmondsworth: Penguin, 1972); Laura Mulvey, "Visual Pleasure and Narrative Cinema," *Screen* 16, no. 3 (1975).

28 Mary Russo, "Female Grotesques: Carnival and Theory," in Teresa de Lauretis, ed., *Feminist Studies / Critical Studies* (London: Macmillan, 1986).

29 Ibid., p. 217.

30 Ibid., p. 219.

31 Ibid., p. 221.

32 Julia Kristeva, *Powers of Horror: An Essay on Abjection* (New York: Columbia University Press, 1982). Barbara Creed has used this analysis in a most interesting way in the discussion of the basis of appeal of horror movies (Barbara Creed, "Horror and the Monstrous-Feminine: An Imaginary Abjection," *Screen* 27, no. 1 [1986]).

33 See, for example, Evelyn Fox Keller, "Gender and Science," in Sandra Harding and Merrill B. Hintikka, eds., *Discovering Reality: Feminist Perspectives on Epistemology, Metaphysics, Methodology, and Philosophy of Science* (Dordrecht: D. Reidel, 1983).

34 Barbara Ehrenreich, "Foreword" to Klaus Theweleit, *Male Fantasies*, vol. 1 of *Women, Floods, Bodies, History* (Minneapolis: University of Minnesota Press, 1987), p. xvi.

35 For a helpful discussion and critique of this term and its uses, see Ann Rosalind Jones, "Writing the Body: Toward an Understanding of *l'écriture féminine*," in Elaine Showalter, ed., *The New Feminist Criticism: Essays on Women, Literature, and Theory* (London: Virago, 1986).

36 Julia Kristeva, *Revolution in Poetic Language* (New York: Columbia University Press, 1984), p. 68.

37 Hélène Cixous, "The Laugh of the Medusa," *Signs* 1, no. 4 (Summer 1976), p. 889. See also Luce Irigaray, *This Sex Which Is Not One* (Ithaca, N.Y.: Cornell University Press, 1985).

38 Lisa Tickner, "Nancy Spero: Images of Women and *la peinture féminine*," in *Nancy Spero* (London: Institute of Contemporary Arts, 1987), pp. 5, 7–8.

39 See, for example, Michèle Barrett, "Feminism and the Definition of Cultural Politics," in C. Brunt and C. Rowan, eds., *Feminism, Culture, and Politics* (London: Lawrence and Wishart, 1983).

40 Elizabeth Gross, "Philosophy, Subjectivity, and the Body: Kristeva and Irigaray," in Carole Pateman and Elizabeth Gross, eds., *Feminist Challenges: Social and Political Theory* (Boston: Northeastern University Press, 1986), p. 140.

41 Ibid., p. 142.

42 Adams, "Versions of the Body," p. 29.

43 Denise Riley, *"Am I That Name?" Feminism and the Category of "Women" in History* (Minneapolis: University of Minnesota Press, 1988), p. 105.

44 Ibid., p. 106.

45 Ibid., p. 112.

46 See, for example, Jane Flax, "Postmodernism and Gender Relations in Feminist Theory," in *Signs* 12, no. 4 (Summer 1987). Also *Feminist Studies* 14, no. 1 (Spring 1988): special issue on deconstruction.

47 Riley, *"Am I That Name?,"* p. 111.

48 Doane, "Woman's Stake," pp. 225–26.

49 Ibid., p. 223.

50 Adrian Stokes, "The Classical Ballet," extract from *Tonight the Ballet*, in Roger Copeland and Marshall Cohen, eds., *What Is Dance? Readings in Theory and Criticism* (Oxford: Oxford University Press, 1983), pp. 244–45.

51 A personal account is the dancer Gelsey Kirkland's autobiography, *Dancing on My Grave* (London: Penguin, 1986).

52 Elizabeth Dempster, "Women Writing the Body: Let's Watch a Little How She Dances," in Susan Sheridan, ed., *Grafts: Feminist Cultural Criticism* (London: Verso, 1988).

53 Mary Kelly, "Beyond the Purloined Image," *Block* 9 (1983). See also Judith Barry and Sandy Flitterman, "Textual Strategies: The Politics of Art-Making," *Screen* 21, no. 2 (Summer 1980); and Lisa Tickner, "The Body Politic: Female Sexuality and Women Artists since 1970," *Art History* 1, no. 2 (June 1978) (reprinted in Rosemary Betterton, ed., *Looking on: Images of Femininity in the Visual Arts and Media* [London: Pandora, 1987]).

4 "THE STORY IS TOLD AS A HISTORY OF THE BODY": STRATEGIES OF MIMESIS IN THE WORK OF IRIGARAY AND BAUSCH

Susan Kozel

In Dance Theater the story is told as a history of the body, not as danced literature. . . . If a logic exists it is not a logic of the consciousness, but of the body, one that adheres not to the laws of causality but rather to the principle of analogy.[1]

The logic of the body unfolding in dance theater is that of analogy, or, to use a richer word, mimesis. Mimesis is a well-rehearsed term in the history of aesthetics, and I am going to work it further. But this reworking, or repetition, is not an exhaustion of the mimetic principle; rather it is the very essence of it. In classical Greece it was the word for artistic representation. Mimetic theory was used to draw a distinction between art and life: the art object was seen to be an imitation of life. Noverre, the eighteenth-century dancer and scholar, saw dance in a similar light: "Poetry, painting and dancing, Sir, are, or should be, no other than a faithful likeness of beautiful nature."[2] However, the mimesis found in the work of the Belgian-born feminist Luce Irigaray and the German choreographer Pina Bausch is based on a principle of repetition or analogy which is not one of identical reproduction or simple imitation. There is always a moment of excess or a remainder in the mimetic process, something that makes the mimicry different from that which inspires it, and which transforms the associated social and aesthetic space. I want to suggest that this remainder is a moment of distortion, and that it contains the great hope for regeneration which emerges from the process. Further I suggest that this distortion is inherently physical, affecting the situation of bodies in time and space.

Physical Mimesis: "A Thorn in Our Eye"[3]

Pina Bausch does not pull her punches. After the 1985 Brooklyn Academy of Music Next Wave festival there was an intense confrontation between the

American postmodern dancers and the descendants of German expressionism, of which Pina Bausch was a focal point. According to the advocates of postmodern minimalism who reject theatricality and emotion, Bausch's work was regressive and indulgent, being an explosion of existential conflict between the sexes. Supporters of tanztheater responded by claiming that focusing on form alone curtailed the aesthetic and political power of dance.

It is impossible to be untouched by Bausch's dance theater: you either love it or hate it for political, psychoanalytical, or aesthetic reasons. What causes such a furor in her work is her mimetic strategy. And the reactions to it are similar to the reactions to mimetic strategy in Luce Irigaray's feminist philosophical writing.

Irigaray accepts the view that at present the political, social, and linguistic structures that shape us are dualistic, and that duality is not a confrontation of different elements, but it is a guise of indifference. The dualisms of male/female, mind/body, conscious/unconscious, good/bad, same/other are all really products of one side of the duality: male, mind, good, sameness. The other side is excluded, yet it is essential to support the dominant side. The side of the other, or "Woman," is necessarily silent, denied a voice in language or politics. Irigaray's project begins with the question: "What happens to a structure if its silent support begins to speak?" Bausch implicitly continues the question by saying, "What happens if this silent support begins to speak and move?"

Irigaray sketches out her mimetic strategy in *This Sex Which Is Not One,*

> One must assume the feminine role deliberately. Which means already to convert a form of subordination into an affirmation, and thus to begin to thwart it. . . .
>
> To play with mimesis is thus, for a woman, to try to recover the place of her exploitation by discourse, without allowing herself to be simply reduced to it. It means to resubmit herself . . . to ideas about herself that are elaborated in/by a masculine logic, but so as to make visible, by an effect of playful repetition, what was supposed to remain invisible.[4]

The idea is that by parodically occupying the place of "The Feminine" it is possible to break out of this mold and unleash our energies into other directions, not shaped and contained by duality. According to Irigaray, this is more effective than a direct challenge to the structure.

Both Bausch's and Irigaray's work engage the issue of framing. Mimesis seems to be stepping inside a frame, but is in fact a constant transgression of the frame, which amounts to charting another territory altogether. Rosi Braidotti in her book *Nomadic Subjects* describes the two moments that make up mimetic repetition: first, the metabolic repossession of meanings and representations (I like the physicality of the word *metabolic*); and second, the aim of finding "points of exit" from these so that alternative figurations of subjectivity, physicality, and interaction can be generated.[5] The points of exit are a stepping out of the frame based on the realignment of meaning through mimesis, a mimesis which is most powerful when it is understood in a physical sense.

As I have indicated, the word for this effect is *distortion*—a highly emotive word which evokes images of twisted limbs and twisted meanings. Distortion implies a challenge to existing senses of order and normality through partially conforming to and partially transgressing the usual. It is the blending of familiar with unfamiliar which makes a distortion so unnerving: it is not totally new; it shows us the otherness within the same, the invisible which animates the visible. Anything that is capable of distorting an order makes us sense the inherent fragility of that order. Or, I would suggest, the inherent fluidity. (Order can refer to political order, language, social conventions, or dance technique.) The aesthetics of distortion is particularly effective in a physical context, since we react viscerally to dance and are less able to screen out elements that do not fit into intellectual categories.

Time, Space, Fluidity, and Desire

Several significant elements of mimetic strategy feature in both Irigaray's writing and Bausch's dance theater. These elements are time, space, fluidity, and desire. They are striking for being at once philosophical and embodied, metaphysical and physical. They can be understood in an abstract sense and can be phenomenologically experienced. When they appear in mimetic strategy they undermine aesthetic, political, and discursive structures, and it is through them that mimetic strategy can be a transformative process.

Irigaray writes that we must reconsider the whole problematic of space and time.[6] In the prose-poetry of her book *Elemental Passions* she speaks of a "fluid density which overturns habitual space-time and yet always already takes place in it."[7] Bausch situates her mimetic portrayal of fear, despair, desire, and exploitation in a context where time and space are constantly challenged (figures 1 and 2). In her choreography, she uses filmic devices such as montage, cross-fades, fade-outs, and foreground/background contrasts to transform theatrical space into swirling layers of movement and emotion.[8] She blurs the distinctions between personal space, theatrical space, and natural space. Her dancers involve us in intimate emotional exchanges or inner monologues, thereby ignoring the implicit distinction between private and public space.

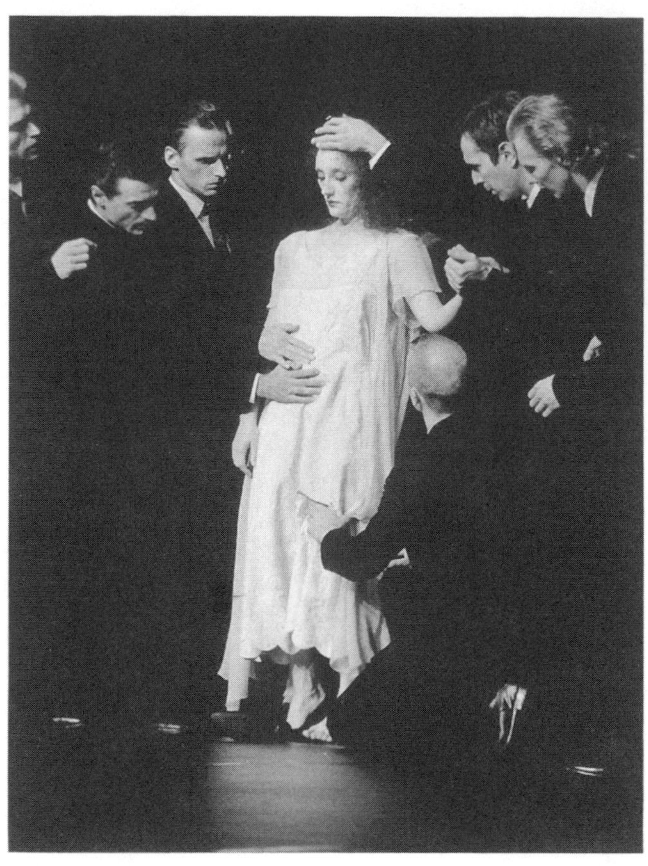

1. Wuppertal Dance Theater in *Kontakthof* by Pina Bausch (1978).
Photo: Maarten Vanden Abeele.

2. Wuppertal Dance Theater in *Tanzabend II* by Pina Bausch (1991). Photo: Detlef Erler

They often call attention to the fact that the audience is watching a performance, breaking the illusion of theatrical space by revealing the convention. Her performances occur in surreally "unnatural" environments. She covers the stage with leaves, water, grass, or dirt. In themselves these are organic elements, but when these natural elements are transferred to a theatrical context they confuse certain crucial categories: natural versus artificial; reality versus theater.

Bausch is just as disruptive of time as of space. She is not concerned with a linear narrative; movement, speech, and even music are repeated and recur at random intervals. Irigaray writes of time: "For me infinity means movement, the mobility of place. Engendering time, yes. Always becoming."[9] Bausch's performances are often very long, causing them to be experienced in "real time" where all parties involved battle exhaustion. Her choreographic talent lies in layering: beginning with a simple movement (walking, running, caressing), she draws out a hidden emotion and lets it transform and distort the movement as it is repeated over and over. The result is a blurring of the boundaries between dance movement and regular movement, between the time structures we associate with reality and with theatricality.

Fluidity is essential to mimesis and its challenge to dualistic structures. Irigaray writes: "Your flowing into me, and me into you. Receiving you melting, molten, and giving that flow back to you. Without end."[10] Bausch's work has been called a scene of transformations, a space where elements work together, contradict and complement each other, combine to provide new insights. The emotional energy of her pieces is not linear; it does not build smoothly. The emotional registers of the dancers slide between affection and rejection, love and hate, humor and despair. There is a further circularity between art and life, for life gives her the raw material for art, yet her work exposes us to our structures of meaning and behavior.

The next major element of mimetic strategy is desire. Irigaray's model for physicality is not dance; rather it is sexual relations from the neglected perspective of female sexuality. Desire spans the interval between people, and this interval has its own space and fluidity. In Bausch's work, embracing people can seem to be separated by an enormous gulf, or personal space can be squashed by manipulation, possessiveness, or jealousy. Desire becomes potent or impotent, and in most cases destructive. It is intimately related to framing, since the opposite of flowing desire is physical or emotional confinement. The portrayal of desire in a Bausch choreography is often shaded with a sort of bitter, surrealist humor—the wry acknowledgment that the absurdity unfolding onstage is a reflection of what we live each day. She makes us laugh at ourselves, our clothes, our mannerisms, the situations we get into with our lovers, but this laughter is not light-hearted. It is laughter emerging from the fertile ground of desire and despair.

A New Poetics

There is an overt relationship between physical and theoretical mimetic strategies. They complement and critique each other. Irigaray provides a framework for understanding Bausch's mimetic project. Her theory offers a context for Bausch's work and adds philosophical depth to it. It is broadened significantly by the notion of the symbolic. Irigaray has as her objective the creation of a "new symbolic." This is a term taken from Jacques Lacan; it is a conglomeration of representations which make up all of our experiences. We do not experience anything naively, but through a web of linguistic, social, structural, cultural, iconic, theoretical, mythical, and religious representations. Although Lacan places little or no emphasis outside language (i.e., no role for a dancing body), Irigaray sees the symbolic as the junction of body, psyche, and language.[11] So when she claims that a new social and political order requires a new symbolic, there is a strong role for the body combined with language, and scope for a physical symbolic. I believe that the arts, particularly the embodied arts of dance, theater, and performance, are essential to the creation of such a symbolic. Without their participation, there is a danger of the symbolic being construed solely in abstract, linguistic terms.

By using Irigaray's insight we see that Bausch is exposing not just the power relations between men and women but the entire web of conventions and representations which shape us. And by stressing the need for a new symbolic, she provides a warning not to let ourselves collapse into amplifying and preserving current experiences for aesthetic or cultural gain—a charge which is leveled at Bausch. Irigaray makes it clear that it is essential not to lose the forward-looking moment of mimesis.

Reversing the perspective, Bausch can be used to gain insight into Irigaray. Through her physical work it is possible both to draw out what is radical in Irigaray's thought, and to see its limitations. The radicality of Irigaray's thought is its rejection of linearity and its embrace of fluidity, its emphasis on developing a new experience of time and space and its use of the body as a base for poetic images.

The limitation of Irigaray's thought which bothers me is not the old essentialist claim that she reduces women to inarticulate and irrational versions of the Eternal Feminine. Instead, I worry about the status of the body in her work. The physical metaphors that she uses are at once a strength and a limitation, for at times she seems less concerned with the actual physical body than she is with the expansion of linguistic and symbolic structures which the movement of the body inspires. As a psychoanalyst and a philosopher, she clearly considers it crucial to create a linguistic space for women, yet I worry that she remains trapped within language. Instead of her highly physical vocabulary making her language embodied, what happens is that the "non-weight" of language tends to render her physical vocabulary abstract and overconceptual, thereby losing the body and the scope for participation in the project by the performing arts.

I suggest that the projects of Irigaray and Bausch are highly complementary, and that they constitute the first stage of mimesis. Irigaray claims that mimesis itself is an initial stage, and that it is up to us to generate a new age of thought, art, and poetry; to create "a new *poetics.*"[12] Rosi Braidotti considers this question and comes up with the idea that points of exit from our current system are approached through a new notion of subjectivity, and she suggests that this involves a certain lightness of touch.[13] Irigaray also suggests that laughter is the first form of liberation from oppression.[14]

This is the note on which I would like to conclude. I strongly believe that Bausch and Irigaray's contributions are essential, yet now I wonder whether mimetic strategy can take on a different direction: less heavy-handed, less labored. It will still have the same revolutionary approach to time, space, bodies, frames, desire, and fluidity, yet could liberate itself somewhat from looking backwards. For mimesis only runs the risk of simple recapitulation if it has an investment in preserving the status quo for aesthetic or discursive reasons. Mimetic critique is not an end in itself, but has to gesture toward new ground.[15]

In the spirit of forward-looking mimesis, I see great scope for the transformation of our cultural symbolic through the overlap between art and technology, particularly between dance and the techno-aesthetics of virtual reality. Donna Haraway, a major theorist in this field, claims that cyborgs (organisms which are part human and part technology) are a compound of the organic, technical, mythic, textual, and political.[16] If a role for art is added to this compound, it sounds very much like the new symbolic for which Irigaray is preparing the ground. A new poetics and a new generation of artistic mimesis can indeed emerge, particularly if the theoretical advancements are animated by the dancing body.

Notes

1 Norbert Servos, ed., *Pina Bausch Wuppertal Dance Theater, or The Art of Training a Goldfish*, trans. P. Stadie (Koln: Ballett-Buhnen-Verlag, 1984), pp. 19 and 22.

2 Jean-Georges Noverre, *Letters on Dancing and Ballet*, trans. C. W. Beaumont (London: C. W. Beaumont Publishers, 1930; first published St. Petersburg, 1803), p. 9. According to Noverre, faithfulness of reproduction is the factor that determines whether or not a work is handed down to posterity.

3 Cited in Johannes Birringer, "Pina Bausch: Dancing across Borders," *Theatre, Theory, Postmodernism* (Bloomington: Indiana University Press, 1991), p. 140. This is a quotation from the German playwright Heiner Müller.

4 Luce Irigaray, *This Sex Which Is Not One*, trans. C. Porter (Ithaca: Cornell University Press, 1985; first published 1977), p. 76.

5 Rosi Braidotti, *Nomadic Subjects* (New York: Columbia University Press, 1994), pp. 36–39.

6 Irigaray, *An Ethics of Sexual Difference*, trans. C. Burke and G. C. Gill (London: Athlone Press, 1993; first published 1984), p. 7.

7 Irigaray, *Elemental Passions*, trans. J. Collie and J. Still (London: Athlone Press, 1992; first published 1982), p. 72. I have selected vivid passages from this highly poetic text to illustrate Irigaray's radical approach to time, space, fluidity, and desire. This approach extends across her other more overtly philosophical work such as *Speculum of the Other Woman* and *This Sex Which Is Not One*, but in a less obvious way. As the objective of this section is not a general textual analysis of Irigaray, I have confined myself to *Elemental Passions*.

8 See Ana Sanchez-Colberg's essay, "You Can See It Like This or Like That," in *Parallel Lines: Media Representations of Dance*, ed. S. Jordan and D. Allen (London: John Libbey and Co., 1993), pp. 220–24, for an interesting account of Bausch's cinematic strategies.

9 Irigaray, *Elemental Passions*, p. 71.

10 Ibid., p. 44.

11 Margaret Whitford's *Philosophy in the Feminine* (London: Routledge, 1991), contains an illuminating explanation of the psychoanalytic basis of Irigaray's thought. See section 1, chapters 2, 3, and 4.

12 Irigaray, *Ethics of Sexual Difference*, p. 5.

13 Braidotti, *Nomadic Subjects*. This was also one of the themes she discussed at the conference "Seduced and Abandoned: The Body in Virtual Reality," at the Institute of Contemporary Art, London, March 1994.

14 Irigaray, *This Sex Which Is Not One*, p. 163.

15 This very act of gesturing causes much frustration in Irigaray's readers who are accustomed to being presented with a political program, or agenda for the future, when they read feminist texts. She resists the temptation to be prescriptive, believing this would be a recapitulation to the normative and prescriptive rhetoric of the structures she seeks to undermine. Instead she opens a space for the new which sometimes feels uncomfortably like a void.

16 Donna Haraway, "A Manifesto for Cyborgs: Science, Technology, and Socialist Feminism in the 1980s," *Socialist Review* 80 (1985), pp. 65–108.

5 CLASSICAL BALLET:
A DISCOURSE OF DIFFERENCE

Ann Daly

When Marie Camargo leaped forward to substitute for a male soloist who had missed his entrance at the Paris Opera in the 1720s, her fame was ensured. She was admired for her speed and her fiery style as well as for her ability to master difficult steps, and was complimented as the first woman to dance like a man.[1] Thus, when the ballerina emerged as a great stage persona,[2] she was defined as difference. For to say that Camargo danced "like a man" was to imply that she appropriated the vigorous style and steps of the danseur rather than sticking with her native feminine abilities.

Those abilities had been quite clearly prescribed. The German dancing master Johann Pasch, for example, had written in his 1707 *Beschreibung wahrer Tanz-kunst* that any sort of technical tours de force such as pirouettes or any movements not *gracieux* or *doux* were improper for women dancers.[3] Even the radical Camargo had internalized a degree of conventional femininity; according to an obituary, she "did not make use of *Gargouillade*, which she considered inappropriate for women."[4] Unlike La Faye who—however left-handedly—appreciated Camargo's bravura, Jean-Georges Noverre disparaged her lively style, which, he implied, was carefully constructed so that spectators had little time to notice the shortcomings in her female form.[5]

In ballet, the female form has long been inscribed as a representation of difference: as a spectacle, she is the bearer and object of male desire. The male on stage—the primary term against which the ballerina can only be compared—is not inscribed as a form, but rather as an active principle. The celebrated danseur Igor Youskevitch wrote only twenty-seven years ago, "The inborn feminine tendency to show herself physically, combined with the natural feminine movements that are the cornerstone of her dance vocabulary, is to me the golden key to feminine dance."[6] And, he continued, "For a man, the technical or athletic side of dance is a rational challenge. Once mastered, it provides him with the opportunity to display strength, skill and endurance, as well as with the vocabulary and means to achieve creativity."[7] Masculinity is not mere shallow display. Masculinity is the strong jumper, the narrative's driving force, the creator rather than the created.

Youskevitch's rhetoric is emblematic of ballet discourse as a whole: it is inextricably rooted in the notion of "inborn" or "natural" gender differences. Across the centuries, these differences have been an unabashed hallmark of classical ballet at every level: costuming, body image,[8] movement vocabulary, training, technique, narrative, and especially the pas de deux structure.[9] Like a thicket grown fat around a fencepost, discourse has entwined itself with stage practice in inscribing gender difference as an aesthetic virtue.

Because of dance's ephemerality and because of the relatively recent development of film and video, discourse has been privileged more completely in dance than in any other art form. And it is as much in discourse as in the stage practice itself that Woman (and Man) has been trapped. Instead of confronting patriarchy in representation, critical and scholarly writing has only rationalized it, often in the guise of "classicism" and "romanticism." Dance classicism is an ideology devoted to tradition, chivalry, and to hierarchy of all kinds—gender, performer's rank, the distinction between types of roles, spectators' placement, stage organization, the canon. Romanticism's emphasis on personal expression also relies on the theatricalized dichotomy of feminine and masculine temperaments.

Very few critics and scholars have investigated the patriarchal underpinnings of ballet. This is largely due, I think, to dance's inferiority complex as a "feminine art." Any systematic criticism would undermine the constant struggle to establish dance as a legitimate art form. The first step in creating an alternative discourse is to ask questions—new, difficult, and even disturbing questions. Perhaps it is the only way to present any challenge to the ballerina icon, given that we can never posit who she would be outside of the male constructs that have created her. And it is only by asking questions that "difference"—the seemingly natural and innocent phenomenon in which the ballet discourse is rooted—will be exposed as a socially and politically constructed "opposition." For, as Monique Wittig has pointed out, the primacy of difference is that which constitutes dominance.

> Before the conflict (rebellion, struggle) there are no categories of opposition but only difference. And it is not before the struggle breaks out that the violent reality of the oppositions and the political nature of the differences become manifest. For as long as oppositions (differences)

> appear as given, already there, before all thought, "natural," as long as there is no conflict and no struggle, there is no dialectic, there is no change, no movement.[10]

Although there have been obvious historical changes in women's lives during three centuries of ballet, Woman's place in representation has never really changed, because its ideology has never really changed. Whether the surface rhetoric is Theophile Gautier's fetishization of the ballerina, or Lincoln Kirstein's separate-but-equal argument, or Clive Barnes's dancing-is-macho stance, the underlying assumption is of female difference / male dominance.[11]

Writing during the Romantic period, Gautier's first requirements for ballet were grace and beauty. For him, dancing consisted of "nothing more than the art of displaying beautiful shapes in graceful positions and the development from them of lines agreeable to the eye."[12] He clearly differentiated, however, between female and male participation in this beauty, their respective roles being very narrowly defined. It was fine, he wrote, for men to take action parts—pantomine and character roles—but they were unsuited for the pure dance (i.e., pure display) parts, because these effeminized men, resulting in "that specious grace, that ambiguous, revolting, and mincing manner which has made the public disgusted with male dancing."[13] Pure dancing befit a shapely young woman, he believed, but it was beneath men, whose presence intruded on the illusion of the Eternal Feminine being played out onstage. To be female was grace incarnate; strength/action was the male's sole domain.

Critic Jules Janin in 1840 expressed a similar philosophy, making clear the derogatory feminization of Romantic ballet:

> Speak to us of a pretty dancing girl who displays the grace of her features and the elegance of her figure, who reveals so fleetingly all the treasures of her beauty [illegible] But a man, a frightful man, as ugly as you and I, a wretched fellow who leaps about without knowing why, a creature specially made to carry a musket and a sword and to wear a uniform. That this fellow should dance as a woman does—impossible! That this bewhiskered individual who is a pillar of the community, an elector, a municipal councillor, a man whose business it is to make and above all unmake laws, should come before us in a tunic of sky-blue satin, his head covered with a waving plume amorously caressing his cheek, a frightful *danseuse* of the male sex, come to pirouette in the best place while the pretty ballet girls stand respectfully at a distance—this was surely impossible and intolerable, and we have done well to remove such great artists from our pleasures.[14]

Gautier and Janin abhorred men dancing because their participation in this spectacle emasculated Man's unquestioned power and authority. That men were effectively banned from engaging in this display during the height of Romanticism does not bespeak a subordination of men, as many critics and scholars interpret it, but rather an attempt to uphold the male's virile image—his dominance—untainted by the "feminine." It is no coincidence that the cult of the ballerina arose at the same time that the Paris Opera, cut loose into private enterprise, was trying successfully to turn a profit by appealing to the rising middle class's desire for entertainment.

Even though women's newfound pointe work monopolized the balletomanes' attention, the men on stage retained dominance in the representation by presenting and displaying (and "creating") these object-forms as their own possessions. And by identifying with these figures, the male gaze of the spectator[15] was active in creating and possessing—and "ogling"[16]—these female creatures. Such is the tone of Gautier's criticism: verbal ogling. He wrote as if each ballerina were but one more specimen in his private collection of femininity—minutely and sometimes cruelly making an inventory of what he considered her every asset and defect. For him, the ballerina embodied his desires. Fanny Elssler, he wrote, "in that hand which seems to skim the dazzling barrier of the footlights . . . gathers up all the desires and all the enthusiasm of the spectators."[17] And as she gathered them up, so she dutifully projected them back.

The rhetoric of gender differentiation continued into the twentieth century, superficially transformed by supposedly more enlightened times. Much of the discourse in this century unblinkingly posits the equality of male and female on the ballet stage. For instance, Balanchine apologist Lincoln Kirstein wrote in 1959 that "in the best dance-theater, there is a polarity of male and female on an equal see-saw of elegance and muscularity. The power of the male for leaps in the lateral conquest of space sets off the softness, fragility, speed and multiplicity of the ballerina's action on pointe and in the sustainment of held, breathless equilibrium. Male dancers make girls more feminine and vice versa."[18]

Male and female—"power" and "fragility"—are "equal" only insofar as they maintain the asymmetrical *equilibrium* of patriarchy—which does not offer equality at all. Lauding women for their marginal characteristics, Kirstein and many like-minded writers never question these accepted notions of "femininity," let alone the bipolar opposition which, as Simone de Beauvoir explained, ensnares women in an illusion of complementarity. "Here," she wrote, "is to be found the basic trait of woman: she is the Other in a totality of which the two components are necessary to one another."[19] De Beauvoir could just as well have been describing the pas de deux, an emblem of classical gender asymmetry.

The ruse of ballet's equality-in-difference deconstructed itself by 1978, when *New York Post* critic Clive Barnes explicitly stated the implicit. Under the headline "How Men Have Come to Rule Ballet's Roost," he wrote: "Male dancing is much more exciting than female dancing. It has more vigor, more obvious power, and an entirely more energetic brilliance. Of course there are different qualities—thank Heaven!—to female dancing, yet there is something about the male solo, its combination of sheer athleticism with art, that makes it unforgettable."[20] Female dancing, he implied, is valuable *only* because it is different; the important—and "unforgettable"—qualities are already and exclusively embodied in male dancing.

Male dancing rose to prominence during the seventies—at the same time, ironically, that the women's rights movement reached its peak. The shift was accompanied by a lot of "dancing is masculine" propaganda in the press (à la Barnes) and in a spate of books. Rudolf Nureyev, Mikhail Baryshnikov, and Edward Villella were hyped as strong, virile, and athletic stars. They, however, were the exceptions that proved the rule. The fervor with which apologists invoked the rhetoric of difference in order to assert male dominance in ballet ironically echoed the very rhetoric—that some activities are "masculine" and others are "feminine"—which had contributed to the "emasculation" of the art form as a whole. The profession will never be truly destigmatized for men (or women) as long as the masculine-feminine difference is maintained, because it is due to this polarity that dance was dubbed "effeminate" in the first place. And yet an extreme version of this argument was used in the seventies to "upgrade" the status of men dancers (masculine = big-money = sports = motivation = action = dance).[21]

Symptomatically, a 1969 issue of the prestigious *Dance Perspectives* was devoted to the "Male Image." Anthropologist and kinesics founder Ray L. Birdwhistell introduced the issue by discussing the invented nature of human gender display and concluding that "art is conventional and erroneous when it allows the binary logic of the primary sexual characteristics to determine the rhetoric expressing human interaction."[22] Despite Birdwhistell's visionary critique of gender codes, four danseurs—including Youskevitch—then proceeded to characterize the art form along rigidly "natural" gender line: female/male, display/action, delicate/strong, emotional/rational, nature/culture.

The civil rights movement demonstrated that "separate but equal" is impossible and even vicious—that "separate" or "different" underlines and perpetuates inequality. Until the struggle—at least in discourse—breaks out in

1. *Serenade* by George Balanchine.
Performers include Mimi Paul and Nicholas Magallanes of the New York City Ballet. Courtesy of the Dance Collection, the New York Public Library for the Performing Arts, Astor, Lenox, and Tilden Foundations.

classical ballet, the political nature of male-female difference remains submerged. This is especially true today, when formerly experimental choreographers are one after the other turning to toe shoes and arabesques for their inspiration. In borrowing from the classical vocabulary, choreographers like Karole Armitage, Laura Dean, Twyla Tharp, and Molissa Fenley are not being subversive or transformative. They may mix-it-up differently, laying their own twist or attitude on top of the classical, but it is essentially the traditional ballet and its ideology borrowed whole, particularly the romantic pas de deux. If choreographers such as these are not going to question themselves, at least the critical discourse can do so.

But contemporary writing, for the most part, has continued to collude in ballet's representation of Woman. When Bill T. Jones and Arnie Zane did some gender-bending of George Balanchine's classic *Serenade* (figure 1) in their 1985 *How to Walk an Elephant*, the *New York Times* critic Anna Kisselgoff scolded them for daring to tangle with Balanchine's "ballet is woman" iconography:

> When they take one of the most celebrated and beautiful moments in "Serenade"—a woman in arabesque revolving in place because a man on the floor below turns the leg upon which she stands—and give us a gawky arabesque for a tall slim man, they are not being respectful of either the choreographer or one of his greatest ballets.
>
> It does matter whether the arabesque in this "quotation" belongs to a man or a woman. Mr. Zane and Mr. Jones might wish to make a valid point about changing attitudes toward traditional gender roles, about men and women sharing the same characteristics. But this was never Balanchine's belief and his well known creed that "ballet is woman" received one of its firmest statements in "Serenade."[23]

Kisselgoff's indignation underscores the integral role of Woman in ballet ideology and particularly in its inscription of pleasure. To her, the sacred authority of tradition is never to be desecrated by critical analysis. For what we risk in questioning pleasure is the very loss of that pleasure. But the liberating potential of the inquiry, as Laura Mulvey has pointed out, is "the thrill that comes from leaving the past behind without rejecting it, transcending outworn or oppressive forms, or daring to break with normal pleasurable expectations in order to conceive a new language of desire."[24]

Notes

1 Although it is usually Voltaire to whom this "compliment" is attributed, it was actually La Faye who wrote the verse appearing on the engraving of the Lancret painting of Camargo dancing (Ivor Guest, letter to author, 16 May 1993).

2 In the sixteenth and seventeenth centuries, gender difference was encoded in court spectacles, which adapted social dances in polished and studied form. In the earliest years of the Paris Opera, women's roles were taken by men in travesty. Four ballerinas finally took the stage in 1681, in *Le Triomphe de l'Amour*, among them Mlle. de la Fontaine. She was succeeded as prima ballerina by Marie-Thérèse de Subligny and then Françoise Prévost. Still overshadowed by the virtuosic men, neither one drew as much attention as Camargo.

3 Marian Hannah Winter, *The Pre-Romantic Ballet* (New York: Pitman Publishing, 1974), p. 46.

4 Ibid., p. 162.

5 See Parmenia Migel, *The Ballerinas* (New York: Da Capo Press, 1972), pp. 37–38.

6 Igor Youskevitch, "The Male Image," *Dance Perspectives* (Winter 1969), p. 16.

7 Ibid, p. 23.

8 The ballet dancer's body image is the product of centuries of patriarchal codification about gender difference. In Carlo Blasis's classic treatise on dancing, *The Code of Terpsichore*, he wrote: "Men must dance in a manner very different from women; the *temps de vigeur*, and bold majestic execution of the former, would have a disagreeable effect in the latter, who must shine and delight by lithsome [*sic*] and graceful motions, by neat and pretty *terre-à-terre* steps, and by a decent voluptuousness and *abandon* in all their attitudes." See Blasis, *Code of Terpsichore* (London: James Bulcock, 1828), pp. 94–95. Reprinted in Brooklyn by Dance Horizons. The phrase "decent voluptuousness" encapsulates the double bind in which women are placed as erotic/aesthetic object: they must be erotic enough to titillate but distanced enough not to offend.

9 For further analysis of the pas de deux, see Ann Daly, "The Balanchine Woman: Of Hummingbirds and Channel Swimmers," *The Drama Review* 31, no. 1 (Spring 1987), pp. 8–21.

10 Monique Wittig, "The Category of Sex," *Feminist Issues* (Fall 1982), pp. 64–65.

11 See, for example, Theophile Gautier, *The Romantic Ballet as Seen by Theophile Gautier*, trans. Cyril W. Beaumont (New York: Books for Libraries, 1980); Lincoln Kirstein, *Ballet: Bias and Belief* (New York: Dance Horizons, 1983); and Clive Barnes, "After All, Don't Men Dance Better?" *New York Times*, 6 June 1971, p. 12, and his "How Men Have Come to Rule Ballet's Roost," *New York Post*, 22 July 1978, p. 27.

12 Gautier, *The Romantic Ballet*, p. 17.

13 Ibid., p. 67.

14 Quoted in Ivor Guest, *The Romantic Ballet in Paris* (Middletown, Conn.: Wesleyan University Press, 1966), p. 21.

15 See E. Ann Kaplan's development of the concept of the male gaze in her *Women and Film: Both Sides of the Camera* (London: Methuen, 1983), pp. 23–35. The pivotal concept of the "male gaze" arises from the structure of representation, in which the position of the spectator (the gazer) is encoded. Thus, women too, under patriarchy, can partake in the acculturated male gaze.

16 See Jack Anderson, *Ballet and Modern Dance* (Princeton, N.J.: Princeton Book Company, 1986), p. 69.

17 Gautier, *The Romantic Ballet*, p. 15.

18 See Kirstein, *Ballet*, p. 400.

19 Simone de Beauvoir, *The Second Sex*, trans. and ed. H. M. Parshley (New York: Vintage Books, 1974), p. xxiii.

20 Barnes, "How Men Have Come to Rule Ballet's Roost," p. 27.

21 It is interesting to note an opposite stream in the gender-conscious seventies: danseurs in

some repertoires had the opportunity to be softer, to display a more pronounced, aesthetic line. Yet women were still not permitted strength. This "androgynous" approach maintained gender difference and asymmetry; it simply reapportioned the polarized attributes, allowing men a much larger range of expression.

22 Ray Birdwhistell, "The Male Image," *Dance Perspectives* 40 (Winter 1969), p. 11.

23 Anna Kisselgoff, "The Dance: Alvin Ailey Performs 'Elephant,'" *New York Times*, 7 December 1985, p. 14.

24 Laura Mulvey, "Visual Pleasure and Narrative Cinema," *Screen* 16, no. 3 (Autumn 1975), p. 8.

6 BALLET AS IDEOLOGY: *GISELLE*, ACT 2

Evan Alderson

In the past few years there has been a growing interest in the social nature of art production. This interest is frequently opposed from within traditional aesthetics on the grounds that it reduces art to a social symptom and thus fundamentally misses the locus of aesthetic value. Conventional aesthetics assumes that artistic expression exists most importantly within an autonomous aesthetic realm—that works of art indeed reflect society, but that this reflection should be understood from within a disinterested "aesthetic attitude." The desire to preserve the aesthetic as a separate realm does not deny that art is a social product so much as it tends to isolate the social meanings of a work of art from those meanings that are seen to develop intrinsically, that are grounded in human universals rather than historical particulars. In this view the continued accessibility of classic works is taken to manifest the transhistorical qualities of art. The local conditions of production and historically specific ideas are seen to fall away, so that our present appreciation is of timeless essences.

In recent years, however, serious questions about this perspective have been raised by various cultural theorists.[1] By focusing on the ways in which an art object expresses the interests and ideas of a particular social group even where the work seems to claim an aesthetic transcendence, some sociological approaches emphasize the constant and necessary entrenchment of both the production and reception of a work of art within the social order. Moreover, the very concept of aesthetic autonomy itself is perceived as exemplifying a social bias, a means whereby social elites privilege some expressive forms over others. This skepticism is partially a response to the different sense of art that arises from its relation to other spheres of contemporary cultural production. The uncertain dividing lines between "high art" and popular culture in a medium such as film, the reinforcement of regressive cultural stereotypes within traditional forms such as ballet, the use of "high art" imagery within advertising media, all suggest that art and the idea of art have a social power that cannot be accounted for either by traditional aesthetic concerns or by study of the overt social messages within some works.

This social orientation toward art must still come to terms with the actual experience of beauty. When we are moved by the beauty of something, it is difficult to see it also as expressing a specific social interest. In particular, classic works of art that have a continuing presence in our culture seem to escape any ideological entrapments of their moment of creation. What do the attitudes toward ballet displayed by members of the Jockey Club during the July Monarchy have to do with our present experience of the immortal *Giselle*? Quite a bit, I will argue, though in intricate and indirect ways. But to understand the connection, we must see how our appreciation of a classic work involves an arcing across historical periods that is ideological as well as aesthetic, and how our sense of the beautiful is itself ideologically conditioned. In order to understand how art functions in society, we have to perceive how ideology is projected in and through aesthetic value and not apart from it. And in perceiving this, we may recognize some of the ways our own subjectivity is socially organized, how the experience of aesthetic transcendence also replaces us in the social order.

In choosing to discuss ideology in relation to ballet aesthetics, I am obviously stalking easy prey. One of ballet's charms is the overtness with which it propagates socially charged imagery as a form of the beautiful. Of course, such insouciance has had its response: much of the tradition of modern dance can be seen as an ideologically grounded critique of the ideals of beauty embodied in ballet. The saints of modern dance from Isadora Duncan forward have characteristically harnessed some idea of the "natural"—that warhorse of ideological conflict—to ride against the dragon of artifice. More recently, several books have criticized the ballet world for its tolerance or even encouragement of anorexia nervosa and other physical and psychological perils. L. M. Vincent's *Competing with the Sylph*, Joan Brady's *The Unmaking of a Dancer*, and Suzanne Gordon's *Off Balance* all, from somewhat different perspectives, describe what can only be regarded as a fairly perverse social order. But for the most part their criticisms appear reformist in spirit: these authors tend to see the perversities they describe as excesses of fashion rather than as phenomena having deep connections with ballet aesthetics. Their works thus remain vulnerable to the most characteristic defense against such charges by the adherents of ballet: "Yes, but it's beautiful."[2]

The invocation of beauty as an absolute defense should remind us that one of the chief characteristics of ideological argument is to make tendentious positions appear natural and inevitable. This feature of ideology accounts for a curious doubleness in most discussions of it from Marx forward. In one of its definitions, ideology is a set of ideas and values that reflect the interest of the dominant group within a given social order. These values become instruments of social domination insofar as they are accepted by subordinate groups as universal truths. But there is a second aspect of ideology that is especially important for my purposes here: ideology is not just a "mask" of the dominant class; it is also a "veil" of perception. It is a structuring of social experience which sublimates group interests into a set of justifying ideals, ideals which from behind the veil appear as socially integrative values.[3] In this definition ideology is an inevitable component of social experience, refracted through both individual experience and cultural history, and as such, necessarily engaged in the experience of art works. But the feeling of "rightness" in a work of art also acts as a persuasion; it may be exactly through the beautiful that ideological naturalization takes place, that the individual subjectivity in all its complexity is rejoined with a social order.

I want to pursue this double theme of joining—of the self with the social order and of the past with the present—through a discussion of *Giselle*, beginning where I believe more criticism should begin, with an account of personal response. I am ordinarily a rather temperate viewer of ballet, with my own biases and resistances to its formal beauties—certainly no balletomane. Yet at a performance of *Giselle* by the Royal Winnipeg Ballet some time ago, my critical response was at one moment thoroughly disarmed. Until well into the second act, I observed the proceedings with considerable detachment, though alive to such qualities in the production as there appeared to me to be. Then, at a moment in the second-act adagio—Giselle *en attitude* downstage right, Albrecht behind and reaching toward her, and both set off against the severe diagonals of the Wilis—a new and beautiful unity appeared whereby Evelyn Hart's virtuosity, the forms of grace given in ballet, the unfolding story, the music and decor all seemed to become one thing. Criticism fell away; I was for that time seized by beauty.

Now, I do not wish to claim any special authority for this response, though I think it is not uncommon; as Théophile Gautier wrote of the work's first reception in 1841, "More than one eye which thought it was seeing only *ronds de jambe* and *pointes* found to its surprise its vision obscured by a tear—which does not often happen in ballets."[4] I do want to suggest that my reaction stemmed from a pattern of affective dynamics within the work itself, one that links ideas and values of the work's time of origin to those of the present. Thinking back on my response, I realized that I had been hooked on the point of my own desire: I had been "let in" through Albrecht's longing for the absolutely faithful, absolutely unattainable woman whose death he had occa-

1. *Giselle* (choreography by Blair after Coralli).
Performed by the American Ballet Theater, with Carla Fracci and Erik Bruhn. Courtesy of the Dance Collection, the New York Public Library for the Performing Arts, Astor, Lenox, and Tilden Foundations, gift of J. Willis.

sioned, because I share with much of nineteenth-century culture an attraction to what is sexually charged yet somehow pristine. I can thus be affected by the unity of longing, purity, beauty, and death which the second act proposes (figure 1). The adagio was for me the time of transformation of Albrecht's burden from guilt to sorrow, from the bearing of blame to an endless forgiveness, the time when I *knew* that he was loved, and that his own longing was justified. The dematerialization of the object of his desire seemed a small cost to pay for such a beautiful redemption.

But there is more here than merely the sentiment of an unattainable ideal. Giselle's gratifying faithfulness, after all, not only forgives Albrecht his own duplicity but also rescues him from a world of feminine vengeance. In the sources on which Gautier drew when creating his scenario, and also in his own writings on *Giselle*, there are numerous linkages among female sexuality, dancing, and vengeance against the male. In the legend that he used, the Wilis are the spirits of maidens who have died before their wedding day and who thus "could not satisfy their passion for dancing."[5] This unsatisfied *Tanzlust* has converted them, in Gautier's words, into "cruel nocturnal dancers, no more forgiving than living women are to a tired waltzer." Their queen, the pitiless Myrtha, "resorts to an infernal and feminine device" in forcing Giselle to tempt Albrecht with "the most seductive and most graceful poses."[6] Giselle's ultimate gift to Albrecht is that despite her newly found sisterhood, she does not finally dance him to death. The fullest mark of her love is that she denies her own power in helping him to survive. Her femininity remains in the service of the male.

I suggest that there is considerable sexual anxiety concealed within the libretto of *Giselle*, and that both the dance's ideality and its aesthetic consolations should be understood in this light. Since Mario Praz's *The Romantic Agony* it has become a commonplace to perceive deflections of sexuality within various motifs of romanticism.[7] Yet in relation to ballet there have been only tentative explorations of the intricate connections between, on the one hand, the resolution of private fantasies through imaginative creation and, on the other, the ideological resolution of social contradictions through the same aesthetic structures. Two critics of romantic ballet, John Chapman and Eric Aschengreen, have commented usefully in this regard. For Aschengreen, Gautier's "idolization of beautiful forms" is part of his search "for something deeper, the very thing that could lift him beyond the primal desires he felt as a man." The "pure, spiritual and completely un-sensual beauty that comes alive in the second act of *Giselle*"[8] thus indicated Gautier's "love of art as a palliative for a painful life," as "all that remained as a prospect for escape in an intolerable world created by the bourgeoisie."[9] The implications of this position are that the desexualization of Giselle is one part of an aesthetic transcendence that stood in opposition to the dominant social order. In contrast, John Chapman emphasizes the direct eroticism of much romantic ballet, placing that eroticism in the context of "the owned woman" of the period, as given in the odalisques and slave girls of *juste milieu* painting, as well as in the actual social practices in the *foyer de danse*. For him, the sylph is just another prospect: "Perhaps just as erotic as the harem girl was the supernatural spirit. . . . The challenge and danger of the seductive *femme fatale* only heightened erotic stimulation."[10]

I believe that both these critics misplace the eroticism of *Giselle* in crucial ways. Certainly, Gautier's attitudes toward dance, as given in his criticism, do include both erotic appreciation and a proprietary sensibility. The spirit of his criticism lies in his declaration that "an actress is a statue or a picture which is exhibited to you, and can be freely criticized,"[11] an attitude which he takes as license for frankly sensualist appraisals of dancers like Fanny Elssler. Yet the "school of Taglioni," with its "modest grace, chaste reserve, and diaphanous virginity,"[12] exercises a different kind of fascination. Here he is moved by just the visible contradiction between sexuality and chastity. Writing on Taglioni's performance in the 1844 revival of *La Sylphide*, he comments: "What rhythmic movements! What noble gestures! What poetic attitudes and, above all, what a sweet melancholy! What lack of restraint, yet how chaste!"[13]

In the tradition of *ballet blanc*, as modified in *Giselle*, there is an alternative to both the sensualist and spiritualist positions, in which the erotic is given and yet simultaneously denied. The "sweet melancholy" that results is a staple of romantic imagery. In the sentimental novel, beginning with Samuel Richardson's *Clarissa* in 1748 and flourishing for a century after, the poignancy of sacrifice and regret is everywhere. What is particularly to be noticed about this imagery is that it stems from a complex and double view of woman, one that is at once heroizing and subtly deprecating: female sexual feeling is deflected toward innocence and virtue, but this virtue both invites victimization and triumphs through it; the feminine power of virtuous self-denial is thus ambiguously both a saving gift and a mode of revenge. The fate of Clarissa herself sets the pattern. She suffers an extended threat to her chastity from an aristocratic admirer, and when her heroic resistance is eventually overcome by Lovelace's deceit and rape, she dies. But she does so only two-thirds of the way through a very long book, so that we may see the powerful working of her virtue on the regretful Lovelace. In effect she, like Giselle, maintains a supernatural and saving presence over the final movement of her story.

Certainly, the two heroines have their differences, but *Giselle* clearly elaborates the pattern. Albrecht's betrayal of Giselle's first-act innocence, even though it is set in a never-never land of happy peasants and princes in disguise, contains the basic lesson that sentimental novels of the time were endlessly and formulaically repeating concerning “the evil consequences of seduction.” The imaginatively more compelling second act makes explicit two possible avenues of femine power—the Wilis' aggressive revenge and Giselle's forgiveness—and “chooses” the latter. But the satisfactions of this resolution depend upon the tensions that have been raised: a woman triumphs, but her power has been channeled in a way that confines male sexual anxiety, subtly condones male sexual aggression, and alleviates male guilt. The “completely un-sensual beauty” of act 2 is a negation that contains its opposite, an example of “the sublimation, camouflage, or subterfuge of . . . elemental appetites and aspirations” that one cultural critic has cited as characteristic of bourgeois art.[14]

It is no accident that the century between *Clarissa* and *Giselle* roughly coincided with the triumph of the bourgeoisie, that family-oriented, capital-accumulating, industrious, and pragmatic social class that Gautier claimed to despise. The bourgeois self-concept required a center of social value apart from those given within an aristocratic order, in which definitions of virtue had tended to coincide with prior definitions of social rank. This center of values was required to be secular, status-conferring, and consonant with the unrestrained acquisition of material possessions. The social values imaginatively embedded within *Giselle* fulfill these requirements in complex ways. As mask, these values are self-congratulatory, evasive, and power-seeking; as veil, these same values appear to manifest a deep respect for women (at least for bourgeois wives and daughters) and a profound interest in private experience, especially the domestic emotions. Moreover, they are infused with the sentiment for beauty. The romantic and ethereal beauty of act 2, then, has a more complex social function than either Chapman or Aschengreen contemplates. Whatever the lusts of the Jockey Club, ideality does not simply “heighten erotic stimulus”; instead it both captures and inverts it in the interests of sentiment and power. Whatever the avowed social oppositions of Gautier's aestheticism, he has not escaped “the intolerable world of the bourgeoisie”; he has become its ideologist.

Gautier called Taglioni “the dancer for Women,”[15] in order to contrast her style with Fanny Elssler's more sensuous appeal to men. Yet to whatever extent *Giselle* or its first star, Carlotta Grisi, combined the two styles, we should remember that it was Taglioni who defined what is now memorable in the style of romantic ballet. This definition was as much as anything a matter of technique: the rising on pointe as familiar practice, the domination of grace over visible effort, the remarkable lightness (“She descends without falling,” said Auguste Vestris[16]). Costumes and decor as well as libretti reinforced this emphasis of the vertical and its association with both ethereality and chastity. But of course the technical innovations also correspond to and reinforce a particular ideal of femininity, an ideal that has been so persuasive because it accommodates both masculine and feminine interests. The "dancer for women" images woman as both cynosure of eyes and epitome of virtue, but both beauty and purity depend upon a sexuality refined to the vanishing point. She presents a demure, perfected, admired body which projects disembodiment. And she is also a dancer for men—men whose attraction to this attenuation of the flesh both sentimentalizes sexual possession and spares them full acknowledgment of a sexuality they cannot control.

It should be clear that this coalescence of gender interests around a particular image of the female body is not an entire historical novelty, but simply a new form for an old pattern. That women might attract men through an ostentatious modesty was no invention of the bourgeois era, nor did the romantic ballerina provide the first feminine image to channel the desires of both women and men. But the emergence of a new and potent image deserves sociological attention. One social theorist has argued that an important transition in gender relationships took place in western Europe at about the time of *Giselle*, when legal and religious structures that had previously supported patriarchy were giving way under the pressures of bourgeois individualism. Thus, "capitalism produces patriarchalism by reaping the advantages of cheap labour and unpaid domestic services within the household; it also destroys patriarchy by creating, at least formally, universalistic values and individualism."[17] In this situation, the persistence of male privilege comes increasingly to depend upon the persuasions of imagery that appears to give women a distinctive place in the order of things, whether this place is her closeness to nature, her moral purity, or the sexual allure created by such punitive engines of glamour as the corset.

Pervaded by a romantic ideal of femininity, ballet has played a part in promulgating its wider social acceptance. The romantic style and its immediate heirs continue to be highly visible in ballet production, even though cognate styles in literature have fallen from view, or at least from our idea of "art." Perhaps the imagery of *ballet blanc* has such staying power because it has entered a discourse of the body. Dance, after all, is an art that depends upon the entrenchment of its conventional imagery in living bodies: the technical training of a dancer maintains and reproduces the social bearing of the dominant style by actualizing it in the dancer's body. In some very important senses, Pavlova—as person, performer, and legend—*became* Giselle. The power her performances had on young women, touchingly described by Agnes de Mille in her autobiography,[18] constituted an invitation also to embody that image. And alongside that invitation to women, the critical response to the romantic ballerina, even by her most sensitive appreciators, continues to reveal the connections among idealization, erotic distortion, and masculine possessiveness. Consider, for example, these words of Adrian Stokes:

> The ballerina's body is etherealized. She seems scarcely to rest upon the ground. She is, as it were, suspended just slightly above the earth so that we may see her better. She seems cut off from the sources of her being, or rather, those dark internal sources are shown by her as something light and white, brittle as are all baubles, all playthings that we can utterly examine; yet, at the same time, so perfect is her geometry that we feel this plaything which our minds may utterly possess, to be as well the veriest essence.[19]

In a slightly less blatant way, Balanchine's equation—"Ballet is woman"—has the same tendency, for it implies that woman is not, or should not be, what ballet is not. In one of his glosses on the famous aphorism, Balanchine contrasts men and women as follows: "Man is a better cook, a better painter, a better musician, composer. . . . Man is stronger, faster. . . . And woman accepts this. It is her business to accept. She knows what's beautiful."[20] The equation works both ways: ballet is the art form of beautiful acceptance.

Balanchine's attitudes toward woman bring us back both to the defense of beauty and to the issue of anorexia nervosa. Balanchine has been called "the man who defeminized women," and has been accused by Suzanne Gordon of establishing the fashion for emaciation in the American ballet world.[21] Such charges are probably not fair to Balanchine, but there is clearly a relationship between "the look" and this particular pathology. Gordon cites estimates that 15 percent of female ballet students in the leading American ballet schools are true anorectics. If this disturbing statistic is anywhere near the truth, then possible reasons for the correlation should be considered. There have been plausible contentions that the ballet environment is compatible with anorectic susceptibilities: competitiveness, discipline, a desire for self-control, and a preoccupation with the body are requisites for ballet training and are also characteristics of the anorectic type. There are also connections between the willful childlikeness of some citizens of the ballet world and the denial of sexuality that is stressed in some interpretations of anorexia. Gordon quotes one authority as saying that "[Anorectics] don't learn, as they grow up, to accept their sexuality and integrate sexual feelings into normal functioning. They don't want to grow up; they want to remain children."[22]

There are deeper possible connections, however, between anorexia and the themes of this discussion, for the anorectic seeks power by means of embodying a culturally given image, an image she can fulfill only at the cost of disembodying herself. The anorectic pursues, with a vengeance, a particular ideal of feminine beauty. But it is an obsession with perfection that bases itself with chilling literalism on a symbolic system. Having within it a strong component of adolescent rebellion, anorexia can be described as at once a drive for autonomy and a cultural invasion of the body. This "compelling, peculiar path to selfhood"[23] is a triumph of negation, deeply infused with the paradox of a sexual idealism that demands desexualization. In this sense the image of the romantic ballerina, and more particularly Giselle's apotheosis in death, is a stylization, a socially sanctioned version, of some of the impulses that take a diseased—and unbeautiful—extremity in anorexia.

Anorexia has been described as an illness of consumerism, a neurotic version of the obsession with appearances within a "culture of narcissism." If *Giselle* in 1841 participated in and expressed a developing bourgeois culture, *Giselle* in modern performance participates in ours. Of course, the terms of its participation have changed, for now it is a classic. As such, the beauties and comforts it offers to us are legitimated as transhistorical. The eternal feminine rearticulates an idealism of feminine sacrifice, whether that sacrifice is for a man, for one's art, or to the labor of glamour. Anyone who surveys the slick dance magazines with sensitivity to cultural signs will be aware that romantic ethereality still occupies a central place in the image of the female dancer, and that the image of the female dancer is largely a servant of the glamour industry. In this way the inherent innocence of dancing bodies—which Giselle also celebrates but converts in act 2 to the poignancy of unfulfilled desire—is turned toward economic purposes. In our present North American culture, the extraordinary continuing popularity of *Giselle* reflects a society in which sentimental imagery has been deeply confused with attainable achievements, and for which the practical exactions of ethereality provide an ironic model of endless consumption.[24]

The conflict between sociology and conventional aesthetics can now be restated as it applies to dance. From the perspective of phenomenological aesthetics, David Michael Levin has called dance the "poetizing" of bodily experience.[25] From the perspective of sociology, Bryan Turner has seen control of the body, particularly the female body, as one pervasive task of Western ideology.[26] My central contention is this: in its poetizing of bodily experience *Giselle* gives us also and at once a poetizing of bodily control. This bodily control has an aspect that faces inward, toward the specificity of ballet and its pleasures—the technical mastery, the sublime tension with gravity that Levin, among others, has analyzed so compellingly. But intricately related to these formal issues, and regardless of the focus of our attention, *Giselle* also poetizes the control *of* bodies, the ways in which the body is socialized in at least partial accordance with the structures of power within society. The bodies we admire in their fulfillment of an extraordinary technique, the sense of a rare perfection, the feeling of ultimate simplicity in the "rightness" of it all—these also invoke our loyalty to a social order.

The ideological persuasiveness of ballet, then, operates at a deep level of the art form, one that is inextricable from its aesthetic values. This integration is deeply historical, most especially in works that have continuing appeal. Thus I have argued that the etherealization of the female body that is imaged in *Giselle* represents a particular moment within the general history of patriarchy in which the ascendancy of private economic relations called forth an image of woman as at once private and powerful, sacred and spectral, a figure of desire that by inversion of physical presence both accommodates and imaginatively controls feminine sexual power. The moment of our response to this classic work is a moment of convergence—of past and present, of self and society, of imaginations at a distance. If we are affected by the work's provisional, aesthetic resolutions to tensions between desire and belief, it is because those tensions are alive in us, as they were in the culture of its creation. Such imaginative resolutions are indeed aesthetic; they may be experienced—quite simply—as beautiful, and are not to be taken for social prescription. Yet our assent to this beauty entails a further assent to a network of social ideas. For this reason, a summary of our tastes is also a summary of our allegiances, however confused and self-contradictory both of these may be. An adequate aesthetics will enhance our awareness of art as social form.

Notes

1 An excellent overview of contemporary issues in the sociology of art is provided in Janet Wolff's *The Social Production of Art* (London: Macmillan, 1981). Her more recent book, *Aesthetics and the Sociology of Art* (London: George Allen and Unwin, 1983), more specifically addresses problems of aesthetic value in relation to the social nature of art production. Another useful discussion of these issues is provided by Terry Eagleton in *Literary Theory: An Introduction* (Oxford: Basil Blackwell, 1983).

2 L. M. Vincent, *Competing with the Sylph: Dancers and the Pursuit of the Ideal Body Form* (New York: Berkley, 1981); Joan Brady, *The Unmaking of a Dancer: An Unconventional Life* (New York: Harper and Row, 1982); Suzanne Gordon, *Off Balance: The Real World of Ballet* (New York: Pantheon, 1983). A fairly typical example of the defense of beauty is given by Debra Cash in a review of the Gordon book: "Suki Schorer, a former NYCB principal and now one of SAB's finest teachers, answered a question about why a student jumped without putting down her heels. Doesn't this cause tendinitis? Yes, Schorer smiled, when people come into this company they get tendinitis—but it's *beautiful.*" *Ballet News* 5, no. 8 (February 1984), p. 43.

3 I have borrowed the metaphor for ideology's double aspect from J. G. Merquior's essay "The Veil and the Mask: On Ideology, Power, and Legitimacy," in his book *The Veil and the*

Mask: Essays on Culture and Ideology (London: Routledge and Kegan Paul, 1979), pp. 1–38. An excellent critical introduction to the very substantial and often contradictory literature on ideology is provided by John B. Thompson in *Studies in the Theory of Ideology* (Cambridge: Polity Press, 1984).

4 *Les Beautés de l'Opéra*, p. 23, quoted in Ivor Guest, *The Romantic Ballet in Paris* (Middletown, Conn.: Wesleyan University Press, 1966), p. 209.

5 Cyril W. Beaumont, *The Ballet Called "Giselle"* (New York: Dance Horizons, 1969), p. 19.

6 *The Romantic Ballet as Seen by Théophile Gautier*, trans. C. W. Beaumont (New York: Dance Horizons, n.d.), pp. 55, 57.

7 Mario Praz, *The Romantic Agony*, trans. Angus Davidson, 2nd ed. (New York: Meridian, 1956). See also Leslie A. Fiedler, *Love and Death in the American Novel*, rev. ed. (New York: Stein and Day, 1966).

8 Erik Aschengreen, "The Beautiful Danger: Facets of the Romantic Ballet," *Dance Perspectives* 58 (Summer 1974), p. 23.

9 Ibid., p. 30.

10 John Chapman, "An Unromantic View of Nineteenth-Century Romanticism," *York Dance Review* 7 (Spring 1978), pp. 28–45, 35.

11 Gautier, *The Romantic Ballet*, p. 20.

12 Ibid., p. 86.

13 Ibid., p. 70.

14 Xavier Rubert de Ventos, *Heresies of Modern Art*, trans. J. S. Bernstein (New York: Columbia University Press, 1980), p. 50.

15 Gautier, *The Romantic Ballet*, p. 27.

16 Quoted in Guest, *The Romantic Ballet in Paris*, p. 86.

17 Bryan S. Turner, *The Body and Society: Explorations in Social Theory* (London: Basil Blackwell, 1984), p. 153.

18 Agnes de Mille, *Dance to the Piper* (Boston: Little, Brown, 1952), pp. 39–42.

19 From *Tonight the Ballet* (1935), quoted in *What Is Dance? Readings in Theory and Criticism*, ed. Roger Copeland and Marshall Cohen (New York: Oxford University Press, 1983), p. 246.

20 Quoted in John Gruen, *The Private World of Ballet* (New York: Viking, 1975), p. 284.

21 Gordon, *Off Balance*, p. 143. The epithet "The Man Who Defeminized Women" appeared as the headline of a newspaper article on Balanchine by Suzanne Gordon reprinted from the Los Angeles *Times* in the Vancouver, B.C., *Sun,* 28 July 1983.

22 Ibid., p. 147.

23 Turner, *The Body and Society*, p. 193. My perspective on anorexia is indebted to Turner's interesting discussion on pages 180–203. A more extensive treatment of the ideal of slenderness and its complex relation to sexuality is Kim Chernin's *The Obsession: Reflections on the Tyranny of Slenderness* (New York: Harper and Row, 1981).

24 In pointing to a special and probably transitory relationship to fashion in contemporary North America, I am not ignoring other regions of *Giselle*'s ideological reach. Ideological forms have some measure of both stability and change, and the capacity to adapt, within limits, to local circumstances of power. An equivalent argument could be made about the place of this ballet in the Soviet Union, which would point to a somewhat different but no less ideological functioning of its current reception.

25 David Michael Levin, *The Body's Recollection of Being* (London: Routledge and Kegan Paul, 1985), p. 293 ff.

26 Turner, *The Body and Society*, pp. 91, 115.

7 DANCING THE ORIENT FOR ENGLAND: MAUD ALLAN'S *THE VISION OF SALOME*

Amy Koritz

Maud Allan, a Canadian-born Californian who had launched her dancing career in Germany, far exceeded the popularity of other "barefoot" dancers who performed in England in the first decade of this century. In 1908, she enjoyed an unprecedented run of over 250 performances at the Palace Theatre, a London music hall, due in large part to the notoriety of her depiction of Salome in a dance called *The Vision of Salome.* Descriptions of this dance by critics and others, including Allan herself, reveal an interaction of racial and gender stereotyping that reinforced English assumptions about the "Oriental." This Orientalism (in Edward Said's sense of the term) in turn depended upon a rhetoric that characterized as female those attributes that denoted the inferiority of England's colonized peoples. The discourse of Orientalism, in other words, deployed a gendered rhetoric available in English culture to define the role and nature of women. The attributes of English, or more generally, of Western women, however, had to be distanced from those of both the feminized and the female native. A Western woman's representation of that fantasy of the Eastern woman—Salome—became, in these circumstances, an ideologically unstable event requiring the careful manipulation of available vocabularies in order to keep the overlapping and mutually reinforcing categories of Western woman and native clearly distinct.

These vocabularies were drawn mainly from a cluster of discourses that defined the place of the Englishman in relation to the colonial subject (Orientalism and imperialism), in relation to Western women (separate-spheres gender ideology), and in relation to other non-English peoples (nationalism). Before exploring how these discourses were activated in discussions of Allan's dance, their relations with each other should be briefly stated. The discourse of Orientalism was inextricable from the policies and ideology of English imperialism. Orientalism, in Said's terms "a Western style for dominating, restructuring, and having authority over the Orient," was not, however, simply coextensive with imperialism.[1] Rather the colonial rule that was the practical consequence of English imperialist policies was, according to Said, "justified in advance by Orientalism."[2] That is, the institutional and discursive practices of Orientalism, practices that established the conceptual polarization of East and West, claimed authority for Western definitions of the Orient, and legitimized the domination of Eastern peoples, were an enabling condition of imperialism, not its post-hoc rationalization.

Although Said's analysis of Orientalism has been faulted for its overreliance on binary opposition and its inability to provide a place from which the colonized subject can speak, both of these qualities characterized the discourse he set out to describe.[3] Orientalism names a powerful and long-lived collection of practices and conventions that cannot, as Said argues elsewhere, be simply brushed aside once their oppressive nature is recognized.[4] The binary, racist rhetoric of Orientalism was pervasive in the England that welcomed Maud Allan.

Imperialism, unlike Orientalism, explicitly named a foreign policy and its supporting ideology actively pursued and contested in late-nineteenth- and early-twentieth-century England. Thus, for example, in 1902 J. A. Hobson attacked imperialism as both a political policy and an ideological stance (what he called its "moral and sentimental factors"). He saw it as an abuse of nationalism which "convert[ed] a cohesive, pacific internal force into an exclusive, hostile force, a perversion of the true power and use of nationality."[5] Many Fabians, meanwhile, including Sidney Webb and George Bernard Shaw, supported imperialism on the grounds of the administrative efficiency of the British Empire.[6] The attraction of imperialism went beyond its justification of English domination of non-Western peoples; it also, as Hobson hints, served to strengthen internal cohesion, thus helping subdue dissatisfaction within England. As the historian Eric Hobsbawm has written, imperialism "made good ideological cement" because it persuaded potentially rebellious internal groups, such as women and the working class, to ignore their own interests in order to identify with the imperial state.[7] The usefulness of the Orientalist/imperialist ideological nexus for reinforcing domestic unity suggests its close alliance with nationalism.

Imperialism worked in concert with Orientalism to define the Oriental as inferior—needing, deserving, even desiring domination—and with nationalism to consolidate the national identity of the English. When the demands of empire required English unity abroad, nationalism gained an ideological ally in the pursuit of conformity at home. Further, the Orientalist racial stereotypes commonly deployed in the service of imperialist policies worked in concert with gender stereotypes that underwrote definitions of the English "national character." By representing the English to themselves as vigorous, manly, direct, and so forth, the discourse of nationalism was couched in a vocabulary that explicitly excluded women.[8] Gender stereotypes, when deployed in the service of nationalist unity and imperialist domination, served at the same time to resist challenges to women's traditional place currently being posed by the New Woman and the suffrage movement. In fact, one of the frequent arguments made against woman's suffrage was the inadequacy of female nature to the demands of empire. In the words of Lord Curzon: "For the discharge of great responsibilities in the dependencies of the Empire in distant parts you want the qualities not of the feminine but of the masculine mind."[9]

Maud Allan's representation of an Oriental princess in *The Vision of Salome* (figure 1) invited discussions that invoked two discourses in particular, Orientalism and a separate-spheres gender ideology. Both discourses deployed the same strategies of rhetorical polarization and tendentious normativeness to contain and define two potential threats this dance posed to its audience—female sexuality and the racial Other. Allan's dance was potentially transgressive in that it violated the supposed polarity between East and West by presenting her, a Western woman, as an Oriental. In addition, Allan violated the terms under which the separate-spheres ideology assigned the "privileges" of (middle-class) femininity by appearing on a public stage in a daringly scanty costume. More often than not, however, the press did not consider Allan's dancing transgressive, and Allan for a time managed to achieve a precarious combination of notoriety and respectability.[10]

During the summer of 1908, when Maud Allan was still enjoying great popularity at the Palace, two other "barefoot" dancers appeared in London—Isadora Duncan and Ruth St. Denis. Although the trajectory of dance history has accorded these two dancers a fame and stature Allan has not shared, they never approached Allan's popular appeal in England. St. Denis, whose "Eastern" dances might have tapped the same audience attracted to Allan's *The Vision of Salome*, was perceived as overly ascetic and scholarly. J. E. Crawford Flitch, whose 1912 book, *Modern Dancing and Dancers*, discussed St. Denis in a chapter on "Oriental and Spanish Dancing" (he considered Allan a "classical" dancer), found her dancing literal and limited in its symbolism, too static and too concerned with ideas "to give itself up wholly to the expression of beauty."[11] Even though St. Denis, unlike Duncan, was willing to appear in a music hall program, she could not reach the English popular audience. During an engagement at the London Coliseum, according to her biographer, St. Denis "suffered indignities from vaudeville audiences impatient for technical tricks and virtuosity." At one performance the management actually had to lower the curtain in the middle of one of her dances, so strong was the

1. Maud Allan in *The Vision of Salome.*
Courtesy of the Dance Collection, the New York Public Library for the Performing Arts, Astor, Lenox, and Tilden Foundations.

audience dislike.[12] Finally, St. Denis, who was accustomed to being compared to Duncan on the Continent, was in London compared to Allan, a dancer St. Denis felt was inferior to Duncan and in some respects—for example, a frequently admired arm ripple—derivative of St. Denis herself.[13] Clearly, a dance history written from the point of view of the English public would not give the same status to St. Denis as she is commonly accorded in the United States.

While it is important to acknowledge that Allan performed in a context of dance practices and conventions that shaped her dancing and its reception, that dance-specific context is not my primary concern in this essay. I would argue that the unusual popularity of Allan's dance in London, when the performances of other solo female dancers such as St. Denis and Duncan (who might on the Continent be considered Allan's betters) received much less attention, suggests the appropriateness of an approach to Allan's dance that focuses more on the specificity of the English cultural context than on the dance as an art form.

Allan's own description of Salome (in her autobiography) treats the character as a naturally spiritual and innocent child. The story of Salome and John the Baptist she claims to depict in her dance is one of spiritual awakening. Salome is transformed in the dance from an obedient child accustomed to Oriental luxury into a woman anxious to submit to the superior power represented by the Baptist. Although the critics did not understand the details of the plot from watching Allan's dance, they did see its narrative structure and sometimes the emotional tenor Allan intended to convey. The dance began with Salome's descent down the palace stairs. She next performed a dance that was, according to Allan's description, supposed to represent Salome's recollection of her dance before Herod. Then the head of John the Baptist appeared in a cistern (this is the "vision"). Allan placed it center-stage and danced again, this time to express the "ecstasy mingled with dread" that signaled her impending spiritual awakening.[14] According to Max Beerbohm's description, in this section Allan "performs around [the head] a mild quasi-Oriental dance, overcomes her repugnance, hears someone coming, puts the head behind her, pops it back into the cistern, dances again, and finally repeats the swoon she did in 'Valse Caprice.'"[15] A more sympathetic review confirms the general structure of the dance as Beerbohm recorded it, while giving a reading of the emotional force of the movements somewhat closer to the one Allan provided in her autobiography:

> Salome dances as one fascinated, slowly advancing towards the head and swiftly receding from it, gradually drawing nearer and nearer, then falling upon hands and knees and gloating, half savagely, half amorously, over it,

> then pouncing upon it like a hawk upon its prey. Thereafter she dances fear, a quivering, shuddering dance, and finally collapses, a huddled—but still graceful, still beautiful—mass.[16]

No critic interpreted the dance as the story of Salome's spiritual awakening, although Flitch presents Allan's own description of the dance rather than his own, thereby endorsing her version of its meaning. A few commentators, particularly those who objected to the dance, asserted an explicit connection between Allan's version of the story and Oscar Wilde's 1893 play *Salomé.* The reception of Wilde's play was shaped by public perception of the writer's character—to be confirmed by his conviction for homosexuality in 1895. The association of Salome with sexual transgression and moral decadence was, in other words, quite strong, while there was no narrative tradition of her conversion or spiritual rebirth. Neither did Allan or the critics dwell on the political subtext of the Salome story. There is no explicit recognition that Salome's request for the Baptist's head was motivated by her mother's political ambitions.[17] Rather, the nature and proper direction of female (or in Wilde's case, male) sexuality seemed to overshadow any other questions Salome might have raised for the English. The representation of sexuality, however, is not irrelevant to politics in the narrower sense of the word. As the interweaving of "masculinity" with definitions of an English national character suggests, gender stereotypes played an integral role in shoring up imperialist and nationalist ideologies.

Stereotypes, although usually presented in terms of binary and mutually exclusive oppositions, are not, as Homi Bhabha has persuasively argued, that simple. Rather, stereotypes are always internally divided and embody, like the Freudian fetish, mastery and anxiety simultaneously. The stereotype of the Oriental woman enacted by Allan embodied anxieties about women and Orientals while also affirming the mastery of both by a Western and male-defined truth. In Bhabha's formulation, "colonial discourse produces the colonized as a fixed reality which is at once 'other' and yet entirely knowable and visible."[18] This contradictory assertion of simultaneous transparency and opacity was encapsulated in *The Vision of Salome.* First, as I shall demonstrate shortly, Allan made the East transparent to the West by representing its essence; but she was not an Eastern native, and therefore could not disrupt its Otherness. Second, she presented a threatening female sexuality in a way that confirmed its Otherness by identifying it only with Oriental women; however, being a Western woman, her performance also implied that Western women as well are impenetrable. The dark continents of Western femininity and Orientalism meet in Allan's depiction of Salome.

Allan's program at the Palace Theatre consisted of approximately twenty minutes of dancing, in which she performed a number of "classical" dances in Duncanesque Greek costume along with *The Vision of Salome.* The impact of this one Oriental number was both mitigated by being the only controversial piece in her program and perhaps exacerbated by the sharp contrast in which it stood to the other, more "Occidental" depictions of femininity. Certainly the presence of dances inspired by Botticelli rather than Wilde gave critics uncomfortable with the Salome dance something to praise.[19] Even the Salome dance, however, did not employ the kind of movement many critics associated with Eastern dancing. Max Beerbohm refers to Allan's movement in this piece as "quasi-Oriental," and the critic for the *Daily Chronicle* notes that her dance "was not, to be sure, very Oriental." At the same time, other observers did not hesitate to characterize Allan's Salome as a "hot-blooded, sensual Oriental."[20]

The quality of Allan's dancing, although not always identified as Oriental, was not recognized as typically Western either. Western dance was thought to focus on the feet—as in ballet and step-dancing—while Allan made striking use of her hands and arms. W. R. Titterton, in an article that compares Allan unfavorably with Isadora Duncan, observes nonetheless that "she makes fine use of those beautiful hands of hers—say when she stretches her arms wide, and makes the music ripple from her shoulders to her fingertips."[21] In general, then, no matter if she were performing *The Vision of Salome* or one of her classical numbers, Allan's movement style stood in sharp contrast to typical stage dancing at the time. The "Palace Girls," a team of dancers drilled to move in unison, illustrated this contrast dramatically for one critic:

> There is a certain satisfaction, a robust, breezy satisfaction, in watching the well-drilled 'Palace Girls' in their violent prancing and whirling and high-kicking. Downright gymnastics of this kind form, at any rate, a piquant contrast to the wonderful instrument of expression, the revelation of beauty, the mysterious power, that dance becomes with Miss Maud Allan, our Lady of Dreams.[22]

If there was not agreement on the exact geographical or historical origin of Allan's dance style, there was agreement that it was not typical of contemporary English dance. Allan's foreignness forms a common denominator in the English reception of her performances.

Allan's success may have had a great deal to do with the notoriety of her Salome dance, but she also managed to acquire a reputation for aesthetic seriousness and feminine respectability. How critics interpreted Allan's rendition of the "East" would have a great deal to do with her ability to establish such a reputation. Several critics did her a great service in this regard by distancing her dancing from the supposedly provocative dances of the East. The review in the *Times Literary Supplement* asserted that "authentic" Eastern dance would have been offensive to respectable British sensibilities. Particularly in the case of belly-dancing, it explained, Eastern dancing was "something lascivious and repulsively ugly."[23] If Allan had been "authentic" she would have been dismissed as vulgar. At the same time, however, the suggestion of Oriental sensuality and lurid sexuality implied by her subject matter attracted a sufficiently large audience to assure Allan (while her popularity lasted) both wealth and celebrity. To achieve these, while retaining her social status, Allan had both to enact the East and to distance herself from that enactment.

The publicity strategy of the manager of the Palace Theatre, Alfred Butt, suggests the power of the East as a sexual lure. The pamphlet he circulated just prior to Allan's debut uses Orientalist stereotypes of aggressive and dangerous—but inviting and available—female sexuality to attract its readers to the Palace. Here is the description of Allan as Salome:

> The desire that flames from her eyes and bursts in hot gusts from her scarlet mouth infect[s] the very air with the madness of passion. Swaying like a white witch, with yearning arms and hands that plead, Maud Allan is such a delicious embodiment of lust that she might win forgiveness for the sins of such wonderful flesh. As Herod catches fire, so Salome dances even as a Bacchante, twisting her body like a silver snake eager for its prey, panting with hot passion, the fire of her eyes scorching like a living furnace.[24]

Obviously, if this passage had accurately described what Allan was doing onstage, she could not have credibly staked any claim to social respectability.

The existence of the pamphlet, however, encouraged critics to distinguish what they saw on stage from what they were led to expect, giving Allan the best of both worlds: a large audience attracted by the prospect of sexual titillation and an assurance of propriety from the critics. Thus, for example, the critic who warned his readers of the "lascivious and repulsively ugly" quality of Eastern dance goes on to distinguish Allan's performance from its presumed original:

> Now it is obvious that this dancer could make no movement or posture that is not beautiful, and, in fact, her dancing as Salome, though Eastern in spirit through and through, is absolutely without the slightest suggestion of the vulgarities familiar to the tourists in Cairo or Tangier.[25]

While "authentic" Eastern dancing calls attention to the sexualized body of the dancer, making it "ugly," Allan's version is "Eastern" but "beautiful." It both alludes to the sexual and evades it. Allan's Salome dance expresses the *spirit* of the East, thereby erasing its supposed sensuous physicality and avoiding, as another critic put it, regressing into the "mere provocative posturing of the body" from which the dance Allan performed was presumed to have evolved. This critic asserts that "the *essence* of this art . . . is Eastern, although Miss Allan has never been to the East."[26] Likewise, Raymond Blathwayt assures his readers that Allan's Salome "was an epitome in itself of Orientalism and yet with scarcely a suggestion of the sensuous, let alone the sensual."[27]

For these critics, *The Vision of Salome* translated the "East" into a spirit or essence. Allan's performance could thereby be abstracted from the explicit expression of sexuality assumed to characterize Eastern dance as practiced in Cairo or Tangier, while at the same time the authority of her rendition can be maintained because of its accurate portrayal of some essential "truth" about the East. This process serves two interrelated functions. First, it reaffirms the West's superiority, since it takes a Western woman to understand and represent the essence of the East. The Orient, as Said notes, cannot represent itself. Secondly, it reaffirms the spiritual nature of (middle-class) womanhood, as posited by the still dominant separate-spheres ideology. Gender and Orientalist ideologies work hand-in-hand to contain Western women within the realm of the spiritual, to affirm the West's superior knowledge of and thus rightful domination of the East, and, finally, to help constitute a Western (male) subject in opposition to both the Oriental and the Western woman.

Ashis Nandy, in his study of the psychology of colonialism, argues that gender ideology cannot be extricated from that collection of beliefs and assumptions that justified England's imperial ambitions. Colonial ideology, in his analysis, depended upon the deployment of categories of discrimination already institutionalized in English culture, one of which was gender. The combination of Western gender stereotypes and colonialism, according to Nandy, "produced a cultural consensus in which political and socio-economic dominance symbolized the dominance of men and masculinity over women and femininity."[28] Mary Poovey has made a related argument. In tracing the contribution of the image of woman provided by the separate-spheres ideology to a definition of the English national character, Poovey makes the case that gender and imperialist ideologies stood in a relation of "mutual rhetorical construction." Thus, for example, just as the mid-nineteenth-century champion of female nurses, Florence Nightingale, used a rhetoric "borrowed from the imperial campaigns England waged throughout the second half of the century, so those nationalistic campaigns appropriated the terms of the domestic ideology that underwrote the separation of spheres, male identity, and female nature."[29] The distinction Poovey makes between "male *identity*" and "female *nature*" is important for understanding how Allan's reception participated in a similar conjunction of gendered and nationalistic rhetoric. The rhetoric of national character was overwhelmingly one of masculinity, while the character of the English*woman* was defined by the perfection of those domestic and maternal qualities felt to be universally present in female nature.[30] While gender ideology and nationalism could mutually construct one another in that Englishness was gendered masculine and non-Englishness feminine, there was, on another level, a fundamental discontinuity between nationalism and gender as ideological constructs.

Although male identity could be specifically national, the rhetorical construction of female nature arguably had more in common with racism. According to Benedict Anderson, a racist ideology, unlike nationalism, "erases nation-ness by reducing the adversary to his [*sic*] biological physiognomy."[31] Nationalism, in other words, has a historical specificity denied the object of racism: "nationalism thinks in terms of historical destinies, while racism dreams of eternal contamination."[32] While men have an *identity*, a historically specific set of characteristics, women have a *nature*—an eternal "contamination." Positive reviews of Maud Allan do not usually make national character an issue, since Allan has in these reviews generally been found adequate to a transnational conception of appropriate femininity. Conversely, the more negative the review, the more likely we are to find some allusion to Allan's or the audience's presumed national character. In these cases, Allan's failings can be in part attributed to her misunderstanding of the English character, or her contamination by a lesser national character, usually American. Before examining such reviews in more detail, however, it is important to acknowledge that dance itself could be characterized as un-English—both as the product of an alien culture and as a manifestation of femininity.

Flitch introduces his chapter "Oriental and Spanish Dancing" with a discussion of the relation between gesture and national character. He observes that different peoples have not only different languages, but different kinds of gestures. The "characteristic gesture" of a "people" in turn forms the basis of its national dance. The foundation of dance in the national character of a people as expressed through their use of gesture explains for Flitch the origin of ballet in Italy, the recent developments in ballet by the Russians, and, of course, the difference between Eastern and Western dance forms. However, Flitch observes, "as a people becomes more intellectual, and learns to express all the nuances of thought by means of language alone, it relies less upon the elucidation of gesture."[33] Gesture (dance) represents a more primitive form of communication which the "Anglo-Saxons" have predictably left behind. Nevertheless, Flitch does find an English national dance—the Morris.

At the time Flitch was writing *Modern Dancing and Dancers*, a revival of morris dancing was under way, led by Cecil Sharp and explicitly linked to the inculcation of nationalist sentiment, particularly in schoolchildren.[34] In a chapter entirely devoted to this dance form, Flitch lets Sharp speak for the character and significance of the morris dance. Sharp's description is a catalogue of the traits of the perfect Englishman:

> It is, in spirit, the organized, traditional expression of virility, sound health and animal spirits. It smacks of cudgel-play, of quarterstaff, of wrestling, of honest fisticuffs. There is nothing sinuous in it, nothing dreamy; nothing whatever is left to the imagination. . . . It is the dance of folk who are slow to anger, but of great obstinacy—forthright of act and speech: to watch it in its thumping sturdiness is to hold such things as poniards and stilettos, the swordsman with the domino, the man who stabs in the back—as unimaginable things. The Morris Dance, in short, is a perfect expression in rhythm and movement of the English character.[35]

In short, insofar as a dance can be English, it must be strictly "masculine." No female dancer can do more than impersonate Englishness.[36] Nationalism, then, was not directly relevant to Allan's dances; rather it functioned either to form the basis of a critique or to provide a measure for the transcendence of historical specificity achieved by womanhood in the service of art.

As opposed to discussions that place Allan's representation of the East in relation to behavior thought appropriate to Western womanhood, those reviews that make nationality an issue frequently do so to criticize either dancer or audience. Christopher St. John, for example, attributed Allan's success to an astute and hyperbolic advertising campaign which she associated with things American. The press, by assuring the public that Maud Allan was, "in the beautiful American phrase, 'the greatest thing that ever happened'" enticed the credulous English masses to the Palace Theatre. Allan herself was equally infected by "Americanness." According to St. John, Allan's strength of character may be admirable: "But it is . . . stupid to mistake this character, this American 'grit' and 'bluff' for beautiful art."[37] In the *Morning Advertiser*, however, Allan's nationality denotes what she has managed to transcend in her dances: "Coming from America, the young lady might have been expected to give an exposition of high-kicking, whirlwind, and cake-walk dances. But hers is the very antithesis of this sort of terpsichorean revelry. She is perfectly artistic and sylph-like in all her movements."[38] The *Daily Telegraph*'s critic cites an implied ideal of English character in condemning "The Vision of Salome." He observes of her costume for the dance that "even the least squeamish in such matters will probably admit that such an exhibition is indifferently suited either to English tastes or to our English climate."[39] Finally, W. R. Titterton uses Allan's success to name and condemn the hypocrisy in sexual matters that he considered to be the "beastliest side of the English national character."[40]

To a large extent, however, nationality, either Allan's or her audience's, was much less of an issue than the relation of her performance to ideals of femininity and to Oriental art and society. The rhetoric of national character generally works to situate Allan's performance in relation to aesthetic ideals or appropriate gender behavior—neither of which are specifically national. Significantly, she was not perceived to be performing a specifically national dance. Her Salome was not Egyptian, Algerian, or Syrian, but "Eastern" in a vague, homogenizing sense of the word. While Westerners might have national identities—American or English, for example—the East, like Woman, is characterized by eternal qualities shared by all its inhabitants. This similarity between Orientalism and Femininity as ideological constructs placed a Western woman performing the East in a complex position. In order to retain the privileges of her ethnicity, she cannot be too closely identified with the Orientalized subject peoples of the British Empire. At the same time, the Oriental has already been defined as "feminine" in relation to the "masculine" colonial power. Allan cannot, in this symbolic system, inhabit the privileged ground of the "masculine" West, but she can avoid the "bad" femininity of the Oriental woman. She (or her reviewers) can manipulate the distinction between a "good" and a "bad" femininity in order to position her performances on the positive side of a symbolic system that denies women full subjecthood in any case.

Many critics performed this function for Allan by asserting the beauty and propriety of her dance, despite her admittedly scanty costume. Even those who disliked her performance frequently helped solidify her respectability. Max Beerbohm, for example, wrote of the Salome dance, "I cannot imagine a more lady-like performance," and St. John's scathing condemnation concludes by calling Allan a "very earnest young lady with a sincere conviction of her mission" who "dances like a revivalist preacher."[41] Although the Manchester Watch Committee refused to let her perform in their town, they were one of a minority who found her performance offensive. Moreover, Allan herself attempted to influence the public construction of her persona in the autobiography she wrote in 1908 to commemorate her 250th performance at the Palace Theatre. In this book Allan explicitly used the rhetoric of "good" femininity to define herself and her dances within the terms of the separate-spheres ideology.

Allan's next to last chapter, "A Word about Women," is devoted to explaining and justifying her opposition to women's suffrage. As an unmarried, childless, and self-supporting woman, Allan violated the dominant ideal of woman as mother and homemaker. However, unlike Isadora Duncan, who critiqued the gender ideology she transgressed, Allan attempted to underplay her transgressions and to locate herself inside that ideology. In opposing women's suffrage, she argued that women are overly emotional, indifferent to principles, easily swayed by personalities, and therefore unsuited to political life and action. This statement of faith in antisuffrage assumptions about women's nature and proper sphere can be read as an indication of what Allan felt she had to lose by allowing herself to be associated with feminism. Her livelihood was dependent on the good will of powerful men—King Edward VII had recommended her to the Palace manager—and on women of the upper class. She was known, for example, to be friendly with the Asquiths, whose patronage added considerably to her wealth and whose sympathies were not with the suffragists.

Despite her rejection of the suffrage movement, Allan's attitude toward women's rights was ambivalent. She believed in equal education and job opportunities for women who did not have men to support them.[42] She also, however, placed great emphasis on the spiritual tasks of moral guidance assigned women within the separate-spheres ideology. Participation in the public realm of politics seemed to her not only inappropriate to the female character but threatening to those activities which it was women's particular talent and duty to pursue: "Woman should be the refining, the inspiring, the idealising element of humanity. In becoming a good politician she would cease to be that."[43] This rhetoric of female spirituality and moral superiority was commonly deployed by the suffragists to authorize their right to participate in politics.[44] As the most positive quality granted women, spirituality (along with maternal instinct) constituted important symbolic capital in any argument for altering the norms of acceptable behavior for "respectable" women. Maud Allan deployed this symbolic capital differently than the suffragists.

Allan displayed her body on the public stage at a time when actors and actresses had only recently become socially acceptable and the association between actresses and prostitutes was still common, despite the influx of middle-class women into the theater in the 1890s. Lisa Tickner's examination of the 1907 mass demonstration (known as the Mud March) organized by the suffrage movement notes the importance of attitudes about female public display in the press response to the march. The distaste that middle-class women were assumed to have for exposing themselves to the public gaze persuaded at least some writers of the deep sincerity of any such woman who was willing to do so for a cause.[45] If, as one paper put it, "it requires some courage for a woman to step out of her drawing room into the street to take her place in a mixed throng,"[46] how much more spiritual resolution must it take to display oneself daily in a music hall? In such a context, Allan's performances could be read either as the product of a powerful aesthetic and moral conviction, or as the consequence of moral laxness in the service of ambition. The *Daily Chronicle*'s report of an interview with the dancer after her first appearance in London indicates which interpretation Allan worked hard to place on her behavior:

> It was, however, while travelling with her parents in Italy, and gazing at the paintings of Titian and Veronese, that she first made up her mind that there was nothing necessarily ugly or shameful in naked feet. It needed enormous courage, she confesses, to make her first appearance . . . as a barefoot dancer.[47]

The writer of this article assures the reader that Allan is in fact "the most modest and ladylike little person imaginable." But, while establishing her modesty was important, it would not explain her continuing apparent willingness to overcome the dictates of that modesty.

To justify her behavior in a way that would not offend the sensibilities of the critics, and presumably the audiences whom they served, Allan needed a stronger motivation than the precedent set by Titian and Veronese. This was to be her conviction that dance was the "spontaneous expression of the spiritual state."[48] This belief in the spiritual value of dance enabled Allan to situate the public display of the female body within the terms of the separate-spheres ideology. Reviews that commented on the "abstraction" of Allan's dancing, or its childlike spontaneity, or its perfect translation of music or emotion into movement, such as those in the *Daily Mail*, the *Daily Chronicle*, and the *Times*, reinforced the relationship between the selfless asexuality of a valorized femininity and Allan's mode of public performance. In simply avoiding being characterized as engaged primarily in a form of physical display, Allan largely achieved the social and aesthetic legitimacy she desired.

Beyond her acclaim in the press, however, her genuine popularity must be considered. One of the most important reasons for Allan's popularity—as opposed to simply being taken seriously by the press as an artist—was, I would argue, the internal contradictions her Salome dance enacted, and perhaps symbolically resolved, for her audience. On the most basic level, these were, first, the contradiction between an unknowable Otherness and an apparent mastery of the Other (embodied in the Western performance of the Oriental) and, second, the contradiction between a stereotype of Western femininity as devoid of sexual knowledge and sexual threat and a Western woman's successful depiction of a character commonly held to embody both.

The stereotypes of the Oriental and Western femininity are both complementary and contradictory in their relationship to each other. Structurally, both constructs are internally divided in the manner suggested by Bhabha's analysis of the stereotype; but further, this structural similarity allowed the combination of the two in Allan's Salome dance to magnify both the anxiety and the sense of mastery each stereotype conveyed. Thus, for example, Allan's performance enacted the possibility of an assertive female sexuality while denying its threat to her audience by displacing it onto an Oriental woman. She was, nevertheless, a Western woman embodying that sexuality. (No depiction of Salome could realistically be considered asexual in early-twentieth-century England.) While simultaneously denying and embodying female sexuality, Allan was also simultaneously denying and embodying the threat of the racial Other. On the one hand, her dance conveyed the "truth" about this Other by distilling its presumed essence or spirit, while on the other hand, the unknowability of the East remained inviolate, since Allan remained a Westerner. Maud Allan as Salome both calms and embodies anxieties about female power and sexuality being raised by the suffrage movement and the incursion of middle-class women into the work force.[49] She both calms and embodies anxieties about English knowledge and imperial domination of the East.

Although the interaction of Orientalism with gender ideology is most direct when femininity rather than masculinity is at issue, masculinity is not irrelevant to the aggregate of mutually reinforcing discourses under discussion. Nationalism and imperialism contributed to the definition of an English identity that was irredeemably masculine. Standing in a relation of opposition rather than ambivalent and reinforcing similarity to Orientalism, English masculinity secured the ground from which both Western women and the East could be mastered. Both imperialism and nationalism employed a rhetoric of homogeneous masculinity as definitive of Englishness. The alliance of Otherness into which femininity and Orientalism were thrown by their mutual opposition to this masculinity lies at the heart of *The Vision of Salome*. This alliance was not a stable one, however, as the disagreements over whether Allan's dance was "Oriental," over whether her costume was offensive or appropriate, and over whether her portrayal of Salome was "lady-like" or sensual, suggest. Allan's performance could migrate in significance from implying the similarities between Western womanhood and the Oriental to asserting their absolute difference.

Because the ways in which Allan's various observers deployed and positioned the discourses of imperialism, nationalism, Orientalism, and gender varied significantly, the picture emerging from this study is not one of stable relationships among clearly bounded ideologies, but of dominant trends and recurring emphases in the context of multiple possibilities. This is not to suggest that there is no limit to the possible relationships in which these discourses could stand to one another. In the particular historical context I have addressed, the variability in their interaction occurred within quite rigid parameters—for example, the Oriental is never "masculine" in the sense that the Englishman is. Indeed the relationship between Orientalism and gender ideology in general was probably the most culturally charged of all the discursive interactions provoked by Allan's dance. In particular, the language used to describe and evaluate *The Vision of Salome* indicates a mutually productive and reinforcing interaction between the rhetoric of Western femininity and Orientalism. Maud Allan was able to benefit from the contradictions inherent in this relationship by appealing to apparently mutually exclusive elements of each. Consistency does not necessarily characterize either the important ways in which these discourses interacted, nor even the internal struggle of any single discourse.

This is where Homi Bhabha's insight into the deep ambivalence characteristic of colonial discourse not only serves as an important corrective to Said's work but also contributes to our understanding of how other ideologies function in discourse.[50] Because the basis for the hegemony of an ideology is the successful assertion of a particular "truth" about the world, a truth which can be contested from other ideological positions, an anxiety necessarily coexists with the mastery claimed by the hegemonic discourse. Allan's dance evoked precisely the kind of internal contradiction in Orientalist and gender ideologies that Bhabha names in his concept of ambivalence and in his analysis of the stereotype.

Finally, the complexity of the context in which Maud Allan found her audience injects another kind of ambivalence into this analysis—an ambivalence about the political significance of her performance. One function the public discussion of *The Vision of Salome* served was to soothe anxieties about women and racial difference, thereby shoring up the myth of masculine mastery that underwrote English nationalism and imperialism. It would be a mistake, however, to assert that this was the only, or even the most enduring, consequence of Allan's success. The combination of unresolvable contradictions within discourses and the instability introduced by the interaction of multiple discourses opened up the ways in which Allan's dance could be interpreted and deployed by its audiences. Thus, for example, the aesthetic and social legitimacy granted Maud Allan increased the possibility that dance would become an acceptable career for middle-class women, thereby further breaking down the taboo against female public display that helped keep the separate-spheres ideology in place. Although such relatively progressive consequences coexisted with conservative and regressive ones, they serve to remind us that determining the political significance of cultural products is not a simple or a straightforward task.

Notes

A much shorter version of this essay was originally presented at the 1992 Society of Dance History Scholars Conference at UC–Riverside. My thanks to Lynn Garafola, Loren Kruger, and Susan Manning, whose comments on that paper were instrumental in shaping my final approach to the subject.

1 Edward Said, *Orientalism* (New York: Vintage, 1979), p. 3.

2 Ibid., p. 39.

3 See Homi Bhabha, "The Other Question—The Stereotype and Colonial Discourse," *Screen* 24, no. 6 (1983), especially part 2. For a generally positive discussion of *Orientalism* from an anthropologist's perspective, see James Clifford's review essay "On *Orientalism*" in *The Predicament of Culture: Twentieth-Century Ethnography, Literature, and Art* (Cambridge, Mass.: Harvard University Press, 1988), 255–76. Clifford does, however, take Said to task for an overly static and dichotomous understanding of cultural difference. Said responds to some of his critics in "Representing the Colonized: Anthropology's Interlocutors," *Critical Inquiry* 15 (Winter 1989), pp. 205–25.

4 Said, "Representing the Colonized," pp. 210–11.

5 J. A. Hobson, *Imperialism: A Study*, rev. ed. (London: George Allen and Unwin, 1938), p. 9.

6 Jonathan Rose, *The Edwardian Temperament, 1895–1919* (Athens: Ohio University Press, 1986), p. 129.

7 Eric Hobsbawm, *The Age of Empire: 1875–1914* (New York: Vintage, 1987), p. 70.

8 Philip Dodd, "Englishness and the National Culture," in *Englishness: Politics and Culture, 1880–1920*, ed. Robert Colls and Philip Dodd (London: Croom Helm, 1986), pp. 5–6.

9 Quoted in Brian Harrison, *Separate Spheres: The Opposition to Women's Suffrage in Britain* (New York: Holmes and Meier, 1978), p. 75. Suffragists tried to counteract this argument by asserting the special contribution that women could make to the empire. See Antoinette Burton, "The Feminist Quest for Identity: British Imperial Suffragism and 'Global Sisterhood,' 1900–1915," *Journal of Women's History* 3, no. 2 (Fall 1991), pp. 46–81. Her analysis of the relation between British suffragism and imperialism concludes that the feminist "appeal to empire was a means of achieving inclusion, and identification with Britain's imperial mission might, it was hoped, persuade opponents of the need for statutory equality" (p. 69). This attempt to usurp a male-identified rhetorical ground for women did not finally relinquish the separate-spheres argument that women would have a refining and purifying influence on the exercise of imperial power (p. 59).

10 Maud Allan was thirty-five when she began dancing in London, and her success lasted approximately two years. After she suffered an injury in 1909 and was forced to stop performing for a while, the public lost interest. In 1910 she embarked on a tour of the United States, but her imitators had preceded her, making her own performance seem secondhand. The rest of her life was a slow decline from the height of her fame in 1908. For biographical information on Allan, see Felix Cherniavsky's series of articles in *Dance Chronicle*; the two most relevant here are "Maud Allan, Part II: First Steps to a Dancing Career, 1904–1907," *Dance Chronicle* 6 (1983), pp. 189–227, and "Maud Allan, Part III: Two Years of Triumph, 1908–1909," *Dance Chronicle* 7 (1984), pp. 119–58. He has recently published

this work in book form: *The Salome Dancer* (Toronto: McClelland and Stewart, 1991). On the appearance of Salome dancers in the United States, see Elizabeth Kendall, *Where She Danced* (New York: Knopf, 1979), chap. 4.

11 J. E. Crawford Flitch, *Modern Dancing and Dancers* (Philadelphia: J. B. Lippincott, 1912), p. 194.

12 Suzanne Shelton, *Divine Dancer: A Biography of Ruth St. Denis* (Garden City, N.Y.: Doubleday, 1981), p. 86. In contrast to her reception in England, St. Denis was to achieve wide popularity in the United States. See also Jane Desmond, "Dancing Out the Difference: Cultural Imperialism and Ruth St. Denis's 'Radha' of 1906," *Signs* 17 (Autumn 1991), pp. 28–49. Desmond discusses the interplay of Orientalist fantasy with gender and race ideologies in St. Denis's dance *Radha*. Her emphasis on women and the Orient as mute visual spectacles within a Western patriarchal symbolic system makes dance a particularly charged site for representing the simultaneous presence of "seemingly incommensurable attributes—goddess/whore, Eastern/Western, and sexual /chaste" (p. 42). The ability of the dancing body to apparently hold these contradictory states in suspension deserves further examination.

13 Shelton, *Divine Dancer*, p. 83.

14 Maud Allan, *My Life and Dancing* (London: Everett, 1908), p. 126.

15 Max Beerbohm, "At the Palace Theatre," *Saturday Review*, 4 July 1908, p. 11.

16 "The Drama: The New Dancer," *Times Literary Supplement*, 25 March 1908, p. 102.

17 My guess would be that this exclusion not only indicates an anxiety over sexuality that overwhelmed other concerns, but a symbolic repression of the potential for effective political action by women. I am indebted to Sue-Ellen Case for bringing this issue to my attention.

18 Bhabha, "The Other Question," p. 23.

19 Although Allan never cites Wilde as the inspiration for her dance while in England, Cherniavsky quotes an interview published in a Budapest paper in which she proclaims Wilde's Salome as her ideal ("Maud Allan, Part II," p. 212). Botticelli's "Primavera" was, according to her autobiography, one of the formative influences on Allan's dancing (*My Life and Dancing*, p. 62). Allan shared with Duncan a tendency to appeal to a valorized tradition of female nudity in the visual arts to authorize her performances.

20 Beerbohm, "At the Palace Theatre"; "Barefoot Dancer," *Daily Chronicle*, 7 March 1908; "A New Dancer," *Daily Mail*, 7 March 1908.

21 W. R. Titterton, "The Maud Allan Myth," *New Age*, 27 July 1908, pp. 171–72.

22 "The Drama: The New Dancer," p. 102.

23 Ibid.

24 Quoted in " 'Maud Allan,' at the Palace," *Truth*, 18 March 1908, pp. 701–2. Deborah Jowitt, *Time and the Dancing Image* (New York: William Morrow, 1988), accepts the accuracy of this description, but most of the reviews I was able to examine would not support that position. Several reviews, such as the one in *Truth*, explicitly took issue with the description offered in the pamphlet.

25 "The Drama: The New Dancer," p. 102.

26 "Miss Maud Allan's Salome Dance," *The Academy*, 21 March 1908, pp. 598–99; emphasis added. This review is the only one that explicitly addresses the issue of empire in its discussion of Allan's dance. The article begins by castigating English audiences for their "instinctive" horror of the East: "We have the largest Eastern Empire the world has ever seen, and yet we not only neglect to study Eastern thought and custom, we even shrink

with horror, which is instinctive, but which we like to believe virtuous, from anything Eastern." Allan is to be praised, the author continues, for educating the parochial English public. The irrelevance of the actual peoples subjected to English colonial rule to an Orient constructed by and for the West could not be made plainer.

27 Raymond Blathwayt, review of Maud Allan in *Black and White*, 18 July 1908, p. 76. This article was found in the clipping file on Maud Allan of the New York Public Library Dance Collection.

28 Ashis Nandy, *The Intimate Enemy: Loss and Recovery of Self Under Colonialism* (Delhi: Oxford University Press, 1983), p. 4.

29 Mary Poovey, *Uneven Developments: The Ideological Work of Gender in Mid-Victorian England* (Chicago: University of Chicago Press, 1988), p. 195.

30 Jane MacKay and Pat Thane, "The Englishwoman," in *Englishness: Politics and Culture, 1880–1920,* ed. Robert Colls and Philip Dodd (London: Croom Helm, 1986), p. 191.

31 Benedict Anderson, *Imagined Communities: Reflections on the Origin and Spread of Nationalism*, rev. ed. (London: Verso, 1991), p. 148.

32 Ibid., p. 149.

33 Flitch, *Modern Dancing and Dancers*, pp. 189–90.

34 See Anne Bloomfield, "Drill and Dance as Symbols of Imperialism," in *Making Imperial Mentalities: Socialization and British Imperialism*, ed. J. A. Mangan (Manchester, U.K.: Manchester University Press, 1990), pp. 74–95. She discusses the incorporation of folk dancing into the elementary school curriculum in 1909 and the role Cecil Sharp played in the folk-dance revival, in the process establishing the nationalistic basis of his motivation (pp. 82–87).

35 Flitch, *Modern Dancing and Dancers*, p. 207.

36 See Penny Summerfield, "Patriotism and Empire: Music-Hall Entertainment, 1870–1914," in *Imperialism and Popular Culture*, ed. John Mackenzie (Manchester U.K.: Manchester University Press, 1986), pp. 17–48. She examines the invisibility of women in patriotic music hall songs of the late Victorian and Edwardian era. Women seldom performed these songs, and when they did, it was frequently as male impersonators. This, she argues, was due to the close association between imperialism and militarism. The need to present oneself as a man in order to legitimize the performance of patriotic songs "serves to underline the masculine identity of . . . popular imperialism" (p. 38).

37 Christopher St. John, "All We Like Sheep," *The Academy*, 2 May 1908, pp. 735–36.

38 "The Palace Theatre," *Morning Advertiser*, 7 March 1908, p. 2.

39 "Palace Theatre," *Daily Telegraph*, 7 March 1908, p. 13.

40 Titterton, "The Maud Allan Myth," p. 171.

41 Beerbohm, "At the Palace Theatre," p. 11; St. John, "All We Like Sheep," p. 736.

42 Allan, *My Life and Dancing*, pp. 112–15.

43 Ibid., p. 118.

44 See Martha Vicinus, "Male Space and Women's Bodies: The English Suffragette Movement," in *Women in Culture and Politics: A Century of Change*, ed. Judith Friedlander et al. (Bloomington: Indiana University Press, 1986), pp. 209–22.

45 Lisa Tickner, *The Spectacle of Women: Imagery of the Suffrage Campaign, 1907–1914* (Chicago: University of Chicago Press, 1988), pp. 95–98.

46 Quoted in ibid., p. 75.

47 "Barefoot Dancer."

48 "Miss Maud Allan on Dancing," *Times*, 22 February 1909, p. 10.

49 On status anxieties caused by the growth of a female work force and the relation of these anxieties to lower-middle-class jingoism in the late nineteenth century, see Richard N. Price, "Society, Status, and Jingoism: The Social Roots of Lower Middle Class Patriotism, 1870–1900," in *The Lower Middle Class in Britain, 1870–1914*, ed. Geoffrey Crossick (London: Croom Helm, 1977), pp. 89–112. Allan attracted a large number of women to her performances, particularly the matinees. One article, "Miss Maud Allan: Palace Crowded with Ladies to See New Dances," *Daily Chronicle*, 13 June 1908, estimated that 90 percent of one matinee audience was female, commenting that "it might have been a suffragist meeting." The Salome dance was not presented on this program, and it is impossible to determine the significance of that absence for the composition of the audience. Nevertheless, if large numbers of women regularly attended Allan's performances, it may have been because they found her dancing liberatory (making the analogy to the suffrage movement more telling than the author no doubt intended). Without concrete information on the response of these women to Allan, one can only speculate that she perhaps modeled for them a use and presentation of the female body that they found attractive and that was not readily available elsewhere in their culture.

50 Important discussions of ambivalence as a characteristic of colonial discourse occur in Homi Bhabha, "Signs Taken for Wonders: Questions of Ambivalence and Authority under a Tree Outside Delhi, May 1817," *Critical Inquiry* 12 (Autumn 1985), pp. 144–65, and "Of Mimicry and Man: The Ambivalence of Colonial Discourse," *October* 28 (Spring 1984), pp. 125–33.

8 THE FEMALE DANCER AND THE MALE GAZE: FEMINIST CRITIQUES OF EARLY MODERN DANCE

Susan Manning

In academic circles it has become a truism that feminisms (plural) have replaced feminism (singular). However, this is not necessarily the case in dance studies, a discipline that has yet to develop and apply the diversity of feminist methods and theories currently found in other fields of the humanities.[1] To survey the recent literature on feminism and Western theater dance is to recognize the extent to which dance scholars have relied on gaze theory as a starting point for their analyses. Not that other approaches—particularly those adapted from anthropology and sociology—have been absent.[2] But to the extent that dance scholars have moved beyond discrete applications and evolved a dialogue on feminist methods, that dialogue centers upon gaze theory.

By "gaze theory" I mean a set of concepts that originated in film studies,[3] migrated to theater studies,[4] and now have found their way to dance studies. From my perspective, these concepts include not only the proposition that women on film and on stage typically are represented from the perspective of the male spectator (the notion of the "male gaze" or, alternately, the voyeuristic gaze) but also the counter-proposition that female spectators possess the potential to look in a way different from their male peers. How and when female spectators are enabled to look differently and thus to realize a subjectivity of their own remains a much disputed issue. In this essay I use the term gaze theory to refer to a broad range of literature that applies the concepts of the voyeuristic gaze and female spectatorship in diverse ways. For my purposes, the divisions within this literature—for example, between formulations that elaborate gaze theory in psychoanalytic terms and those that recast the theory in other disciplinary contexts—are less important than the ways that gaze theory, broadly defined, has entered dance studies.

Surveying the literature, one notes first that feminist critics who have applied gaze theory to ballet have reached strikingly similar conclusions. With varying emphases, one scholar after another has demonstrated how candidly the form of ballet positions the spectator as voyeur.[5] In contrast, feminist commentators who have examined modern dance have disagreed over whether and how the form engages the voyeuristic gaze. Their disagreement is particularly vehement when it comes to early modern dance, a practice innovated by female performer-choreographers in the first decades of the twentieth century. Assuming that the more contentious the conversation the more interesting, I have chosen to track the dialogue among feminist scholars of early modern dance. Yet my choice is not disinterested, for at the end of this survey of the literature I enter the conversation and propose an alternate position that may resolve the seemingly contradictory positions staked out in the debate among feminist dance scholars.

The disagreement over early modern dance centers upon two issues. The first is the degree to which successive generations of modern dancers have realized the potential of their practice to undermine the voyeuristic gaze. While some commentators credit early modern dancers with subverting the eroticization of the female dancer,[6] others reassign this achievement to later generations, in particular to postmodern dancers.[7] The second point of contention among feminist critics is the degree to which the works of early modern dancers reflect dominant conceptions of race and nationality during the early decades of the twentieth century. This second issue has as its corollary the question of how essentialized notions of national and racial identity interact with conceptions of gender in the works of early modern dancers.[8]

As this review of the literature will make clear, the debate among feminist critics centers upon the question of whether early modern dancers resist or reinforce dominant conceptions of gender. On the one hand, commentators note how deliberately early modern dancers dramatized female subjectivity and authority and, in so doing, introduced the possibility of female spectatorship. On the other hand, commentators note how clearly, though perhaps unwittingly, early modern dancers dramatized essentialized notions of gender, race, and nationality that seemingly worked against their staging of female subjectivity.

It is my intention to propose an alternate position, an analysis of early modern dance that gives equal weight to the resistive and recuperative dimensions of the practice. Indeed, I would like to propose that it was precisely the double move of subverting the voyeuristic gaze while projecting essentialized notions of identity that defined the practice of early modern dance. It was this double move—along with the rejection of balletic conventions, the fashioning of idiosyncratic movement styles, and the adherence to the modernist program of highlighting the essence and independence of the medium—that made a shared tradition of the individual styles of Loie Fuller, Isadora Duncan, Maud Allan, Ruth St. Denis, Mary Wigman, and the early Martha Graham.

In "Founding Mothers: Duncan, Graham, Rainer, and Sexual Politics," Roger Copeland celebrates modern and postmodern dance as the one art form where "women have been not only prominent, but also dominant."[9] Drawing on the distinction Luce Irigaray makes between the visual and the tactile, Copeland associates nineteenth-century ballet with the male choreographer's (and, by implication, the male spectator's) privileged looking at the ballerina. In contrast, early modern dancers, notably Isadora Duncan, "placed a much higher premium on kinetic empathy than on visual experience."[10] Thus Duncan reversed the hierarchical ordering of visuality over tactility characteristic of Western (and masculinist) thought. In so doing, Duncan danced out her own—and her generation's—rebellion against the Puritanism of the Victorian era. This rebellion culminated in the theater of Martha Graham, whose works dramatized the conflict between Puritanism and sexual expression.

The postmodernists in turn reacted against the physicality and overt sensuality of Duncan and Graham. Copeland explains this reaction in terms of the feminism of the sixties and seventies, which "eyed the sexual revolution with considerable suspicion, fearful that it hadn't really liberated women, but had simply made them more available."[11] Yvonne Rainer's 1973 film *"This Is the Story of a Woman Who . . ."* investigated the dynamics of the gaze, drawing an analogy between the spectator's relationship to the performer and the man's relationship to the woman, two years *before* Laura Mulvey published her seminal essay "Visual Pleasure and Narrative Cinema."[12] In pointing out the convergence between Rainer's and Mulvey's concerns, Copeland acknowledges the divergence between Rainer's and Irigaray's positions, that is, the divergence between Rainer's suspicion of sensuality and Irigaray's celebration of physicality. The author himself does not take sides in this debate, but rather notes how postmodern dance reflects the divisions in contemporary feminist thought.

From one perspective, Copeland historicizes the relations between early modern dance, postmodern dance, and varieties of twentieth-century feminism. From another perspective, he reduces these relations according to a model that posits art as more reflective than productive of social relations. His concluding paragraph walks a fine line between contextualizing dance in its historical setting and assuming that dance *mirrors* its historical setting:

> Obviously, none of the choreography I've been discussing can, or should, be reduced purely and simply to its feminist dimensions. The aesthetic and political path that leads from Duncan to Rainer . . . is long,

> circuitous, and complicated. Feminism is one of many influences exerted on, and reflected in, these works. But the fact remains that modern and postmodern dance are probably the only art forms in which various stages of feminist thinking are literally *embodied.*[13]

Despite his disclaimer, Copeland ultimately does view dance as a reflection of its society and thus commits what some scholars label the fallacy of reflection theory.

Like Copeland, Elizabeth Dempster presents broad contrasts between ballet, early modern dance, and postmodern dance in her essay "Women Writing the Body: Let's Watch a Little How She Dances." Unlike Copeland, however, she consciously rejects the assumptions of reflection theory and premises her argument on the observation that "social and political values are not simply placed or grafted onto a neutral body-object like so many old or new clothes. On the contrary, ideologies are systematically deposited and constructed on an anatomical plane, i.e., in the neuro-musculature of the dancer's body."[14] Carrying through this claim, Dempster bases her analyses on the technical methods of the dance styles under discussion.

Her argument sets up a clear opposition between classical ballet and postmodern dance. "In the classical dance," Dempster writes, "the spectator is invited to gaze upon a distanced, ideal world where the female dancer is traced as sylph and cipher, a necessary absence."[15] In contrast, "the body, and by extension 'the feminine,' in postmodern dance is unstable, fleeting, flickering, transient—a subject of multiple representations."[16] It is the shifting quality of the body and subject in postmodern dance that Dempster finds so liberating.

Her attitude toward earlier modern dance styles is far more ambivalent. She recognizes that Duncan and Graham "proposed a feminist dance practice which would return the real female body to women." Yet she also recognizes that Duncan and Graham posited a natural and interiorized body that seemed to reiterate traditional assumptions about the relatedness of women, nature, emotionality, and the body. It was Graham's codification of her technique, she believes, that led to the cooptation of modern dance. Once "one woman's speech [became] 'women's language,'" the ability of early modern dance to challenge dominant conceptions of gender was rendered null. Postmodern dance avoids such cooptation by defining itself not as a newly innovated dance vocabulary but as "an interrogation of language itself."[17]

Although in an endnote Dempster cites Susan Foster's distinction between resistive and reactionary modes of postmodernism,[18] her description of postmodern dance never becomes less than celebratory. She does not address the specific example Foster gives of reactionary postmodernism—the dancing of

Twyla Tharp. Indeed, her argument makes little reference to specific choreographers or specific works but remains an idealized description of postmodern dance *sui generis*. And she never resolves the question of the gender politics of early modern dance. If Martha Graham was largely responsible for the cooptation of the practice, then where does that leave Isadora Duncan? Dempster ends her discussion of Duncan without being able to decide whether to place more weight on her historical significance or her theoretical incorrectness:

> Duncan's vision of the dance of the future presumes an unproblematic return to a body of untainted naturalness and to an essential purity which she believed was fundamental to women. To recognize that Duncan's vision is unrealizable and perhaps, from a 1980s perspective, in some degree complicit with the concept of "natural" sexual difference is not to deny the power of her rhetoric, nor to dismiss the considerable impact her dancing had upon audiences of her time.[19]

In "Reinstating Corporeality: Feminism and Body Politics" Janet Wolff echoes many of Dempster's judgments. Yet Wolff does not write primarily as a dance critic but rather as a feminist theorist and sociologist of art. She structures her essay as a review of recent literature on the body and proceeds to question which model of the body best serves a "feminist cultural politics."[20] With impressive erudition, she summarizes the insights of Mary Douglas, Norbert Elias, Michel Foucault, Mary Russo, Julia Kristeva, Luce Irigaray, and Hélène Cixous. For Wolff's purposes, none of the available models quite work, for all presuppose either a purely constructed body or an essentialized body, and she is looking for an alternate position that acknowledges the female body "as discursively and socially constructed and as currently experienced by women."[21] This she finds in postmodern dance and in related modes of performance art, film, and visual art. Her essay concludes:

> Beginning from the lived experience of women in their currently constituted bodily identities—identities which are *real* at the same time as being socially inscribed and discursively produced—feminist artists and cultural workers can engage in the challenging and exhilarating task of simultaneously affirming those identities, questioning their origins and ideological functions, and working towards a nonpatriarchal expression of gender and the body.[22]

Wolff's essay includes a cursory survey of dance history. In agreement with other feminist commentators on ballet, she sees the form "[colluding] in a discourse which constructs, in a medium which employs the body for its expression, a strangely disembodied female."[23] She then acknowledges the transgressive potential of early modern dance, in particular its "commitment to women's stories and lives." But in the end, she believes, the essentialism of early modern dance, the "notion of women's natural body or women's universal essence," undercut its potential to resist the patriarchal status quo. Following the lead of Elizabeth Dempster, Wolff asserts that "dance can only be subversive when it questions and exposes the construction of the body in culture" and credits postmodern dance with this achievement, citing the examples of British choreographer Michael Clark and American choreographer-turned-filmmaker Yvonne Rainer.[24]

Although she mentions Clark and Rainer by name, Wolff provides no further analysis of their works. Even more than Dempster, she relies on an abbreviated, idealized description of postmodern dance. In the end postmodern dance becomes more of a metaphor than a practice in Wolff's account, a metaphor for the alternate position she stakes out in the debate between essentialists and anti-essentialists. Moreover, her metaphorical figuring of postmodern dance introduces a teleological narrative to her survey of dance history: that is, postmodern dance realizes the transgressive potential that early modern dance failed to achieve. A less pronounced version of this teleological narrative underlies Dempster's dance history as well.

To summarize my review of the literature thus far: the overviews penned by Copeland, Dempster, and Wolff necessarily rely on schematic arguments and broad generalizations supported by a few specific examples. Copeland's survey can be reduced to a single proposition: the evolving practice of modern dance reflects evolving notions of feminism. In other words, art reflects culture. Deliberately avoiding the reflection theory that informs Copeland's account, Dempster and Wolff risk another sort of reductive generalization. Their arguments come down to the proposition: early modern dance produced a corrupt feminism, postmodern dance an authentic feminism. In other words, contemporary theory becomes the yardstick by which the critic measures history.

It is telling that the surveys under discussion fall on opposing sides of the debate over whether early modern dance resisted or reinforced the status quo of gender. Copeland believes that early modern dance did resist dominant conceptions of womanhood during the Victorian era. On the contrary, Dempster and Wolff believe that early modern dancers' resistance to the status quo was coopted by, alternately, their codification of techniques first developed experimentally and their essentialist notions of woman and the body. There seems no middle ground between the two perspectives. The critic either endorses or dismisses the feminist aspirations of early modern dance.

The same either/or judgments inform the specific case studies of early modern dancers penned by Ann Daly, Jane Desmond, and Amy Koritz. Yet the case studies complicate the rhetorical opposition by introducing issues related to racial and national identity. Whereas Wolff and Dempster criticize early modern dance for its essentialized notions of gender, Desmond and Koritz compound the critique by pointing out how solos choreographed by Ruth St. Denis and Maud Allan, respectively, essentialized not only gender but also race and nationality. In contrast to Desmond and Koritz, Daly downplays the national self-fashioning implicit in the dancing of Isadora Duncan, focusing instead on issues surrounding the voyeuristic gaze. Yet none of the authors extends her case study to the practice of early modern dance as a whole. And so the question remains of how their insights can be applied to understanding the larger trajectory of early modern dance from Loie Fuller to Martha Graham.

Ann Daly boldly challenges the applicability of gaze theory to Isadora Duncan's dancing in her essay "Dance History and Feminist Theory: Reconsidering Isadora Duncan and the Male Gaze." Writing an implicit rebuttal to the position staked out by Wolff and Dempster, Daly remarks:

> The male gaze theory forces the feminist dance scholar into a no-win situation that turns on an exceedingly unproductive "succeed or fail" criterion. We expect the choreographer to topple a power structure that we have theorized as monolithic. The dancer or choreographer under consideration will always be condemned as a reinforcement of the patriarchal status quo, despite any transgressive behavior, because, by definition, that which is communicated arises from within the fabric of culture, that is to say, within patriarchy.[25]

As a way out of, or around, this "no-win situation" Daly focuses on the kinesthetic quality of Duncan's dancing (figure 1), building on Julia Kristeva's notion of the chora as the realm of the "ineffable." In dance terms, Duncan "rendered [the ineffable] intelligible" by "choreographing the drama of the kinesthetic—the sense of intentionality communicated through activated weight, the attentiveness signalled through spatial sensitivity, and the impression of decisiveness or indecisiveness gained through the manipulation of time." In so doing Duncan projected a "dancing subject-in-process . . . constantly reimagining herself." Daly concludes: "Dance was no longer about the spectacular display of the legs for entertainment's sake; it was about the self's inner impulses made manifest through the rhythmic, dynamic expression of the whole body."[26] Focusing on Duncan's performances during her first American tours from 1908 to 1911, Daly argues that Duncan did not perform Woman but rather staged her own complex subjectivity. In other words, the

1. Isadora Duncan. Photo: Arnold Genthe.
Courtesy of the Dance Collection, the New York Public Library for the Performing Arts, Astor, Lenox, and Tilden Foundations.

2. Ruth St. Denis in *Radha.*
Courtesy of the Denishawn Collection, the New York Public Library for the Performing Arts, Astor, Lenox, and Tilden Foundations.

kinesthetic power of Duncan's dancing countered not only the voyeuristic gaze but also the essentialism that commentators such as Dempster and Wolff have perceived in the form.

However, Daly does acknowledge that American spectators of Duncan's early tours did generalize her performances of the "subject-in-process" in national terms. Noting that this was a time "when America was obsessed with finding for itself a national selfhood, a cultural identity, and a means of individual self-expression,"[27] Daly believes that Duncan's American audiences projected their own self-fashioning onto her performances. In the eyes of progressive liberals, Duncan "embodied an optimistic belief in the reformability of the social and political system," while in the eyes of the radicals, the dancer "enacted a paradigm of complete social rupture."[28] Limiting her comments to the early phase of Duncan's career, Daly presents the association between Duncan's dancing and the fashioning of an American identity in terms that are more celebratory than critical.[29]

In contrast to Daly's attitude toward Duncan, Jane Desmond and Amy Koritz harshly judge Ruth St. Denis's and Maud Allan's engagement with agendas of racial and national self-fashioning. Drawing on the theorization of Orientalism by Edward Said and others as well as on feminist theory, Desmond and Koritz interpret solos by St. Denis and Allan, respectively, and point out how transparently the two choreographers staged Western stereotypes of the East. Neither critic sees much redeeming value in such thoroughgoing assent to Orientalism.

In "Dancing Out the Difference: Cultural Imperialism and Ruth St. Denis's *Radha* of 1906," Jane Desmond reads St. Denis's solo as a multilayered performance text. Her analysis turns on the solo's framing of female sensuality within a narrative context of renunciation and transcendence, the evocation of Indian temple dancing suggested by the dance's title (figure 7). Desmond sees the juxtaposition of female sensuality and representational pretext working in a complicated way, both subverting and reinforcing strictures on the sexuality of middle-class white women while projecting the Oriental Other as a figure of dangerous and excessive sexuality and redemptive spirituality. Yet despite her acknowledgment of the complexity of *Radha*, Desmond in the end views the solo as far more recuperative than resistant. Indeed, her concluding remarks call attention to the "invisible links that bind racism, sexism, and cultural imperialism so tightly together,"[30] in St. Denis's oeuvre and in society at large.

Amy Koritz extends Desmond's argument about how early modern dance conflated the staging of Woman and Oriental in her essay "Dancing the Orient for England: Maud Allan's *The Vision of Salome*." To a greater degree than Desmond, Koritz explores the potential disjunction between the Western woman as performer and the Oriental Other as subject matter. Koritz first notes how Allan displaced the threat of her assertive female sexuality onto her representation of an Oriental woman. But Allan could not afford to identify herself wholly with an Oriental Other. Rather, she "made the East transparent to the West by representing its essence,"[31] thus simultaneously embodying and distancing herself from her performance of the spiritual and sensual Oriental. Yet Allan's embodiment of the essence of the East also circled around and reinforced her staging of the Western women's separate sphere, for her dance reaffirmed "the spiritual nature of (middle-class) womanhood."[32] Thus her solo resolved the potential disjunction between Orientalism and the ideology of separate spheres, as "the dark continents of Western femininity and Orientalism [met] in Allan's depiction of Salome."[33]

Koritz surmises that the reason why *The Vision of Salome* enjoyed such popularity among English audiences when Allan appeared at the Palace Theatre in 1908 was that the dance "both [calmed] and [embodied] anxieties about female power and sexuality being raised by the suffrage movement and the incursion of middle-class women into the work force. [The dance] both [calmed] and [embodied] anxieties about English knowledge and imperial domination of the East."[34] Although Koritz casts her analysis of early modern dance in less judgmental terms than does Desmond, she nonetheless concurs with Desmond's conclusion that *The Vision of Salome*, like *Radha*, functioned to contain potential threats to the social order.

What both Koritz and Desmond overlook, however, is the kinesthetic dimension of Allan's and St. Denis's performances, a dimension that surely informed their dancing as well as Duncan's. Like Duncan, both Allan and St. Denis innovated their own movement vocabularies that drew on methods of physical culture—aesthetic gymnastics and Delsartism—widely practiced among middle-class women of the time. Unlike spectators of nineteenth-century ballet, whether male or female, who rarely had direct experience of the movement techniques presented onstage, many female spectators of early modern dance did have such direct experience, which surely intensified their kinesthetic response to the performances they witnessed. Although few women wrote reviews of early modern dance, more than a few recorded their enthusiasm in letters and memoirs, and these sources suggest that they viewed the kinesthetic power of early modern dance as a metaphor for women's heightened social mobility and sense of possibility. It may well be the case that the representational frames of Orientalism were less central to the responses of contemporary female spectators than they were to the responses of male reviewers of the time.

Neither Daly, Desmond, nor Koritz extends her argument to the practice of early modern dance as a whole. But if they did, their arguments would fall on opposing sides of the same rhetorical axis that divides Copeland from Dempster and Wolff. Like Copeland, Daly focuses on the resistive potential of early modern dance. Like Dempster and Wolff, Desmond and Koritz draw attention to the recuperation of the subversive potential of the practice. It seems that pursuing the debate over early modern dance in terms of whether the practice transgressed or upheld dominant conceptions of race, gender, and nationality results in a dead end comparable to the "no-win situation" Daly posits as a consequence of applying gaze theory to dance.

As a way around this impasse, I propose an alternate position that accepts the validity of Daly's argument as well as Desmond's and Koritz's and extends the implication of their case studies to the practice of early modern dance as a whole. That is, I would like to pay as much attention to the kinesthesia (Daly's focus) as to the representational frames (Desmond's and Koritz's focus) of early modern dance. To do so is to recognize a complexity in the formal structure of early modern dance that traced a distinct ideological profile, the dismantling of the voyeuristic gaze and the reliance on essentialized notions of identity. And it was this ideological profile that marked the paradoxical social function of the form, its ability to contest and to conform at the same time.[35]

In my view, it was the kinesthesia of early modern dance that allowed for its choreographic dismantling of the voyeuristic gaze and its address to the female spectator. Here I would like to extend Daly's analysis and suggest that not only Duncan's dancing but also the dancing of her contemporaries projected a kinesthetic power that challenged male viewers to see the female dancer as an expressive subject rather than as an erotic object. At the same time the kinesthesia of early modern dance engaged female viewers in ways that the spectacle of late-nineteenth-century ballet did not. In fact, since many female spectators had experienced the same movement techniques that the dancers transformed in performance—Delsarteanism and aesthetic gymnastics—their kinesthetic response was particularly intense and led more than a few to identify the dancer's flow of bodily motion as reflective of their own. As Mabel Dodge Luhan once wrote about her experience of seeing Isadora Duncan: "It seemed to me I recognized what she did in the dance, and that it was like my own daily, nightly return to the Source."[36]

Whereas the kinesthesia of early modern dance challenged the voyeuristic gaze, its representational frames deployed essentialized images of identity, images of a universalized Woman or generalized ethnic or national type. Here I would like to extend Desmond's and Koritz's analysis and suggest that just as the Oriental frames of St. Denis's and Allan's dancing countered the performance of their individual subjectivities, so too did the representational frames employed by their contemporaries. Indeed, I would like to suggest that the kinesthesia and representational frames of early modern dance often worked at cross-purposes. Or perhaps more accurately, the juxtaposition of individualized kinesthetic subjectivity and generalized representational type created a dynamic tension underlying the form of early modern dance, a tension that grounded the paradoxical social function of the form. Whereas the representational frames reiterated and updated preexistent images of gender and ethnicity, the kinesthetic dimension introduced a new image of the female body in motion that was without precedent.

Stated in these terms, my analysis is necessarily schematic. What is required now is a precise comparison of how different dancers inflected the dynamic tension between kinesthetic flow and representation frame, between undermining the voyeuristic gaze and deploying essentialized images of identity, between resisting and reinscribing dominant cultural values. Although this is not the place to detail such a comparison, it does seem an appropriate occasion to call upon dance scholars to acknowledge and confront the tensions and paradoxes of early modern dance. For until we do so, we will remain limited in our ability to write early modern dance into the history of a "feminist cultural politics." And that is where the practice clearly, if complicatedly, belongs.

Notes

1 Christy Adair's *Women and Dance: Sylphs and Sirens* (New York: New York University Press, 1992), begins the project of bringing diverse methods of feminist analysis to bear on dance studies. However, since her book does not present a view on early modern dance that differs from the perspectives outlined below, it is not included in my survey of the literature.

2 See, for example, Judith Lynne Hanna, *Dance, Sex, and Gender* (Chicago: University of Chicago Press, 1988), and Helen Thomas, ed., *Dance, Gender, and Culture* (New York: St. Martin's Press, 1993).

3 See Mary Ann Doane, "Film and the Masquerade—Theorizing the Female Spectator," *Screen* 23, nos. 3/4 (September/October 1982), pp. 74–88; and her "Masquerade Reconsidered: Further Thoughts on the Female Spectator," *Discourse* 11, no. 1 (1988/1989), pp. 42–54. See also Laura Mulvey, "Visual Pleasure and Narrative Cinema," *Screen* 16, no. 3 (Autumn 1975), pp. 6–18, and her "On Duel in the Sun," *Framework* 15 (1981), pp. 12–15; and E. Ann Kaplan, "Is the Gaze Male?" in *Women and Film: Both Sides of the Camera* (New York: Methuen, 1983), pp. 23–35.

4 See Sue-Ellen Case, *Feminism and Theatre* (New York: Methuen, 1988), and Jill Dolan, *The Feminist Spectator as Critic* (Ann Arbor: UMI Research Press, 1988).

5 See Evan Alderson, "Ballet as Ideology: *Giselle*, Act II," *Dance Chronicle* 10, no. 3 (1987), pp. 290–304, and reprinted in this volume; Ann Daly, "The Balanchine Woman: Of Hummingbirds and Channel Swimmers," *Drama Review* 31, no. 1 (Spring 1987), pp. 8–21; and her "Classical Ballet: A Discourse of Difference," *Women and Performance* 3, no. 2 (1987–

1988), pp. 57–66, and reprinted in this volume. See also Lynn Garafola, "The Travesty Dancer in Nineteenth-Century Ballet," *Dance Research Journal* 17, no. 2, and 18, no. 1 (Fall 1985 and Spring 1986), pp. 35–40.

6 Roger Copeland, "Founding Mothers: Duncan, Graham, Rainer, and Sexual Politics," *Dance Theatre Journal* 8, no. 3 (Fall 1990), pp. 6–9 and 27–29; Ann Daly, "Dance History and Feminist Theory: Reconsidering Isadora Duncan and the Male Gaze," in *Gender in Performance*, ed. Laurence Senelick (Hanover, N.H.: University Press of New England, 1992), 239–59.

7 Elizabeth Dempster, "Women Writing the Body: Let's Watch a Little How She Dances," in *Grafts: Feminist Cultural Criticism*, ed. Susan Sheridan (London: Verso, 1988), pp. 35–54, and Janet Wolff, "Reinstating Corporeality: Feminism and Body Politics," in her *Feminine Sentences* (Berkeley: University of California Press, 1990), pp. 120–41, and reprinted in this volume.

8 Jane Desmond, "Dancing Out the Difference: Cultural Imperialism and Ruth St. Denis's *Radha* of 1906," *Signs* 17, no. 1 (Autumn 1991), pp. 28–49; and Amy Koritz, "Dancing the Orient for England: Maud Allan's *The Vision of Salome*," *Theatre Journal* 46, no. 1 (March 1994), pp. 63–78, and reprinted in this volume.

9 Copeland, "Founding Mothers," p. 6.

10 Ibid., p. 9.

11 Ibid., p. 7.

12 See note 3.

13 Copeland, "Founding Mothers," p. 29.

14 Dempster, "Women Writing the Body," p. 37.

15 Ibid., p. 49.

16 Ibid., pp. 48–49.

17 Ibid., p. 51.

18 Susan Foster, "The Signifying Body: Reaction and Resistance in Postmodern Dance," *Theatre Journal* 37, no. 1 (March 1985), pp. 45–64.

19 Dempster, "Women Writing the Body," p. 51.

20 Wolff, "Reinstating Corporeality," p. 120.

21 Ibid., p. 134.

22 Ibid., p. 138.

23 Ibid., p. 136.

24 Ibid., p. 137.

25 Ann Daly, "Dance History and Feminist Theory: Reconsidering Isadora Duncan and the Male Gaze," in *Gender in Performance*, ed. Laurence Senelick (Hanover, N.H.: University Press of New England, 1992), p. 243. For more on Isadora Duncan, see Isadora Duncan, *The Art of the Dance* (1928; New York: Theatre Arts Books, 1969).

26 Daly, "Dance History," pp. 252, 254, 255.

27 Ibid., p. 254.

28 Ibid., p. 247.

29 In a book published after this essay was written, *Done into Dance: Isadora Duncan in America* (Bloomington: Indiana University Press, 1995), Ann Daly does carry her discussion into the later phases of Duncan's career and confronts the racism of Duncan's 1927 essay, "I See America Dancing." As Daly writes, Duncan "effectively [constructed] the genre of American modern dance as whiteness" (p. 219).

30 Desmond, "Dancing Out the Difference," p. 49.

31 Koritz, "Dancing the Orient," p. 68.

32 Ibid., p. 70.

33 Ibid., p. 68.

34 Ibid., p. 76.

35 This position is implicit, though not explicit, in my book *Ecstasy and the Demon: Feminism and Nationalism in the Dances of Mary Wigman* (Berkeley: University of California Press, 1993).

36 Mabel Dodge Luhan, *Movers and Shakers* (1936; Albuquerque: University of New Mexico Press, 1985), pp. 319–20.

9 SOME THOUGHTS ON CHOREOGRAPHING HISTORY

Brenda Dixon Gottschild

We all see things through our personal histories, with their parts rooted in convention and their parts that became subject to change. These histories come to include reflections on what made us enter into them. Through such reflections I believe we become political, because they address questions of gender, race, class, nationality and family origins. With political consciousness . . . some knowledge of self and place . . . change becomes possible.—Jill Johnston[1]

History is a fable agreed upon. So too is identity, which is a story not only arrived at by the individual but conferred by the group.—John Lahr[2]

For historians in any discipline the process of writing about the past is an exercise in metaphoric choreography. Deconstruction theory has taught us that to formulate a history means to interpret selected events. Besides the subjectivity of any one interpretation, the researcher/historian also risks the danger that theory/philosophy will come loose from context an untenable situation, as the two quotations above indicate. In order to avoid that occurrence, I find it helpful to remind myself that I am first cause / first context. As an erstwhile theater professional, I find that choreography and the dancing body play a role in shaping my approach to research. I arrive at ideas affectively and kinesthetically, as well as cognitively. For example, I was actively at work on this essay in times of vulnerability and intuition: waking from sleep (especially from naps!); in the midst of my movement workout; as I lay sunbathing in midday summer heat. Such is the way in which I am seduced into a topic, listening to my accumulated research as it begins to speak to me. It parallels the way in which I worked as a performer, choreographer, and director. It approximates the findings noted in literature on the creative process.[3] Other performing artists who have become writers and scholars may note similar processes. In the same vein, I advise my doctoral students, most of whom are/were performers, to regard research writing as "choreography for the page."

I mention the example of my personal process in order to arrive at my first premise: namely, that we bring our cultural, social, and preacademic habits and predilections to bear upon both the topics that we choose to research and the manner in which we go about it. Although this proposition may seem obvious and simple, the denial of it feeds the subjective/objective fallacy. If we accept this first premise, then it becomes apparent that it is a categorical error to speak of subjective/objective as contending approaches.[4] The two are binary opposites which do not oppose each other but work together and coexist. They are processes which reflect, embrace, and require each other. The fact that we as a culture have made such a big deal of the oppositional nature of binary concepts, ignoring the symbiotic relation of opposites defining each other, says a lot about how we perceive, what we value or devalue, what we do, and how we do it. It is heartening that some groups in our contemporary culture are showing signs of receptivity toward Asian and African concepts which are more sophisticated than ours in embracing competing opposites, or contrarieties. Living with the opposite, "the other," is no longer a luxury of choice but a necessity of survival for our planet and for the conception and execution of our research.

Recent research has begun to take these matters of process into consideration. Scholars have presented conference papers as performances.[5] A decade ago Victor Turner called for a "performative and reflexive anthropology" in which "we should not merely read and comment on ethnographies, but actually perform them," a concept which he put into practice with his students.[6] Earlier researchers like Katherine Dunham and Maya Deren immersed themselves in the cultural experiences of the "other" and proceeded in their work from the perspective of a subjective/objective (or intuitive/cognitive) continuum. Integrative approaches are also central to the work of Robert Farris Thompson and Cornel West—both visionaries in their own right. These efforts represent processes of experiential methodologies and deal with the horizontal interplay of content/context, rather than the vertical determination of cause/effect. They parallel efforts by performers and other artists to turn to the "-ings"—the dancing, not the dance; the singing, not the song—that is, to apprehend the vitality and energy of the subjunctive mode of process as an antidote to overdoses of the declarative, full-stop mode of a product-oriented tradition.

This horizontal, subjunctive, processual model offers some means by which we might "theorize the relationship between a given artistic/bodily endeavor and general cultural values relating to the body."[7] From some process of "lived research" we might deduce principles about kinesthetic and affective ways of knowing. These observations lead to my second premise: that it would be wise should we researchers and historians listen to our materials and let the context suggest a methodology. This premise is a way of checking or restraining the force of the first premise. If we allow our context to lead us, we might travel paths that would not present themselves when we take the lead and travel the paths we already know. "Traditional scientific method can't tell you where you ought to go, unless where you ought to go is a continuation of where you were going in the past."[8] We know that, regardless of what we do, we will see the world through the lens of our specific, individual histories and our generic, sociocultural, economic, and political backgrounds. However, we need to continually test our approaches against the mirror of our personal biases. Like the power of the sun, this mirror both blinds and illuminates. The idea of listening to one's text/context and playing with its lead offers some balance.

This premise requires that we also listen to the language that we use. Language is one of our major reflectors as academics; it holds a mirror to the world we live in and, reflexively, it molds our thoughts. People and systems are not different because of their language but because of their experiences in the world, which made different things important to different people. We can use language to build bridges or to make barriers. Take for example the devious language of dehumanization used in the Persian Gulf war: a "patriot missile" surely has a noble mission; "collateral damage" gives "us" the right to decimate "them" without having to bear the guilt of acknowledging their deaths; and "friendly fire" exonerates us even when we attack ourselves. On the other hand, terms like "exotic," "primitive," and other such descriptors may serve the reverse purpose in dance writing. By using such terminology, the object of those terms is put in a category below that of the academic, Europeanist concert dance ideal.[9] In a very real sense, these words are almost always negative-value indicators. They are important tools in the language of disenfranchisement and have been used in describing concert dance by people of African lineage from the beginning of the concert dance era. But such choices of vocabulary may have more to say about who is writing than who is performing or what is being seen.

As an African-American woman—a status described in some circles as one of double jeopardy—I am acutely aware of the language of empowerment and disempowerment. To give one example, I cite a dance review published in a national monthly magazine wherein the European-American male writer used basically the language of Europeanist ballet aesthetics (line, form) to discredit—disempower, if you will—the New York season of a major African-American concert dance company.[10] Here is his opening paragraph:

> For dancerly directness, simplicity, cohesion, and strict kinetic pleasure, the most rewarding moment in a performance by Garth Fagan Dance occurs during the curtain calls. Neatly lined up across the stage, standing in recognizable First Positions [*sic*], the company bends forward into smooth and unaffected bows. The uncomplicated actions, clearly centered in consistently loose lower backs, give a potently elemental effect: They tell of plumb-line stretch, central force, and plastically easy articulation.[11]

This introduction, praising the postperformance bows, states that none of the criteria the writer values appear in the performance and that virtually the only "rewarding moment" is after the performance proper is over. That is the only time that the performers show a clear-cut, linear arrangement. The phrases "neatly lined up across the stage" and "plumb-line stretch" give us the message that linearity and verticality matter a lot to the writer. He goes so far as to have the phrase "first position" placed in the upper case. These value indicators reveal that the writer perceives Fagan's work as though it were bad ballet.

His assumption is a major categorical error and an example of comparing pigs to fish. It is clear to any dance critic or scholar who takes the time to study Fagan's choreography and its sources that his work is not based upon adherence to ballet precepts any more than Alvin Ailey's work is an example of Louis Horst's principles of modern dance forms—and Ailey's work has suffered in this skewed equation in the same way that Fagan's suffers at the pen of this writer. Fagan's work is not based on the centered verticality of ballet, so of course that will not be a value exhibited in his choreography. His canon is a synthesis of Africanist and Europeanist influences with a strong emphasis on the fluid, articulated torso, which is a strong aesthetic value in African dance. It is a forceful, dynamic, and effective marriage of cross-cultural influences.

This critic does not see the merger as the measure. Instead, he holds onto one side of the equation—namely, European ballet—as his standard, implying that the African side is lesser because it doesn't uphold that standard. He reinforces this point of view in the next paragraph: "Beyond a pervasive air of unaffected gentility, the company of fourteen tends to bypass the structural niceties of theatrical dancing for the quirky, hard-to-follow idiosyncrasies of Fagan's choreography."[12] Well, what are the "niceties of theatrical dancing"? Who sets those criteria? Is the critic privy to them and not the choreographer? Is theatrical dancing meant to be nice? The "unaffected gentility" line has a bit of the "noble savage" implied in it, but updated for a 1990s readership. The implication in these excerpts and, indeed, throughout the review is that Fagan doesn't know the rules nor how to abide by them, but the critic does.

My assessment is the reverse: it is this critic who doesn't know the rules—or the aesthetic criteria underlying Fagan's work. To simply characterize it as idiosyncratic is to fail to come to terms with the style of dance. In the phrase "hard-to-follow idiosyncrasies" he reveals that he really does not know what is going on, how to look at it, or how to write about it. It veers from the only norm the writer knows and reveres—but which the choreography was never intended to obey. I won't belabor the point. The review continues in this vein; it is demeaning and small-minded. No matter that the review was written several years ago: such distortions continue as old-school critics trained in one aesthetic perspective are faced with a panoply of dances that simply do not fit. One of the easiest ways to disempower others is to measure them by a standard which ignores their chosen aesthetic frame of reference and its particular demands. In examples such as this one, language is deployed as an intercultural weapon.

I am also reminded of an example in Michael Kirby's article "Criticism: Four Faults."[13] The point I make here was probably unnoticed by European-American readers, whether male or female, and probably unintentional on the part of the author. It is an example of disempowerment for African-American females. In order to prove that criticism is subjective but that there still exists some consensus regarding aesthetic values, Kirby states that it would be possible to take a poll and ascertain that Marilyn Monroe is considered a beautiful woman in our society. He explains his argument, using the term *woman* to refer to the (European) female who is characterized as beautiful. He states that "the 'beautiful' woman that Rubens painted and the 'beautiful' woman photographed in the last century are quite different from the 'beautiful' woman of today."[14] Fine. Then he claims that in spite of the "subjective nature of experience," it is still possible to be objective in describing a performance. His example is what interests me. He states, "If I say that there are three performers on stage, that one of them is a black girl, that none of them is speaking, and so forth, these statements are both value free and objective."[15] In using the term "black girl," he has used the language of disempowerment in referring to an African-American female, since the other females referred to, all Europeans, were referenced as women. His inconsistency shows that even the most innocent, supposedly simple and straightforward language is in fact subjective and value laden. Mature African-American women and men were referred to by European Americans as boys and girls until very recently. Dancers, too, have been subjugated to the less-than-full-person status of the boys-and-girls terminology.

I find this example noteworthy because it comes from a researcher and historian whose work has been about breaking stride with traditional currents. It suggests that listening to one's materials to hear personal biases is not a bad idea for any of us, whether we are categorized as avant-garde or traditional, liberal or conservative. Of course, there are examples throughout our culture which are more blatant than the two offered here that illustrate the debasing use of language in reference to the other. However, these subtle manifestations are potentially more dangerous than their overt counterparts. It is ironic that this seemingly tangential "slip" (after all, "black girls" were not the subject of the essay) is one of the points upon which one may justifiably hang a refutation of Kirby's thesis regarding objectivity. Frequently it is the seemingly insignificant elements—the pieces that look as though they are filler in the cracks of our research—which are essential to the full picture of what we experience and how we report it.

My third premise is that, given the first two premises, we need to keep ourselves off center in order to stay on target. Some ways of doing this include the use of reversals/inversions; an awareness of intertextuality; and an awareness that aesthetics and performance history, theory, and criticism, like all constructs, are functions of power (which is the real message of the foregoing examples). None of these are new ideas, but the configuration that I bring to them from my particular perspective may shape them in ways to suggest new applications to the reader.

Reversals/inversions can be invaluable in offering alternative approaches. In the same sense that the hatha yoga headstand is performed not only to physically stimulate circulation to the brain but also to psychically offer the practitioner the experience of seeing the world in chaos—upside down—and to find one's center off-center, feminist and cultural activist Jill Johnston recommends gender reversals: "I recommend reversing many things in your mind's eye when looking at dance, just to see where we still stand in our sexual politics. I can't watch TV or movies without doing this myself. When a woman cries, I put the man in her place and imagine the unthinkable when a man tells a woman what she thinks. I turn it all around."[16] Likewise, I recommend culture reversals. What if we stand on our heads and look at our culture as African based? In visual arts classes students occasionally are assigned a similar exercise and must make a representation by depicting only the "negative spaces," the spaces in and around the "subject." The exercise shows by the experiential process and its result that subject/object and foreground/background are relative—and, from this informed perspective, the dichotomy between subject/object blends into a dialogic relationship.

The Africanist reversal provides a similar perspective. For example, Duke University historian Peter Wood suggested to the planners of Colonial Williamsburg that, in the reconstruction of that village, the plantation owners be played by African Americans and the enslaved workers by European Americans. As we know, the idea did not catch on, but it was a good one and would have allowed an exchange of information for both cultures.[17] Historian Eric Foner points out that an Africanist perspective on the American Revolution would conclude that that event was not the harbinger of liberty and equality but worsened the situation for African Americans and strengthened the institution of slavery.[18] Likewise, Florida State University psychologist Naim Akbar commented that, from a European perspective, the "Old World" is Europe and the "New World" is America; but, from an Africanist perspective, the "Old World" is Africa, and the "New World" is Europe.[19] An Africanist perspective on the roots of Greek culture is based on the "Ancient Model" which acknowledges Greece's Egyptian and Levantine roots, while the Eurocentric or "Aryan Model" posits Greece as a "pure" culture and purposefully excludes acknowledgment of nonwhite influences. Similarly, we could look at the works of Picasso and Braque in their African-influenced, wedge/plane period and term them Africanist, rather than Cubist.

I have been engaged for the past several years in investigating the Africanist presence in European-American culture by focusing an Africanist mirror on European-American performance, and dance in particular. In making my observations I discuss signature characteristics of African-based aesthetics in contrast to European-based aesthetics and pointed out their exemplary occurrence in the Americanized ballet style of George Balanchine.[20] If we take the African-American presence as the foreground and look at European-American performance from this perspective, we begin to see the Africanist influences in places we didn't dream it existed, such as ballet. My intention in all my examples is to show that the Africanist aesthetic is part of the air we Americans breathe—part of the negative/positive space continuum to which we all are born as Americans, black and white.[21]

Intertextuality goes hand in hand with inversions/reversals. This theory, developed and utilized by Roland Barthes, Julia Kristeva, Mikhail Bakhtin, Jacques Derrida, and others, can be summed up in a phrase that is reductive but bears repeating: all texts are intertexts. That is, forces, movements, motifs, trends, languages—text, in other words—of previous and contemporary societies influence us, live within and around us, and constitute the threads through which we weave our "new" patterns. They are the anonymous, unauthored codes of a given culture. What this implies is that there really is nothing new under the sun, only variations on prior patterns and processes assimilated and reconfigured in any present moment. Every culture, then, is a panoply of quotations from a wide spectrum of past and present conditioning forces. Also implicit in the theory are, first, the idea that the anonymous, unauthored, multifold sources feeding into any given text are so thoroughly interwoven that their origins are difficult, if not impossible, to sort out, and, second, the assumption that the fusion process is unconscious and automatic.

My contentions both affirm and depart from intertextual theory. I agree that there are forces afoot which interface with other forces and that the process of interchange/intertextuality is largely subliminal. However, in the case of the Africanist influence in American culture, it is wrong to assume that sources and influences cannot be attributed and that the formulae are anonymous. My contention is that, indeed, we do not need to reduce the intertextuality of the African-American/European-American equation to a laundry list of sources and influences, but we desperately need to get beneath the convoluted web of racism which has obscured the affirmation and celebration of the fact that African-based culture is, indeed, an interface touching almost every part of American life. In the case of the black/white American equation, intertextuality is more than an anonymous field of generalized sources and influences. We are able to trace threads and see the jazz aesthetic in the art deco architecture of Miami Beach and in the inspiration for works by Jackson Pollock and George Balanchine, alike. We see the codes, formulae, rhythms, patterns, and fragments that derive from the Africanist aesthetic as a frequent visitor in European-American endeavor. The concept of intertextuality invites the application of reversals and inversions, for no text is unaffected by other texts, and thus it can be regarded from a number of perspectives.

In suggesting these ways of keeping oneself off balance in order to rebalance, let me return to the concept of the subjunctive as a working model to replace the declarative nature of most research. We need modes of inquiry that are intersubjective, intertextual, subjunctive, phenomenological, processual. For those who have used these approaches—now and even before the existence of the literary and aesthetic jargon we have adopted to designate them—it becomes evident that previously assumed boundaries have been ruptured, and performance falls between boundaries and between genres. As writers and historians we can choose to communicate process and contexts instead of following the traditional, deterministic route of Europeanist scholarship which looks for linear, vertical flashpoints—trends and hierarchies—in the evolution and development of our histories. Indeterminacy is a valid approach. We don't need the answers: we need the questions; we need the dancing, not the dance.

Afterword: Whose History?

I was shocked when a dance writer who had read the conference version of this essay approached me to inform me that she was "sick and tired" of my complaints about irresponsible writers, and that she wanted me, next time, to address "the critics who have been writing responsible criticism for the past twenty-five years." In my defense, and to orient the reader to my perspective, let me make myself clear. Of the numerous articles and conference papers I have published, this essay and one other[22] are the only ones that focus on the myopia of particular European-American reviews of specific African-American choreographies. I am not a one-issue person. In fact, the above essay is not a one-issue statement. It reflects the multilayered convolutions that power plays and hierarchies have wrought upon our cultural potential as Americans, black and white.

As far as I know, there are no mainstream dance critics who have been "responsible" to world cultural practices until the past few years, when deconstruction theory, Afrocentricity, and related new developments forced their card. I do not even consider myself—an African American schooled in European-American institutions in New York, dwelling in environments and moving in circles dominated by European Americans where I am often the only person of color—as having practiced responsible criticism. The irony is the fact that, regardless of color, class, or gender, those of us who were educated in traditional, Europeanist institutions hadn't the slightest suspicion that we were not responsible. And we still have much to learn. I look back at the reviews I wrote even ten years ago and see how I, too, evaluated African-American modern dance groups using Europeanist criteria as the sole frame of reference. It should have been clear to me that the African-American aesthetic (as evidenced in the work of a choreographer like Dianne McIntyre, for example) fuses and integrates forces and influences in a way that begs a knowledge of Africanist aesthetic threads in order for the work to be appropriately assessed. But, like this angry woman, I too was raised and programmed to recognize only one stream—conveniently tagged as the mainstream—even though our American context and the dances we critique represent multiple currents.

In spite of her status and renown, this woman was isolated, angry, frightened, and threatened by my essay. Her response may have worked in her favor, because, since her encounter with me, she has noticeably expanded her range of inquiry in examining dance. The important point is that there is some change in her perspective, and she has listened. She is called upon far more frequently than I am to talk about dance and culture, and she has cleverly incorporated a multicultural approach in her recent work. I hope I am around to witness the time when people of color will be called upon as frequently as she is to consult, give presentations, and publish; and when the organizations and institutions that call upon them are not chiefly European or European-American gatherings, but include a proportionate representation from people of color, as both presenters and sponsors.

Notes

The original version of this essay was prepared as a presentation for the University of California–Riverside conference, Choreographing History, 16–17 February 1992.

1 Jill Johnston, "How Dance Artists and Critics Define Dance as Political," *Movement Research Performance Journal 3* (Fall 1991), pp. 2–3.

2 John Lahr, "The World's Most Sensational Absence," *New York Times Book Review* 84 (June 1990), p. 10.

3 For example, see L. Humphries, "How Ideas Take Shape," *Yellow Springs Newsletter*, Fall 1986, pp. 6–8.

4 The methodologies of some phenomenologists and ethnographers consciously aim to approach subjective/objective as a continuous, reflexive process. For a succinct discussion of how these efforts (by scholars Maurice Merleau-Ponty, James Clifford, and Clifford Geertz, among others) are put to use by contemporary dance scholarship, see Deirdre Sklar, "On Dance Ethnography," and Sondra Fraleigh, "A Vulnerable Glance: Seeing Dance through Phenomenology," *Dance Research Journal* 23, no. 1 (Spring 1991), pp. 6–16.

5 For example, see "Reports," "Performance Studies International," *Dance Research Journal* 23, no. 1 (Spring 1991), pp. 55–57.

6 Victor Turner, "Dramatic Ritual / Ritual Drama, Peformative and Reflexive Anthropology," *From Ritual to Theatre* (New York: Performing Arts Journal Publications, 1982), pp. 89–101.

7 Susan Foster, conference organizer, preliminary materials for Choreographing History conference.

8 Robert Pirsig, *Zen and the Art of Motorcycle Maintenance* (New York: Bantam Books, 1972), p. 275, as quoted in Molefi Asante, *The Afrocentric Idea* (Philadelphia, Penn.: Temple University Press, 1987), p. 114.

9 I use the terms *Europeanist* and *Africanist* throughout this manuscript. The term *Africanist* includes concepts, practices, attitudes, or forms which have roots or origins in Africa and are found in the diaspora of African peoples. My precedent for using this term is set in recent scholarship. For example, see Joseph E. Holloway, *Africanisms in American Culture* (Bloomington: Indiana University Press, 1990), and Toni Morrison, *Playing in the Dark: Whiteness and the Literary Imagination* (Cambridge: Harvard University Press, 1992). I coined the term *Europeanist* to use as its counterpart and to denote concepts, practices, attitudes, or forms which have roots or origins in Europe.

10 Robert Greskovic, "Garth Fagan Dance," *Dance Magazine*, February 1991, pp. 112–15.

11 Ibid., p. 112.

12 Ibid., p. 113.

13 Michael Kirby, "Criticism: Four Faults," *Drama Review* 18, no. 3 (September 1974), pp. 59–68.

14 Ibid., p. 61.

15 Ibid., p. 67.

16 Johnston, "How Dance Artists and Critics Define Dance as Political," p. 3.

17 Peter Wood, in conversation with the author, American Dance Festival, Durham, North Carolina, June 1988.

18 Eric Foner, "Morning Edition," National Public Radio, 3 November 1989.

19 Naim Akbar, "Morning Edition," ibid.

20 See Brenda Dixon Gottschild, "Stripping the Emperor: The Africanist Presence in Ameri-

can Concert Dance," in David Gere, Lewis Segal, Patrice Koelsch, and Elizabeth Zimmer, eds., *Looking Out: Perspectives on Dance and Criticism in a Multicultural World* (New York: Schirmer Books, 1995).

21 See Brenda Dixon, "The Afrocentric Paradigm," *Design for Arts in Education* 92, no. 3 (January/February 1991), pp. 15–22.

22 See Brenda Dixon (Stowell), "Black Dance and Dancers and the White Public: A Prolegomenon to Problems of Definition," in Gerald E. Myers, ed., *The Black Tradition in American Modern Dance*, American Dance Festival publication, Durham, N.C., 1988; reprinted in *Black American Literature Forum* 24, no. 1 (Spring, 1990), pp. 117–23.

10 AUTO-BODY STORIES: BLONDELL CUMMINGS AND AUTOBIOGRAPHY IN DANCE

Ann Cooper Albright

As I advance in these memoirs, I realise more and more the impossibility of writing one's life—or rather, the lives of all the different people I have been. Incidents which seemed to me to last a lifetime have taken only a few pages: intervals that seemed thousands of years of suffering and pain and through which, in sheer defense, in order to go on living, I emerged an entirely different person, do not appear at all long here. I often ask myself desperately, what reader is going to be able to clothe with flesh the skeleton that I have presented? I am trying to write down the truth, but the truth runs away and hides from me. How find the truth? If I were a writer, and had written of my life twenty novels or so, it would be nearer the truth.[1]

How does this statement, written near the end of her autobiography, reflect on the lively account of art and love which Isadora Duncan has given her reader? Faced with the daunting task of creating a coherent literary account of her life, Duncan tries to tell her story only to realize (some three hundred pages later) the impossibility of such an attempt.[2] She claims, instead, that were she a novelist, the "truth" of her life would be found in her novels, not in her autobiography. In "Writing Fictions: Women's Autobiography in France," Nancy Miller tackles this issue of "truth" in autobiography and proposes a new reading similar to the reading that Duncan alludes to. Although Miller calls for a "double reading—of the autobiography with the fiction," she is quick to note that her dual reading is not suggesting (as others have) that all women's fiction is autobiographical. Rather, what she proposes is "an intratextual practice of interpretation which . . . would privilege neither the autobiography nor the fiction, but take the two writings together in their status as text."[3] Miller concludes the chapter with her usual panache by declaring: "The historical truth of a woman writer's life lies in the reader's grasp of her intratext: the body of her writing and not the writing of her body."[4]

But what if the body of her writing is the writing of her body? What if the female signature that we are trying to decipher is a movement signature? What if its "author" is a dancer? At the risk of distorting Miller's comments by switching their context from writing to dancing—from the literary muse to the moving one—I want to explore some ways in which autobiography is staged in dance, not so much to focus on the nature of identity per se, as to examine the complex ways in which dancing can at once set up and upset the various frames of the self. How does the presence of a live body create a representation of identity that differs from literary autobiography? How closely intertwined with its own physical reality is the "self" of dance?

While feminist critics concerned with the representation of women in film, art, and popular culture have dubbed the eighties the decade of the body, those working in literary theory tend to see these years as framing various debates over the nature of identity and the social construction of gendered writers and gendered readers.[5] So far, few feminist scholars have tried to connect the two realms in order to address issues of identity by looking at the representation of the performing body within the context of gender and race. In this essay, I intend to use the frame of autobiography in dance as my own intratext—of writing and dancing—in order to explore the complex issues involved in representing a self through the dancing body. Beginning with a rereading of Isadora Duncan's *My Life* in terms of her actual dancing, I will discuss the ways in which feminist approaches to autobiography have shifted their focus from seeking to identify (or constitute) a "self" in the name of "woman," to questioning the very possibility of a unified writing subject. Turning to contemporary dance and focusing on three works choreographed by Blondell Cummings, I will then ask what it might mean to represent these conflicting positions within a live performance.

The emphasis on fluid and constant motion in many contemporary forms of dance (such as contact improvisation) suggests an intriguing analogy to recent explorations of the autobiographical self. Duncan's autobiography is framed by a rhetorical stance which asks how she is to find the "truth" of her "self" among all the different people she has been. This ambiguity of identity can be seen as reflecting the radical nature of an art form whose very medium insists on changes in location, on moving through spaces. Nonetheless, the physical presence of a dancer's body refuses any loose assumptions about the playful postmodern multiplicity of dancing, by relentlessly insisting on the cultural moorings—the social implications of gendered, racial and historical ties—which that live body can never escape. The existential questioning with which Duncan, a white, middle-class bohemian artist from the early twentieth century, interrupts her conventional autobiographical voice holds very different meanings in a solo dance by Cummings, a black, middle-class, contemporary choreographer. By looking at issues of identity and representation within a discussion of the body in dance, I hope to keep these differences in mind by focusing on how they are played out on the stage.

Referring to a moment in the beginning of her choreographic career, when her family had just arrived in Paris, Duncan writes:

> I spent long days and nights in the studio seeking that dance which might be the divine expression of the human spirit through the medium of the body's movement. For hours I would stand quite still, my two hands folded between my breasts, covering the solar plexus. . . . I was seeking and finally discovered the central spring of all movement, the crater of motor power, the unity from which all diversities of movements are born, the mirror of vision for the creation of the dance.[6]

These sentences, which are woven into more explicitly autobiographical facts such as when Duncan went to school and the economic plight of her family after her mother's divorce, establish the mythopoetic voice which carries the narrative themes of *My Life.* Again and again, Duncan recites a litany of inspired performances in which her body becomes a medium for her soul, registering with Cixousian euphoria the swells of ecstasy—both her own and the audience's—which her performances create. Although Duncan calls her dance performances "representations," she never discusses them critically as a representation of the self and only rarely expresses any ambivalence about who she is in terms of her dancing. While her memoir comments on the changing selves of her life experience, her meditations on dance reveal her most fervent belief in a joyous, unified expression of the self through movement.

Sorting through Duncan's zealous expressions of her selfhood in *My Life*, Patricia Spacks analyzes Duncan's autobiography as a psychological portrait and looks for the psychic attributes of what she calls the "female imagination"—"the ways of female feeling, the modes of responding, that persist despite social change."[7] In *The Female Imagination*, Spacks interprets Duncan's autobiography as a narcissistic tale of the artist as a visionary, seeing it as emblematic of woman's need to resist societal constrictions by way of her creative imagination. "The woman as artist may help to illuminate the woman as woman."[8] Not attuned to the potency of Duncan's experience as a dancer, Spacks reads *My Life* only for a coherent portrait of the artist as a visionary and the visionary as a woman. "The woman's most potent fear is likely to be of abandonment, her most positive vision, of love. . . . She dreams of herself as beautiful, therefore beloved; as powerful because beloved."[9] Spacks insists that Duncan's construction of the monumental self in *My Life* is adolescent, and she searches Duncan's "tawdry prose" for the discrepancies between Duncan's vision of her dancing and the "facts" of her loves and woes in a way which subsumes Duncan's connections with dance in her own analysis of a "female imagination." Spacks continues: "The disproportion between the way she sees and the way she reveals herself creates much of the interest of her autobiography, testimony to a mind that refuses to accept the domination of external circumstance. Her vision more compelling than any conceivable reality, she declares her ultimate power to deny facts, transforming them into myth."[10] In giving us a portrait of Duncan as an obsessive artist, Spacks skims over the cracks in Duncan's writing, reinforcing a vision of the artist as a creative genius working outside of society and never probing the social constructions underneath that facade.

Taking my cue from Miller's intratext, the "double reading—of the autobiography with the fiction," I propose to read *My Life* in conjunction with what we know of her actual dancing; not in order to validate her mythopoetic voice by citing reviewers' praises of her dancing persona, but rather to point to the possibility of a different kind of attentiveness in reading autobiography. In addition to the obvious translations from a literary context to a performance one, the differences between Spacks's and my readings of Duncan's autobiography illustrate a shifting approach to issues of identity in feminist studies. Published in 1975, Spacks's *The Female Imagination* came from a women's studies tradition which sought to analyze women's writing for the uniquely "female" perspective created by the marginalization of women in Western society. Even while she is remarking on the tensions between Duncan's desire and the socially defined possibilities for women at the time, Spacks is interested, finally, in locating a specific female subjectivity. I am less interested in defining the characteristics of a female signature per se, than in exploring the intratextual autographs of writing and dancing: in other words, I want to look at the ways in which the performing body physicalizes the autobiographical voice to produce a representation of subjectivity which is at once whole and fragmented.

Unfortunately, there are no known films which could help dance scholars re-create Duncan's dancing. Most reconstructions of her solos are based on the memories of her six adopted "daughters," especially Irma, Anna, and Theresa.[11] Nevertheless, the wealth of photographs, drawings, paintings, and written descriptions by her contemporaries bear witness to Duncan's extraordinary performing presence and give us possible clues as to what her dancing was like. Take, for instance, a remarkable description of the first time he saw Duncan dancing by Gordon Craig, son of the famed British actress Ellen Terry and one of Duncan's lovers:

> Quite still. . . . Then one step back or sideways, and the music began again as she went moving on before or after it. Only just moving—not pirouetting or doing any of those things which we expect to see, and which a Taglioni or a Fanny Elssler would have certainly done. She was speaking in her own language—do you understand? her own language: have you got it?—not echoing any ballet master, and so she came to move as no one had ever seen anyone move before.[12]

Craig's written evocation connects with Duncan's own passages in *My Life* to represent the writer as dancer and the dancer as writer. The language of Duncan's dancing, which Craig describes as "her own language," parallels Duncan's description of waiting for the movement to start in her solar plexus, that "crater of motor power." It is also important to note that Craig fuses dancing and writing in order to give Duncan a certain authority over her own text.

Duncan's mythologizing of her experience in *My Life* can be heavy-handed at times: "I was possessed by the dream of Promethean creation that, at my call, might spring from the Earth, descend from the Heavens, such dancing figures as the world had never seen."[13] However, one can learn to read beyond the tone of her writing and into her dancing. Spacks describes Duncan's allusions to Prometheus in the passage quoted above as "conventional romantic rhetoric," paradoxically placing Duncan in the very phallocentric category of the artist as tragic hero.[14] When read next to a well-known photograph by Edward Steichen of Duncan standing in the Parthenon, however, her reference to "Promethean creation" not only suggests an invocation to Zeus—at once a challenge and an appeal to "see me," but also makes me aware of the physical implications of that invocation; the lines of movement streaming through Duncan's body, her outreached arms calling energy from the skies, and her legs receiving a grounded support from the earth. Even the passage in which Duncan describes how she stood in the studio waiting for inspiration affords the reader who looks beneath its mythic veneer an insight to the importance of breath and central chest initiation of her movements. It was Duncan's strength of vision which gave her the physical and moral fortitude to actually go out there on stage and dance. Acknowledging the importance of her dancing self enables the reader of *My Life* to look for another story—a movement story—threaded among the pages of her autobiography.

Giving little weight to Duncan's extraordinary achievement in radicalizing the theatrical dancing of her time, Spacks simply condemns Duncan for recording so convincingly her illusions about her art: "As an autobiographer, Isadora Duncan is dreamer rather than observer of her life: not an artist despite all her assertions of artistry."[15] Read within the context of her dancing, however, Duncan's autobiography reveals the very real tensions between her need to justify her work to a society which she feels has misunderstood her art and her desire to share the experience of creative momentum which sponsored her dancing. To efface that dancing body from her writing is to negate a powerful force in the creation and representation of Duncan's life.

Doubly circumscribed by the theatrical frame of her dancing experience and the literary frame of her writing, Duncan's autobiography is riddled with intriguing gaps produced by her shifts in identity. Inspired by the memory of a successful performance, Duncan proclaims the universality of her mission and refers to her work as Art and herself as an Artist in order to highlight the aesthetic and spiritual aspects of an art form based on the display of bodies, which had strong connotations of entertainment and still carried traces of an earlier association with prostitution and loose morals. The fact that she rarely calls herself a dancer—though she writes of the Dance—points to Duncan's acumen with regard to the cultural milieu in which she performed as well as her attentiveness to the subtle precariousness of a publicly defined identity for women. At times, this strident sense of individualism carries her along for pages, bolstering her confidence in her mission. Other times, however, Duncan disrupts the self-congratulatory tone of her writing by directly confronting her readers with a speech aimed at defending her unorthodox lifestyle in the name of art. Her usual exalted, self-assured pace is broken up by periodic moments of introspection when Duncan is likely to ask, "Where can I find the woman of all these adventures? It seems to me there was not one but hundreds."[16] Discussing the difficulty of translating the memory of one's life experience into a literary medium and the impossibility of completely escaping the influence of others' perceptions of who you are, Duncan allows her readers to see the gaps in her identity, these black holes of absence in the otherwise smooth narrative of her extraordinary presence. Writing her life story is difficult for Duncan; for it is on the autobiographical stage, more so than on the dancing one, that her various identities—like so many illustrious ghosts—emerge to confront and question one another. The act of writing places a shadow over her dancing: "Words have different meaning. Before the public which has thronged my representations I have had no hesitation. I have given them the most secret impulses of my soul. From the first I have only danced my life."[17]

Duncan feels more in control of her self-representation when she is dancing than when she is writing. Her supreme confidence about the authenticity of the former contrasts dramatically with her ambivalence about the latter. Duncan's preferred means of self-expression is clearly the language of dance. In *My Life*, Duncan tries to find words which can translate her elated experiences of dancing to her readers. What she finds, however, is that in spite of a dramatic, mythopoetic voice, the project of writing one's life exposes the fragility not only of the writing self, but also of the dancing self. As readers, we can negotiate this rocky languagescape by redirecting our goal of looking for a coherent self in the autobiographical signature, into a more open, double reading which might examine how writing and dancing combine to create different, interwoven signatures.

In his essay "Self-Invention in Autobiography: The Moment of Language" Paul Eakins coins a phrase that is particularly resonant in the present context.[18] Discussing the realization of selfhood through language, Eakins refers to this process as "the performance of the autobiographical act." Eakins's use of a theatrical metaphor in discussing this "art of self-invention" is echoed in much of the recent spate of feminist scholarship on autobiography. In this new body of literary work, autobiography is treated less as a truthful revelation of the singular inner and private self than as a dramatic staging—a representation—of the public self. What this performance paradigm emphasizes is the acutely self-conscious public display inherent in the act of penning one's life, especially for women, who must deal with a double jeopardy: they are both on display and often never really feel in control of the terms of that representation. Even though current theory is less interested in reading autobiography as a mirror of women's experiences, we can still ask: What does it mean for women to write the stories of their lives?

The blossoming of women's autobiographies in the twentieth century has been celebrated by feminist scholars as an awakening, a speaking of life stories that have historically been silenced. Collections of critical essays such as Jelinek's *Women's Autobiography*, Mason and Green's *Journeys: Autobiographical Writings by Women*, Benstock's *The Private Self: Theory and Practice of Women's Autobiographical Writings*, Stanton's *The Female Autograph*, and Smith's *A Poetics of Women's Autobiography* all comment on the growing feeling of emancipation from the scripts (mostly by men) that have traditionally written women's lives. More than a factual document or realistic description of their lives, women's autobiographies often create a selfhood by virtue of that very process (performance?) of writing. The struggle to mediate between private ambitions and public conditions may fragment a woman's sense of her self, but if these layered bits of experience do not add up to the traditional depiction of one grand unified identity, they nonetheless reveal a productive authority—a writing self. In much of the feminist scholarship on autobiography, "voice" is seen as a metaphor for the act of inscribing one's self in the world. "To find her own voice" implies a great deal more than expressing a thought or opinion; it also carries a healthy blend of satisfaction and bravado. The whole world is a stage, the autobiographical self may be a representation, but it is her voice. In the coda at the end of her book, Sidonie Smith speaks of the contemporary woman autobiographer: "Fashioning her own voice within and against the voices of others, she performs a selective appropriation of stories told by and about men and women. Subversively, she rearranges the dominant discourse and the dominant ideology of gender, seizing the language and its powers to turn cultural fictions into her *very own story* [emphasis added]."[19]

It is, of course, important to celebrate women's finding their voices—as much of women's literary criticism so joyfully does. However, with the influence of poststructuralist thought on feminist theory and the internal debates concerning whether "woman" is not, in fact, completely a social construction, feminists have begun to question what it means to call something our "own." While the written signature is conventionally associated with authorship, performances are less clearly signed because they are based on an indeterminate dialogue between performer and audience. Dance performances are extreme examples of a fluidity of authorship, since it is virtually impossible for a choreographer to transpose exactly her or his movement onto another body. This past decade has witnessed an increase in autobiography included within the context of dance. The various connections between the writing self and the dancing one—the movement and the text—can range in these performances from a loose juxtaposition of sound and gesture (as in the solo work of Ishmael Houston-Jones and Simone Forti) to a carefully orchestrated tableau which meshes these verbal and physical elements to produce an intricate web of movement and meaning (as in the recent group work by the Bill T. Jones and Arnie Zane dance company). Translating reader-response theory into the performance context, one could say that not only is each dance "read" and interpreted by the audience members, it is constantly "read" and reinterpreted by the person performing those movements. In many ways, then, the presence of the performing body can challenge and stretch even the most recent explorations of the autobiographical self. Although the act of performing itself (or one's self) foregrounds the fact that the self is always performed, this constructed performative self is also always reinvented by a physical body which cannot be so easily or neatly fragmented. In the very act of performing, the dancing body splits itself to enact its own representation and simultaneously heals its own fissure in that enactment.

Reading *My Life* next to Duncan's dancing provides us with an intratext—of the body and the writing—which can refocus our thinking about the autobiographical self. By inserting the dancing body into a study of autobiography, I do not mean to reduce women (once again) to being *only* their bodies. I am aware that phrases such as "speaking through the body," which can be envisioned as a means of authorizing the "self" in dance, can also connote social inscriptions which reflect the powerlessness of hysteria and summon up historical moments when women did not have the option to use their voices assertively—when their only option was to "speak through the body." But I think it is important not to shy away from a theoretical engagement with the female body and its representations in dance just because they comprise a network of layered contradictions and cross-referenced significations.

One of the earliest published accounts of Blondell Cummings's choreography appeared in the 14 March 1971, *New York Times.* Anna Kisselgoff, the *Times* dance critic, was reviewing an afternoon showcase of young choreographers which took place at the New School in New York City.

> Particular promise was shown in "Point of Reference" by Blondell Cummings who composed a touching encounter between herself, a twenty-two year old black girl born in South Carolina, and Anya Allister, also twenty-two, a Jewish girl born in Russia. Each girl recited her biographical information on tape. The honesty of the movement matched the direct statement about minority background.[20]

While Cummings's publicity statements mark 1978 as the year she began to choreograph regularly, it is telling how many of the elements that Kisselgoff mentions in this early dance are still motivating concerns in Cummings's dance-making almost two decades later. The theatrical correspondence between the dancers, their movements, and taped biographical stories, the "honesty" of the emotionally vivid gestural movements, and the juxtaposition of different cultural and racial backgrounds have informed Cummings's work throughout her choreographic career.

Cummings spent most of the seventies working with Meredith Monk / The House, a performance ensemble which blended music, movement, and text to present imagistic theater rituals. While she was developing one of the company's seminal pieces, "Education of the Girlchild," Monk asked the various performers to create a stage persona that embodied an important aspect of their own identities. In an interview with Marianne Goldberg, Cummings describes the process of shaping her particular character: "I tried to find a way of representing an archetypal figure that I would understand from a deep, personal, subconscious point of view that at the same time would be strong enough to overlap several Black cultures."[21] Cummings's character in "Education of the Girlchild" is autobiographical in that it was developed directly from Cummings's personal experience of African American cultures. These memories and sensations were then distilled into repetitious movements (as in her continuous swaying during the traveling section) or large, emotional gestures (such as her silent compulsive scream). They are meant to strike the viewer as archetypal, somehow so basic that they could be a part of everyone's experience. This movement from memory to gesture, from a specific life experience to a formal movement image, underlies much of Monk's work with The House and is also the central source in Cummings's own work. As Linda Small predicted in a 1980 article on the then emerging choreographer, Cummings was to "become recognized for her ability to recycle experience into art."[22]

This comment by Small pivots on an assumption about autobiography which I feel is valuable to take up here. When she coins the phrase "recycle experience into art," Small suggests that Cummings is taking the raw material of a life experience and representing it through formal "artistic" means. But as I have already noted, Eakins's use of the trope of performance to discuss autobiography reflects just how layered with representation the self already is. Even in the "raw" experience of life, the "self" is performed; autobiographical performances are often complex ways of consciously taking responsibility for the terms of that experience. Yet it is critical to realize that within the context of a dance performance these different levels of representation are contained within one physical, racial, and gendered body.

In 1978 Cummings began a collaboration with writer Madeleine Keller that exploded into the multidimensional performance piece called "Cycle." She was working as an arts administrator with the now defunct CETA program and her organizational abilities were funneled into this mammoth artistic project which included group workshops and taped interviews, visual and literary contributions from a widely diverse cross-section of people, as well as a solo performance by Cummings and a video document. The interconnecting theme was individuals' reactions to women's menstrual cycles. The name *Cycle* refers not only to the menstrual cycle but also to the way in which ideas and images are re-cycled throughout the piece. Cummings recalls that the genesis of the whole project took place in the back seat of a car while she was on tour with Meredith Monk / The House. Curled up in agony because of her menstrual cramps, she declared that some day she would make a performance piece based on this experience. The momentum of the project peaked in August 1978 when Cummings performed her solo at the Warren Street Performance Loft, New York City.

Cycle proved to be a catalyst in Cummings's choreographic career not only because it lent inspiration and a name to Cycle Arts Foundation, the multifaceted arts organization that supports her choreographic projects and collaborations, but also because it affirmed her artistic process. Taking a subject that she was intimately connected to, Cummings created a variety of forums in which to collect other people's reactions to this same issue. In an interview,

Cummings spoke about her desire to appeal to multiple cultures, to transform her personal interest into an experience that many people could relate to. "Cycle" was an appropriate vehicle for this work. For Cummings a topic such as menstrual cycles could potentially involve women from practically every class and cultural experience. It also affects women in an age range of about forty years, and most women can talk about it with the confidence and authority of being an expert in the matter. Finally—significantly—this piece even allowed her mother to interact with Cummings's artistic projects, a realm of her daughter's life with which she rarely had much active interaction.

Cummings is interested in finding a way to universalize or, at least, extend her particular concerns in order to allow many people to identify and engage personally with her work. For instance, *Cycle* was not meant to speak just to women. Cummings believes that men, by way of their family or friendly connections to women, are implicated in this topic of menstrual cycles as well. Cummings does not want to essentialize or separate women from men. In this sense, her desire to expand a personal issue into an umbrella which could cover many people's experience suggests that she feels that the personal is not only political, but also can create cross-cultural affinities.

Although her work is not always explicitly autobiographical, Cummings's solo choreography repeatedly presents the audience with links between the character she is portraying and her own self. As one reviewer explains: "[She] conjures up both a personal history and an entire culture."[23] Unlike the genre of art/life performances which seek to blur the distinctions between representation and "real" life, Cummings uses performance as a formal means to explore more general cultural and psychological influences (friendships, relationships, working, money) that shape her life. Yet specific movement material often reappears in subsequent solos. These repetitive gestures combine with an underlying narrative thread (often augmented by bits of personal stories and anecdotes by a woman's voice on the soundtrack) to create a woven fabric of dancing and autobiography. Cummings herself articulates the way these characters evolve from her life experience:

> My characters might seem like they're coming out of the blue, but they take a long time to develop. . . . I've done a lot of traveling alone, which has made me a real observer, real interested in detail, and in basic but universal things—food and eating styles, friendship, the menstrual cycle. Sure my pieces come from being a woman, black and American, but they're mostly concerned with the human condition.[24]

Despite that fact that Cummings tries to abstract personal material into portraits that have a wider connection to her audience, she has a vivid and

1. Blondell Cummings in *Chicken Soup*.
Photo: Kei Orihara. Courtesy of Cycle Arts Foundation.

quirky movement style which leaves little doubt that she is performing her own story. Cummings's performing presence is intensified by her quick hand gestures and split-second changes of facial expression which contrast dramatically with her slower, more fluid shifts of weight. While she wants to affect audience members with a broad range of life experiences, Cummings does not dissolve into a nondifferentiated character in an attempt to be everything for anybody. Her dancing rarely uses the abstract and formalized positions and movement styles of more traditional dance techniques. Often the audience assumes that her portraits are dramatic extensions of the various facets of her life. This autobiographical association in her work is accentuated by the fact that when she is onstage, she is often dancing alone. Although she has choreographed for her own company and the Alvin Ailey Repertory Ensemble, among others, Cummings rarely appears in these group pieces. When she is dancing, there is often the sense that she inhabits a private space, moving around and through her world with the intuitive frankness of a woman alone in her apartment. Cummings speaks of her solo work with a hint of existential resolve:

> I feel strongly about solo work, because I think that basically we are soloists. And yes, we couple with other people, we socialize with other people; but you're born alone and you go through certain periods of your life that change and the only thing that is consistent is you—yourself. When you die, you die alone. I feel that when one is being solo, it allows the solo sorts of self to be able to identify with that person and hear that inner voice.[25]

Significantly, though, it is the images, voices, gestures, and memories of other people that filter throughout one of Cummings's most popular solos, *Chicken Soup* (1981–83). Danced independently or as the first section in the evening-length collection of solos called *Food for Thought*, *Chicken Soup* (figure 1) presents Cummings as a woman whose life revolves around the community and loneliness of the household kitchen. The first image is the back of a woman dressed in a long white skirt and white shirt, swaying from side to side with her shopping bag in hand, just as if she were walking down a country lane on her way to market. This image dissolves into another picture of a woman seated primly on the edge of a chair. As a nostalgic, wistful melody plays, her face and hands become animated with a variety of gossipy—"Oh, you don't mean it!"—expressions. During this silent, cheerful chatter, Cummings begins to rock in a movement so old-fashioned and yet so hypnotically soothing that it is hard to imagine that she will ever stop. As Cummings banters away with herself, a woman's voice reminisces in a calm, thoughtful manner. Phrases such as "the kitchen was the same" melt into the tableau of the woman rocking in the chair. The constant repetition of rocking makes time seem somehow irrelevant. Soon, however, the pleasant conversation turns to one of grief and pain, and Cummings's body encompasses the change with full central contradictions. The quick, flickering hand gestures which traced years and years of passing out cards at a bridge table and cups of tea get caught for a moment in a posture of pain or anger and then release back into the repetitious flow of rocking and talking. Joining the music on the soundtrack, a woman's voice haltingly describes afternoons spent around the kitchen table talking of "childhood friends, operations, abortion, death, and money." It seems as if the scene we are watching is her memory. Participating in the merged memory of voice and body, Cummings's character is selectively responsive to these words, periodically breaking into a stop-action series of emotional gestures which mime the spoken words and which have become a trademark of her work.

"Moving Pictures" is the phrase Cummings uses to describe her uncanny ability to segment movement into a series of fast stop-action bits that give the impression of movements seen under a strobe light or of a film strip seen frame by frame. Cummings explains their genesis by telling a story about her childhood fascination with photography and the excitement of getting her first camera. This movement technique is the result of grafting photographic images onto the kinetic energy of dance. By freezing her movement in an evenly rhythmic succession, she gives the effect of being in a strobe light, without the flickering darkness. In this choreographic process, Cummings forces the viewer to take a mental picture, so to speak. The zest and physical intensity of Cummings's living body coupled with the timeless quality of photography, its overwhelmingly memorable specificity of character, creates a fascinating conflict between stillness and movement—death and life. Reviewing an early concert of Cummings's work, Burt Supree, a dance critic for the *Village Voice*, writes of her "silent wildness." "She's most astonishing, though, in a section where she moves as if caught in the flicker of a fast strobe, no sounds coming from her gaping mouth, sliding from worry to fear to screaming terror, blending into laughter which merges again into wailing."[26] Cummings describes her unique movement images as "an accumulation of one's life" and speaks of how they are pregnant with memory for her. Interestingly enough, she also discusses these "moving pictures" as autobiographical, not because they have become a signature style of moving which can be found in almost every solo she has choreographed, but because they are a way of picturing herself with an outside eye. At once the photographer and the image, she creates an unusual mode of self-reflexivity in dance.

While Isadora Duncan actually needed to write her autobiography in order to see herself with an outside eye and only realized in retrospect that "from the first I have only danced my life," Cummings has found a method of including this process of self-reflection into the dancing itself. The exalted and unified dancing self that is so emblematic of the autobiographical voice in *My Life* has been transformed by time, culture, and aesthetics into a fractured combination of image, gesture, and movement in Cummings's dancing. How are we to find a single "self" amid all these split-second portraits of women crying, rocking, laughing, and talking?

Chicken Soup continues. Stepping away from the picture gallery of women that she animates in the rocking chair, Cummings sinks to the floor and picks up a scrub brush. Her body bobs with the rhythm of her work and the action of the bristles across the floor creates a swish swish accompaniment. The audience sees her in profile, her body stretching and contracting with the strong, even strokes of her arms. The broad sweeps of her movement are more important than the task of cleaning the floor. Although the image could be one of contracted menial labor, there is a caring, authoritative quality in Cummings's motion that suggests that this work is immensely satisfying. Cummings notes: "There is poetry to scrubbing the floor. Scrubbing the floor is scrubbing the floor, but the way you scrub it can reflect your own physicality, your own background, your culture."[27]

The direct, spare physicality and its affirmation of life in work diffuses when Cummings trades her brush for a long black scarf. As a nostalgic hummed melody floats into the scene, Cummings swirls the scarf in the air and crosses the stage with joyous, exalted skips and leaps. This moment of whirling happiness fades into a sad sweep of the scarf as Cummings walks to the back of the stage and waves "good-bye." Loss and mourning crush the previous gaiety. Her heavy, tired body is dwarfed by a huge shadow of herself projected on the background. The figure, swelled by grief, looms behind Cummings. Then, the emotional tides change once again as a chicken soup recipe is recited and Cummings picks up a cast-iron frying pan with all the assurance and sassiness of a woman who could cook in her sleep. Like a simmering soup, there is a constant rhythm and bubble in her body. Chopping, mixing, and frying actions are literally embodied by full motions that spread through her body and down into her feet as well. With cooking coursing through her body, Cummings comments on the images she has made by a series of wonderfully comic facial expressions. Innuendo wafts, like the imagined aroma of her cooking, in and around this figure, and when the recipe directs her to "simmer until tender," Cummings ironically, and with a knowing smile directed to the audience, shimmies her hips.

Chicken Soup is generally referred to as, in the words of one critic, "a fond memory of black rural life."[28] Considering Cummings's very urban experience, one might wonder whose memory this is and where it comes from. Memory, of course, is most peculiar. What parts are "remembered" and which ones are invented is quite a difficult thing to discern, particularly when the "memory" serves as a basis for a work of art. In an article called "The Site of Memory," Toni Morrison discusses how memory influences her writing, merging fiction with autobiography. She describes how she fills an "image" of her relatives with a "memory" of them. "These people are my access to me; they are my entrance into my own interior life. Which is why the images that float around them—the remains, so to speak, at the archeological site—surface first, and they surface so vividly and so compellingly that I acknowledge them as my route to a reconstruction of a world, to an exploration of an interior life that was not written and to the revelation of a kind of truth."[29] I think that memory serves a similar purpose for Cummings in *Chicken Soup* by allowing her to connect to women in her history and to participate in their worlds. Seeing her gossip in a chair or shake a skillet, I feel as if this is the first time as well as the hundredth time Cummings has gone back inside these images to merge past and present, dancing bits of stories from all these women's lives.

When Cummings introduced *Chicken Soup* during an informal lecture-demonstration at Franklin and Marshall College in the fall of 1987, she spoke of her interest in food and how she could guess someone's characteristics just by looking in their refrigerator. Cummings described *Chicken Soup* as a solo about women—many different women—who use food to nourish and connect to other people. Her intention was to make a dance that spanned a variety of cultures—Jewish, African American, Italian—and that desire is reflected in her choice of texts, which include pieces by Grace Paley as well as a recipe from *The Settlement Cookbook*. Despite this multicultural tapestry in the text, the dance is generally received as being specifically about black women. In fact, when Cummings presented the work on television in the "Alive from Off Center" program during the summer of 1988, the cover of the *New York Times* "Television" section announced her work as a vision of "traditional roles of black women in America."[30] A curiously intrusive interference by the television producer had Cummings performing the dance in a generic formica kitchen, wearing a housedress and a flowered apron. The effect, especially to someone who had seen the solo in a theater space, with no set and white costuming, is quite bizarre. The tacky television realism stages a very narrow definition of "traditional roles of black women in America," removing the wonderful ambivalence of Cummings's earlier version of this dance. Unlike the stage portrayal of this solo where it is unclear whose memories she is dancing, the television production reduces this woman to a generic two-dimensional figure who is trapped in the specific context of her own spic 'n span kitchen.

The publicity for this video underlined how many reviewers discussed *Chicken Soup* as exploring a specifically black heritage. This insistence on viewing the dance only within one cultural tradition, the one referenced by her race, disturbs Cummings. In an interview, she spoke of wanting to sound a resonant note in everyone's background—to create a common memory.

> What happens for me is that it [the sense of familiarity] stops when you start saying that you see me as a black person in the chair because then it might stop your ability to have it go back into your own background. Because if you see it as black and you're not black, then it seems to me you will not allow yourself the same liberty to identify with that character and then you start bringing all the references to a black person and why that makes that black.[31]

The issues of identification which Cummings touches on in this statement are rife with complexity. Self versus other, difference versus sameness, individuality versus community are indicative of polarities deeply rooted in this culture's social, political, and religious epistemologies. The last few decades in America have witnessed celebrations of sameness in the political industry and difference in those strangely allied realms of intellectual theory and fashion. Most feminists have begun to negotiate between the need for recognizing crucial racial, class, and cultural differences among women and the persistent feeling that women share some sort of affinity, if only in their common awareness of the practical risks of being a woman in today's society. Cummings is caught in this sticky web of identifications, for although she claims she wants to create a "universal" image of a woman that anyone could relate to, she has also described with tears in her eyes the moving and self-affirming experience of dancing *Chicken Soup* for a predominantly black audience in the "Black Dance America" series at the Brooklyn Academy of Music. "It was wonderful. . . . And I thought to myself, so this is what it is all about!"[32]

Doubly inscribed (by the culture) as black and as a woman, Cummings must confront these multiple identities as she places her self-representation on the public stage. It would be as simplistic to assume that elementary addition—black plus woman equals black woman—delivers a specific and singular identity as it would be to assume that Cummings can figuratively erase the signs of these social categories in her dancing.

In her essay "Women's Autobiographical Selves: Theory and Practice," Susan Friedman critiques certain theoretical models of autobiography which are predicated on a singular self. "The individual concept of the autobiographical self. . . . raises serious theoretical problems for critics who recognize that the self, self-creation, and self-consciousness are profoundly different for women, minorities, and many non-Western peoples."[33] Because they are isolated and alienated from the powerful sense of "self" in a white patriarchal society, women and minorities, Friedman asserts, need to approach autobiography as a way of building another kind of identity from the raw materials of "interdependence" and "community." This sense of defining a selfhood in relationship to others is a concept which is strikingly absent from the earlier visions of the autobiographical self. Friedman cites a variety of sources, from Nancy Chodorow on developmental identity to Regina Blackburn on African American women's autobiography, which attest to and explain the "collective consciousness" of a "merged" identity of "the shared and the unique."[34] Although the consciousness discussed here originally arises negatively from a sense of marginalization or a feeling of oppression, it acquires power by connecting the individual to a group identity. It is important to realize, though, that this groupness is not a sameness. While every essay I read on African American women's autobiography mentioned the profound connection between individual identity and a sense of blackness, each autobiographer relates to her community differently. Zora Neale Hurston ironically illuminates this interconnection of "the shared and the unique" in a comment from her autobiographical writing *Dust Tracks on a Road.*

> I maintain that I have been a Negro three times—a Negro baby, a Negro girl and a Negro woman. Still, if you have received no clear-cut impression of what the Negro in America is like, then you are in the same place with me. There is no *The Negro* here. Our lives are so diversified, internal attitudes so varied, appearances and capabilities so different, that there is no possible classification so catholic that it will cover us all except My people! My people![35]

Cummings's relationship to the performance of her African American identity shifts in terms of the context of her performing. In other words, when there is a positive connection to be made, as in the Black Dance America program, when the condition of being black is expansive and not limiting, Cummings embraces that identification. Within an evening-length dance program which is focused on the many varieties of dance forms coming out of the African American heritage, Cummings's solo could be seen as encompassing one aspect of that multidimensional experience. In that context her work will not be interpreted generally as speaking about black culture as it so often is in other situations. But when she is touring or guest teaching at academic institutions around the country and the audience is predominantly white, Cummings seeks to transcend the specificity of her blackness. What Cummings does not allow for and what I feel is essential to postulate (at the very least), is the ability of a predominantly white audience to recognize a familiarity with these rocking, grieving, simmering portraits by a black woman. Of course, I am not suggesting that this audience could inspire the same communal feelings that Cummings experienced at the Black Dance America program. But I do insist that it is categorically different (not to mention politically disastrous) to suppose that the only way a white audience member can relate to a black performer is by figuratively covering over the fact of her race.

Cummings is a woman and she is black, but her dances can frame that identity very differently. *Basic Strategies V* (1986) is the last section of a cycle of dances called "Basic Strategies" which explores how people deal with work and money. *Basic Strategies I–III* were originally created for college dancers and *Basic Strategies IV* was commissioned by the Alvin Ailey Repertory Ensemble. Many of the movements in these earlier pieces are repetitive motions loosely based on a work activity. Mixed in with the music soundtrack are voices telling stories of a business success or describing an early memory. *Basic Strategies IV* is prefaced with a still tableau of arranged figures. Although they are all dressed in white, some characters are recognizable as a nun, a nurse, a farmer, a soldier, and a hospital attendant. The dancing begins as a clump of these figures in white shuffle across the stage chanting "For love or for money." Breaking off from the group, several dancers come to the center of the stage to mime a work activity as a voice on the soundtrack describes a memory of that figure. The realism of story and gesture in these early "Basic Strategies" is replaced in *Basic Strategies V* with a formal juxtaposition of the movements and their contexts.

Basic Strategies V begins with a group section and ends with a solo for Cummings. Although I want to concentrate on the complicated images in her solo, I will take some time to sketch in the first part of the dance, for it sets up many of the double readings within the dance. Originally commissioned by Williams College and the Massachusetts Council on the Art and Humanities, *Basic Strategies V* is a collaboration with the writer Jamaica Kincaid and composer Michael Riesman. In what Cummings terms her process of "collage," this work layers sets, costumes, music, taped texts, and movement to create multiple references of self and community. Unlike *Chicken Soup*, however, *Basic Strategies V* uses the texts, sets, costumes not as background accompaniment for the dancing, but rather as primary elements which create the basic irony and dramatic tension in this piece and make it so compelling to watch. The remarkable text by Kincaid, who was born in St. John's, Antigua, focuses the dancing in the first group section. The fluid and rhythmic carrying, pushing, pulling movements are juxtaposed to a story (spoken by a soft woman's voice) which braids a history of her people with a history of an Anglican colonial cathedral. The slaves built this cathedral for their masters, but now the descendants of both the slaves and their masters worship there. Noting the ambiguity of her history, the narrator's liquid voice on the sound tape loops back on itself repeatedly:

> My history before it was interrupted does not include cathedrals. What my history before it was interrupted includes is no longer absolutely clear to me. The cathedral is now a part of my history. The cathedral is now a part of me. The cathedral is now mine.[36]

It is never entirely clear how the story of the cathedral relates to the dancing on stage. This section, which is subtitled "Blues I," is cast in a cool blue light with a large luminous moon in the background. Dressed in nondescript dance clothes, Cummings's dancers seem much more abstracted than in the earlier versions of *Basic Strategies.* Moving back and forth across the stage while they stay low to the ground, squatting or walking, their movements seem to serve as a background texture for Kincaid's words. Toward the end, a recognizable character of an elder crosses the stage, gradually growing more and more hunched over with the passing of each small shuffling step.

During a brief interlude, Kincaid's second text begins. Although it is read by the same smooth voice, this one is much less personal and describes with encyclopedic detail the habitat, production, and reproduction of the silkworm. Coming after the storytelling intimacy of the first section, this new factual tone strikes an odd, almost dissonant chord. Read like an article from *National Geographic*, the information seems tame enough, if somewhat irrelevant. As the interlude finishes and Cummings's solo begins, however, the context changes and the spoken text transforms into a series of metacomments on the politics of colonial enterprise, cheap third-world labor, and the production of Western luxuries.

At the beginnings of her solo "Blues II," the lights fade up very slowly to reveal a statuesque Cummings, wearing a shimmering black evening gown and cape. Slowly raising and lowering a champagne bottle and fluted glass, she turns in a curiously disembodied and vague manner, as if she were a revolving decoration in the middle of the ballroom floor. Her impassive face and glittering dress are reflected in the large mirrors which fan out to either side of her. Functioning as a kind of "Huis Clos," these mirrors confine her movements, meeting each change of direction with multiple reflections of her body. Sometimes Cummings moves with proud, grandiose strides, covering the space with a confident territoriality. Other times, she seems possessed, pacing the floor in this prison of mirrors only to meet up with another reflection of the woman she wants—was—intended—to become.

On one level, these mirrors function as reflections of common cultural representations of women. Glamorous in the evening gown that connotes a romantic lifestyle and independent income, Cummings's many mirrored figures are visually more enticing than the body they reflect. In a way Cummings seduces the viewers through these images in order to disrupt our visual pleasure and, presumably, the economy which supports it. For instance, in the midst of a waltzy section where she is swirling around the stage, she abruptly drops to her knees and, drawing her skirt over her face, begs for money. This split-second transformation of her body from ease to despair and back again reminds the viewer of the fragility of that seductive world. This early fracture is quickly smoothed over by the romantic music and Cummings's lyrical dancing. But the crack in the illusion widens as slides are projected on a screen above her head. Alternating images of third-world famine refugees with Western signs of wealth and power (i.e., Ralph Lauren advertisements), these slides throw Cummings's whole persona into question. Is she attempting to buy into these white, patriarchal images? Is she happy? Or is this whole scenario a tragic pretense? At this point in the solo, Cummings launches into an energetic stream of repetitive actions that pull her back and forth across the stage. The lively rhythm of her feet and hand gestures soon borders on mania as the tranquillity of the earlier dancing gives way to a literal dis-ease with the costume. Eventually, she takes off the black dress and in the closing moments of the dancing she sits on a chair in her underwear, restlessly gesturing and pointing, in an effort to "speak" her tangled emotions.

Seen within the context of Kincaid's texts and the slides, the apparent glamour of Cummings's persona is undercut by the insistent issues of race, class, and gender. The pristine image of self-involvement—the private satisfaction initially projected by the mirrored glittering gown, champagne bottle, and solipsistic dancing—is clouded by the recognition that both idealistic (advertising) and realistic (photojournalism) images pervade the very fabric of our consciousness. Confronted at every turn with the cultural reflections of who she is, the woman in "Blues II" is fragmented into a series of confusing and conflicting images.

Once the gown and all that it represents has been taken off near the end of this solo, the persistent question of "Who am I?" seems to remain for the character. Although Cummings intended that this disrobing should suggest a symbolic stripping away of cultural masks to reveal basic human needs and emotions, there is little sense of resolution or closure. Amidst the bombardment of media images, the woman without the dress is still tragically searching for a single identity that fits. Restlessly turning her head or bent over with an extreme expression of pain, she tries on the very same gestures of hugging, talking, and rocking a baby which seemed so solidly soothing in *Chicken Soup.* Yet in this new context, these movements are not quite so comfortable and the woman onstage flits through a seemingly endless succession of gestural memories until finally the music stops and the lights fade out.

These two solos, *Chicken Soup* and "Blues II," enact a struggle also found in many contemporary women's autobiographies. In *Chicken Soup*, the body is represented as the condition of the self, the place from which memories arise. The still photographic images of the first tableau and the vague reminiscences of the voice provide a setting appropriate to an expression of a woman's community. Gestures of rocking a baby, cooking and eating, waving good-bye, and grieving are consciously portrayed with a belief in their universality—in the archetypal engagement of women in community. In this dance, the body is opened up very wide and presented as a well of remembering and knowing. In "Blues II," however, the dancing figure is less comfortable with her embodiment. Although some of the movements are similar to *Chicken Soup*, there is an increasingly restless quality in their motion which creates a sense that this female character would like to escape her own skin. Surrounded at every turn by reflections of her body which she is unable to control or escape and which insistently clash with one another, as well as the slides and the soundtrack, this woman seeks to disengage her body from these pervasive images by taking off her gown. Yet, black and female, her body has been "written" over in so many ways by these background images of black women in her culture that it is still difficult to find an "original" signature.

While both solos begin with distilled, almost photographic images of women that are recognizable as cultural icons (woman as nurturer and woman as beautiful object), Cummings's *Chicken Soup* solo presents a person who can effectively connect with her memory to create images of herself, for herself. This character is a movement storyteller; she speaks through her body. Scholars of African American literature often connect autobiography to a cultural experience of storytelling in the black community. Presented in the context of a dialogue with the community audience, "telling one's own story" is an empowering act which affirms a selfhood in connection with other people. In the section "Writing Autobiography" in her recent book *Talking Back: Thinking Feminist, Thinking Black*, bell hooks also locates her own autobiographical impulse in that tradition. "Within the world of my childhood, we held onto the legacy of a distinct black culture by listening to the elders tell their stories. Autobiography was experienced most actively in the art of telling one's story."[37]

This ability to tell one's own story is missing in "Blues II." The potency of this dance lies in the very fact that there does not seem to be any possibility of communication—any community to whom to tell this life story. The gowned woman in this dance is at once connected to and disconnected from the many narratives suggested by the visual images and Kincaid's texts. Because her body is a figurative screen for the contradictory meanings of these visual images and the powers who control their representation, it is impossible for her to find a useful identity or a comfortable way of moving. Physically dwarfed by the mirrors and the slides, the woman drifts through this melange of cultural representations like a ghost through a maze. The mirrors amplify her spatial (and psychological) disorientation, reflecting and fragmenting the visual definition of her self. As a result, her internal physical equilibrium is disrupted and she either floats aimlessly about the stage or rushes frantically from one reflected image to another in a bewildered attempt to find one that looks right. Whether she is physically inert or psychically distraught, the dancing seems to be compelled by a restless scarching for a visually and physically satisfying self. Even when she rejects the "lie" of the dress, even when she takes off the costume of "high" culture, there is no reassuring "natural" self underneath it all. The dance ends without closure, continuing its ambivalence about the intertwining issues of race, culture, and gender and identity.

Although critics often interpret *Chicken Soup* as a nostalgic portrait of the lost companionship of a women's community, and "Blues II" as a vision of the pressures and conflicts embedded in the identities of middle-class African American women, it would be reductive to imply that these characters are simply derived from Cummings's immediate experience. Like all autobiographical material, they are representations. As hooks points out, autobiography "is a very personal storytelling—a unique recounting of events not so much as they have happened, but as we remember and invent them. [My autobiography] seemed to fall in the category of writing that Audre Lorde in her autobiographically based work *Zami*, calls bio-mythography. As I wrote, I felt that I was not as concerned with accuracy of detail as I was with evoking in writing the state of mind, the spirit of a particular moment."[38]

If we cycle back to the beginning discussion of Isadora Duncan's autobiographical "intratext" (of the dancing and the writing), Lorde's term *bio-mythography* stands out as particularly intriguing. I like how it emphasizes the activity of writing one's body and the mythic dimensions inherent in performing this representation. As she stood still in front of her famous blue curtains,

Duncan must have appeared as a grand figure onstage; a being not unlike the mythic dancing self whom she describes in *My Life.* Yet her writing reveals the conflicts between her self-representation as an artist and her personal sense of herself as a woman *and* the prevalent cultural images and ideologies about women which circulated during her lifetime. Read together, these two autobiographical texts suggest the inevitable contradictions within a representation of any self, bio-mythological or not.

Seven decades and several cultural revolutions later, Blondell Cummings expresses this very tension as a central theme in her solo dance performances. The resulting portraits of women represent a struggling identity which can only be pieced together through the negotiation between the inner voices of memory, bodily experience, and public representation. Wresting the power of seduction and colonialization from the media images projected above her head, Cummings shows not only the cracks and flaws in these cellophane narratives but also the possibility of other stories emerging from their gaps. Her disrobed figure at the end of "Blues II" has refused the closure implicit in the commodified image of a glamorous woman complete with champagne bottle. She may not have yet found another ending; but, at the very least, she is looking forward to writing many more stories.

What happens, however, if we step away from the dance stage in order to place Cummings's work within the current discussion of cultural politics? How can we look at the layered identities danced out in "Blues II" in terms of a shared community? In her recent book *Yearning: Race, Gender, and Cultural Politics*, bell hooks articulates both her interest in and resistance to postmodern (and poststructuralist) theories of identity. While she acknowledges the Eurocentric and elitist origins of most postmodernist discourses, hooks sees these theories as useful alternatives to the traditional narratives of the self sponsored by black nationalism. "The critique of essentialism encouraged by postmodernist thought is useful for African-Americans concerned with reformulating outmoded notions of identity. We have too long had imposed upon us from both the outside and the inside a narrow, constricting notion of blackness. . . . Such a critique allows us to affirm multiple black identities, varied black experience."[39] Unlike the mirrored woman in "Blues II," who seems tragically alone among her disparate selves and therefore unable to connect fully to any community, hooks imagines the postmodern self being able to establish new sorts of collective identities. "Radical postmodernism calls attention to those shared sensibilities which cross the boundaries of class, gender, race, etc. that could be fertile ground for the construction of empathy—ties that would promote recognition of common commitments and serve as a base for solidarity and coalition."[40]

Given hooks's optimistic espousal of "Postmodern Blackness," it is ironic that her next essay in this collection, "The Chitlin Circuit: On Black Community," begins with a highly nostalgic portrayal of her southern, black, rural childhood. In a description that evokes a number of the images in Cummings's *Chicken Soup*, hooks writes: "It was a world of single older black women school teachers, dedicated, tough: they had taught your mama, her sisters, and her friends. They knew your people in ways that you never would and shared their insight, keeping us in touch with generations. It was a world where we had a history."[41] Once she has pictured her "beloved black community," however, hooks realizes the uncomfortable confinement implicit in any notion of one "authentic" black experience. Still longing (her term is *yearning*) for a sense of home much later in the book, hooks ends up redefining that space in a way that can accommodate her radical sense of identity. "Home is no longer just one place. It is locations. Home is that place which enables and promotes varied and everchanging perspectives, a place where one discovers new ways of seeing reality, frontiers of difference."[42] In this passage, hooks envisions home in such a way that it connects meaningfully to her sense of personal history and still opens up to possibilities beyond that experience.

This strategy of re-appropriation—sizing theory to fit a cultural experience or personal need—is echoed in an excerpt from Ralph Ellison's "The Little Man at the Chehaw Station," which Houston A. Baker cites as an epigraph to his book *Blues, Ideology, and Afro-American Literature: A Vernacular Theory*: "So perhaps we shy from confronting our cultural wholeness because it offers no easily recognizable points of rest, no facile certainties as to who, what or where (culturally or historically) we are. Instead, the whole is always in cacophonic motion."[43] In the introduction, Baker uses the image of blues music as a kind of "cacophonic motion" which illustrates at once the historic specificity of an African American heritage and the multiplicity of its subjects. "To suggest a trope for the blues as a forceful matrix in cultural understanding is to summon an image of the black blues singer at the railway junction lustily transforming experiences of a durative (unceasingly oppressive) landscape into the energies of rhythmic song. The railway juncture is marked by transience . . . and is simply a single instance in a boundless network that redoubles and circles, makes sidings and ladders, forms Y's and branches over the vastness of hundreds of thousands of American miles."[44]

Taking my cue from Baker's metaphorical understanding of African American identity in terms of the blues and the blues in terms of incessant motion, I want to suggest another way to look at the woman in Cummings's "Blues II." Some feminist scholars object to a representation of autobiography which situates identity as inherently fractured and multiple, insisting that this decentered subject loses any viable connection to a political community. Seeing instability only in view of its rather frightening psychic consequences, these scholars are nonetheless hard pressed to find a representation of the unified self which does not seem romantically nostalgic. But what if we switch tracks and look at instability as motion—as the beginning of a dance. While at the same time that the woman character in "Blues II" can be seen as drowning in the existential refractions of too many self images, there is a certain fluidity and ease of movement from one mirror to the next, an internal shifting of weight and context. If we think of "Blues II" in terms of Baker's use of the blues (another intratext), we can position Cummings's dance at the intersection of several cultures while still figuring its connection with an African American community. If the blues give us a rich image of incessant motion within a culturally specific identity, "Blues II" suggests its logical sequel—in dance.

Notes

1 Isadora Duncan, *My Life* (New York: Liveright, 1955), p. 323.
2 There is some speculation as to whether Isadora Duncan actually wrote her own autobiography or whether it was mostly written and edited by Duncan's close companion Mary Desti. For the purposes of this essay, the "authenticity" of this work is not of primary concern. Mostly, I am interested in the changes in tone from the self-assured mythopoetic voice to the questioning one. Even if Duncan did not actually write *My Life*, it has certainly become part of her history.
3 Nancy Miller, "Writing Fictions: Women's Autobiography in France," in *Subject to Change: Reading Feminist Writing* (New York: Columbia University Press, 1988), p. 60.
4 Ibid., p. 61.
5 See, for example, a special issue of *The Drama Review* on movement analysis, particularly Elizabeth Kagan and Margaret Morse on "The Body Electronic," pp. 164–80 (*Drama Review* 32, no. 4 [Winter 1988]).
6 *My Life*, p. 75.
7 Patricia Meyer Spacks, *The Female Imagination* (New York: Alfred A. Knopf, 1975), p. 3.
8 Ibid., p. 160.
9 Ibid.
10 Ibid., p. 163.
11 For more information about the historical sources on Duncan see Deborah Jowitt, *Time and the Dancing Image* (New York: William Morrow, 1988), pp. 69–102.
12 Quoted in Francis Steegmuller, *Your Isadora* (New York: Random House and the New York Public Library, 1974), p. 23.
13 *My Life*, p. 213.
14 Spacks, *The Female Imagination*, p. 161.
15 Ibid., p. 163.
16 *My Life*, p. 2.
17 Ibid., p. 3.
18 Paul Eakins, *Fictions in Autobiography: Studies in the Art of Self-Invention* (Princeton: Princeton University Press, 1985).

19 Sidonie Smith, *A Poetics of Women's Autobiography* (Bloomington: Indiana University Press, 1987), p. 175.

20 Anna Kisselgoff, "Music's Absence Marks Five Dances," *New York Times*, 14 March 1971.

21 Marianne Goldberg, "Transformative Aspects of Meredith Monk's 'Education of the Girlchild,'" *Women and Performance* 1, no. 1 (1983), p. 21.

22 Linda Small, "Best Feet Forward," *Village Voice*, 10 March 1980, p. 35.

23 Paula Sommers, "Blondell Cummings: Life Dances," *Washington Post*, 30 November 1984.

24 Quoted in ibid.

25 Interview with the author in New York City, 7 February 1989.

26 Burt Supree, "Worlds Apart," *Village Voice*, 17–23 December 1980, p. 109.

27 Quoted in Debra Cash, "Blondell Cummings: Melds Two Worlds of Dance," *Boston Globe*, January 1985.

28 Nancy Goldner, "Electric Cooking," *Saturday Review* 9 (May/June 1983), pp. 37–38.

29 Toni Morrison, "The Site of Memory," in *Inventing the Truth*, ed. William Zinsser (Boston: Houghton Mifflin, 1987), p. 115.

30 *New York Times*, 7 August 1988.

31 Interview with the author.

32 Interview in Michael Blackwood's film *Retracing Steps*, 1988.

33 Susan Friedman, "Women's Autobiographical Selves: Theory and Practice," in *The Private Self*, ed. Shari Benstock (Chapel Hill: University of North Carolina Press, 1988), p. 34.

34 Ibid., p. 40.

35 Quoted in Regina Blackburn, "In Search of the Black Female Self: Afro-American Women's Autobiographies and Ethnicity," in Jelinek, ed., *Women's Autobiography: Essays in Criticism* (Bloomington: Indiana University Press, 1980), p. 139.

36 Jamaica Kincaid, 1987. This text was commissioned especially for Cummings's dance.

37 bell hooks, *Talking Back: Thinking Feminist, Thinking Black* (Boston: South End Press, 1989), p. 158.

38 Ibid., pp. 157–58.

39 bell hooks, *Yearning: Race, Gender, and Cultural Politics* (Boston: South End Press, 1990), p. 28.

40 Ibid., p. 27.

41 Ibid., p. 33.

42 Ibid., p. 148.

43 Houston A. Baker Jr., *Blues, Ideology, and Afro-American Literature: A Vernacular Theory* (Chicago: University of Chicago Press, 1984), p. 1.

44 Ibid., p. 7.

11 DANCE NARRATIVES AND FANTASIES OF ACHIEVEMENT

Angela McRobbie

Dance and Culture

At first the child sat numbed, tense. Then chills began going up and down her spine. Her hands clenched. She could feel the nails piercing the flesh of her palms, but it didn't matter. Nothing mattered, only this—only loveliness mattered. . . . Yes, she would dance—and nothing would stop her, nothing, nothing in the world.—Gladys Malvern, *Dancing Star*

So what will be a girl's reactions? . . . She dances, thereby constructing for herself a vital subjective space. . . . The dance is also a way of creating for herself her own territory in relation to the mother.—Luce Irigaray, "The Gesture in Psychoanalysis," in *Between Feminism and Psychoanalysis*

It is surprising how negligent sociology and cultural studies have been of dance. As a leisure practice, as a performance art, and as a textual and representational form, dance continues to evade analysis on anything like the scale on which other expressive forms have been considered. And while dance theory and dance criticism are well-developed fields in their own right, they do not offer the kind of broader social and cultural analysis which is still so much needed. Dance history tends to be either empirical (and anecdotal) or else collapsed into the biographical details of great dancers. Some of this work is, of course, a useful resource for the sociologist of dance. It is here that we come across the many accounts of the impact of Isadora Duncan's techniques and the descriptions of the network of artists, painters, and dancers, mostly Russian exiles who came to live in Paris in the early years of the century. The immensely interesting biography of Nijinsky, written by his widow in 1933 (with a postscript in the 1958 edition), provides a fascinating glimpse of dance culture and its links with the other high arts in the early years of the century.[1]

Most of the other easily available dance history volumes are published as lavishly illustrated coffee-table books or else as exhibition catalogs. The only piece of cultural studies analysis which intrudes into this area marked out by the dominance of taste and connoisseurship is Peter Wollen's recent essay.[2] Wollen argues that while theorists of modernism are loath to admit it since ballet has always been regarded as a less important art, the Russian ballet directed by Diaghilev, choreographed by Fokine, and with stage sets by Leon Bakst was enormously influential in the uneasy lurch which was made in the early years of the century toward a modernist aesthetic. By documenting the central importance of Diaghilev, and the way in which his most popular ballet, *Scheherazade*, looked to the Orient as a way of unsettling sexual and cultural mores, Wollen reinstates ballet as a crucial vehicle for the expression of radical ideas. The Russian ballet was poised between the old and the new order, and its decadence and excess accounted for what was an unfair marginalization in the writing of modernist history.[3]

Wollen's essay shows not just the importance of ballet in the broader sphere of the arts but also the extent to which the boundaries which are used to demarcate aesthetic forms are frequently artificial. Diaghilev's *Scheherazade*, with Nijinsky as the athletic, effeminate, and androgynous center part, with music by Rimsky-Korsakov and with lavishly colored and Oriental sets by Bakst, was on the cusp of the shift into modernism. This ballet and those that followed posited the dancer's body as unconfined, as more natural and "modernist" in its movements than had been the case before.

Most interesting, perhaps, is Wollen's comparison between the balletic body of that moment in history and the ambiguously extravagant body which was part of punk style of the early 1980s: "We can perhaps see a link between the Russian ballet and punk, the radical excess of the last years of the ancien regime and that of postmodern street culture, complete with its own scenography of bondage, aggressive display and decorative redistribution of bodily exposure." This analogy is important because it locates ballet outside the narrow terms of high culture, and posits it as something which has connections with the aesthetics of everyday life. The Russian ballet was as prefigurative as punk was when it reverberated across British society in the late 1970s and early 1980s.

In a sociology of dance it would also be important to consider the role of dance journalism and the way in which it shapes our perceptions of ballet in a number of ways. Ballet is simultaneously a "low" high art, a spectacle for virtuoso performance, a part of the "national heritage," a showcase for other national identities, and an opportunity for promoting international relations. Since the review is the most widespread and accessible form of writing which accompanies a text or performance, what journalists do with dance and how they make sense of it would form an important point of inquiry. It is unfortunately the case, however, that the dance columns which fill the pages of the Sunday newspapers rarely move beyond either a descriptive account of a performance focusing on the star, an assessment of an adaptation, or a retrospective account of a dancer's life. The pity of this generally uncritical and unreflexive writing is that it remains largely unread by those who do not count themselves within the small enclave of committed dance fans. It rarely opens up dance to a new audience because it does not consider dance in a wider context. It seems not to be interested in the complex pleasures of watching dance and it never sets out to explain to the uninitiated how dance is staged, cast, produced, and performed. Most importantly it fails to prise open the momentum of the particular relationships set up between the dance company and its audiences, and the sociocultural basis of such a relationship.

Dance theorists and critics do not relish the idea of dance being appropriated by sociology and cultural studies. In much the same way as musicologists complain about how sociologists rarely talk about the music outside all the other social relations within which it is "packaged," dance critics dislike the thought of others trespassing on their terrain. But dance comes to us packaged in the messy social contexts of consumer capitalism, class culture, and gender and race relations. Ballet is a form which occupies a specific position in the high arts and popular culture spectrum. It is the poor relative of opera, but like opera is increasingly marketed not for an élite but for a mass market. On these grounds alone dance should be of great interest to the sociologist, and not just as a cultural product and a form of mass entertainment (one which moves from ballet to the chorus line, from *Swan Lake* to *Top Hat*) but also as a form which invites a participative response, speaking to and with the body.

Dance would have to be considered, therefore, in all its diversity. Its history in folk and urban culture as well as its status in contemporary culture would necessarily entail an investigation of key cultural overlaps including, for example, dance in the cinema, the popularity of the musical, and the place of dance in the history of rock'n'roll. Running alongside this would be the place of dance in African American culture and the relationship between black and white culture in the postwar period. Finally it would also be important to consider dance in terms of its place within the state-funded arts.

For the purposes of the following analysis the crucial point about dance is that as an art, a representational form, a performance and a spectacle, it has an extremely strong, almost symbiotic relationship with its audience. For girls and young women, particularly for those not brought up in a cultural background which sees it as part of its duty to introduce young people to the fine arts—to painting, literature, classical music, great drama, and so on—dance exists as a largely feminine and thus accessible practice. It also comes to life as a set of almost magical childhood narratives in the form of girls' ballet stories. In each of these forms dance carries within it some mysterious transformative power. Its art lies in its ability to create a fantasy of change, escape, and of achievement for girls and young women who are otherwise surrounded by much more mundane and limiting leisure opportunities. Dance is also different from the other arts in that it is readily available to young girls as a legitimate passion, something that, unlike painting or classical music or even writing, they might be expected to want to do. It has a more "interactive effect" than the other high arts. The Royal Ballet speaks to the thousands of preteen and teenage girls who learn ballet each week in the same way as the film and TV series *Fame* and *Flashdance* speak to those children and teenagers who dream of going to stage school, or who learn disco dancing at school or on a Saturday morning. Images of dancing have the effect of making people want to do it. Which images or which performances they watch is of course dependent on a wide range of social and cultural factors.

Ballet lessons cost money and they are not usually provided during school time. This limits the range of those who can learn ballet. Disco dancing and modern dance lessons are often provided free by local authorities. Pop and jazz dancing are therefore more widely available forms. Ballet requires leotards, shoes, tights of the right thickness, "block shoes," and so on. Pop dancing requires only tights and a T-shirt. (These differences crop up repeatedly in ballet fiction when a girl who dreams of being a ballerina is forced to make do with disco-dancing lessons because she cannot afford all the extras that go with ballet.) Ballet is therefore an activity favored within the middle and lower middle classes while disco dancing is more likely to be linked with working-class girls. Ballet, however, occupies an uncertain place in middle-class culture. It does not carry the same value as classical music. Proficiency in music and knowledge of the great composers carries greater cultural weight than knowledge of dance and a proficiency on points. The "cultural capital" of music holds the pupil in much better stead than that acquired in dance.[4] Pupils are encouraged to join the school orchestra while those who want to dance will rarely find a school which takes dance (as a gender-specific subject) as seriously as it does music.

A sociology of dance would have to consider this cultural ambivalence. The middle-class preference for music reflects the connotations dance carries as a pleasure of the body rather than of the mind. And because dance is also a popular leisure activity where the female body has been allowed to break free of the constraints of modesty, dance has aroused anxiety about sexual display.

It was for this reason, for example, that the early middle-class pioneers of the youth club movement discouraged dancing as a legitimate club activity. And since dance halls were associated with working-class leisure, the middle classes, anxious to define themselves as different in all aspects of taste from their working-class counterparts, preferred to have their daughters taught piano (though a degree of gracefulness on the ballroom floor was a necessary accomplishment for the middle-class girl in search of a husband). This parental preference for music was also a reaction against the "dangerous" popularity of dance fiction among girls of all social classes which romanticized the stage and which invariably focused on some dramatic escape on the part of a girl who wanted to dance but was thwarted by her strict and narrow-minded parents.

It was mentioned earlier how it was strange that dance had proved of so little interest to sociology and cultural studies. Strange because, despite the absence of a sociological language which would embrace the formal dimensions of dance, there is nonetheless a diversity of wider social questions and issues which are immediately raised by even the most superficial consideration of dance. Some of the most richly coded class practices in contemporary society can be observed in leisure and in dance. The various contexts of social dancing tell us a great deal about the everyday lives and expectations of their participants. Dance marks out important moments in the life-cycle and it punctuates the more banal weekly cycles of labor, leisure, and what Ian Chambers has labeled the "freedom of Saturday night."[5] It is perhaps not insignificant in this context that in the Thatcher years the last night of the annual Tory party conference was usually highlighted on television with Mrs. Thatcher taking to the floor with a partner who was neither her husband nor a member of her cabinet. This might well be a gender-specific leisure choice. Mr. Kinnock used this same slot and television time to sing with a male voice choir

Dance and Club Culture

> Dancing, where the explicit and implicit zones of socialized pleasures and individualized desires entwine in the momentary rediscovery of the "reason of the body" . . . is undoubtedly one of the main avenues along which pop's sense travels.[6]

A sociology of dance would have to step outside the field of performance and examine dance as a social activity, a participative form enjoyed by people in leisure, a sexual ritual, a form of self-expression, a kind of exercise and a way of speaking through the body. Historians of working-class culture have acknowledged the place occupied by dance in leisure and the opportunities it has afforded for courtship, relaxation, and even riotous behavior. Unfortunately, in most cases the nature and form of the dance remains in the background, something more enjoyed by women than by men and therefore marginal to the real business of working-class life. This imbalance is slowly being redressed by American social historians like Elizabeth Ewen, who has attempted to chart the various histories of immigrant and working-women's leisure in the early years of the century.[7] However, in this country it remains an uncharted ground coming through only in fleeting references in oral history or in collections like Sheila Rowbotham and Jean McCrindle's *Dutiful Daughters*.[8] Even here memories of dancing are always associated with pleasure and with loss as though the rest of the woman's life can be measured against such moments. Social history generally has tended to be more concerned with the problem of order and with the policing of the working class in its leisure time. Robert Roberts makes a few telling comments about the social anxieties which came into play around the dance halls in the years following the end of the First World War.[9] These fears and anxieties hinged upon the possible promiscuity of the working-class girls who flooded into the dance halls as many nights a week as they could and who also dressed up and wore makeup for the occasion in a way that was seen as shocking and indicative of some immoral intent.

This strand continues right into the postwar years. Dance halls remain a key feature in working-class leisure and a focal point for the expression of concern about working-class youth. Outside the evangelical thrust of youth clubs and other forms of state-provided or religiously controlled leisure, the dance hall or disco, run for profit by "uncaring" businessmen, exists as a site for the kind of moral panics which have marked the field of "youth" for many years. However, the target for the moral panic revolves not so much around dancing (though rock'n'roll dancing and jiving were linked with sexual license) but rather around the other activities accompanying dance: drinking, drug taking, or violence. Dancing is the least of the worries of the moral guardians. If the boys did more of it, there would be less to worry about. The girls are less likely to fight, less likely to drink themselves into a stupor (partly because of the risks of not getting home safely), and less likely to consume drugs on the same scale as their male peers, because of the double standard which still holds that a girl out of control is less socially acceptable than her male equivalent. Because of these social constraints and sexist sanctions girls are less of a problem and therefore remain largely in the shadows, dressed up, dancing, and immersed in the "reason of the body."

Geoff Mungham is the only sociologist who has turned his attention to the more mundane aspects of social dancing.[10] In *Youth in Pursuit of Itself* he locates the importance of dancing in the life-cycle of working-class girls for whom getting a husband at a relatively young age is a social and an economic imperative, and for whom also the dance hall provides the main opportunity for finding a possible partner. Like Richard Hoggart he sees the enthusiasm of young girls for dancing and having a good time as a "brief flowering" before they settle down to the hard work of being a wife and mother.[11] For older working-class women memories of these good times sometimes burst through the surface as they take to the dance floor on the odd night off, or at the "girls' night" at the local pub. Ann Whitehead graphically describes this kind of married women's leisure in her classic study of rural life in Herefordshire.[12] But beyond these fleeting comments and fleeting images, and since Mungham's essay on dance hall culture, there is and has been very little else. Dance, like fashion, seems to find expression more at the level of "popular memory." Film footage of hundreds of couples crowding the dance floor after the end of the Second World War is immediately evocative of a whole social moment, in the same way as footage of couples jiving or of early Mods moving to the black "sounds of the city" conjure up in a flash what the early 1960s were all about.

The link between dance and youth culture is reflective of how a crucial element in subcultural activity was played down, if not altogether ignored. Despite Phil Cohen's early listing of subcultural components—argot, ritual, and style—dance has hardly merited any attention whatsoever.[13] With the notable exception of Dick Hebdige's description of the short, sharp movements of the "pogo" dance and its articulation with the other elements of punk style,[14] and Ian Chambers's extensive documentation of the clubs and dance halls which have provided the backdrop for urban youth culture and music in the postwar period,[15] there has been little or nothing said about the various dances and movements which have been a constant feature of urban youth cultures.

A trivialized or feminized form? A ritual without resistance? A sequence of steps some steps removed from the active, creative core of youth cultural activity? Chambers mentions a range of dance styles by name: the shake, the jerk, the northern soul style of athletic, acrobatic dance, as well as the break dancing and "body popping" associated with black youth. He also makes connections between white youth culture dancing and the black music and dance from which it has continually borrowed. But he is faced with the same difficulties which seem to have beset other sociologists when it comes to locating the movements in the context of the culture. He evades the issue by referring to the "rich tension of dance" and then going on to engage more critically with the music.

Chambers's work is important because it recognizes the centrality of dance in leisure and it makes connections between dance and African American music, suggesting that it is this, and in particular soul music, which has provided the corporeal language for white youth culture dancing over the past forty years. Chambers is certainly not blind to gender dimensions in dance. Indeed, he articulates a sharply differentiated means of experiencing dance according to gender. Dance for girls represents a public extension of the private culture of femininity which takes place outside the worried gaze of the moral guardians and indoors in the protected space of the home. Male youth stylists, however, take to the floor within the direct ambiance of the subculture, hence the dominance of boys in the northern soul scene, or in black jazz dancing, break dancing, and so on. Chambers also seems to suggest that because boys in youth subcultures have been closer to the music in a technical sense so too have they been closer to the dance. The problem with this is that it posits a static and sexually divided model which is not in fact reflective of the active involvement of both girls and boys in dancing and in the various club cultures (in particular the recent "Acid House" phenomenon). Chambers's analysis is the outcome of an approach to dance conducted through the medium of music and musical taste where boys have undeniably been at the controls and where girls have been in the background. Such an emphasis lets the author off the hook in relation to dance itself. "But dancing is itself an obscure reality, the not-so-innocent refuge of many a social secret."

It is the clubs and dance halls which have provided a whole series of subcultures with their own private spaces. It is here that the distinctive styles have found a place for their first public appearances. It is from the clubs that the first reports and snapshots filter through to the public and to the readers of the color supplements. The already privileged place occupied by youth cultures in the style glossies and in the fashion pages means that the incubation period of subcultural style is speeded up to the point that this is only a momentarily privatized space. Within a flash the details have been itemized, and the customized ripped jeans, the cotton headscarf knotted behind, and the "granny specs" have been installed in yet another ever-extending subcultural history related by the style experts. The function of the club in this context is simultaneously to construct the distinctiveness of the new style as different from what went before (cool is out, *un*cool "jollity" is in; one style of dance is out, another is in; and so on) and to spread the word before moving on to something else, to new musical sounds and new dance steps. The essence of these processes in the age of the postmodern mass media, with their thirst for new copy and their space for lifestyle items, is the rapidity with which an emergent style is killed off through instant overkill.

What remains are the same old cultural cocktails of dress, music, drugs, and dance and the way in which they create an atmosphere of surrender, abandon, euphoria, and energy, a trancelike state and a relinquishing of control. As Dick Hebdige has suggested, these cannot be understood without reference to the "phantom history" of youth subcultures—that is, to the black experience and the impact of African American culture on white youth culture.[16] In the same way as rock'n'roll music bears the traces of its origin in African American culture, so too does jazz dancing, pop dancing, and the kind of funky sexy movements demonstrated by generations of black performers (Little Richard, James Brown, Tina Turner, Michael Jackson, and Prince) which were copied step by step by white singers and dancers and drawn into the mainstream entertainment business as a result.

It is this latter process which feeds into and shapes the whole popular dance experience of the postwar period and particularly that pursued within the youth subcultures. No historian of dance should be able to ignore the way in which a range of cultural forms, mainstream and subcultural, have drawn on black dance. The steps in Hollywood musicals are as derivative of black culture as those carefully copied in the clubs and dance halls by generations of young white people from the 1950s right up to the present day. Even the most cursory glance at footage of black dancers reveals the debt owed to them by Fred Astaire, Gene Kelly, Ginger Rogers, and many others. Likewise in social dancing. There is a slow process where black American dance styles are taken over, adopted, and extended by white dancers and performers. Jagger acknowledges his debt to James Brown and Tina Turner, while soul fans remember the impact of the Philadelphia TV show *Soultrain* for the new dance ideas it provided. If, as Paul Gilroy has argued, black dance addresses the body in a different register from that of formal ballroom dancing or folk dance, if this urban soul dancing traverses the entire body surface, shifting the center of erotic gravity away from the narrowly genital and allowing instead a slow spread, then the meaning of this hypereroticism must be seen in the broader context of racial discrimination and prejudice.[17]

Lurking behind the fears of the moral guardians has also been the specter of racial difference and otherness, the hysterical anxieties about the black rejection of work and labor discipline, the assumptions of sexual license and drug abuse and the contaminating effect these might have on white youth. At the other end of the spectrum is the equally racist assumption about black "ability" in the sphere of entertainment—an ability which of course has its own material history, its own dynamics of necessity. Within this rhetoric of racial inferiority is also the debased positioning of black song and dance, and black-influenced forms, as lower arts or even native art.

This has certain consequences for the remaining sections of this essay, especially those dealing with two popular and contemporary dance narratives,

Fame and *Flashdance*. In each case a narrative tension is set up around this divide (ballet/jazz, classical/pop) and in each case it is "satisfactorily" resolved within the framework of the story. In the film *Fame* the resolution hinges on the multicultural performances and the range of "abilities" demonstrated by the kids (black, white, and Hispanic) and highlighted in the graduation show which also marks the end of the film where the performance moves seamlessly from classical to "progressive" pop and then to gospel. In *Flashdance*, Alex, who is poor, orphaned, and part Hispanic, is able to give up her sleazy disco-dancing job when she wins a place at the prestigious ballet school.[18] Even in the novel *Ballet Shoes*, which I shall also be considering, there is evidence of the classical/pop divide, though here it is characterized by two of the three sisters making choices in opposite directions—Polly toward Hollywood, where she will sing, dance, and act, and Posy to a European ballet school.

Dance Fictions

The experience of learning to dance as a child or as a young girl, and then later, in adolescence, the almost addictive pleasure of social dancing to an endless beat in the darkened space of the disco or nightclub, are relatively unchanging forms in the landscape of female leisure culture. They also provide a multiplicity of narrative possibilities in popular entertainment, in film, on television, and in fiction. These narratives will be the focus of attention in this section. It will be part of my argument that dance occupies a special place in feminine culture because for many women and girls whose upbringing or education does not involve any direct relation to the world of art or culture, ideas about dance made available through texts and stories serve as an introduction to these spheres. The meaning of art in this context is sufficiently wide (and conventional) to allow it to signify a "realm of the senses," an arena for self-expression and a form which is capable of transporting the reader or viewer away from the difficulties of everyday life. In this heightened state the reader or viewer is also invited in fantasy at least to identify and become part of the spectacle. In the language of the narratives, dance exists as a passion. As such it awakens a strongly emotional response on the part of the girl. The attraction of dance narratives, therefore, lies in the fantasies of achievement they afford their subjects.

The three chosen narratives for analysis are the girls' novel *Ballet Shoes*, the film and TV series *Fame*, and *Flashdance*, the 1983 film which attempted to build on and extend *Fame*'s earlier and enormous success.[19] Along with a focus on achievement, passion, dedication, and self-discipline, each of the chosen works also engages with the terrain of what in psychoanalysis is called "the family romance." These two poles act as the framework for the development of the narratives. As the stories unfold they move backwards and forwards between the desire to achieve and the constraints and expectations of the family. Work becomes an alternative romance, a dream to be pursued even if it is against the odds. Dance operates as a metaphor for an external reality which is unconstrained by the limits and expectations of gender identity and which successfully and relatively painlessly transports its subjects from a passive to a more active psychic position. What is charted repeatedly in these stories is this transition from childhood dependency to adolescent independence, which in turn is gained through achievement in dance or in the performing arts and therefore in the outside world.

All three texts are conventionally feminine texts, though *Flashdance* also attempts to extend its audience to men and boys. The readers and viewers, however, are largely female and all three products are marketed accordingly. These are unique cultural objects for the reason that they define an artistic mode as a kind of utopia and as a symbolic escape route from the more normative expectations of girls and young women found in most other forms of popular culture. It will be my contention that these narratives have proved so popular precisely *because* they depart strongly from the kind of narrative submissiveness associated both with girls' magazine stories of the type outlined by Valerie Walkerdine in her short study of girls' comics, and with teenage romantic fiction.[20] The romance of work and achievement simultaneously resolves the difficulties posed by the family romance (in psychoanalytic terms) and postpones the difficulties envisaged in the transition toward adult feminine sexuality. It does this either by disregarding sexuality altogether (*Ballet Shoes*) or by reducing romance to a minor episode, a fleeting embrace (*Fame*), or else, in the more adult world of *Flashdance*, by treating it as something which can be an additional, unexpected pleasure, but subordinate to the real business of work.

In both *Fame* and *Flashdance* pop or disco dancing plays a major role in the narrative development and both are associated either with being poor or else with being black (or both). In *Fame* jazz dancing of the type associated with African American culture is given equal status with ballet, and this is taken as a symbol of the school's commitment to multiculturalism and racial equality. In *Flashdance*, however, Hispanic-born Alex is pleased to be able to leave her disco-dancing days behind her when she eventually wins a place in the Pittsburgh Ballet School. This is partly because throughout the film her go-go dancing is portrayed as overtly sexual and therefore sleazy. Unlike the "funky" dancing of Leroy in *Fame*, Alex's dancing in Mowby's bar is choreographed to arouse sexually and this is accentuated in the film by the effect she has on the men sitting around watching her perform. However, for her audition to ballet school she returns to a more acrobatic disco style and despite the initial frosty looks from the panel she eventually manages to get them tapping their feet in enjoyment. In this penultimate moment in the film we see a small act of validation of pop dancing and by implication of pop culture, even though it remains a sign of Alex's untutored ability.

I have chosen these three narratives for a number of reasons. They address specific ages of readers and viewers (teenage and pre-teenage girls) and have been immensely popular with them and with a wider constituency of even younger children, as well as adults. As well as reflecting different historical moments (*Ballet Shoes* first appeared in 1936), the texts also range from the classical to the popular in terms of taste and cultural preference. *Ballet Shoes* is a classic of girls' fiction, a specifically English and middle-class portrait of fantasized childhood in interwar Britain. *Fame* was first a film, directed by Alan Parker in 1980, and then it became a TV series achieving almost cult status two years later. Although describing the lives at the New York School of Performing Arts of a group of teenagers, the *Fame* narratives were focused on a much younger viewer. *Fame* (the film) was also reflective of a number of media strands emerging in the early 1980s. It functioned not just as a narrativized showcase for pop music and dance performances, where the soundtrack was strongly publicized and then released as an album, it also worked visually as a high-fashion text. The early 1980s saw the mass popularity of dance-exercise style. *Fame* helped to trigger the leggings, sweat-band, and leotard look and helped also launch the success of thousands of dance classes and exercise centers, of which in Britain the Pineapple Centre in London is still the best known. *Fame* is also interesting because of its strongly multicultural emphasis. This is more strongly highlighted in the film than in the TV series. Indeed the film might well be credited as one of the most racially mixed pop musicals to have been produced in recent years.

Flashdance is different in a number of respects. It is more overtly trashy than *Fame*; its visual overlaps with other media forms are more obvious and more derivative (critics described it as a prolonged pop video or a movie-length advertisement); and its narrative was recognized as extremely unlikely (critics also suggested that the story had been created with the help of a computer which was able to bring together a combination of highly marketable features). Even here, however, we find a number of themes pertinent to the concerns of this essay. Ridiculous as its narrative might be, the film still holds a peculiar attraction. It is regularly shown on TV and has a healthy shelf-life in video shops across the country (though this might be partly attributable to the film's erotic appeal). But what marks it out as different from *Fame* is not so much the sex or the romance but rather that Alex is presented as more sexually knowing than her counterparts in *Fame*. *Flashdance* was marketed for a slightly older teenage audience and for a less exclusively female viewer. While the narrative disavows the vulgarity of the dancing that Alex is forced to perform in her early days as a dancer, the visuals contradict this message and at key points throughout the film allow the audience to dwell at length on the purely sexy gyrations of the dancers.

Let us look then in more detail at the individual texts. *Ballet Shoes* was written in 1936 by Noel Streatfield and has been reprinted almost every year since then. It is read by prepubescent girls of all social and ethnic backgrounds, and the narrative is heavily overladen by the kind of themes that make it more than open to a psychoanalytic interpretation. Three foundlings are brought back to England over a period of time by the man whom the children come to refer to as Gum (great-uncle Matthew). They are left under the care of Nurse and Sylvia with very little money as absent-minded Gum disappears abroad to continue with his work as an explorer. The three children are called Pauline, Petrova, and Posy and they give themselves the surname of Fossil, as befits their strange and unknown parentage. Orphaned and without any secure financial future, the Fossils, with the encouragement of Nurse and Sylvia, set about finding ways of earning their own keep. One of the boarders living with them in genteel poverty in Kensington teaches in the Children's Academy of Dance and Stage Training in Bloomsbury and she manages to get them lessons in return for payment at a later stage when they begin to work.

> The Fossils became some of the busiest children in London. They got up at half-past-seven and had breakfast at eight. After breakfast they did exercises with Thea for half an hour. At nine they began lessons. Posy did two hours reading writing and kindergarten work with Sylvia and Pauline and Petrova did three hours with Dr Jakes and Dr Smith. . . . At twelve o'clock they went for a walk with Narnie and Sylvia. . . . Narnie thought nicely brought-up children ought to be out of the house between twelve and one even on a wet day.

As pupils at the academy the girls receive an education in the arts by reading and performing *Richard III*, *Midsummer Night's Dream*, and Maeterlinck's *Blue Bird*. Pauline shows an increasing talent as an actress; Petrova, the tomboy, manages to get a few parts while preferring the unfeminine world of cars and aeroplanes, and Posy develops the temperament of the talented ballet dancer destined for great things. The narrative spans a predictable number of auditions and disappointments and successes. It also dwells on financial difficulties and on ways and means of overcoming them such as pawning necklaces and making dresses from old hand-me-downs and so on.

Through successions of wet summers, rainy winters, and endless bouts of flu, the Fossils eventually realize both the prospect of fame and the likelihood of fortune. Pauline is offered a part in a Hollywood movie and will be escorted by Nurse. Posy is to be the most famous of the three and wins a place in a leading ballet school in Europe, and Petrova is rescued by the sudden return of Gum, whose masculine interests coincide with her own.

What makes an old-fashioned story like this so popular with preteen readers? What accounts for its continuous success in a world now marked out by much more sophisticated interests? And what are the links between *Ballet Shoes* and the other chosen narratives of this chapter? *Ballet Shoes* is not just a middle-class story about scrimping and saving and then succeeding, as many critics would have it. (*Ballet Shoes* is the kind of unfashionable book which is disapproved of by librarians for precisely these reasons.) Nor is its popularity expressive of a nostalgia for a particular kind of English household management and child rearing as exemplified by Nurse's preference for brisk walks and self-reliance. *Ballet Shoes* works as a text of transition and development. It simultaneously allows its readers to fantasize a family space unencumbered by sibling rivalry and parental dictate (a state of affairs experienced negatively in one or another by boys and girls of all ages and social backgounds) and to contemplate a future state of being which promises reward, recognition, and happiness. The narrative also works through, in fictional form, the kind of psychic material which in itself is a product of the difficulty girls face in moving toward achieving a feminine identity.

The Kensington household, inhabited by people among whom there are no blood relatives, plays a role similar to that of the boarding school in school stories (*Malory Towers*, *Trebizon*, *The Chalet School*, etc.) or indeed in ballet-school stories (the best-known of which are the stories of Sadlers Wells by Lorna Hill). These nonfamilial spaces provide readers with a kind of fantasy playground where they can contemplate what it would be like without the symbolic constraints of the mother, father, and siblings, and where they can explore over and over again what it would be like to be an orphan, or to be without close contact with parents or relatives, to be simultaneously relieved and relinquished. More than this, readers can also take up and experiment with non-gender-specific activities. In the ballet school or boarding school there are echoes and replays of the child's original bisexual disposition played out here as a kind of *grande finale* before the real world once again intrudes.

Bruno Bettelheim has suggested that the role of children's fiction is to "manage life in an age-appropriate manner."[21] To the sociologist this sounds excessively normative, prescriptive, and unalert to the material circumstances which have a much more dramatic effect than any work of fiction on a child's ability to manage its own life appropriately. It is easy to imagine sociologists also arguing that Bettelheim's is a conservative and adaptive model of childhood socialization where the text propels the child into his or her allotted role, becoming in effect a vehicle for social control. However, as teachers and researchers testify, the popularity of this story transcends the divisions of social class and race. Gill Frith's study shows that this kind of novel is read repetitively and addictively by schoolgirls aged between ten and twelve. *Ballet Shoes* sits comfortably alongside the Sadler's Wells stories already mentioned and Enid Blyton's popular *Malory Towers* series.[22] Many of Frith's respondents were Asian girls living in the poorest parts of Coventry and for whom the reality of boarding-school life was far removed. They knew it was a fantasy structure they were reading over and over again, but they enjoyed both the exciting plots and the predictable endings. The highly ordered routinized world of the boarding school was at once reassuring and thrilling.

Frith's argument could be extended by drawing attention to the absence of parents in the narratives she describes. Bettelheim has marked upon the absence or death of parents in classic fairy tales. The real parent is replaced by a wicked stepmother or sometimes by a cruel stepfather. This repeats a theme described by Freud where the child frequently imagines that he or she is not the child of his/her parents but rather a child of some "exalted personages" from whom for some reason she has been parted.[23] In fiction this fantasy is frequently developed into a full-blown narrative. In *Ballet Shoes* it represents the trigger which sets the whole narrative in motion. The anxiety about origins is revealed in the children's choice of a surname. The "Fossils" which Gum collects are also symbolic expressions of what the childish unconscious ponders over, the mystery of its origins, the question of its identity. A sign of some unfathomable time. Fictional articulations of the drama of parentage play an important part in allowing the child to explore this dilemma and also to speculate on what in reality might be too terrible to contemplate—the child's anger or even fury against the parent and most often the mother, and the cruelty of which he or she perceives the parent being capable. Hence the desire for another parent. The "orphan" narrative signifies the parental fall from grace, the disappointment felt keenly by the child as the parent is revealed as less than perfect. It also charts the shifting ground of dependency as the child approaches adolescence.

In *Ballet Shoes* the absence of both real and adoptive parents and their replacement by the more anonymous "Nurse" and Sylvia is transformed into an opportunity to achieve, unencumbered by the rivalries and other difficulties which, in real life, act to contain or restrict the child's desires. The reward for Pauline, Posy, and Petrova's achievement, however, is the sudden and unexpected return of Gum. Removed from the Oedipal scene for as long as is psychically reasonable, Gum is then able to take up the mantle of paternal authority. He allows Pauline to go to Hollywood and Posy to go to a ballet school in Europe.

In psychoanalytic terms, the Fossil household, with its rooms full of respectable lodgers, like the boarding schools with their dormitories of girls, legitimates the reader's desire to imagine a hypothetical space where the dilemmas and difficulties of everyday life are magically resolved through the working out in fantasy of precisely that which cannot be consciously admitted—that is, their ambivalent and changing relations with their parents, their rivalries and resentments against their brothers and sisters, their desire to move toward the outside world which because it is too threatening is itself contained in the narrative in the form of a school or house full of boarders.

Central to *Ballet Shoes* is the question of feminine identity, and it shares this concern not only with other classic girls' novels, like *Little Women* and *What Katy Did*, but also with the magazine stories consumed each week by teenage and pre-teenage girls. The narrative equivalent of *Ballet Shoes* would be the line-drawing stories found in *Bunty*, *Mandy*, and *Tracey*, comics addressed to the eight- to ten-year-olds and containing between six and seven stories each week. There is no boys' equivalent to these forms. There are classic boys' stories which also use the setting of the boarding school, but these tend to be individual texts; they do not connect with the kind of genre of writing described here. And there is certainly no boys' equivalent to *Bunty* or the other girls' comics. Boys' comics of the sort described by George Orwell in his well-known essay written in the 1930s are no longer in existence.[24] It might be surmised that the leisure activities of similarly aged boys are quite differently constructed.

The repetitious reading described by Gill Frith, the continuing popularity of a form which might otherwise have been superseded by the modern mass media, and the continual working and reworking within the texts of the question of what it is to be a girl point to the kind of ambivalence and uncertainty which psychoanalysts from Bruno Bettelheim to Juliet Mitchell have seen as part of the intractable difficulties in the fixing of feminine identity and indeed in the impossibility of achieving a satisfactory resolution to this problem.[25] What Bettelheim has referred to more cryptically ("most women do not painlessly slip into their roles as women") Juliet Mitchell has examined and reexamined in a variety of different contexts.[26]

In *Ballet Shoes* feminine identity is split in three and represented in the different personalities of the three girls. Pauline is good, hard-working, and responsible; Posy is gifted but spoiled, indulged and therefore extremely selfish, and Petrova is the "boy," the narrative reminder of the child's bisexual disposition. This splitting allows the reader to see her own internal but coexisting divisions made manifest but also handled—and therefore resolved—through the distinct personalities of the girls. Each of these separate characteristics is validated in the end. It is not just that each girl gets what she wants, but that each of their individual quirks is recognized as necessary for them to achieve their goals. No one is punished, not even Petrova whose unfeminine interests are allowed to be pursued. In *Ballet Shoes* an active if internally divided femininity is projected into the text and is seen as enabling. It is this which makes the book so appealing to its generations of readers. It certainly stands out in sharp contrast to the stories described by Valerie Walkerdine mentioned earlier.

Many of these picture stories in young girls' comics like *Bunty* and *Mandy* paint an altogether different portrait. They too are preoccupied with aspects of the family romance, but the narrative emphasis and the outcomes are different. Walkerdine's argument is that in most of these stories the girl is encouraged to put up with the enormous suffering imposed upon her by a cruel stepmother or father or by jealous siblings. In suffering passively, however, the girl can be sure that eventually she will be rewarded and that it is therefore worth being a "good girl." Stories like these located within a pre-teenage scenario anticipate a future when the good girl who has successfully learned all the codes of femininity will find her "prince." *Ballet Shoes* and all the other school stories mentioned create an entirely different scenario first by effecting an escape from the site of potential trauma or cruelty (i.e., the home) into a more neutral sphere such as the school, and then by plunging headlong into an activity, ballet or gymnastics or whatever. These are then pursued with all the passion of a great love, a fabulous obsession. The shoes in *Ballet Shoes* are a symbol of effectivity and escape and of prepubescent female desire.

Fame, Flashdance, *and Fantasies of Achievement*

Fame was first released as a feature film in 1980 and its success led to the creation of a TV series of the same name based on several of the characters who appeared in the film. The series focused each week on a number of narrative dilemmas which in the course of the episode would be satisfactorily resolved. These programs were broadcast on BBC 1 in the U.K. during 1982 and 1983 and they were immediately successful with young viewers and particularly young girls. *Fame* soon began to develop a kind of cult status, with its stars becoming household names. Interest then moved back to the film which was rereleased, and to a variety of commercial spin-offs. The "Kids from Fame" performed a number of live stage shows in London and in other major cities, the soundtrack reached the Top Ten, the single "Fame, I'm Gonna Live for Ever" reached number one, and an additional album of *Fame* hits was released. The stars appeared on chat shows and the whole *Fame* phenomenon added momentum to the exercise craze of the early 1980s.

There were a few key differences between the film and the TV series. The film version was visually a great deal more adventurous than the TV show, with its style verging at points on cinematic naturalism. The camera seemed to "drop in" on rehearsals or simply record in an understated kind of way the day-to-day life of the school. The plot was skeletal. It merely followed the paths of a number of young hopefuls from the first auditions to graduation day three years later. Throughout the course of the film various individuals emerged. Each had some personal dilemma to work through, and most of these related to a parental relationship. In each case the strength of the peer-group friendships helped in this process. Emphasis on the family in the TV series was even more marked, sometimes dominating all the action. In the film version, however, the viewers' attention was directed more toward the performance, and those few narrative strands that did emerge were more controversial. One boy was forced to come to grips with his homosexuality; a girl called Coco became involved unwittingly with a porn filmmaker, and Leroy's girlfriend became pregnant and had an abortion. Four-letter words were scattered generously across the text as the film tried to achieve a realistic effect.

The film also engaged more directly and in greater depth with the split between high culture and pop. It did this by drawing on a number of assumptions and popular stereotypes. The first of these involved crediting black music and dance with a kind of spark of authenticity that was missing in the colder and more austere world of the white classics. These qualities of warmth, humor, and style extend, in the film, in two directions simultaneously. They include both personalities and performances. Thus Leroy is a "wide boy." He knows how to manipulate the system to his own advantage. His poverty and his time spent on the street lend an even more attractive edge to his personal image. He is both sexy and stylish, admired by all and especially by his dance teacher, Lydia. His talent is also a reflection of many of these attributes. Even without tuition he is a born dancer. His ability amazes his white, ballet-educated peers. He is continually late for class, to the annoyance of his teachers, but when it comes to it, he shows himself to be as disciplined and committed as any of the others.

Popular culture and high culture occupy the same status in the school and are seen as equal to each other as long as they are pursued with the same degree of dedication as is needed to achieve in these highly competitive fields. In the world of entertainment what is important is success, not what side you come down on in the high-culture/pop-culture divide. Individual dedication and determination negate such unhelpful distinctions. At a personal level these are registered as choices (Bruno upsets his father and his music teacher by preferring to play electronic progressive pop rather than the classics), and as signs of difference they can add an exotic edge or frisson to interpersonal relationships between the pupils. In one of the favorite scenes in *Fame*, a rich white girl who looks and acts aloof and snobbish, is practicing alone in the long mirrored rehearsal room. Wearing a pink leotard and dancing on blocks, she performs a beautifully executed solo to a piece of classical music on tape in the background. The viewer can see that Leroy is watching, spellbound by her classical performance and attracted by her beauty. But it is unclear whether she knows that he is watching right up until the last second when the tape finishes and she completes her final pirouette. Her body language and expression convey a sense of distance, until she suddenly winks at Leroy and invites him to join her in the changing room. The asexual image of classical ballet is thus debunked and the distinction between high and pop culture is shown not to be insurmountable.

In performance terms this moment in the film is paralleled by an earlier sequence which also acts as its reverse. Leroy and his black female dancing partner perform their audition piece to gain a place at the school. The dance teachers, all white save for Lydia, are lined up, unsmiling, severe, and, it appears, biased wholly in favor of classical dance. Only Lydia, who looks softer and is wearing makeup, would seem to have any time for jazz dancing. To a loud soul track Leroy and partner take to the floor and perform an extremely sexual and gymnastic routine. At one point Leroy passes his hand over his crotch as though in sexual pleasure, in time to the beat. The camera cuts to the panel who look horrified and embarrassed except for Lydia, whose expression is one of slightly shocked enjoyment. She begins to move to the music as the short scene comes to an end. In doing so she is indicating that she identifies with this black culture and that it does have a legitimate place in the school.

This strand is further developed and resolved in the final moments of the film. This sequence consists of an end-of-term performance for the graduating students and is performed as a kind of non-stop showcase for each of the characters to display their talents. The audience is made up of parents and teachers and the camera cuts to and fro between the adults and the young performers as they get their chance to appear in the spotlight. Once again this provides an opportunity for celebrating race and cultural equality. In the closing moments of the performance, where emotions have already been roused to a peak, the performance moves quite suddenly and entirely unexpectedly from a classical mode into a strong black gospel mode. Black parents and children sing and clap and are joined by their white peers as gospel is also given its place in the school's multicultural repertoire.

The New York School for the Performing Arts is therefore a perfect meritocracy and as such is a metaphor for America as it would like to see itself. Popular culture (particularly music) is a unifying force. When the kids spontaneously break into dance outside the context of the rehearsal room it is always to the backdrop of black urban dance music. Even the ballet dancers "get down." Race therefore becomes just another obstacle to be overcome. Black students are prepared for the outside world of discrimination by one of the black teachers who warns them that they are going to have to be able to stand up for themselves by not letting prejudice overwhelm them. But his message is little different from that of all the other teachers, black or white. In this register race is not much different from any other difficulty they are going to have to face in their struggle to make it. In the context of Hollywood entertainment this is an entirely appropriate way of understanding racial inequality. The more there is of it, the more reason to overcome it and get to the top. Race becomes an incentive to work even harder, a self-regulating form of labor discipline.

This is also a useful idea in a society where young black males are increasingly passed over as a result of a combination of racism and structural changes in technology and the labor market. There is indeed a real question of labor discipline for that section of society deemed most "dangerous." Leroy in *Fame* is a figure of white fantasy, a kind of black "head boy," a rough kid turned good, a symbol of all that young black males in reality are not. The melting-pot mentality of *Fame* is predicated on there being sufficient difference to highlight the way that different races—with all their idiosyncracies—coexist, without those differences arousing racism or conflict. In both the film and TV series racism is avoided by stressing the rich ethnic mix of the pupils where black is only one of many identities and where each of these identities is portrayed through a range of familiar stereotypes. Thus Doris in the TV series might come from a comfortably-off Jewish family, unlike Leroy or Coco, but they still give her a tough time emotionally. Again in the TV series "ethnic" is interesting where "white" can be neurotic. Julie—white, beautiful, and unconfident—is continually failing to accept her parents' divorce as final and trying unsuccessfully to engineer their reconciliation. When this fails she returns to her cello for consolation, and channels all her anger and emotional disturbance into her classical music.

This raises an additional, related point. In both the film and the TV series art plays an emotionally cathartic and therapeutic role. It helps each of the characters to overcome the difficulties they face, particularly in relation to their families, and it also provides them with something in which they can lose themselves. When Coco's or Lydia's romance goes wrong, when "he" doesn't turn out to be the right guy, their recognition of this fact is almost always punctuated with a solo dance—alone at night in the studio; the dance movements are at once an expression of pain and a means of getting over it. A shared commitment to art is also the basis for friendship in *Fame.* Art is always an emotional space. Achievement or disappointment in the "performing arts" is a cause for great floods of emotion. In *Fame* the characters each have to learn to cope with disappointment. These move with great regularity from family to art and back again. Only occasionally are the romances those of the kids themselves. They are kept at a few steps removed from adult sexuality. Instead their relationships are still focused on the family or the peer group.

It is this which makes *Fame* such a satisfactory prepubescent text. As in *Ballet Shoes* there is a concern with separation. In the film version a shy timid girl is only able to discover her acting talent once she has summoned up the courage to show anger to her anxious and overprotective mother. And the gay boy with whom she strikes up such a friendship is haunted by his mother's early separation from him. Indeed it is his monologue: "We spent two whole days together and it was just like we were sweethearts" which opens the film. As in other preteen texts this journey of separation is made safe by the boundaries and limits set by the institution. Teachers act as surrogate parents without any of the messy emotional strings. Friendships which for the most part do not develop into sexual relationships give the kids the confidence to try out new experiences and to work in an environment where there is a shared commitment to the same kind of work. This is the utopian element. This is what makes *Fame* a modern version of *Sandra at the Ballet School* or *No Castanets at the Wells* or *Ballet for Drina.* In *Fame*, as in these more traditional novels, work is a grand passion, never just a means of earning a living. The romance of work in these feminine texts is particularly resonant and even poignant, since achievement in work rapidly fades into the background in most girls' teenage fiction.

Flashdance, in contrast, sits unevenly between these two genres. It is a ballet story for teenage viewers and it suffers under the strain of the conflicting expectations of what constitutes a ballet story and what constitutes a successful teen film. Like so many of her counterparts in ballet fiction, Alex is motherless. Her only adult friend is an elderly Russian woman who takes her to the ballet and who encourages her to apply to ballet school even though she has never had any lessons. Alex practices alone at night in her shabby warehouse apartment by copying the steps from ballet videos. Since the narrative deals with that period of time running up to her successful audition, there is no space for peer-group culture or the institutional life of the school. Alex's only institutional support comes from the girls with whom she dances in the sleazy working-men's club at night after work. And this environment is cheap, nasty, and somewhere to be escaped from. Psychologically Alex is alone until she strikes up a relationship with the handsome son of the owner of the steelworks where she works as a welder. This introduces the sexual dimension, which is a necessary part of the teenage text but which in this case has to be reconciled with Alex's great desire to get into ballet school. The narrative solution to what would otherwise be a generic difficulty lies in the introduction of a feminist slant. Alex is not typically feminine. She is doing a man's job, while managing to retain her glamorous good looks. She is not scared to live alone and until Michael comes along she is single. This emancipated image is emphasized throughout the film. Alex cycles to and from work and through the city streets at night. She has only a large dog as companion and protector and she is fiercely independent. She is also sexually liberated and actively initiates sex with Michael. She does not mind selling her body in Mawby's bar if it helps her to earn money to pay her way. And, finally, she is proud of the way she lives. She is neither looking for nor wants a man to rescue her, though in a sense that is what she gets.

Alex is pretty but poor. She does pop dancing because that is all she has managed to teach herself. At her audition she performs a gymnastic dance routine where the sexuality is toned down. Her energy impresses the panel of judges who, in a scene strongly reminiscent of that described earlier in relation to *Fame*, reluctantly end up tapping their feet in time to the beat. It is being modern and up-to-date which works in favor of Alex. It is not that her pop-culture dancing is vindicated in the way it is in *Fame*, rather that it is taken as a sign of raw talent, rough at the edges but with potential for learning real, that is, classical, dance.

Unlike *Fame*, *Flashdance* is a narrative of desired social mobility. Alex is disadvantaged by her poor background but her aspirations are to escape. She does not want to do this through a man or a romantic relationship, but she wants to get to where "high art" is found and that is undeniably on the other side of the tracks, in the "Grand Met" or its Pittsburgh equivalent, in the austere and beautiful building in the city center where perfectly outfitted students practice pliés and arabesques with complete disregard for anyone outside their privileged world. Alex's achievement is that she gets there and by implication leaves behind her the steelworks and the working-men's bar. The visual double bind in the film comes into play around Alex's body—she speaks through her body in dance, it is her only "commodity," her labor power and her artistic raw material. Cinematically, however, it is also the object of the male gaze. Michael is immediately attracted to her body as she dances in the bar. The camera lingers voyeuristically over every inch of her body as she performs. It is this which marks out the cinematic style from that of *Fame.* While the dancing is sexy in *Fame*, the bodies remain the possession of their owners. The camera at no point takes over and dwells upon them fetishistically. But it is this which makes *Flashdance* a more adult and a more male-oriented film. In narrative terms it is this sexual "looking" which Alex will escape when she moves into the environment of the ballet school, but in cinematic terms it is the sexual looking which counterpoints the feminine desire to dance which motivates the action. This creates an unevenness and imbalance which cannot be resolved in the course of the film. *Flashdance* remains a film for girls, to be looked at also by boys.

Dance, Culture, Art

The purpose of this discussion has been to sketch out some possible parameters for the construction of a sociology of dance. It has been argued that, whereas such a sociology would by necessity include a number of areas beyond the scope of this essay (for example, the dance labor process, the dance institutions, dance and the national heritage), of equal interest and importance would be the kinds of areas frequently bypassed in the world of cultural theory. Dance representations and the presence of dance images in a variety of media forms would form the basis of a study of the place of dance in contemporary consumer culture. Dance fictions and their role in preteenage feminine culture, as well as dance as a leisure practice enjoyed by thousands of young girls, would be of vital importance in building up a gender oriented model of dance, as would the practices and conventions surrounding social dancing and its place in contemporary youth culture.

The role of dancing in the development of romantic or sexual relationships has not been considered in depth here, nor has the presence of girls as dancers in the postwar youth subcultures. Instead attention has been focused on a moment which precedes teenage dancing and which has generated its own particular cultural expressions around dance. In dance fiction, and especially in "ballet books for girls" the reader is presented with an active and energetic femininity. In these books and in *Fame*, a more contemporary cinematic example, it is assumed that girls will be overwhelmed by a grand passion to dance or to perform. This passion will take them through a number of difficulties which with extreme dedication and hard work will be overcome. The emphasis is not so much on achieving "fame" but on the processes of getting there. Dance fictions are therefore about work, the sacrifices that have to be made, the relationships that have to be cast aside. In these narratives young female readers are also introduced to the idea of art and the special place it occupies in culture. Despite the conventional and perhaps mystified definition of art which crops up repeatedly in these stories, art is, for many readers, an enabling concept. Art is presented as something which can change the course of a life. It can give a young girl a legitimate reason to reject the normative expectations otherwise made of her and can provide her with a means of escape. This is the kind of language in which dance is presented to preteen readers, as something worth giving up a lot for, something that will pay off later in terms of great personal fulfillment. While some might argue that this is a damaging, pernicious, and misleading myth more likely to end in "the back row of the chorus line" than on stage at Covent Garden, the point is that it acts as a participative myth, a fantasy of achievement and a way of taking one's destiny into one's own hands.

The romance of dance and the importance of work combine in these popular narratives. There are few other places in popular culture where girls will find such active role models and such incentives to achieve. In almost all the examples discussed here success requires the absence or the marginalization of the family and familial relationships. Because the girl is more tightly ensconced within the family than her male peers, it is all the more important for her to free herself of these ties if she is to achieve her potential. Indeed it would be possible to attribute the success and popularity of these fictions with preteen girls to these factors—that they continually and repetitively explore the dynamics of moving into a more independent space which carries with it the promise of achievement while simultaneously holding at bay the more adolescent dynamics of sexual success where a whole other set of competencies come into play. In these fictions the physical body seems to be speaking in a register of its own choice.

Notes

1 R. Nijinsky, *Nijinsky* (Harmondsworth: Penguin, 1960).

2 Peter Wollen, "Fashion/Orientalism/The Body," in *New Formations* 1 (Spring 1987).

3 See also Eric Cahm, "Revolt, Conservatism, and Reaction in Paris, 1905–1925," in M. Bradbury and J. Macfarlane, eds., *Modernism* (Harmondsworth: Penguin, 1976), for an interesting discussion following the same lines as Wollen and concentrating on the dramatic effect which Diaghilev's *Rite of Spring* with music by Stravinsky had on Paris audiences: "Fighting broke out and the hubbub practically drowned the music; the refined innovations of Debussy were one thing, but these private rites of Russian tribalism another."

4 Pierre Bourdieu, *Distinction* (London: Routledge and Kegan Paul, 1984).

5 Ian Chambers, *Urban Rhythms: Pop Music and Popular Culture* (London: Macmillan, 1985).

6 Ibid.

7 E. Ewen, *Immigrant Women in the Land of Dollars* (New York: Methuen, 1986).

8 J. McCrindle and S. Rowbotham, *Dutiful Daughters* (Harmondsworth: Penguin, 1977).

9 R. Roberts, *The Classic Slum* (Harmondsworth: Penguin, 1971).

10 Geoff Mungham, "Youth in Pursuit of Itself," in G. Mungham and G. Pearson, eds., *Working Class Youth Culture* (London: Routledge and Kegan Paul, 1976).

11 R. Hoggart, *Uses of Literacy* (Harmondsworth: Penguin, 1956).

12 A. Whitehead, "Sexual Antagonism in Herefordshire," in D. Barker and S. Allen, eds., *Dependence and Exploitation in Marriage* (London: Longman, 1976).

13 Phillip Cohen, "Subcultural Conflict and Working Class Community," in Stuart Hall, ed., *Culture, Media, Language* (London: Hutchinson, 1980).

14 Dick Hebdige, *Subculture: The Meaning of Style* (London: Methuen, 1979).

15 I. Chambers, *Urban Rhythms.*

16 Hebdige, *Subculture.*

17 Paul Gilroy, "There Ain't No Black in The Union Jack," in *The Cultural Politics of Race and Nation* (London: Hutchinson, 1987).

18 *Flashdance* was marketed as a teen dance film. The publicity still and the TV advertisements for the film drew attention to the erotic dimension, focusing particularly on one moment in the film when Alex appears to be dancing under a shower. It might be suggested that the narrative was designed to attract a female interest and the visual subtext to appeal to men.

19 Noel Streatfield, *Ballet Shoes* (1936; Harmondsworth: Puffin, 1984); *Fame*, directed by Alan Parker, MGM, 1980; *Flashdance*, directed by Adrian Lyne, MGM, 1983.

20 V. Walkerdine, "Some Day My Prince Will Come," in A. McRobbie and M. Nava, eds., *Gender and Generation* (London: Macmillan, 1984).

21 Bruno Bettelheim, *The Uses of Enchantment* (London: Thames and Hudson, 1976).

22 G. Frith, " 'The Time of Your Life': The Meaning of the School Story," in G. Weiner and M. Arnot, eds., *Gender under Scrutiny* (London: Hutchinson, 1987).

23 Freud quoted by Bettelheim in *Uses of Enchantment.*

24 George Orwell, "Boys Weeklies," in *Inside the Whale and Other Essays* (Harmondsworth: Penguin, 1969)

25 See, for example, Angela McRobbie, "Interview with Juliet Mitchell," [illegible] (August 1988).

26 Juliet Mitchell, *Women: The Longest Revolution* (London: Virago, 1985).

III EXPANDING AGENDAS FOR CRITICAL THINKING

12 DANCING BODIES

Susan Leigh Foster

If you are asked to describe an object, you answer that it is a body with a surface, impenetrable, shaped, coloured, and movable. But subtract all these adjectives from your definition and what is left of that imaginary being you call a body?—Denis Diderot, "Letters on the Deaf and Dumb"

As a dancer working with, in, and through the body, I experience it as a body-of-ideas. I believe it is, as Diderot observed, the sum of all the adjectives that can be applied to it. I know the body only through its response to the methods and techniques used to cultivate it.

When I read recent critical writing about the body, I am, on the one hand, delighted at this new interest in it, and on the other, dismayed by the tendency to treat it as a symbol for desire or sexuality, for a utopia, for that which is unique to woman or for the elusive nature of the text. These writings seldom address the body I know; instead, they move quickly past arms, legs, torso, and head on their way to a theoretical agenda that requires something unknowable or unknown as an initial premise. The body remains mysterious and ephemeral, a convenient receptacle for their new theoretical positions.

Alternatively, these writings scrutinize and analyze the body, but only as a product of the various discourses that measure it. Here it exists as the referent for genres of calculation that concern the historian of science or sexuality: we learn intriguing details about the significance of sundry anatomical parts and how they have been subjected to study—and, by extension, incorporated into the larger workings of power.

What I miss in both approaches—the synecdochic substitution of the body for a theoretical topos or its metonymic replacement by a set of measurements—is a more meat-and-bones approach to the body based on an analysis of discourses or practices that *instruct* it. Roland Barthes refers to it in this way when he describes Bunraku puppet performances or the involvement of his own body in the physical organization of his desk and chair, his daily routines and habits of writing.[1] Michel Foucault delineates aspects of the instructable body when he describes the disciplinary procedures, the lines, hierarchies, and spatial organizations that bodies are asked to maintain as part of the disciplinary lineaments of culture.[2]

These two examples hardly suffice, though, when one considers what might be done toward studying methods of cultivating the body—whole disciplines through which it is molded, shaped, transformed, and in essence created. Such disciplines include all sports and physical-culture pursuits; regulations governing posture, etiquette, and comportment, and what is dubiously titled "nonverbal communication"; habits in the workplace or place of worship; conduct in the performing arts; patterns of standing, lying, sitting, eating, walking, as well as all practices that contribute to the development of what Marcel Mauss has called "techniques of the body."[3] Such practices, Foucault has demonstrated, are part of the fabric of culture itself. They "invest, mark, train and torture the body; they force it to carry out tasks, to perform ceremonies, and to emit signs."[4]

The daily practical participation of a body in any of these disciplines makes of it a body-of-ideas. Each discipline refers to it using select metaphors and other tropes that make it over. These tropes may be drawn from anatomical discourse or the science of kinesiology; or they may liken the body to a machine, an animal, or any other worldly object or event. They may be articulated as verbal descriptions of the body and its actions, or as physical actions that show it how to behave. Whether worded or enacted, these tropes change its meaning by re-presenting it.

In what follows, I shall attempt to describe one such body-of-ideas, that of the theatrical dancer. I have imagined that I am addressing someone who has seen but never participated in theatrical dance. My comments fall into two sections: the first focuses on the formation of dancing bodily consciousness, and the second situates this bodily consciousness in a cultural and aesthetic moment. Both are firmly rooted in a Western framework for considering the purpose and value of dance; they cannot avoid, even as they try to provide a perspective on, Western assumptions about the body, the self, and the expressive act.

The Perceived and Ideal Dancing Bodies

Typically, a dancer spends anywhere from two to six hours per day, six to seven days per week for eight to ten years creating a dancing body. During the course of this travail, the body *seems* constantly to elude one's efforts to direct it. The dancer pursues a certain technique for reforming the body, and the body seems to conform to the instructions given. Yet suddenly, inexplicably, it diverges from expectations, reveals new dimensions, and mutely declares its unwillingness or inability to execute commands. Brief moments of "mastery of the body" or of "feeling at one with the body" occur, producing a kind of ecstasy that motivates the dancer to continue. Clear sensations of improvement or progress—the result of a momentary matching of one's knowledge and awareness of the body with a developing physical capacity—also provide encouragement. The prevailing experience, however, is one of loss, of failing to regulate a miragelike substance. Dancers constantly apprehend the discrepancy between what they want to do and what they can do. Even after attaining official membership in the profession, one never has confidence in the body's reliability. The struggle continues to develop and maintain the body in response to new choreographic projects and the devastating evidence of aging.

Training thus creates two bodies: one, perceived and tangible; the other, aesthetically ideal. The dancer's perceived body derives primarily from sensory information that is visual, aural, haptic, olfactory, and perhaps most important, kinaesthetic. Dancers see large portions of their own bodies, a vista that changes as they move. They hear the sounds produced by locomotion, by one body part contacting another, by the breath and by joints and muscles creaking, popping, and grinding as they flex, extend, and rotate. They feel the body's contact with the ground, with objects or persons, and with parts of itself, and they sense its temperature and sweat. They smell sweat and breath. They sense kinesthetic indications of the tension or relaxation, tautness or laxness, and degree of exertion for every muscle, the action of any joint, and consequently the proximity of one bone to another, the relationship of any part of the body to gravity, and the entire body's equilibrium. Any of this information about the perceived body may be incorporated into the dancer's ideal body, where it combines with fantasized visual or kinesthetic images of a body, images of other dancers' bodies, and cinematic or video images of dancing bodies. The dancer's ideal body may specify size, shape, and proportion of its parts as well as expertise at executing specific movements. Both bodies, the perceived and the ideal, consist of the skeletal, muscular, and nervous systems and any fat tissue of the biological body. The lungs, stomach, sense organs, circulatory systems exist only minimally; other organs and the endocrine system not at all.

Both bodies are constructed in tandem; each influences the development of the other. Both result from the process of taking dance classes, as well as watching dance and talking about it. Cumulatively, these activities help the dancer to develop skills at attending to, duplicating, repeating, and remembering bodily movement. A third kind of body, the demonstrative body, mediates the acquisition of these skills by exemplifying correct or incorrect movement. Where the ideal body eludes the dancer with its perfection, the demonstrative body didactically emphasizes or even exaggerates actions necessary to improve dancing: it isolates moments in a movement sequence or parts of the body in order to present an analysis of the ideal. The demonstrative body displays itself in the body of the teacher, and sometimes in one's own image in the mirror and in the bodies of other students in the class and their mirror images. For example, when I look at another student in the class, I see her or his body not as that of a friend or an acquaintance, but as the bodily instantiation of desired or undesired, correct or incorrect, values.

Several systematic programs of instruction, known as "dance techniques," exist for studying the perceived body, organizing the information its presents, and correlating it with demonstrative and ideal bodies. Each technique cultivates bodily strength, flexibility, and alignment, the shapes made by the body, the rhythm of its movement, and the quality and amount of tension throughout it. Most techniques offer both a body topography, a mapping of key areas on or in it, as well as principles governing the proper relations of these areas. In dance technique classes, this topography is put in motion by performing sequences of movement usually designated by the demonstrative body of the teacher.

Unlike the private classes offered in the technique of playing a musical instrument, dance classes are usually attended by fifteen to fifty students at a time. They occur daily, rather than weekly or monthly, and they rarely present for study and performance an entire dance composition. Phrases or sections of dances may be taught, but the issues of interpretation, development, coherence, or style of performance are more often addressed in rehearsal for a specific work rather than in technique class. Furthermore, dancers are not expected to practice extensively on their own. Their training is communal and highly regimented, but it is also context specific. As students learn to duplicate the correctly demonstrative body and to avoid the mistakes of the incorrect body, they present (and are presented with) endless new variations on right and wrong. The demands of both the perceived and the ideal bodies are thus redefined by each teacher with each group of students.

Each dance technique relies on an extensive nomenclature, sometimes literal and sometimes metaphoric, for designating key areas of the body and their relations. A dancer may be asked to "rotate the head of the femur in the hip socket," "lift the floating ribs," or "increase the space between the skull and top cervical vertebra"; alternatively, to become "a balloon expanding with air" or "a puppet." Techniques might visualize the body as a set of abstract lines running close to the bones, as a set of points or regions of the surface and interior, as a set of forces that lift, descend, expand, or condense specified areas of the body. Dancers pull, tuck, extend, lift, soften, and lengthen areas of the body throughout the duration of the technique class. They learn the curves or angles that body parts can form, and to place these in a particular shape at a given time. They learn to delineate rhythmic structures, to regulate the flow of effort from one part to another, to sculpt, trace, and imprint these parts in space.

Both the exercises themselves and any directives offered by the teacher are usually highly repetitive. Drilling is necessary because the aim is nothing less than *creating the body*. With repetition, the images used to describe the body and its actions *become* the body. Metaphors that are inapplicable or incomprehensible when first presented take on a concrete reality over time, through their persistent association with a given movement. For example, it may at first seem impossible to lift the leg forward using the back thigh muscles, but continued attempts to execute the movement with this image in mind subtly reorganize muscular involvement so as to produce the clear perception that precisely this is happening.

Over months and years of study, the training process repeatedly reconfigures the body: it identifies and names aspects or parts that were previously unrecognized, and it restructures the whole in terms of dynamic actions that relate the various parts. Neither the perceived body nor the ideal body remains constant throughout this process: definitions of both are altered and refined. The mastery of one area of the body's topography enables the dancer to comprehend new images and to reconsider familiar ones from a new perspective. Once one can "lift" the leg from "underneath," one can appreciate anew how to avoid "leaning into the hip" of the "supporting" leg.

Metaphors open out into related metaphors, leading the dancer further into a given system for conceptualizing the body. The daily routines of training consolidate metaphoric knowledge and thereby produce bodily habits, some "good" and some "bad." Good habits form the basis for the newly perceived body, and they allow the student to attend to assimilating additional information. Bad habits (only recognizable as such once they already exist) indicate problems that require special attention. If the metaphoric system in use proves ineffective in eliminating bad habits or in preventing or curing injury, the dancer may discard it in favor of alternative systems. The dancer must decipher each new interpretive framework, however, using as reference the body of metaphors built up through prior training.

As dancers labor to meet the standards for the ideal body—determined sometimes by themselves, at others by a choreographer, style, or tradition—they inevitably encounter areas of bodily resistance or incapacity. These deficits are exaggerated by the intensity of training, and they produce highly distorted, often obsessive images of the perceived body. The training regimen reveals the perceived body to be horribly deficient in the size and proportion of its parts. Its areas of inflexibility and lack of strength or endurance can take on grotesque dimensions. Its inability to imitate shapes, to hear rhythms, or to relax or tense appropriately become an aberrant inadequacy.

Working to correct bad habits, to modify the body's aberrations, and to increase its capabilities, the dancer frequently incurs pain and learns quickly to distinguish between several kinds: constructive pain that will lead to greater strength or flexibility; destructive pain caused by the incorrect positioning or use of a part of the body; chronic pain, the cumulative result of bad habit; pain resulting from too much tension, too little strength, activities other than dance, overambition, inattentiveness, and so on. Some pains remain constant and reliable, and the dancer carries them around as constant features of bodily topography. Others, intermittent and unpredictable, cause the dancer to chase after them in search of a diagnosis that could prevent their recurrence.

As both the perceived and the ideal bodies develop, they increasingly occupy the dancer's consciousness. Over time, dancers increasingly monitor their alignment, the quality of their movement, and their bodily pain—not only in the dance studio but in quotidian situations as well. They may or may not apply technical principles learned in the dance class to daily chores and routines, but they certainly attend more fully to these activities. They also retain kinesthetic information from past performances of these activities so as to begin to acquire a historical sense of their own bodily movements.

Most dance classes emphasize seeing a movement and then performing it, which further heightens the dancer's kinesthetic awareness of others. Dancers, more than those who do not dance, strongly sense what other persons' bodily movements feel like. Walking down the street, they register the characteristic posture and gait of passers-by; in conversation, they sense the slouch, strain, and gesticulations of others. This capacity for kinesthetic empathy, however, rarely includes erotic feelings. The metaphors used to train the dancing body seldom, if ever, refer to the sexual body. The frequent use of mirrors in learning to dance promotes a form of narcissistic enthrallment with the body, but this is usually mitigated by the tendency to focus on, and criticize, bodily inadequacies. The musculoskeletal empathy developed by dancing usually involves an appraisal of the other's and one's own perceived bodies. The sexual bodies, perhaps adjacent to, and informed by, the dancing bodies, remain clearly separate.

A dancer's daily consciousness of the body thus ranges between her or his perceived body—with all its pains and distortions—and images, both fantasized and real, of other bodies. Dancers alternate between, or sometimes fuse together, images from all these bodies as they objectify, monitor, scan, regard, attend to, and keep track of bodily motion throughout the day. The metaphors learned during instruction serve as both markers and interpreters of developing bodily consciousness. They also integrate the training of the body with aesthetic, social, and moral beliefs about dance. The repertoire of metaphors learned in class functions not only to define the dancer's body but also to establish the epistemological foundation for performing dance.

The Body of Dance Techniques

I have tried to describe the development of dancing bodily consciousness in a way that would apply to most programs of instruction. Each dance technique, however, constructs a specialized and specific body, one that represents a given choreographer's or tradition's aesthetic vision of dance. Each technique creates a body that is unique in how it looks and what it can do. Generally, the style and skills it imparts can be transferred only partially to another technique; thus, ballet dancers cannot assume the bearing or perform the vocabulary of movements found in contact improvisation, and vice versa. Training not only constructs a body but also helps to fashion an expressive self that, in its relation with the body, performs the dance. Aesthetic expression can result when a self uses the body as a vehicle for communicating its thoughts and feelings, or when the self merges with the body and articulates its own physical situation. Body and self can also coexist, enunciating their own concerns and commenting on each other's. Many other relations are also possible, each producing a specific aesthetic impact on dancer, dance, and viewer.

In order to illustrate the different forms that expression, both felt and enacted, can take, I have compiled brief descriptions of five twentieth-century techniques that formulate distinct bodies and selves. These descriptions, which emphasize the differences among the techniques, derive from choreographers' and critics' writings about the techniques, as well as from observations I have heard or have made as a student in class. Far from comprehensive, they present only a few key features of each technique in order to suggest possible relationships between body and self that result from instructing the body in a given dance technique.

Ballet Technique. The dominant and most familiar of all theatrical dance techniques is ballet. Of the five bodies to be considered here, it is the only one with requirements for the dancer's physique. Success in this technique depends in part on thin, long limbs capable of displaying the formal geometric features of the tradition (figure 1). The ideal body—light, quick, precise,

1. Ballet class at the School of American Ballet, New York City. Courtesy of the Dance Collection, the New York Public Library for the Performing Arts, Astor, Lenox, and Tilden Foundations.

strong—designates the linear shapes, the rhythm of phrases, even the pantomimed gestures, all with lyrical effortlessness. Success also requires the promising student to make an early and dedicated commitment to intensive training. The perceived body, never sufficiently thin or well proportioned, must mold itself repeatedly into the abstract forms presented in class and then on stage. The dancer's self exists to facilitate the craftlike acquisition of skills: it serves the choreographer and, ultimately, the tradition by ordering the body to practice and then to perform ideals of movement.

Classes, organized into several levels of competence, measure the student's progress through a standardized set of physical skills. As with the level of classes, the exercises in a given class progress from simple to more complex. Dancers begin a standard daily sequence with one arm stabilizing the body by holding a barre. They perform movements, announced (in French) by the teacher, originating in, and returning to, basic positions—first on one side and then, switching arms at the barre, on the other. The movements work the legs (always in a turned-out position) and, to a lesser extent, the arms to create variations and embellishments on circular and triangular designs. The torso provides a taut and usually erect center connecting the four appendages and the head. Approximately one half of a class session takes place at the barre. Students then move to the center of the room for longer, more intricate combinations at varying tempos. Class ends with sequences of leaps and turns in which dancers travel across the room diagonally, two or three at a time. Descriptions of movements and corrections are phrased so as to ask parts of the body to conform to abstract shapes; they place the pelvis or head in specific locations, or extend the limbs along imaginary lines in space. Additional criteria based on the precision of timing, clarity of shape, and lightness of quality all measure the student's performance.

The teacher illustrates the correct approach by performing a small excerpt from the phrase—seldom, if ever, an entire sequence. The ideal body glimpsed in performances of the premier dancers thus remains distinct from the demonstrative body that models proper practice. From the teacher's unchallenged authority, students assimilate the system of values and internalize the impulse to evaluate and rank their own and others' performances. Competition, although quiet, is fierce—in part because standards for perfection are so clearly defined. The aesthetic rationale based on the pursuit of classical beauty offers dancers no alternative conceptions of dance: inability to succeed at ballet implies failure at all dance.[5]

Duncan Technique. Reacting in part against the artificial and hierarchical organization of ballet, Isadora Duncan and several other early-twentieth-century choreographers and performers pioneered a radically new dance aes-

2. Isadora Duncan. Photo: Raymond Duncan. Courtesy of the Dance Collection, the New York Public Library for the Performing Arts, Astor, Lenox, and Tilden Foundations.

thetic and a concomitant approach to training the body. Claiming for the body an intrinsic freedom and merit, Duncan transported those for whom she danced into an evanescent realm of feeling-filled forms (figure 2). Her work has been reconstructed by a number of companies that currently perform and teach regularly throughout the United States. It has also been preserved in the practices of dance camps that offer summer study, primarily to women, in interpretive dancing.

For Duncan and those following in her tradition, the dancing body manifests an original naturalness. Unadorned by the contrived distortions of movement that modern society incurs, the ideal body inheres in a primal experience of integration both within one's self and within society. Its harmonious passages for the limbs and graceful phrasing emanate from the protean ductility of the respiring central torso. It is here, in the region of the solar plexus, that soul and body meet and converse. The ideal body resides within every body but deforms at an early age in response to social pressures. By requiring dance study of all young children, it is thought, society will make itself over, for dance is a revolutionary force that evokes noble and pure motives in all its participants.

In order to cultivate the natural body and to allow it to relinquish affected habits, Duncan's approach advocates the study of "basic" human movements such as walking, running, skipping, lying down, standing, turning, and jumping—all performed with a graceful, relaxed fullness, initiated by patterns of breath. These basic movements form sequences practiced to music of great nineteenth-century classical composers. Dancers also act out simple imaginary scenarios guided by the music's meter and harmonic development. Since music is considered to be the truest expression of the human soul, dance, which replicates its compositional structure, can likewise indicate the soul's ephemeral but fervent states of being. When students are asked to "retreat, shielding themselves from an evil force moving toward them," or to "fall to the earth, lie quietly, and then rise to greet the sun," they are participating, body and soul, in primordial human situations.

Students imitate the unpretentious intent and full-bodied commitment of the teacher, who frequently dances alongside them. The actual shape of the limbs is less important than the degree of involvement in the dance, evident in the face, the quality of movement, and the graceful connections among areas of the body. These criteria for success discourage critical evaluation of one's own or others' bodies (such a pronounced distance between perceived and ideal bodies could only result in pretentious performance). Instead, through repetition in a communal setting, movement and music work their elevating, liberating charm. The ideal body, then, one that has achieved simplicity in its movement and harmony with the self, issues from a nurturing collective of bodies.[6]

Graham Technique. For Martha Graham, the dancing body must possess the strength, flexibility, and endurance necessary to provide the expressive self with a fully responsive instrument (figure 3). The goal of dance, to represent in archetypal form the deep conflicts of the human psyche, can be realized only through a rigorous training program. As with Duncan, the body functions as a perfect index of the self's feelings. The self's ability to express those feelings, though, like the body's ability to manifest them, shares none of Duncan's exuberance—the self is too dark and repressed, the act of expression too tortured for movement to be light and free-flowing. The ideal body, then, even as it manifests an agile responsiveness, also shows in the strained quality and definition of its musculature the ordeal of expression.

Graham's technique coalesced out of the vocabulary she developed in her earliest dances. The basic set of exercises, which became routine by the 1950s, dominated the American university dance curriculum for many years, and it continues to provide a coherent and viable alternative to ballet training in dance schools around the world. The first half of a class—as much time as the ballet student spends at the barre—consists of exercises performed in a sitting or lying position; students then practice sequences standing and, finally, traveling across the floor. The exercises privilege movements originating in the torso and radiating out with restrained tension to the periphery of the body. The slow progression from sitting to standing to traveling, and the tensile successions from central to peripheral body, affirm both the possibility and the difficulty of bodily expression. Exercises, repeated with slight variations composed by the teacher each day, cause the body to spiral around a spinal core, extending out and then pulling back into dynamic positions. The body, galvanized into action as much by its own potential energy as by the dissonant textures of the musical accompaniment, arrives on the downbeat, but then surges almost immediately in a new direction. Although the precise metric requirements for these miniature cycles of attraction and withdrawal give the class an almost military appearance, tensile elasticity predominates over visual pattern in the overall movement.

The principal metaphor explored in these exercises, that of contraction and release, promotes a connection between physical and psychological functioning. Students introspectively delve into the interior body as they contract and relate internal to external space through various pathways of release. Unlike Duncan's classes, in which the student is cast into imagined situations, the comments made in Graham's classes refer only indirectly to psychological experience: they allude to the self's condition by contextualizing physical cor-

3. Martha Graham in her *Cave of the Heart.*
Courtesy of the Dance Collection, the New York Public
Library for the Performing Arts, Astor, Lenox,
and Tilden Foundations.

rections within the larger and arduous project of becoming an artist. Just as the choreographer must submit to constant self-interrogation concerning the validity of the dance's message, so the dancer scrutinizes self as well as body in a search for the causes of the body's unresponsiveness. The dancer's perceived body, always lacking either in integration or articulation, must struggle to become more than it is—a quest that, in turn, strengthens and sensitizes the self.[7]

Cunningham Technique. Merce Cunningham, a member of the third generation of American modern dancers, left Martha Graham's company in the late 1940s to develop his own approach to choreography and technique.

Cunningham's method presents the physicality of multiple bodies inscribing complex spatial and temporal patterns (figure 4). His conception of the dancing body fuses body and self by immersing the self in the practical pursuit of enhancing the body's articulacy. The self does not use the body for its own expressive purposes as in Graham or Duncan; rather, it dedicates itself, as in ballet, to the craftlike task of preparing and presenting movement. Unlike ballet, however, a radically nonhierarchical definition of competence and distinctive value prevails. Cunningham's approach celebrates unique physiques, quirkiness, and the unanticipated. This is, in part, the open-ended message his dances convey.

Exercises for the technique class vary from day to day as they systematically explore the body's segments and their possible range of movement. They present spinal curves, arches and twists, leg lifts, knee bends, brushes of the foot—all using quotidian names for parts of the body and their actions. Sequences of these moves, complex in duration, meter, and rhythm, form subtle relations with the surrounding space. Students focus on accomplishing clear bodily enunciations of these spatiotemporal relations. The dancer is asked to enhance bodily accomplishment by remaining alert and concentrated, to be "quick on his or her feet." Where ballet's ideal body privileges certain joint actions over others, Cunningham's ideal body is imbued equally throughout with animated alertness.

The teacher presents movement sequences as problems to be solved. Students are asked to focus on and to demonstrate, through their articulacy, the choreography inherent in the movement sequences. The height of a jump or extended leg matters less than the clear presentation of complex directives—quick changes of weight or focus, polyrhythmic patterns in different body parts, carefully patterned paths of movement across the floor. The accompanist reinforces the emphasis on composition by experimenting with different tonal and timbral frameworks, even for the repetition of a given exercise. Such a strong and contrasting musical presence affirms the autonomy of dance and

4. Merce Cunningham and Barbara Lloyd in *Rainforest.* Photo: Oscar Bailey. Courtesy of the Dance Collection, the New York Public Library for the Performing Arts, Astor, Lenox, and Tilden Foundations.

music as expressive media. Students must attend to the two distinct forms simultaneously and to their unpredictable relationships, rather than to fuse one with the other.[8]

Contact Improvisation Technique. If the Cunningham body is a jointed one, the body cultivated in contact improvisation is weighted and momentous. This technique, developed collaboratively in the early 1970s by Steve Paxton, Nancy Stark Smith, Lisa Nelson, and others, explores the body's relations to gravity and to other bodies which result from its ability to flow as a physical mass (figure 5). Contact improvisation gained popularity rapidly in the United States during the 1970s and early 1980s as an artistic and social movement. Its technique classes were complemented by frequent informal practice sessions known as "jams," which allowed dancers to learn from, perform for, and socialize with one another. Its lyrical athleticism has been incorporated into the movement style of many dance companies in the United States and also in Europe, where it offers one of the few alternatives to ballet training.

Unlike any of the other techniques discussed here, contact improvisation sets parameters for how to move but does not designate a set vocabulary of movements for students to learn. Students explore through improvisation the movement territory established by the stylistic and technical rules of the form. Classes include practice at simple skills of weight transfer as well as opportunities to use them through improvisation with others. Exercises present ways to "drain weight" out of one area of the body, to "collect" it in another, and to transfer weight across any of the body's joints. Certain lifts or rolls are practiced again and again; other exercises direct students to experiment for several minutes at a time with methods of regulating and channeling the body's weight on their own or with a partner. As in Duncan's approach, the body is believed to have its own intelligence—though one encumbered by its artificial and ungainly habits. Dancers can be advised on how to roll, jump into another's arms, or land from a great height, but they are also encouraged to "listen" to the body, to be sensitive to its weight and inclinations and to allow new possibilities of movement to unfold spontaneously by attending to the shifting network of ongoing interactions.

The teacher's guidance, like the students' participation, is based on an assessment of the needs of the moment. Rather than specifying a series of preconceived forms, both teacher and students must determine what movement is appropriate for the group at a given time. In this democratic, unpredictable, and highly physical situation, the dancer's self becomes immersed in the body, as it does for Cunningham. The body, however, is not invested with an ongoing identity: its definition is constantly renegotiated in the changing context of the improvised dance. Ideally, its strength should be sufficient to

5. Contact improvisation by Nancy Stark Smith and Andrew Harwood. Photo: Bill Arnold, 1985.

bear the weight of another; but even more important, it must manifest an ability to go with the flow.[9]

Both contact improvisation and Duncan technique cast the teacher in the role of facilitator, and both ask students to appreciate and encourage one another. Each of these techniques embraces all participants in the class, whatever their age or level of expertise, as members of a community of dancers. In ballet, by contrast, the hierarchy of values evident in the levels of classes and companies, in the choreography itself, and in its viewers' responses all incite competition among students. Teachers, as they introduce the tradition's standards for success and rank the students' performance against them, embody the authority of the tradition's abstract ideals. Graham's technique, on the other hand, places dancers in competition with each other but also with themselves. Criteria for success revolve around the dancer's ability to perform fully Graham's vocabulary of movement, but the dancer is also asked to fuse inner motivation with physical form. The teacher encourages the student to measure this psychological and physical participation through comments that question one's commitment to discipline. Cunningham's technique, with its emphasis on composition, encourages dancers to interest themselves in making dance as well as in performing. Students take from class whatever insights may be relevant to their own careers as choreographers and dancers.

The structure of authority developed in each class helps to connect the dancing body to its aesthetic project. Ballet's prescribed pairings of positions and steps, and its emphasis on outwardly rotated legs and arms, constructs a flexible, elegant, lifted body that displays the classical linear and aerial forms that are the hallmarks of that tradition. The teacher's concise directives place the student within that tradition. Duncan's walks and skips, different from the quotidian in their rhythm and quality, embody an ideal of naturalness. Their graceful, grounded litheness seeks to render the body transparent to the luminous inclinations of the soul. The teacher's enthusiasm and conviction help to incorporate the student into the dancing community. The restrained successive movements of Graham's contraction and release build a sinewy, tensile, dynamic body that symbolizes a self full of turbulent feelings and the struggle inherent in expressing those feelings. The teacher's intimation of the arduous training ahead warns students of their need for commitment as it summons them to the dance. Cunningham's matter-of-fact inventory of the body's structural capabilities produces a lanky, intelligent, alert body that eloquently declaims its own physicality. Cunningham teachers tend to approach their students as junior colleagues, instructing them while preserving their autonomy as potential artists. Contact improvisation's athletic, fleet body realizes itself through the act of contact with others. Its teachers must consistently empower students with the ability to improvise an innovative and sensitive response to the collective gathering of dancers.

Much more could be said about each of these techniques—how each elaborates a set of relations among parts of the body, and among dancing bodies, and how each develops the body within a sonoral and architectural environment. Ballet dancers, for example, have insisted on practicing before a mirror since the middle of the eighteenth century, whereas Duncan preferred teaching outdoors on a carefully groomed lawn. Through choices such as these, reiterated daily in distinctive routines, each technique introduces students to the set of metaphors out of which their own perceived and ideal bodies come to be constructed. It also instructs them in the rhetorical relations that bind body to self and to community.

The "Hired" Body

Prior to the last decade, each of these techniques was considered to be unique. Not only did each mark the body so deeply that a dancer could not adequately perform another technique, but each aesthetic project was conceived as mutually exclusive of, if not hostile to, the others. Recently, however, choreographic experimentation with eclectic vocabularies and with new interdisciplinary genres of performance has circumvented the distinctiveness of these bodies. A new cadre of dance makers, called "independent choreographers," has emerged; their aesthetic vision can be traced to the experimental choreography of the early 1960s and 1970s, a period when choreographic investigation challenged boundaries between dance and day-to-day movement and claimed any and all human movement as potential dance. Because these choreographers' work neither grows out of, nor is supported by, any of the academies of dance, classical or modern, their success depends largely on their own entrepreneurial efforts to promote their work. New institutions of "arts management and administration" have grown to meet the needs of producing their work. Issues of fashion and fundability have increasingly influenced their aesthetic development.

These choreographers have not developed new dance techniques to support their choreographic goals, but instead encourage dancers to train in several existing techniques without adopting the aesthetic vision of any. They require a new kind of body, competent at many styles (figure 6). The new multitalented body resulting from this training melds together features from all the techniques discussed above: it possesses the strength and flexibility found in ballet necessary to lift the leg high in all directions; it can perform any

6. Mark Morris with Susan Hadley and Rob Besserer in Morris's *Pièce en Concert.* Photo: Beatriz Schiller, 1987.

movement neutrally and pragmatically, as in Cunningham's technique; it has mastered the athleticism of contact improvisation, enabling a dancer to fall and tumble, and to support another's weight; it articulates the torso as a Graham dancer does; it has the agility of Duncan's dancers.

This body exists alongside others that remain more deeply involved in, and consequently more expert at, the techniques I have outlined. It does not display its skills as a collage of discrete styles but, rather, homogenizes all styles and vocabularies beneath a sleek, impenetrable surface. Uncommitted to any specific aesthetic vision, it is a body for hire: it trains in order to make a living at dancing.

The hired body has been shaped partly by contemporary practices of physical education, whose goals for such activities as sports, aerobics, and individual exercise programs—jogging, swimming, weight lifting, and so on—have been set by the scientization of the body's needs. Like the ideal body promoted by these activities, this hired body should achieve a certain heart rate, a general level of strength and flexibility, and a muscular tonus. The criteria for evaluating its training share physical education's specialized and scientific orientation. They use the language of biology and kinesiology to appraise the strength, flexibility, and endurance of the body's muscle groups. Through this scientific language of the body, the body's character is reduced to principles of physics: it can be enlarged here, elasticized there. This body, a purely physical object, can be made over into whatever look one desires. Like one's "lifestyle," it can be constructed to suit one's desires.

Of equal influence on the hired body is the video dancing body, which is as familiar to "dancercize" and MTV enthusiasts as to theatrical dance choreographers, performers, and viewers. The video dancing body is often constructed from the edited tapes of dance movement filmed from different angles and distances. Its motion can be slowed, smeared, or replicated so that it performs breathtaking feats, and yet it projects none of the tensile qualities of movement, the body's situation in space, or the charisma of a live performance. Nonetheless, it offers to performers, choreographers, and scholars the irresistible promise of a "permanent" record of the dance, which can be viewed and reviewed indefinitely. This record, helpful as a tool in the choreographic process, has become increasingly mandatory as a promotional device required by all dance producers and funding agencies as an unproblematic simulacrum of live dance.

Although the video body bears little resemblance to any of the bodies perceived in the dance class, it shares with the hired body certain ideals. Both feature a rubbery flexibility coated with impervious glossiness, and both are equally removed from the aesthetic vision that implements them. Training to construct it primarily takes place standing behind the camera and sitting in the editing room. The techniques it manifests, along with the aesthetic orientation it supports, belong properly to the medium of video, not to dance as a performing art. Training to construct the hired body occurs in rooms full of bodybuilding machines or in dance classes whose overall aesthetic orientation may hold little appeal. Still, both video and hired bodies appear as the products of an efficient and "unbiased" training program, assumed to be neutral and completely adaptable; as a result, they mask the process through which dance technique constructs the body.

Of course, there is nothing new about the assertion of a normative or original body, or an efficacious way to instruct the body. Duncan and the other early modernists, for example, obscured their approach to constructing the body by insisting on the "naturalness" of their training. Their "natural" body, however, contravened prevailing aesthetic ideals and presented a profoundly different alternative, whereas the multipurpose hired body subsumes and smooths over differences. The modernist approach to dance making, even as it promoted the body's movement as material substance to be worked into art, assumed an irrevocable connection to a self. The hired body, built at a great distance from the self, reduces it to a pragmatic merchant of movement proffering whatever look appeals at the moment. It not only denies the existence of a true, deep self, but also proscribes a relational self whose desire to empathize predominates over its need for display. The hired body likewise threatens to obscure the opportunity, opened to us over this century, to apprehend the body as multiple, protean, and capable, literally, of being made into many different expressive bodies.

Notes

1 See, for example, Roland Barthes, *The Empire of Signs*, trans. Richard Howard (New York: Hill and Wang, 1978); and *Barthes by Barthes*, trans. Richard Howard (New York: Hill and Wang, 1977). Barthes, however, also uses the body as a symbol for desire and the unconscious.

I am indebted to Cynthia Novack and to Kim Benton for their insightful comments on this essay.

2 Michel Foucault, *Discipline and Punish: The Birth of the Prison*, trans. Alan Sheridan (New York: Pantheon, 1978).

3 Marcel Mauss, essay in *Incorporations*, ed. Jonathan Crary and Sanford Kwinter (New York: Zone, 1992), pp. 454–77.

4 Foucault, *Discipline and Punish*, p. 25.

5 Descriptions of the ballet class can be found in Merrill Ashley and Larry Kaplan, *Dancing for Balanchine* (New York: Dutton, 1984); Cynthia Lyle, *Dancers on Dancing* (New York: Drake, 1977); and Joseph Mazo, *Dance Is a Contact Sport* (New York: Saturday Review Press, 1974).

6 For more detailed accounts of Duncan's approach to dance technique, see Irma Duncan, *Duncan Dancer* (Middletown, Conn.: Wesleyan University Press, 1966); Irma Duncan, *The Technique of Isadora Duncan* (Brooklyn, N.Y.: Dance Horizons, 1970); and Isadora Duncan, *The Art of the Dance* (New York: Theatre Arts, 1928).

7 Graham's philosophy of dance technique is summarized in her article "The American Dance," in Merle Armitage and Virginia Stewart, eds., *Modern Dance* (New York: Weyhe, 1935), pp. 101–6; idem, "A Dancer's World" (transcript of the film *A Dancer's World*), *Dance Observer*, January 1958, p. 5; and in Alice Helpern, "The Evolution of Martha Graham's Technique" (Ph.D. diss., New York University, 1981).

8 Cunningham describes his approach to dance technique in his article "The Function of a Technique for Dance," in Walter Sorell, ed., *The Dance Has Many Faces* (New York: World Publishing, 1951), pp. 250–55; and, in conversation with Jacqueline Lesschaeve, *The Dancer and the Dance* (New York: Boyars, 1985).

9 For a comprehensive and insightful analysis of the development of contact improvisation, see Cynthia Novack, *Sharing the Dance: An Ethnography of Contact Improvisation* (Milwaukee: University of Wisconsin Press, 1990); and *Contact Quarterly*, a journal featuring articles on contact improvisation.

13 SPECTACLE AND DANCING BODIES THAT MATTER: OR, IF IT DON'T FIT, DON'T FORCE IT

Anna Beatrice Scott

Now I pride myself on being a post-essentialist black person, but when I went to a *bloco afro* rehearsal in San Francisco intent upon doing some Black Atlantic research this past March only to discover that I was one of only five black people out of at least fifty participants, including the drummers and teacher, I was having a hard time controlling my proprietary and protective instincts regarding black culture. I stood amidst the collection of Anglo, Asian, and Latino participants in the room, questionnaires in hand, smile on face, and wondered to myself, "Where are the black people?" Why did it matter to me? And why was everyone staring at *me*, the materialization of the adjective in *bloco afro*?

In this essay I want to begin addressing what has been a central part of my life as a black dancer/performer of African cultural practices—spectacle. Displaying my otherness as impressive and striking entertainment and politics, I desire, indeed need to be seen by white spectators, even while I am repulsed by the scene. "I" as subject materialize before their eyes only as a flash of excessive material. Placing in plain view my desire to become every black 'other' in order to reclaim my pre middle passage self, my race-specific appropriations dissimulate through their apparent appropriateness the restrictions/regulations on my dancing black body. Spectacle, spectator, and specter, I precede myself as always and already racialized.[1]

I am invested in understanding "traditions" separated from their moorings, a free play that costs $8 at the door or $13.99 in the record store. This free play is a spectator sport even while one participates. Me, a dancing black hole in which the white dancer and any spectator may pour her desire, extract their fill of embodied knowledge, authenticating themselves by making me a spectacle. The questions I want to ask are, "Through what regulatory norms of spectacle is race itself materialized? Is there anything at all liberating or useful created in transgressing those laws? Sister-girl has a lot of issues to work through. So there I was looking for recognition, that one friendly face that would say with its smile, "Oh yeah. I remember you. You used to dance with *Orixa Baba* a couple of years ago. How you been?" But let me ease up and enter this story from an eddying whirlpool of a start, to mark Benjamin.

For the past few years I have been conducting research on a particular *Carnaval* dance form that has its undisputed origins in Salvador, Bahia-Brasil, by undisputed inventors collectively called Ilê Aiyê, with an undisputed date of the year 1974. However, it was much disputed if *bloco afro* really counted as a Brazilian folklore form, given: (1) the hybridity of its music, known as samba reggae, (2) non-Brazilian themes and costumes, and (3) critical distance embedded in the performance, or more precisely, its overt political stance of black nationalism. This in a country that was ruled by a dictator wielding propaganda for pride in its racial democracy and the great Brazilian past. In short, *blocos afros* are performance groups based on looks—skin colors, nose widths, hair textures, eye colors—and a belief that those looks are the signs of a body that needs to matter, be counted, accepted, and celebrated. These signs function as unity-texts and are materialization of the unseen spiritual world that validates and connects all those beautiful black bodies. Conversely, in certain *blocos*, these signs become restrictions on the "complexion" of the collective body, demanding a uniformity in appearance of each individual body.

The directors and creators of *bloco afro* performance see themselves as members of the global struggle for black liberation and self-determination. The musicians and dancers consider themselves the heirs to a vast cultural richness that stretches across the Atlantic Ocean engulfing the United States, the Caribbean, Europe, and Africa. Bob Marley is a very big influence on the music, as are traditional Yoruba rhythms and practices that were imported along with enslaved Africans. James Brown and Michael Jackson influenced dance styles on the street and the I-Threes influenced carnival queens on floats. All groups were influenced by Yoruba ritual dances. Moreover, many dances and costume designs were researched in the most unlikely places: coffee-table photo collections on primitive art and peoples, album jackets and descriptions in songs, ethnographic dissertations, pan-African literature, tourist, ethnographic and fictional films, and postcards, to name a few.

Blocos afros perform in various places: at *Carnaval*, in smaller club venues, or as mass political actions to shut down traffic for a few hours in order to demonstrate the unity of the burgeoning black community. They hold weekly rehearsals or *ensaios*, where you can go and learn the latest songs and dance steps or get political information about the Black Atlantic, get your pockets picked, maybe get caught in a crossfire, get a contact high, or pick up some

1. Members of the *bloco afro* Malê do Balê participate in the 1995 Caminhada do Axê in Salvador, Bahia, Brazil. This particular performance was done with the general theme of "axê," stressing the life force/power of Afro-Brazilian cultural heritage. Photo: Anna Scott.

comfort for the evening. Basically it is your typical big-city urban festival. Although it sounds as if *bloco afro* is *the* black *Carnaval* expression, it's misleading to envision all the "black" people in the city of Salvador participating in *bloco afro* performances.

Aside from a colorist instead of racist paradigm of classification, one other fact complicates the picture of a unified black performance style in Salvador: there are several different types of carnival performances. *Bloco afro* is just the latest in a long line of performer options. There are *cortejos*, *embaixadas*, *afoxês*, *trio electricos*, *escolas de samba*, *bloco de indios*, simple *blocos*, and I'm sure a handful of other styles that I don't even know about. So why has *bloco afro* style blown up so large that you can join one in San Francisco, Notting Hill Gate, D.C., or Brooklyn—and not even be black?

Recently, *samba reggae* music has taken off on its own and joined the "world music" family. More politically active *blocos* like *Olodum* have always had a pan-African agenda and traveled nationally and internationally to spread their gospel, leaving groups of imitating aficionados in their wake. They cut records locally that circulate internationally through public radio shows like *Afropop Worldwide* and researchers and ethnographers like myself. This conversion from the folk to the world music, or local to the global, has made for interesting creations in points of purchase. Paul Simon, as one of the first white collectors on the scene, moved *Olodum* into the recording studio to capture their sound for his album *Rhythm of the Saints.* Not too much later, and with much more awe and respect, David Byrne of the Talking Heads went to Salvador around 1988 and made a video documentary about black cultural practices, including blackitude *Carnaval* forms, entitled *Ilê Aiyê: The House of Life.* Years later, *samba reggae* can be heard on jazz records, local pop recordings, and even a Michelob beer commercial. You can read about it in the *New York Times* or watch it on Entertainment Tonight or a PBS series on dance. But most importantly, you can buy their records, tapes, and CDs, minus the non-Brazilian front men.

What does all this have to do with the question, "Through what regulatory norms of spectacle is race itself materialized?" Part of the power of the label "world music" in the mid-eighties was that the bodies making the music did not need to originate from or match the music—one world, one music. Those mismatched bodies were usually white bodies, making money while having a bit of the other in public. But in the world of marketing, where to sell is bound up with creating desire for the "new" or "dangerous" or "different," once the novelty of the sound not matching the body, of watching other white bodies transgress, making spectacle of race by passing it off as style, has worn thin for the white consumer, how can the products of "world music" be sold? An obvious answer is to create new markets by changing the appearance of the product itself, or manufacture more consumers. Frequently, world music is a colored body or "original" body playing its colored music. It's real authentic roots music, no fluff. Hard, primal, passionate rhythms played by exotic, wild, dangerous others, the way *they* like it. Excuse my parody, but even the aural must submit to the hegemony of vision where race is involved. The color/race and origins stories of the musicians printed on the packaging as mere information increases the consumption and exchange value of the product. Race, then, materializes as a matter of taste in spectacles of marketing. Divorced from its politics and identity base, *samba reggae* is just another great dance music, making converts (or addicts) wherever it is played.

Oju Oba was created to perform with *Olodum* this past carnival in San Francisco. A majority of the participants seemed to be less than informed about black material reality in Salvador, not to mention *o swingue Bahiano*, kind of an attitude of Soul in popular dance. The group billed itself as "the baddest *bloco afro* north of Brazil," but a good number of the people who showed up the day I attended rehearsal appeared more like a collection of rhythm junkies. As I paid my $8 participation fee for the rehearsal, I noticed a certain amount of tension/anxiety building at my presence. "Oh yeah. I remember you. You used to dance with . . ." but no one aside from Betho, the instructor, came to greet me, even though I could clearly remember dancing and changing costumes together at tacky nightclub floor shows with several of the women in the room.

The space was too cold and dark, but Betho was beaming nonetheless, as he moved his lithe long body through space toward me. It was a smile I had seen once before when I brought two of my black friends to rehearse with *Orixa Baba*. It was a recognition of a commonality that Betho, who calls himself "Brazilian of African descent," never presses into service as a unity text. I do not belong to him because of the inevitability of the power of blood; my brown skin and twisted hair remind him of home, Brazil that is. He also knows that I speak Portuguese and that I know Afro-Brazilian dances, not as his student but as a fellow dancer. There is an illusion of equality, commonality between us. I am Brazilian to Betho. I often have to remind him who I am, especially when he wants to talk about these "African Americans" and their separatist ways. So Betho and I almost invariably end up looking at each other and dancing together during most of the rehearsal because we get tired of dancing next to people who don't know what they are doing, or are overdoing it in an attempt to show that they *have* it. In our self-absorption we become a spectacle of authenticity and a reminder of the threat of aesthetic laws governing proper racial behavior in the dance studio.

Welsh-Asante in her piece "Commonalities in African Dance: An Aesthetic Foundation" lists seven "senses" of African dance that must be present for it to be perfectly aesthetic and correct: polyrhythm, polycentrism, curvilinearity, dimensionality, epic memory, holisticness, repetition.[2] There is another set of seven basic characteristics of African dance. It is low to the earth, undulating from the center outward, and polyrhythmic, and it emphasizes the pelvic girdle, body part isolations, the whole foot touching the ground, and bent knees. I could show you several Senegalese steps that don't adhere to any of those characteristics and utilize only a few of Welsh-Asante's senses. But to many students of African and African-derived dance, these are nothing short of regulations of appropriate dance behavior and conduct. They become laws of African-derived dance that are sedimented in the repetition of the performative, "dancin like a white girl." This utterance, in turn, pronounces who may materialize the matter of African dance on the stage. A dancing black body, moving to African riddims cites the belief of racial blood memory, reiterates it as cultural norm, and sediments it as a law of racial capability—a funky threat to trespassers and transgressors alike: "this is how it should be done."

Was a performativity of African, better yet, black dance at play when I walked into that ballroom on 18th street in the Mission? Even though I feel confident in my ability to consciously choose not to believe in seven senses or characteristics of African dance, when I dance next to Betho I am aware of searching for and finding all those things, and I am equally distracted by their absences when I find myself surrounded by a group of white bodies new to body isolations, polyrhythmic motion—in effect novices, beginning dancers who would not even have those qualities if they were black. Dancers who would not dare to walk into an advanced ballet floor-barre class looking as raggedy as they did now. What was it about Afro-Brazilian dance, aside from Betho's good looks, that made these people want to learn it and do it with the assumption that they could acquire it without any consideration to training or technique?

I needed to find out so I passed out a questionnaire—thirty with a response rate of 100 percent. I asked very basic questions of twenty-four women and six men, with plenty of room for self-expression, women ranging in age from 23 to 46; men, 25 to 45. I was sensitive to difference and people who lived in various intersections. Of the women, fifteen were white, two black, one Asian, two Latina, one mestiça, one nonrespondent. Of the men, three were white, one Latino, one mestiço, one nonrespondent. The questions were nonthreatening and not accusatory, just basic data about what they thought of the music and the dance.

Betho leaves me to go discuss with the drum corps what he plans to do. I catch myself being an anthropologist, mentally mapping the distribution of race, gender, and skill of the subjects in my mind as I watch the age-old universal dancer psyche-out—the preclass stretch. "Oh, I'm so tight," as the perpetrator puts her ear to her knee. I make a note to collect material culture and curse the fact that I don't have my camera. Betho has signaled that he's ready to start—late, as is customary. "Okay. We're preparing for carnival, you know, so we have to begin to develop, um, we'll be dancing the whole time and walking so we have to develop strength. So make a circle." He turns and nods to Mark, the drum corps leader, who begins the rhythm. I am always amazed when Mark starts the rhythm. He looks like a benevolent orderly or something—pony tail, beard, white. We did the warm-ups in a large circle, leaving very little room for extravagant motion. Having previously studied street dancing in a studio setting in preparation for *Carnaval* performance, I knew that this was not Betho being flighty, but purposeful. The necessity of dancing in close quarters, however, did not sit too well with many people. If ever you have danced like that, you know that if everyone is not moving at the same time, in the same direction, on the same foot—it does not work. Somehow I had ended up sandwiched between two groups of beginners, who seemed to grow timid in their movements as I danced among them. Participant observation is supposed to give you a sense of the quality of actions of the subjects. Yes? My rather long arms took a beating, as did my aura from the glares that the one "I'm a white girl with rhythm" babe was throwing me from across the room every time Betho approached me to dance.

The circle began to move, a sign, I figured, of the end of warm-ups. Now we were working moves, moves that needed to be large and exuberant to be adequately seen by the crowds on the sidelines at *Carnaval.* I realized that I suddenly had a lot of space, and that my torso was hurting from trying to out-isolate the white girl with rhythm. "Stick to your own pace and observe, you don't even want to dance in the front," I told myself.

We were now doing a lot of the dances of the *bloco afro Carnaval* queens. Since they ride the floats, they are usually boxed in as a safety measure. What those structures have done to the dance style of the queen is to have created a situation where either she's on top of a big truck, so from the ground she's only seen from the waist up, or she's on a flat-bed truck close to the ground with her entire body visible, but in a narrow, long space. Needless to say, these are dances of attitude, and special favorites of long-armed and leggy gals like myself. "Oh excuse me." To rest up, Betho halted the circle where we danced *Orixa* samples. All of a sudden, he waddled out to the center of the circle in a *samba de galinha*, spun, and headed back out. Nothing happened. We all held the rest step. Then out of the corner of my eye, I saw him coming toward me.

Pushing me out into the circle, giving me directions that I could not hear over the music. I mimed "do you want me to samba?" He nodded "yes" and I got down to it. He continued to move around the circle pushing other women in—we were all black—and he was pointing at our butts and then waddling around to complete the demonstration. But I was the only woman out there who knew what *samba de galinha* was. We were all relieved when it was our turn to exit and pick someone else to come in. The samba solos went on for a while, Betho meticulously making sure that every one in the circle gave one.

When the white girl with rhythm came out with her best friend, who is decidedly nicer, I thought I would pass out from trying not to laugh. Often, dancers confuse the fluidity of the torso and limbs as a slackness, missing the fact that the torso is not jostling around on the pelvic girdle, but is being placed at certain points in space by playing with the time of the rhythm. They looked like they were punching each other. Finally Betho signaled the drummers to stop. And then he spoke, "Um, that was a *samba de galinha* from Bahia. It's not like, uh, the samba that the *escolas* do; not like this. Okay? It's here, you know, and your feet are flat on the floor. No, no. It looks like, come here." He motioned for me, but I verified and he said, "Yeah. Watch her. She knows how to do it." I began to dance as he continued to explain the way the body should look when doing the dance and closed by saying with a big grin, "But she knows. She's practically Bahiana! She already been to Brasil—oh, and, um, so has," remembering the white girl with rhythm that had danced and traveled with him for the last five years. "You watch her, she's good." "So much for observation," I thought as I was backing out of the circle toward the back wall when an older woman called out half joking, half mocking—"Can we touch you?"

It was clear that, in that space, I was functioning as a measure or indicator or even regulator of "authentic," "real," "proper"—not "knowledge," "skill," "technique." I was a dangerous threat in this safe place for white transgression of the taboo of white passing in colored spaces: I mattered too much. I was what the dance was *supposed* to look like. By the time we moved to the choreography, which I didn't even know, white women novice dancers smiled at me timidly as if to apologize, the seasoned white girls with rhythm either tried to ignore me or glared at my audacity to show up on their turf, and the few black women there stood back and watched me intently from a distance. One woman did dance with me, secure in her skills and knowledge of the choreography. She made no apologies for her whiteness, relishing the movements and rhythms. The rest either danced against me or on me, scared that they had missed some nuance in the movement that they could only pick up if they stood less than an arm's length away.

At the end of class I reminded people about the questionnaire and passed them out quickly, still missing most of the drummers. I passed out pens and waited patiently—okay, impatiently—for people to complete them. As I was gathering the completed forms, a woman walked up to me and inquired about my field of "performance studies," what was it? what do you do with it? and finally she asked, "Well exactly what is *samba reggae* and *bloco afro*?" As I was finishing a quick sociopolitical historical synopsis/definition, a cloud of anger swept across her face. "I didn't know this! I didn't know any of that. Nobody ever told me," she said, as if she had accidentally mistaken a sacred object for a toy.

Excerpts from Questionnaires

Women:

Hispanic, aged 40, graphics artist, mixed origin: *bloco afro* defined as "beat of the street/city—Afro-Brazilian; unity of rhythm and people"; *samba reggae* defined as "Brazilian/Jamaican rhythms."

American, aged 26, sales representative, of Italian origin: "Any form of dance is a universal language for me; however, Afro-Brazilian jives with my particular body rhythms and movements."

American, aged 25, teacher, white: "I don't know the origins or technical aspect of this music. I have more intuitive sense of the music, perhaps due to spending part of my childhood in Bahia. The music makes me happy beyond words and fills me with energy and the desire to move, move, move!"

Swiss, aged 34, accountant, white with a Brazilian heart: "It makes me very happy, it is good for my body and my soul and mind."

American, aged 26, no occupation given, Caucasian: "It means 'soul' to me—the ultimate expression of celebration and joy!"

American, aged 46, legal secretary, WASP: "I consider myself Born Again Brazilian. Many past lives with this music and dance."

American, aged 24, ESL instructor, Haitian-American: "As *definitions*, I don't know. But the music *makes* my body dance, and I take lessons to "keep up with" my body—It's my favorite and most complete creative outlet."

American, aged 23, administrative assistant, Chinese American: "Part of American Multicultural experience. I'm not understanding it as a native Brazilian event but an American cultural one. It's a lot of fun for me because it's just dancing and music but it's also part of Brazilian culture I personally get to appreciate, understand and experience."

Brazilian, aged 33, student, Latin: *bloco afro* defined as " 'roots' music from America as well as South America connected with our African heritage. I simply enjoy dancing to primitive beats—it's quite 'organic' and just feels right and good." *Samba reggae* defined as "a Brazilian style of dance—mixing African and other percussive rhythms."

American, aged 27, student, Irish origin: "I am not familiar with either of these terms so I cannot comment."

Men:

American, aged 24, painter, Caucasian: "I'm very drawn to the 'vibrance' of the movement—the 'letting loose.' Yes, it's very *loose* and seems to require a full body coordination (i.e., disciplined)."

Brazilian, aged 27, dance instructor: "Samba reggae is one of the most fun and powerful dance and music movements originating from Bahia, Salvador."

American, aged 36, paralegal, white (on the outside): "Bloco Afro and samba-reggae are powerful musical and cultural expressions for me. It's fun, strong, and I like the community spirit."

Notes

1 In this connection, I draw on Judith Butler's theory of the materializing effects of regulatory power to consider the issues of spectacle and black bodies in a supposedly "black space." See Judith Butler, *Bodies That Matter: On the Discursive Limits of "Sex"* (New York: Routledge, 1993).

2 Kariamu Welsh-Asante, "Commonalities in African Dance: An Aesthetic Foundation," in Molefi and Kariamu Asante, eds., *African Culture: The Rhythms of Unity.* Contributions in Afro-American and African Studies 81 (Westport, Conn.: Greenwood, 1985), pp. 71–82.

14 SENSE, MEANING, AND PERCEPTION IN THREE DANCE CULTURES

Cynthia Jean Cohen Bull

Our own immediate experiences of dancing can be remembered and transformed into observations relevant to our understanding of society and culture. Reports on dance by other dance participants, spectators, and observers can be understood as a source of information and analysis, used to create and crystallize important and often ignored aspects of our shared cultural knowledge. In these events, the sensible is inextricable from the intelligible: a close study of the physical, sensuous experience of dancing provides us with knowledge as unmistakable as that provided by the more conventional study and analysis of cultural beliefs and concepts and of other aspects of social life.

When I dance, I experience kinesthetic, visual, tactile, and auditory sensations, and my *sensible* dance experience includes and implies *intelligible* choreographic and social meanings.[1] As I dance I feel the shifting of my weight and the changing shapes of my body. I see my surroundings and sense the rush of air past my skin; I hear, and feel, the percussive rhythms of my footfalls. All these physical, sensible experiences combine to create, for me (and perhaps, in performance, for my audience) a particular atmosphere and feeling; the physical act of dancing creates a kind of cultural meaning. My dancing also stirs very personal associations and images within me as I move, while my audience creates many different narrative and imagistic interpretations of my dancing.

These various interpretations of the act of dancing stem not only from personal inclinations but from a range of life experiences in cultural settings, both theatrical and social. The challenge of dance anthropology lies in finding ways to reveal and understand the webs of meaning created through the dance event. The challenge is a difficult and complex one, for, often, writers on dance either leap quickly to generalized cultural conclusions, not taking the time to notice what is actually going on in the dance they are writing about, or they emphasize the experiential and descriptive at the expense of commentary and analysis. Phenomenological accounts can sometimes capture the sensual qualities of experience, but they tend to ignore how shared meanings shape the most "natural" of human actions and perceptions in dance and in life, slighting the cultural content inherently implied by physical and cultural experience.

Concepts such as "the body" and "choreography" are, of course, based in human biological capacities to move, speak, and symbolize in both motion and words. Yet *how* any individual moves, speaks, and symbolizes emerges from the intricate process of living in society. While innate capacities or talents make someone a "born" dancer, only experience in the world will turn that person into a specific dancer whose movement embodies meanings both sensible and intelligible to her audience. And while a spectator may be alert to experiences of movement and receptive to the most foreign of choreographies, only a spectator familiar with the cultural references and frameworks of that choreography can respond on many levels simultaneously that correspond to the intentions of the creators. As American modern dance choreographer Charles Weidman succinctly explained it, "The performers and audience enter the house—although through different doors—from the same street."[2]

Writing dance ethnography necessitates abstracting, reducing the multiplicity and chaos of experience to articulate expression, but ethnographic explanations and theories can easily overwhelm the sense of what people do when they dance. Capturing and evoking the dance event, and teasing out its meanings and implications are not counterposed; they are simply difficult to combine in the linear act of writing. The text of dancing exists in the nonlinear space of memory, and its impressions and structures must be reconstructed by the writer even as they are interpreted.

The staples of anthropological analysis—considerations of social functions, symbolic systems, philosophical meanings, or political implications—can apply powerfully to dance and are important because they are often overlooked in aesthetically oriented commentary. The challenge in writing about dance from an anthropological perspective lies in simultaneously evoking the particular experience and the shimmering life which it refracts and reflects; the meanings and implications of dance, indeed, of all performed art, are embedded in the experiences of the art itself—learning, teaching, creating, performing, watching.

A primary interest of recent ethnographies of dance is the conjunction between the sensible and the intelligible, taken as different but profoundly interrelated levels of analysis, description, and understanding. This orientation locates the anthropology of dance within a larger contemporary project in anthropological theory: to consider experience as intrinsic to meaning, action in dialogue with thought, and the actor (dancer) improvising within the social and cultural rules of her environment.[3]

The project of this essay is to compare the realms of the sensible and the intelligible through an examination and analysis of the significance of three physical senses—touch, hearing, and sight—in three different contemporary dance forms.[4] I examine ballet and contact improvisation in their American settings, and traditional dance as currently practiced in Ghana, West Africa. I view the senses not as fixed biological or psychological mechanisms but as dynamic processes shaped by and through culture.[5] Exploring the significance of the cultural context, I hypothesize a unique association between the sense of sight and the ballet; the sense of touch and contact improvisation; the sense of sound and Ghanaian dance.[6]

Comparing the role of the senses in these dance forms evokes both the similarities and the differences of emphasis in how sensation and intelligibility are shaped within each form. Conversely, juxtaposing three kinds of dancing in a discussion of their relationship to the realm of the senses points to the embeddedness of social and political meanings in behaviors and practices. This kind of discussion is not truly ethnographic, although it is based on ethnographic research (I have been a participant-observer in all three dance forms). Because my account generalizes about many versions of a kind of dance without describing the specific events from which the idealized description has been derived, exceptions, contexts, and nuances disappear in favor of a more generic characterization and hyperbolic categorization. These generalizations should not be essentialized, as the ethnographic realities are more complex and varied. But my aim here is to write on a more general level in order to compare analogous events in different cultures. I take a playful, heuristic attitude toward this venture, using it as the basis for interpretation, speculation, and question raising.

Ballet: The Primacy of Seeing[7]

The quality of motion [ballet dancers] show—now heavy, now light, rapid or still, gliding and stabbing, soaring or darting, successively solo, duet, or in chorus—gives the situation onstage its special imaginative meaning. You sense it in the clear shapes their bodies make, in their contact with each other in dance figures and in the cumulative transformations of choreographic architecture.—Edwin Denby[8]

Ballet has a tradition which dates back to the European courts of the sixteenth and seventeenth centuries. During the Renaissance, royalty presented dance as part of lavish political spectacles in which movement and bodily deportment were seen to constitute visible signs of moral states, political power, political resistance, and divine association. Louis XIV's founding of the first dance academy in 1672 initiated a long process of technical development and professionalization of the court dance as a performance form; by the early nineteenth century (the romantic period), the vocabulary of the contemporary ballet can be clearly recognized. In romantic ballet, the former specific meanings of the movement had been nearly transformed into a more generalized signification of beauty and elegance, while the visual design of individual bodies in the stage space assumed primary importance. Today, ballet, as the premier art dance form in America (as well as many other countries), represents ideals of exquisitely controlled technical precision and emotional expression combined within a classical (traditional) framework (figure 1).

The ballet vocabulary consists of a number of positions of the feet and arms, shapes of the entire body, and movements with names describing their physical actions—*plié* (bend), *tombé* (fall), *glissade* (slide), *relevé* (rise); these discrete segments may be variously combined to produce choreographic sequences. These technical specifications meet the demands of ballet performance spaces, "determin[ing] the greatest frontal legibility and launch of the upper body as silhouette framed in a proscenium," as ballet theoretician Lincoln Kirstein explains.[9] Accordingly, the ballet student begins to dance by learning positions, shapes, and separate "steps," all of which centrally concern space and its visual organization. Ballet training, while attending to the feel and the flow of movement, emphasizes sight as the primary process of artistic conception, perception, and kinesthetic awareness.

Since some time in the nineteenth century, the mirror has played an ever present partner to the ballet student and performer: ballet dancers practice by executing repetitive movement patterns while being watched by a teacher or choreographer and by watching their own reflected image.[10] As a dancer moves, she or he carries a mental picture of the perfect performance of each step, comparing the mirrored image with the ideal.

Consequently, for the dancer, the edges and lines of the body as perceived by a viewer became paramount. Students who do not possess "a good line," that is, a slender, long-limbed body which can form geometrically proportioned shapes, know that they will never be successful performers and are told so by teachers and administrators of professional schools. They may enjoy studying ballet, but they know that they do not "have the body"—the physical appearance—to be a "real" (professional) ballet dancer. While having the body by no means provides sufficient basis for success, it is the necessary prerequisite.

For the ballet viewer, vision also predominates. The proscenium stage, the

1. American Ballet Theater in *La Bayadère*.
Photo: Johan Elbers, 1995.
2. Contact improvisation. Karen Nelson and
Alito Allessi in *Hoop Dance*. Photo: Cliff Coles, 1988.

three-sided box in which events unfold, shines brightly in contrast to the darkened space in which the audience sits. In large theaters, spectators in the balconies may be at a great distance from the performers, so that they cannot hear the sound of the dancers' footsteps and breathing (ballet dancers also strive to minimize these sounds), and their kinesthetic sensation of the movement may be greatly diminished. What always remains are the moving pictures, the extended lines which make the images visible from a distance.

Ballet choreography pays great attention to spatial precision. Shifting lines and clusters of dancers constitute major organizing principles of its composition, and formations of symmetrical bodies create visual harmony and hierarchy which frame and set off solo performers. The corps de ballet members strive to look as much alike as possible and to move in perfect unison; individuals must control inclinations to curve an arm less or lift a leg higher than the group ideal or they will ruin the overall visual design and motion. In contrast, the soloist may, indeed should, cultivate an ability to perform movement that looks stylistically unique, and to phrase movement—to delay or hurry an action slightly—in order to create a visible shaping through time and complement the music. Thus the soloist stands out by going beyond the basic pictorial unity of the ballet, playing at the edges of the strict boundaries to which the corps must adhere, and enhancing visual design with individual variation and rhythmic intricacy.

While the sense of sight is not, of course, the sole mode of perception in ballet, it seems to organize all the other senses so as to tie them inextricably to the visual appearance of design in space. For example, most ballet choreography bears a close relationship to the rhythm and mood of the music, often providing a demonstration of the music, a graphic realization of what is being heard. At the same time, the musicians producing the sound remain hidden in the orchestra pit so as not to disturb the stage picture. For both dancer and spectator, aural perception is cultivated in relation to visual perception.

The sense of touch also plays a significant role in ballet choreography, most prominently in the pas de deux, the duet of the male and female soloists. The sense of touch, like that of sound, is inseparable from sight for both dancer and spectator. What the touch looks like to a spectator always merits attention; physical interaction which carries emotional and dramatic metaphor remains technical as well and must, therefore, also create a visual design. An audience learns to interpret the intention of touching correctly: in classical ballet, the touch which signifies the characters' social encounters usually involves arm gestures and conventional embraces, while the danseur's physical manipulation of the ballerina (his hands on her back, waist, armpits, hips, pelvis, and thighs) signifies "dancing." Some twentieth-century ballets more graphically depict sexual gestures and actions, yet the meaning of different kinds of touch (explicitly expressive, implicitly expressive, purely technical, and various combinations of these) become evident by the dancers' execution of touch and the choreographic context.

Finally, the kinesthetic sense of energy or force (the amount of effort needed to execute a movement), also bears close relationship to vision, one which contributes to the characteristic gendering of ballet movement. While all ballet dancers must cultivate considerable muscular strength and control, in a substantial portion of the classical repertory, a man must generally appear to exert force strongly, a woman, lightly. Lifts demand the participation of both dancers, the woman in many cases jumping with great energy and holding the position of her body in the air as the man catches her and utilizes the momentum of her movement. Yet the ballerina looks as if she does very little, the lightness of her upper torso and arm motion in particular (as well as her slender body and her ability to balance on the point of her foot) conveying weightlessness, airiness. The danseur, in contrast, appears solid, stable, either firmly connected to the floor or propelled from it by virtue of his own strength. Paradoxically (magically), in many classical pas de deux in particular, the nearly disembodied female provides the primary image of the dance, while the fully embodied male nearly disappears from sight.[11] As spectators, our eyes confirm the reality of the unreal, the fantastic disembodiment of the body.

I will return to the implications of the primacy of seeing in ballet. How practices of dance differently construct perception and link to cultural meaning becomes clear, however, when more than one dance form is considered.

Contact Improvisation: The Primacy of Touching[12]

What is revealed [in contact improvisation] is mutual understanding, a basic system, a mode of communication. Touch. The fast and subtle skin processing masses, vectors, emotions, giving the muscles the information to correctly move the bones, so the duet can fall through the time and space of demonstration, neither partner hurt, hampered, subjected, objectified.—Steve Paxton[13]

Contact improvisation began formally in 1972, when a group of Americans experimented with catching each other and falling together. The form developed into a practice of moving while constantly touching, leaning on, lifting, balancing on, or supporting another person. The resulting duet intertwines two bodies in a fluid metamorphosis of falls and suspensions, propelled by the momentum of the dancers' weight. Performed from its inception as an informal demonstration, contact improvisation has also been practiced as a kind of social dance which people simply get together and do, sometimes in conjunction with other kinds of popular and/or improvisational dancing. Both contemporary American ballet and contact improvisation draw a largely middle-class viewing audience, but ballet, a highly institutionalized performance form, involves many more people as both performers and spectators and holds a privileged position in the mainstream of American art dance.

Practitioners of contact improvisation have explicitly conceived of what they do as an alternative dance activity and, in many cases, as a kind of political statement. The sense of touch, which guides the dancing, assumes importance both technically and symbolically for teachers, students, performers, and spectators. Awareness of touching a partner and following "the point of contact" provides the impetus for movement, which adheres to no preset pattern and relies on a general vocabulary of falling and rolling varying from one individual to another (figure 2). Touch joins the two dancers, attuning them to each other's weight and momentum as they move.

Students often begin to learn contact improvisation by lying on the floor and closing their eyes, shutting off the stimulus of sight and thereby focusing more attentively on the skin of the whole body. Deliberately excluding sight, they focus more simply on the kinesthetic. Teachers instruct students to investigate simple movements for long periods of time, suggesting that they sense, feel, experience, notice, and give in to the changing patterns of their own bodies on the floor. These patterns do not concern the shape of the body as perceived by a spectator (as in ballet), but rather have to do with the performer's perception of touch, and, through that touch, the perception of weight and momentum.

People learn to partner in contact improvisation by practicing different touching and weight-bearing patterns. While some specific catches or lifts may be taught, longer improvisations based on simple movement ideas—rising and falling, or dancing with heads constantly touching—predominate. Almost all classes, including those with beginners in them, include "open dancing," in which people do whatever they can and wish to do within the structure of staying in contact. Teachers often dance with students throughout the class, helping students when they practice technical ideas and sometimes offering more general commentary about their improvisations. Unlike most American dance techniques, however, the teacher acts more as a guide for a certain kind of experience than as the primary purveyor of knowledge in the class, a condition which contributes to the emphasis on internal experience rather than external appearance.

No ideal physical type for contact improvisation exists, nor is there a single physical prerequisite for skilled performance. Willingness to coordinate one's efforts with another person and to give up control over one's own movement could be called prerequisites to learning the form, but then every dance form could be said to require a willingness to participate. The absence of physical prerequisites for contact improvisation has encouraged people of different body types and backgrounds to participate and to consider themselves dancers.[14]

For the dancer, the body's edges seem to change and to meld with one's partner; likewise, the sense of weight shifts in response to the partner's movement and the movement itself seems generated by and through the points of contact. Emphasis on touch, weight, and momentum supersede attention to visual design of movement, rhythmic control, or choreographic sequencing. In social settings, the connection of one's self and one's partner in contact tends to be the sole focus, while in performing situations awareness of the audience and choreographic considerations may become part of the dancing. Also, skilled contact improvisers, like skilled ballet dancers, have the ability to stretch the form beyond its most simple defining boundaries and may call attention to spatial design, rhythm, or sequencing in their movement, as well as to touch and weight.[15]

The viewers of contact improvisation perceive the dancing as less presentationally directed than ballet. Most performances occur in small spaces with the audience in close proximity to the dancers, so that the audience is invited by this setting and by the emphases of the movement to concentrate on the unification of people through physical contact and interaction (rather than through unison movement—the replication of visual design and exact rhythms). Dancers' noises—breathing, grunting, the sound of falling or catching—are clearly audible. The spectators' empathetic perception of dancers using weight and momentum encourages them to identify physically and kinesthetically with the dancers. Because performers either dance in silence or tend to use music as general ambiance rather than as rhythmic definition or complement, spectators perceive the rhythm of movement phrases largely through identification with the dancers' impulses. Thus, as the movement structure of ballet stimulates the dancer to visualize herself, and the spectator to admire visual design and musical visualization, so the movement structure of contact improvisation stimulates the dancer to sense herself in mutual motion with a partner, and the spectator to identify with the sensual, proprioceptive experiences of the dancers.

The use of the skin as sensory indicator influences not only the dancer's perception of body and self but also the relative importance of aspects of the body as perceived by the audience. The conventions of touch in contact improvisation differ dramatically from those in ballet. First, any parts of the body may be touched without an accompanying signification of "technique" or "expression." Depending on specific performers and specific viewers, different interpretations of touch (technical and/or expressive) may be called for, but the conventions of the dance form do not assign particular meanings to particular body parts. Only those contact improvisers who wish to draw out the expressive or dramatic connotations of physical encounter deliberately utilize hand gesture or eye focus. The structure of contact improvisation thus reconstitutes the body in a way different from that of everyday social interaction as well as from many other American dance forms.

Second, the contact improvisation duet may be danced by two women or two men, as well as a man and a woman, contributing to an avoidance of gendered attributes in movement. Within the dance, any person may support or be supported by another, regardless of size or sex, so that many kinds of gender configurations and relationships may be implied or interpreted. Use of force varies according to individual dancers and the particular moment in the sequence of movement—gender does not prescribe styles or roles. The mutual experience of touch thus creates the central impetus for dancing, felt directly by the performers and vicariously by the spectators.

Traditional Ghanaian Dance: The Primacy of Hearing[16]

Above all, then, a good dancer dances in a steady relationship to the beat. . . . Spectators watch dancing style with the same concerns they bring to music, hoping to see the drummer and the dancer demonstrate their reciprocal involvement in a dialogue on the relationship of time and presence.—John Chernoff[17]

The last dance form I want to consider belongs to a culture different from that which has embraced ballet and given rise to contact improvisation. Ghanaian dance provides an ethnological comparison which helps to clarify further how perceptions may be differently shaped in different cultural circumstances.

The fifty-eight ethnic groups that officially comprise the West African country of Ghana encompass a variety of dance and music traditions. These dance traditions characteristically involve simultaneous rhythmic movement of different body parts—limbs, hips, shoulders, ribs, head—in undulating isolations. Fluid gestures close to the body and feet hugging the floor predominate, although some dances are quite percussive and spatially expansive. Most Ghanaians learn the dancing of their own village and often those of neighboring villages, or, if living in a city, learn the traditional dances of their family, neighbors, and friends. Within the traditional performances, dances cannot be separated from musical structures, in particular from drumming patterns. The rhythmic interrelationship of different drums with each other, and with the movement of dancers and spectators, constitutes the aesthetic and symbolic core of the event (figure 3).

In Ghana, a good dancer is first and foremost one who listens and responds, communicating with the music. No one shows a dance step in silence—it only exists as part of a larger pattern of sound and silence, movement and stillness. Instructors admonish young dancers to "say the drums in your mouth" and to know all of the rhythms, so that they may understand their relationship to the whole. Individual variation is supposed to emerge in response to dance partners and to music, with full awareness of how one fits into the larger event. "Self-expression" does not appropriately describe these individual statements, because they are explicitly musical-choreographic in nature, shaped so as to enhance the entire performance. The experience of dancing and playing realizes and creates social values: flexibility within clear formal structures, participation by everyone, attentiveness of each individual to the group, maintenance of a sense of overall balance. The kinesthetic is tied to social relationships.

A Ghanaian dance and the music to which it is performed share the same name. Each particular piece consists of sets of movements, and of bell and drum patterns which have a particular rhythmic relationship to each other but are played in differing meters. Characteristically, the drum parts retain their pattern vis-à-vis the bell part but do not sound in unison with it or with other drums, except on isolated beats. Rather, they engage in what John Chernoff calls "apart playing," holding one pattern as cross-rhythm to another and all together creating a polymetered music.

The complex accumulated rhythm repeats again and again, augmented and embellished by the improvisations of the master drummer and the dancers. At signs from either the master drummer or a lead dancer, the musicians shift to a new pattern. Dancers may perform certain steps to each pattern, creating appropriate variations in response to the music and to other dancers. Each spectator is also expected to participate by moving some part(s) of the body in a rhythm that complements those of musicians and dancers.

When the dancers are not improvising variations, they dance in rhythmic unison with each other, matching their movement impulses to those of a drumming pattern. However, while dancers may appear unified, they seldom produce an exact spacial unison because the emphasis of their movement lies in rhythmic, dynamic action rather than on achievement of a shape or line, as in ballet. Within the general framework of a step, one may let an arm swing slightly higher or lower or emphasize a movement more or less percussively—in other words, one may improvise subtly within a tight rhythmic and spacial framework. A dancer who solos does so at the invitation of others (the rest of

3. Ghana dance ensemble: the Agbekor-Patience Kwa-Kwa Ensemble. Photo: Cynthia Stephan, 1994.

the dancers may stop and watch, or the master drummer may call a dancer to perform). He or she (or, in some cases, a pair of dancers) performs in the service of the group, playing with variations in response to the group's encouragement. Thus, choreography becomes shaped by the rhythmic interaction of many people, rather than by a choreographer's vision (as in ballet), or by the mutual momentum with a partner's touch (as in contact improvisation).

It is said that a child learns to dance in its mother's womb, hearing and feeling drumming rhythms before it is born. Children learn dance and music by watching, listening, and imitating. A more or less skilled dancer will develop depending on a child's access to traditional dance and on a family's encouragement, the child's individual talents, and so forth. However, the general level of dancing and musical ability in Ghana ranks very high in comparison with the general level among most populations in the United States, for instance. Virtually everyone in Ghana expects to participate in dance at a variety of events. Thus, a continuum exists between everyday dance and special performance, and between everyone who dances and those who are especially skilled.

As with contact improvisation, one qualifies to participate in Ghanaian dance (and, indeed, is expected to do so) by being willing to participate, and at social events and ceremonies people of all ages and sizes dance. While some dances require athleticism or belong to a specific age group, many do not, and older people may be recognized, without condescension, as skilled and subtle performers. Also, those dances associated with specific social occasions and historical traditions often require gender roles. These usually display movement qualities felt to be characteristic of a social action—quick, slashing gestures and percussive accents in a men's war dance, for instance. In many group dances and male-female partner dances, however, everyone does the same movement, that is, movement within the same rhythmic and spatial parameters varied according to each individual's style, regardless of gender.

As in the other dance forms I have discussed, perception never remains confined to a single orientation when discerning valued qualities and skills; a good Ghanaian dancer above all keeps the beat, but also appears visually harmonious, "cool" even in moments of great complexity or rapid motion. It has been my experience that American audiences tend to react with excitement and enthusiasm to the most visually athletic and exuberant aspects of West African dance (and I suspect that companies on tour ensure an abundance of such dancing in order to communicate with their audiences). However, the Ghanaian dancers and musicians I have known tend to admire subtlety and finesse, appreciating understatement, responding to what gets left out or implied. While connoisseurs of any dance form better understand its subtleties than do new audiences, the value of understatement or omission in

Ghanaian dance also reflects the perception shaped by the structures of the dance and music (a music that may be "best considered as an arrangement of gaps, where one may add a rhythm, rather than as a dense pattern of sound."[18]

The close relationship of Ghanaian music and dance may seem similar to the interdependence of the two arts in ballet. However, the nature of the interdependence in fact differs because the structures of the music and choreography differ. The various instrumental and vocal parts in Western classical music join in synchrony within a single meter at a time, and sometimes even within unison rhythm patterns. In like manner, ballet choreography creates frequent points of conjunction with melodic and rhythmic phrases, often matching them in unison, each note with an accompanying movement.[19] While a good dancer in Ghana must feel his or her own rhythmic pattern at all times, what matters is not *synchrony* with other patterns but the steady *relationship* with them. By dancing one among many independent patterns, the dancer becomes another part of the rhythmic dialogue of participants, holding his or her own among the competing countermeters.[20]

The focus on listening in traditional Ghanaian dance shifts attention to social relationships among dancers, musicians, and viewers, and to the ceremonial occasion in which the dance occurs, placing particular constraints on the individual's movement innovations or variations. As with contact improvisation, a sense of group participation prevails. However, whereas contact improvisers generate the dance through touch and the physical interaction of two or more bodies, Ghanaian dancers join with musicians to mutually generate dance and music, listening to the rhythms and responding, seeing the rhythms and playing. The sense of hearing shapes the body itself as a social, ceremonial instrument through which dancers and spectators simultaneously perceive and participate in the event.

Processes of Perception and Dancing Bodies

Even the brief descriptions of dancing offered above indicate patterns and processes of organizing perception in which dancers, teachers, and spectators participate. These perceptions are not just cognitive; they involve both emotional and kinesthetic knowledge. Nor, on the other hand, are such understandings merely natural or intuitive; they are shaped in every aspect by artistic-social ideas and practices.

Ballet practice and performances hone visual sensibility, giving the dancer an acute awareness of the body's precise placement and shaping in space, and demonstrating to the spectator the remarkable possibilities of bodily design and the architecture of moving people in space and time, often viewed from a distance. Ballet choreography shapes actions designated as highly athletic and emotional, encouraging a dancer to feel both mastery over the body and expression through it. Performers learn to see themselves "from the outside," even while they "express" themselves "from the inside," and audiences learn to comprehend the codes of gender and touch which the movement signifies.

The visual priorities of ballet can be seen to complement what Johannes Fabian has called the "visualism" of Western philosophy (and anthropology), a tendency to fix phenomena in space and time, to gravitate toward the "pictorial-aesthetic."[21] The objectification of the body as an instrument to be mastered also fits familiar American patterns in medicine and sport, as well as dance. Performers and spectators learn from the dance that technique and expression constitute separate capacities, which, in ideal circumstances, may be joined. At the same time, the perception of athleticism and expression joined creates stereotypes of male dancers, given the American association of expression through the body with the feminine. Women confront other associations: the dual representation of embodiment and disembodiment by the female performer provides a powerful example of ambiguity in female social images and roles.

While the practice of ballet takes many forms, its general choreographic structure of corps de ballet/soloist and the star system of ballet companies coincides with ideals of competitive individualism. Corps members must try to look alike, but they will become soloists only by virtue of their distinct differences.

Contact improvisation offers an almost opposite set of experiences, yet, as an oppositional practice, it engages some of the same cultural concerns as does ballet. In order to shift focus from the visual, beginning dancers close their eyes. When they dance, the body, as in ballet, remains the focus, but rather than being objectified as viewed from the outside, the body ideally becomes the subject of experience from the inside. The practice of contact improvisation seeks to create a sensitivity to touch and to inner sensation (as opposed to the inner expression of ballet), and the sense of self becomes located in the body, as people experience the contact duet as a dialogue with another person through the skin. The viewer learns to identify with the kinesthetic reflexes and dynamic momentum of the dancers by sitting in close proximity to the performance space.

Contact improvisation exemplifies physical practices formed as alternatives to dominant cultural emphases on visualism, differentiation of gender, and the use of bodies in the service of art. The parameters of the dancing emphasize an egalitarianism of roles and the ability of each individual to move idiosyncratically yet in concert with others. This ideal of egalitarianism became difficult to maintain historically in the practice of performance, particularly as dance groups applied for government grants and formed themselves into professional companies. Yet this "democratic" orientation continues to characterize much of the practice of contact improvisation and how contact improvisers see themselves.

Explicit structures and control have little place in this dance form; hence the perceptual training, which focuses on "feeling free," "letting go," and the experience of self and others, differs greatly from that of ballet. The contact improviser feels herself an individual and a dancer, immersed in and led by physical sensation, responding to another without thought or premeditation, sharing this experience with an audience. The ballet dancer feels herself a special being, a dancer, controlling physical capacity and emotional representation at a choreographer's direction, realizing pre-set choreography and music in presentation to an audience.

The Ghanaian dancer feels herself a social being and a dancer, immersed in rhythm, responding to musicians, other dancers, and spectators in complementary variation within a fixed structure. The body, so prevalent in discussions of training and in the critical literature about American dance forms, does not predominate. Ghanaian dance seems not to posit a theory of "the body"; rather, movement by dancers and drummers creates the patterns of sight and sound which altogether constitute the event. The individual makes no sense outside of the relationship to the whole, so that movement takes on socially communicative, rather than personally expressive, associations. For those dancers who would innovate, social pressure to maintain traditions may pose problems; just how rapidly and in what ways the tradition changes may become a matter of disagreement among dancers, musicians, and spectators.

The practice and performance of Ghanaian dance seems consonant with an assumption of mind/body/spirit/society as interconnected and not separable, and with a society in which artistry is not the opposite of utility. A person dances, enacting a social role as a male or female of a certain age, status, ancestry, and so on. Individuality as defined by social relationships to other people is cultivated in the experience of the dance. The structural parameters of Ghanaian dance encourage a balance of control and variation and a sense of participation by all.

In this essay I have discussed the relationship between the sensible experience of dance and its intelligible cultural and social significance. I have explored a very particular vision of how dance creates meaning, emphasizing aspects of the actual experience of dancing for both participants and observers. I am proposing that the particular characteristics of each dance form and its unique manner of transmission and performance encourage priorities of sensation that subtly affect the nature of perception itself. Dance finely tunes sensibilities, helping to shape the practices, behaviors, beliefs, and ideas of people's lives. At the same time, a multiplicity of ethnographic realities shapes the unique and historical occasion of any dance. All this raises questions about the transmission and transformation of dance from one cultural setting to another, as well as from one historical period to another. The changes in movement and choreography which accompany historical changes in dance forms must also be seen in relation to teaching practices, performance settings, and aesthetic-philosophical beliefs. What do these changes indicate about the mutability of the body? How malleable are our perceptual processes, and what effect might exposure to different dance experiences have on our social perspectives?

The three dance cultures analyzed in this essay are, of course, distinct and identifiable, but they are not isolated, "pure" forms of dance. There are people who practice or study ballet, contact improvisation, and Ghanaian dance, and there are viewers who attend many different kinds of dance concerts. Indeed, many of us have available, at least potentially, a great range of perceptual experiences. Exposure to different dance experiences has the possibility of affecting our social perspectives, encouraging a greater flexibility in our sensual and intelligible understanding of our lives.

Notes

I wish to thank Wesleyan University's GLSP DanceTalk Series, Maria Jose Fazenda and the Bienal Universitaria de Coimbra in Portugal, Susan Foster and the U. C. Irvine Dance Research Group, and Kay Shelemay for opportunities to present and discuss this essay. I also extend my appreciation to Richard Bull for his extensive editorial and critical assistance.

1 I borrow the formulation of "sensibility" and "intelligibility" from Paul Stoller, *The Taste of Ethnographic Things: The Senses in Anthropology* (Philadelphia: University of Pennsylvania Press, 1989).

2 Jean Morrison Brown, ed., *The Vision of Modern Dance* (Princeton, N.J.: Princeton Book Company, 1979), p. 65.

3 Among anthropological works, see, for example, Sally Ann Ness, *Body, Movement, and Culture: Aesthetic and Visual Symbolism in a Philippine Community* (Philadelphia: University of Pennsylvania Press, 1991); Cynthia J. Novack, *Sharing the Dance: Contact Improvisation and American Culture* (Madison: University of Wisconsin Press, 1990); Paul Spencer, ed., *Society and the Dance: The Social Anthropology of Process and Performance* (Cambridge: Cambridge University Press, 1985); and Helen Thomas, ed., *Dance, Gender, and Culture* (London: Macmillan, 1993). Other writing in dance history and cultural studies have also considered these issues, in particular, the work of Susan Foster—see *Reading Dancing: Bodies and Subjects in Contemporary American Dance* (Berkeley: University of California Press, 1986), "Dancing Bodies," in J. Crary and S. Kwinter, eds., *Incorporations, Zone 6* (New York: Ur Zone, 1992),

and reprinted in this volume, and *Choreography and Narrative: Ballet's Staging of Story and Desire* (Bloomington: Indiana University Press, 1996).

4 It goes without saying that all of the senses are involved, to one degree or another, in each of the dance forms to be discussed here. The kinesthetic sense, especially, is often primary for the dancer, who experiences the act of dancing within her own body and feels the physical sensations of dancing as basic and fundamental; the kinesthetic may be a primary and characterizing mode of experience for a dance observer or audience member as well. For the purposes of this essay, I analyze and compare associations between selected specific senses and selected specific dance forms as a strategy for creating insight and understanding.

5 David Howes's anthology, *The Varieties of Sensory Experience: A Sourcebook in the Anthropology of the Senses* (Toronto: University of Toronto Press, 1991), provides examples of how the senses might be culturally described and understood. Paul Stollar's ethnography on the Songhay (in *The Taste of Ethnographic Things*) discusses methodological and theoretical problems posed by understanding the senses in fieldwork and writing about them in ethnography. See also Diedre Sklar, "Can Bodylore Be Brought to Its Senses?" *Journal of American Folklore* 107, no. 423 (Winter 1994), pp. 9–22.

6 The order of discussion was chosen to begin with the dance form that is probably the most familiar for the majority of readers, ballet. Contact improvisation, as an oppositional practice to ballet, follows, and then Ghanaian dance provides a cross-cultural contrast. The order is not intended to connote a hierarchy of value (ballet as the most "developed" or Ghanaian dance as the most "holistic"). Rather, each dance form has its own parameters, possibilities, and limitations.

7 My analysis of ballet relies on over thirty years of involvement, first as student, amateur performer, and teacher, then as dance historian and anthropologist.

8 *Dance Writings*, ed. by Robert Cornfield and William MacKay (New York: Knopf, 1986), p. 508.

9 "Classic Ballet: Aria of the Aeriel," in Roger Copeland and Marshall Cohen, eds., *What Is Dance?* (New York: Oxford University Press, 1984), pp. 238–43.

10 Jerome Robbins's ballet "Afternoon of a Faun" (1953) literally identifies the mirror with the audience by situating a narcissistic dancer in a studio "watching" himself in the mirror of the proscenium opening.

11 The classical *pas de deux* bears an ironic resemblance to the Japanese *bunraku* puppet theater, in which the fully visible puppeteers sink into the background and one's attention is held by the vitality of the puppets which they maneuver. Of course, the ballerina, who may appear to be maneuvered, is not a puppet but a fully participating agent in her own movement.

12 My study of contact improvisation occurred over a ten-year period beginning in 1980. See Novack, *Sharing the Dance: Contact Improvisation and American Culture.*

13 Untitled statement, *Contact Quarterly* 12, no. 2 (1987), p. 44.

14 It is probably fair to say that the athleticism of the form favors younger people, although, theoretically, older dancers could practice contact improvisation and modify their movement according to whatever physical capacity they felt they had. In fact, contact improvisation has been practiced by some older dancers and also by people with disabilities.

15 Even in performance, however, the more skilled dancers are rarely singled out from the group in any way; dancers maintain the egalitarian conception of the form by structuring a concert so as to give "equal time" to each performer.

16 I began my study of Ghanaian dance in 1975, during a period of residence with the Ghana Dance Ensemble at the University of Ghana in Legon and continued studying through 1978 with Ghanaian teachers at the State University of New York at Brockport. Having acknowledged my ballet and contact improvisation teachers elsewhere, I take this opportunity to offer my grateful thanks to my teachers of Ghanaian dance and music: Professor Albert N. Opoku, Edna Mensah, and Gideon Foli Alorwoyie.

17 *African Rhythms and African Sensibility: Aesthetics and Social Action in African Musical Idioms* (Chicago: University of Chicago Press, 1983), pp. 146–47.

18 Ibid., pp. 113–14.

19 When poorly done, dancers call this practice "Mickey Mousing"—moving like a cartoon character in a pantomimic music visualization. When well done, the effect evokes great admiration. Igor Stravinsky claimed that he better understood his own music when George Balanchine, a choreographer acclaimed for his musicality, visually realized Stravinsky's scores.

20 Robert Farris Thompson, *African Art in Motion: Icon and Act* (Berkeley: University of California Press, 1964), p. 16.

21 *Time and the Other: How Anthropology Makes Its Object* (New York: Columbia University Press, 1983), p. 107.

15 SOME NOTES ON YVONNE RAINER, MODERNISM, POLITICS, EMOTION, PERFORMANCE, AND THE AFTERMATH

Mark Franko

This essay reflects on the aftermath of performance, a term Richard Schechner has used for "the long-term consequences or follow-through of a performance" with relation to "theorizing and scholarship."[1] One aspect of aftermath in Yvonne Rainer's work is her switch from dance to film, which positioned dance in an aftermath generating much discussion. Why did Rainer abandon dance? What did film offer as an alternative to dance? A second aspect of the aftermath of Rainer's dance is found in the issue of emotion and its relation to suggestions of narrativity, an issue which arose relative to Rainer's trip to India in 1971 and her subsequent avant-garde cinematic practice.[2] Emotion evoked the aftermath of avant-garde asceticism in "postmodern" dance. Hence, a certain anxiety about emotion and narrative (even deconstructed) toward the end of Rainer's choreographic career. Rainer's turn to cinema subtly countered an avant-garde fashion in dance to deemphasize the theatricality of affective states. As Peggy Phelan has remarked, "Most avant-garde films work so hard to thwart narrative structure that the rigidity of exclusion paradoxically increases the spectator's desire for its presence."[3] Responding to imputations of artistic/political backsliding, Rainer parried that emotion itself does not imply narrative: "Emotions . . . whether exposed or hidden, are facts and can be described as such."[4]

The critical motifs that accompanied Rainer's turn from dance to film invoke what Francesco Pellizzi called the two mainstays of modernism: "the very notion of surface as it appeared in its [modernism's] last two formal orthodoxies—the 'gestural' one of expressionism and the 'rational' one of minimalism."[5] But my evocation of expressionism is not an overture to claims about Rainer's paradoxical expressivity.[6] Nor will I identify Rainer with modernism, as does Sally Banes, to argue that her dance was "truly" modernist while historical modern dance was not.[7] In this view, modern dance becomes modernist for the first time in the sixties inasmuch as minimalism is an extreme-limit case of doctrinaire modernism, and postmodern dance is known in many cases to be minimalist.

I take a historically expanded view of dance modernism with reference to a series of aesthetic innovations during the twentieth century (the canonical figures are Duncan, Graham, and Cunningham) designed to institute a more direct rapport with nature and requiring ever new methods to thwart subjectivism (natural attitudes) and arrive at essences. With regard to these historical goals I believe it is fair, and indeed accurate, to describe much historical modern dance as modernist. The other issue of dance modernism is political engagement with social space. Having said that much canonical historical modern dance was modernist, I hasten to add that dance modernism was "impure" because laced through with covert political intentions.[8] This is not only because an antimodernist strand of American modern dance engaged unambiguously in class politics. In addition, historical modern dance and modernist ballet engaged in a variety of polemics over gender identity.[9] Thus, from both the modernist and antimodernist perspective, Yvonne Rainer does not lack precedents. Certainly, her intent must be allied with the antimodernist tradition. But her discursive involvement in modernism, especially via her referencing of Greenberg, also allies her to dance modernism in the "impure" sense alluded to above.

Rainer's work itself is central to the modernist/postmodernist debate because her choreography consolidates those issues and questions so well. Banes has stated that Rainer's "*Trio A* is the signal work both for Rainer and for the entire post-modern dance."[10] The purpose of this essay, however, is not to reopen that debate with all its terminological complexity. What interests me is the relation of emotion to the American radical tradition of performance within which Rainer belongs historically. Her involvement in modernism, emotion, and politics makes her work part of a choreographic/critical continuity which includes but is not limited to cultural production of the sixties.

Further remarks on modernism are nevertheless in order since I am framing these notes on Rainer within a historical conflict between dance modernism and the performance of politics whose roots are in the thirties. The conflict between modernism and cultural politics is already implicit in but not controlled by Banes's critical framing of postmodern dance. On the one hand, she views postmodern dance as a development permitting the historical emergence of "true" modernism in dance via adaptations of minimalism. On the other hand, Banes also sees this development issuing from a disillusionment with an unfulfilled political promise of historical modern dance.[11] The conflict between autonomous art and the need for a politics—which conflict is a less-acknowledged mainstay of ("impure") modernism—is not problematized. With these two reference points in mind—the advent at one and the same time of a reputedly "true" or "real" modernism, and of a performed politics stemming from an antimodernist tradition—what Banes claims for postmodern dance of the early 1960s seems to be a spontaneous resolution of the realist/modernist debates that arose in German Marxism of the 1930s.[12] When citing aesthetic modernism in its "purity," one inevitably evokes, if not the precise aesthetic and historical context of those debates, at least their philosophical content. With regard to the contemporaneous developments in North American modern dance during the 1930s, I understand emotion as an antimodernist and specifically political modality.[13] What I wish to show in this essay is that the issue of emotion in its relation to a politics is at the basis of Rainer's switch from dance to film.

My second point with regard to debates over modernism centers on the status of minimalism itself. It is well known that Rainer formulated a verbal discourse about minimalism in dance with reference to sculpture. In an early manifesto, she established an interplay between minimalist sculpture and her own compositional methods.[14] A chart stipulated correspondences between "objects" (sculpture) and "dance" (movement), indicating what of dance should be eliminated or reduced with reference to sculptural practice. For example, eliminating or minimalizing the monumentality of the sculptural object corresponded to the subtraction of "the virtuosic feat and the fully extended body" in dance; "figure reference" in objects corresponds to "character" in dance, etc.[15] These statements and their like are usually invoked when linking Rainer's work to modernism understood as "the reduction of dance to its essentials."[16] However, Michael Fried distinguishes sharply between the goals of minimalism as originally enunciated by Clement Greenberg (as paraphrased above by Banes) and those of objecthood in sculpture (particularly in the sculpture of Robert Morris), which Fried calls literalism. I propose to shift the terminological debate on modernism/postmodernism to minimalism/literalism.

The issue of autonomy with respect to sculpture had a different inflection than that associated with painting. "The autonomous and literal nature of sculpture," wrote Robert Morris, "demands that it have its own equally literal space—not a surface shared with painting." The qualities of sculpture are not those of the "medium" as in painting's flatness, but "proportion, shape, mass": they are, as with dance, "physical."[17] As Fried makes us realize, the basic difference this introduces into an autonomy aesthetic is critically significant. Minimalist painting, despite its focus on the concreteness of the medium, aspires to undo its own objecthood by reconstituting itself as an essence, the essence of the medium itself. It is from within this visual aesthetic that Banes can say of Rainer's *Trio A* that she makes "a historical shift in the subject of dance to pure motion."[18] This orientation presupposes the beholder as transcendental ego perceiving the essence of the art object instantaneously and thoroughly: "*at every moment the work itself is wholly manifest.*"[19] The autonomy of minimalism is, in effect, an autonomy from time: "It is this continuous and entire presentness, amounting as it were, to the perpetual creation of itself, that one experiences as a kind of *instantaneousness.*"[20] In Morris's work, on the other hand, "only one aspect of the work is immediate: the apprehension of the gestalt. The experience of the work necessarily exists in time."[21] With time comes a play of differences which contaminate the reproductive capacity of essence to appear as self-identical.[22] As Fried specifies: "The literalist preoccupation with time—more precisely, with the *duration of the experience*—is, I suggest, paradigmatically theatrical: as though theatre confronts the beholder, and thereby isolates him, with the endlessness not just of objecthood but of *time.*"[23] In his strongest anti-theatrical formulation, Fried asserts: "Theatre and theatricality are at war today, not simply with modernist painting (or modernist painting and sculpture) but with art as such—and to the extent that the different arts can be described as modernist, with modernist sensibility as such." "Theatre," he adds, "is now the negation of art."[24] As Fredric Jameson points out, such negations amount to spatialization: "the will to use and to subject time to the service of space."[25] Thus dance and sculpture would be exemplars of theatricality thus conceived.

While I have no sympathy for Fried's anti-theatrical prejudice, the distinction he draws can be ignored only to our peril. To reconsider Rainer's aesthetic in tandem with Morris's literalism is, I think, inescapable. This means that minimalism is merely a descriptive term with regard to Rainer's choreography. Literalism, as it turns out, is the relevant theoretical term. As Rainer specified in the title of one essay, her dance was "quantitatively minimal." Rainer was careful to exclude "qualitative" tendencies which are concerned with essences.

Thus the pressing terminological issue for dance history at this juncture is not, I would argue, modern/modernist—postmodern/postmodernist as previously supposed, but minimalist/literalist. One difficulty with all such terms is that they tend to lead double lives: one life within the artistic milieu where the term minimalism was used by Rainer to signal reduction, a rejection of inflated values[26]; another life within art-critical discourse where Clement Greenberg, for example, elaborated quite different meanings for minimalism. Shifting critical thought on Rainer from issues of modernism/postmodernism to those of minimalism/literalism should also allow us to reformulate the relation of performed emotions to aesthetic modernism on the one hand, and to left avant-garde production on the other.

Rainer's work with the objecthood of dance apparently did not produce the desired effects. Rainer comes to view dance as a space without agency, a space locked into the performer's narcissism and the spectator's voyeurism. Yet, it is only thanks to her literalist choreographic practice and its work with time that her critique of dance becomes possible, such that, as with Eisenstein, the cart (of theater) breaks and the driver falls into cinema. The aftermath of this fall is repeatedly signaled in writings by and about Rainer with a reflection on the place of emotion in her work.

The discovery of emotion occurs three times in her 1971 "Indian Journal." For instance, during part of a Kathakali performance by an old performer playing Nala in one story of *Ramayana*:

> But this guy actually projects *emotion.* His cheeks vibrate, he seems about to cry, he looks startled, he looks afraid, he looks puzzled, he looks proud. But all through extremely small changes in particular parts of his face. . . . You notice a change and then register the reading. Perhaps it is a lesson. I don't watch most people's faces that closely, but it must all be there.[27]

The second instance of note in the "Indian Journal" occurs during a visit to Maya Rao's studio in Old Delhi when Rainer is asked to perform. She does her solo *Trio A.* One of her hosts, Sonar Chand, interpreted the work "to be about 'human frustration.'" In this particular encounter with Indian performance culture, Rainer is understandably less receptive, in that her own work is being read from a radically different perspective than her own. Finally, regarding a performance of Bharata Natyam, she notes: "I refuse to believe that my enjoyment of it must be dependent on understanding the meaning. But maybe we in the Western avant-garde are really fooling ourselves in our contempt for that question, 'What does it mean?'"[28]

These three moments, it seems to me, enjoyed a privileged relation. Indian performance and performance reception, as the journal entries recount them, impinge on Rainer's artistic consciousness because they reference a social space across which people are observed and interpreted: a space of meaning. Interpretation, emotion, externality are symptoms of what comes after Banes's modernism—not as a progress or shock of the new ("purging" and "melioration"), but as a shattering, an aftermath. My point is that Rainer comes *after* modernism in a very literal sense. This literalization of temporal duration, while it spatializes dance in an ahistorical manner, also opens dance to a politics in a parallel manner to the way viewers unfamiliar with avant-garde aesthetic positions observe its openness to emotions.

Can these Indian experiences have influenced Rainer one year later in New York when corresponding with Nan Piene? The exchange of letters was motivated by a question Piene posed from the audience after a showing of Rainer's first film, *Lives of Performers* (1972). The question had "something to do with my passage from dance to film."[29] Rainer makes a number of very interesting points regarding dancing, film, and emotion. "Dancing," she writes, "can no longer encompass or 'express' the new content in my work, i.e., the emotions." Film enables her to emerge from a personal isolation that dance—"the narcissistic-voyeuristic duality of doer and looker"—had imposed.

> This is what allowed me permission to start manipulating [in film] what at first seemed like blatantly personal and private material. But the more I get into it the more I see how such things as rage, terror, desire, conflict, et al., are not unique to my experience the way my body and its functioning are. I now—as a consequence—feel much more connected to my audience.[30]

These remarks indicate a certain dissociation of emotion from the personal experience of bodiliness. They indicate that emotions are the body's *social* material, whereas dance only allows the expression of an insuperable privacy or a kind of seduction. In the most positive sense, "my body and its functioning," although not related to the unconscious as in much historical modern dance, are still highly subjective because they are "unique to my own experience." The letter to Piene articulates the possibility of a new synthesis which brings meaning and emotion to avant-garde practice:

> The implications of this change as they concern art and the avant garde must be most complex, something I would like to see a historian cope with. For example, is there some connection and polarity between formalism/alienation/'humanism'? Or indeterminacy/narrative? Or psychological content/the avant garde?[31]

It seems to me fairly obvious that Rainer locates avant-garde practice on the side of formalism, alienation, and indeterminacy, whereas a more traditional (or expressionistic?) artistic tradition, the analog of which she discovered in India, involves humanism and narrative. Film allows her to merge these two previously antithetical traditions while still maintaining a considerable tension between them. Her work with narrative is obviously not that of classical Hollywood cinema, but in line with avant-garde cinema.

The discovery of emotion conjoined with her transition from dance to film organizes a thinking on politics and aesthetics which Rainer later developed critically. In 1981 she critiqued John Cage for the "troubling implications of his ideas," citing the "Cagean effect" as an aesthetics of political paralysis:

> What are the implications of the Cagean abdication of principles for assigning importance and significance? A method for making indeterminate, or for randomizing, a sequence of signifiers produces a concomitant arbitrariness in the relation of signifier to signified . . . a denial and suppression of a relationship altogether.[32]

Rainer contends that Cage's denial of a relationship as a fixed human reality confounds the need for political perception in art. Indicating disillusionment with Cage's aesthetics and their pervasive influence on the avant-garde, she also reflects in this article on her own abandonment of dance for film. Here again, social (read meaningful) relationship emerges in cinematic work: "The thing that pushed me toward narrative and ultimately into cinema was 'emotional life.' "[33]

A kind of modernism, understood in Greenbergian terms as formal innovation in the visual field, was the discursive vehicle for Rainer's aesthetics and politics during the mid-sixties and early seventies. By 1973, she began to depict her switch to film as the abandonment of remoteness for emotion,[34] the abandonment of a bounded self on a personal, narcissistically self-reflecting inside for a politicized self engaged with others through a social outside. Film offered options for the manipulation and representation of the gaze (as in *Film about a Woman Who . . .*) because film could objectify interpersonal power relations. Paradoxically, however, film enabled politics to enter the creative endeavor via psychologism, that is, in the name of cinema's traditional commitment to an expressivist surface.

Rainer did not need to "express" emotion, as she made clear, but rather to acknowledge emotion as fact. Far from the old ideas of inwardness associated with emotion, Rainer saw it as a relation to the social. Narrative, for its part, furnished a *real* possibility of intersubjectivity through gaze and object encompassed together (power relations) rather than an *apparent* presence simulated for a gaze. Real and apparent are also terms Rainer had used to discuss her choreography. It is therefore worth tracking them through her own account, particularly in the light of Piene's response to Rainer's letter:

> It appeared to me then [at a Judson performance in 1965] that within the apparent neutrality and banality lay a kind of virtuosity all the more

> compelling, poignant really, for its surface absence or cloak. Perhaps what moved me most, in addition to exposure to your unique stage presence, was the strong feeling of being present at the raw creation or certainly bold enactment of a Style.[35]

Piene links Rainer's choreographic practice to her filmic practice with reference to "indeterminacy/narrative and psychological content/avant-garde" binaries: "Is it too simple," she asks, "to say that your manipulation of style in the film induced and *permitted* access to being moved by the mimetic?"[36] Taking this bit of historical spectatorship as a cue, let us reexamine the spectator position in Rainer's *Trio A*.

A four-and-a-half-minute solo performed in street clothes and sneakers, *Trio A* focuses ingeniously on avoiding a series of options confronted at each step, and on the formalization of negated options as a procedure.[37] Rainer has described its performance in terms of "differences in energy investment" through which a battery of kinetic protocols are short-circuited. For example, the body does not stretch its frame through space, propel its mass into the air, or shape volume about a tensile center. It rejects, in other terms, the options of classical and modern dance alike. Here is Rainer's description of how the piece looks: "For four and a half minutes a great variety of movement shapes occur, but they are of equal weight and are equally emphasized. This is probably attributable both to the sameness of physical 'tone' that colors all the movements and to the attention to the pacing."[38] Performing *Trio A* is a task, in the technical sense, one of whose purposes is to accomplish an objectification: "movement-as-task or movement-as-object."[39] The task demands a "sameness of physical 'tone.'" "It is my overall concern," noted Rainer in the original program notes, "to reveal people as they are engaged in various kinds of activities . . . and to weight the quality of the human body toward that of objects and away from the superstylization of the dancer."[40]

Rainer also describes the relationship of the work's production to its perception, the relationship of what she calls elsewhere its "real" to its "apparent" effort. An earlier statement on "neutral doing" is helpful here: "I wanted it [the dance] to remain undynamic movement, no rhythm, no emphasis, no tension, no relaxation. You just *do* it."[41] Uninflected neutrality characterizes the task as movement objectified. (The temptation of a catapult from such stylistic requirements to a discourse of purity and essences is easy to see.) Absence of inflection is only achieved, however, by a very real energy expenditure. *Trio A* is more difficult to perform than one might at first suppose. "In order to achieve this look [of the "factual quality" of movements] in a continuity of separate phrases that does not allow for pauses, accents, or stillness, one must bring to bear many different degrees of effort just in getting from one thing to another."[42]

"Just doing it" inaugurated a performance *style* (as Piene's remarks indicated) with hidden technical challenges underlying its programmatic voluntarism. For Jill Johnston, "the gestures tend to be completely abstract or completely natural,"[43] which might be rephrased to say they were *both* abstract *and* pedestrian in that the task's claim on bodily instrumentality manifested a visible absence of both *dancerly* and *practical* intent. What could be identified as abstract and/or pedestrian movement served to isolate the body's actions from any ideology of actions. "Just when one saw a familiar dance shape," writes Susan Foster, "the configuration of the body would shift, sometimes to a foreign shape, sometimes to a commonplace shape that seemed oddly out of place in the dance."[44] The precision of Rainer's instructions for performing *Trio A* lead one to consider it as a formal exercise. "In the end," writes Maurice Berger, "it was the task itself and the stresses sustained by the body in expediting that task that determined the dance's structure."[45] The production of neutrality as revealed behavior, and reciprocally, the identification of behavior *après coup* with a choreographic object aesthetic, constitute a sort of ideological closure obscuring "differences in energy investment." The intent was to minimize but not entirely to eliminate "performance" by substituting "nonreferential forms" for "illusionism."[46] Tasks unveil the everyday as performance, but task work is stylized at the level of its own production, as arbitrary in its own way as procedures governing conventional "performances." Let us retain the double sense of the rhetoric of reduction: reducing movement toward the natural and toward the neutral or instrumentally abstract.

These thoughts could lead to others on minimal art as analytic art given to the externality of meaning. Yet the goals of *Trio A* are also resumed by Rainer's earlier statement about her *Parts of Some Sextets* (1965):

> NO to spectacle, no to virtuosity no to transformations and magic and make-believe no to glamour and transcendency of the star image no to the heroic no to the anti-heroic no to trash imagery no to involvement of performer or spectator no to style no to camp no to seduction of spectator by the wiles of the performer no to eccentricity no to moving or being moved.[47]

This powerful and beautifully wrought proclamation was reiterated in the program for the first performance of *The Mind Is a Muscle* (1968), in which *Trio A* was premiered, as "my rage at the impoverishment of ideas, narcissism, and disguised sexual exhibitionism of most dancing."[48] The "NO to" manifesto is substantively concerned with the status of dance as culture, and is simultaneously political in that its concerns about the dancer as spectacle are equally about the situation of woman in culture. Reduction or minimization is only a consequence of this manifesto's negativity expressed in emotional and political terms. In *Trio A*, Rainer's own gaze—consistently averted but without any reactive dynamic—abstains from confronting her audience: although one can see her face, she denies the spectator a full view of it in any static position. She thus elides an identifiable gendered "self" and weights the literal objectification of appearances. A fetishizing or desiring potential in the beholder's gaze is somewhat paradoxically neutralized by an excess of bodily presence (objecthood) outdoing the reproduction of a gendered self. The task of *Trio A* itself is the performance of that negation. A performative and gender political dimension enters the work precisely at its most "analytical" juncture: that is, in its literalist focus on objecthood as bodiness. When Rainer later wrote: "Dance is ipso facto about *me* (the so-called kinesthetic response of the spectator notwithstanding, it only rarely transcends that narcissistic-voyeuristic duality of doer and looker),"[49] she seemed to indicate the abiding presence of subjectivity in her performance. By the same token, it seems to me that the originality of *Trio A* is precisely in the way it both preserves the subject but removes her from the narcissistic-voyeuristic relation. It is also for this reason that I find it erroneous to consider *Trio A* a minimalist reduction to the essence of the medium, since in some sense, the essence of the medium would then have to become herself, and this is precisely what *Trio A* removes from scrutiny via its agenda of negations.[50]

In his critique of Greenberg's theory, T. J. Clark points out that "*practices of negation* in modernist art . . . seem to me the very form of the practices of purity (the recognitions and enactments of medium)."[51] Given the politics of Rainer's practices of negation, they cannot also be thought of as practices of purity since, even if we were perversely to equate her*self* with dance (as in fin-de-siècle symbolism), the politics of Rainer's negation effectively opposes the underlying essentialism this equation purveys. "Practices of negation" as pedestrian motor purity engender a spectatorial double bind, a substantial irony on minimalist surface in the qualitative sense. To the degree that modernist purity exists in this dance, Rainer sets modernism and politics at odds. This dichotomy, I argue elsewhere, is germane to the dance-modernist continuum. But inasmuch as Rainer works in the aftermath of historical modernism, she carries it to the breaking point.

Nevertheless, even if a spectacular or stylized dancing subject is discarded in favor of "real" energy—neutral and natural because pedestrian—an abiding "apparent" energy testifies to signifiable subjectivity.[52] Rainer's body desires not to appear, yet it appears. Thus her ambiguity and, indeed, her charisma. This is also why Rainer does not eliminate artifice, but repositions it:

> The artifice of performance has been reevaluated in that action, or what one does, is more interesting and important than the exhibition of character and attitude, and that action can best be focused on through submerging the personality; so ideally one is not even oneself, one is a neutral "doer."[53]

"The irony here," she wrote, "is in the reversal of a kind of illusionism: I have exposed a type of effort where it has been traditionally concealed and have concealed phrasing where it has been traditionally displayed."[54] By reversing the stakes of illusionism, Rainer exposed concentration where it was presumed absent (in the literal execution) and absented it where it was supposed present (in theatricalized self-presentation). Rainer's neutral doing is a reversed illusionism—quite precisely "a reevaluation of artifice"—because it entails the concealment of calculated phrasing on a scale that simulates phrasing's absence. Apparent lack of intent would then become a sign of the body's "real," of its alienation from the "apparent" as artificial. Yet illusion is still exerted by apparent energy's concealed performativity. Also exerted is agency, artifice, and style. Doing's detachment from agency is precisely task's *illusion*, task's *effect* of externality. What does reversed illusionism accuse if not the unavowed (yet performed) theatricality of Rainer's work, its commitment to time, and its politicization of literalism? I would argue on this basis that Rainer is modernist in a sense analogous to the canonical dance modernists: Duncan, Graham, and Cunningham. Manipulations of impersonality in the work of those artists promoted—each quite differently—the performance of (differing) sexual politics.[55] And so did Rainer's. Yet, at the same time, Rainer's adherence to literalism allowed her to break what I have described elsewhere as the double bind of the female soloist in historical modern dance. She cuts the Gordian knot of dance modernism in that she stops dancing, ceases to appear as a live dancer. In this way, she is located not in modernism but in its aftermath.

Rainer's reception has been largely framed in art historical terms. This framing is what permitted the issue of her so-called modernism to emerge in critical discourse. Recent critical reevaluations of modernism in new art history are stimulating a parallel reassessment of historical modern dance in terms which also translate between visual and performance culture. This very critical possibility can be said to have been encouraged by the precedents Rainer's work set and the breadth of its reception. Dance and theory are not historically incompatible.[56] The theorization of dance history appears to be a task of the nineties. The next question becomes: What role will dance take in this critical breakthrough? What will dance look like in the aftermath of theory's performance? Or, how will theory coalesce a dance of its own aftermath?

Notes

I would like to thank Susan Foster, Lena Hammergren, Peggy Phelan, Linda Tomko, and Francesco Pellizzi for their critical responses to an earlier version of this essay presented at the Humanities Research Institute at the University of California–Irvine. I also thank the Scholar's Program of the Getty Research Institute for the History of Art and the Humanities for the time to complete this essay, and the extremely helpful input of Jane Desmond, Randy Martin, and Yvonne Rainer in completing the present version.

1 Richard Schechner, *Between Theater and Anthropology* (Philadelphia: University of Pennsylvania Press, 1985), p. 19.

2 B. Ruby Rich has claimed that Rainer's films have "arrived at a redefinition of melodrama for our times." She adds: "To be sure, the elipsis of time, the flat nonemotive voice, nonnaturalistic 'stagy' movement, verbal cliché, tableaux vivants, and unidentified pronouns, all combine to engage the spectator in the shaping of the film. At the same time, however, it is evident that these techniques precipitate a complete abstraction of the narrative. The only constant left to the film, finally, is emotion itself." See "Yvonne Rainer: An Introduction," in *The Films of Yvonne Rainer* (Bloomington: Indiana University Press, 1989), p. 9.

3 See Peggy Phelan, "Spatial Envy: Yvonne Rainer's *The Man Who Envied Women*," in *Unmarked: The Politics of Performance* (New York: Routledge, 1993), p. 83.

4 Yvonne Rainer, "Letter," in *Artforum* 12, no. 1 (September 1973), p. 10.

5 Francesco Pellizzi, "Fragment on Ornament," in *Parkett* 26 (1990), p. 101.

6 See, for example, Deborah Jowitt: "No matter how much she [Rainer] flattened out phrasing . . . she remained inherently expressive." "Expression and Expressionism in American Modern Dance," in *Dance History: An Introduction*, ed. Janet Adshead-Lansdale and June Layson (London: Routledge, 1993), p. 175.

7 Banes's claim actually has two parts: (1) "historical modern dance was never really *modernist*"; (2) postmodern dance is above all modernist because of its "acknowledgment of the medium's materials [and] the revealing of dance's essential qualities as an art form." See Sally Banes, *Terpsichore in Sneakers: Post-Modern Dance* (Middletown: Wesleyan University Press, 1977), pp. xiv–xv. Banes identifies dance modernism with the sixties on the strength of Rainer's Greenbergianism. See "Yvonne Rainer: The Aesthetics of Denial," in ibid., pp. 41–54. "The achievement of *Trio A* is its resolute denial of style and expression, making a historical shift in the subject of dance to pure motion" (p. 54). For further discussion of Rainer's connection with "new sculpture," see Rosalind E. Krauss, *Passages in Modern Sculpture* (New York: Viking, 1977), esp. chap. 6: "Mechanical Ballets: Light, Motion, Theater," pp. 201–42. For Krauss, the goals of "task performance" are "to exchange illusionism for real-time and to de-psychologize the performer" (ibid., pp. 235–36). Banes's position was disputed in Susan Manning, "Modernist Dogma and Postmodern Rhetoric: A Response to Sally Banes' *Terpsichore in Sneakers*," in *Drama Review* 32, no. 4 (1988), pp. 32–39, and further debated in an exchange of letters (*Drama Review* 33, no. 1 (1989), pp. 13–16), which debate I joined in Mark Franko, "Emotivist Movement and Histories of Modernism: The Case of Martha Graham," in *Discourse* 13, no. 1 (Fall–Winter 1990–91), pp. 111–28.

8 This argument is developed in *Dancing Modernism / Performing Politics* (Bloomington: Indiana University Press, 1995). The present essay is a sequel to that book.

9 See Susan Manning, "Ideology and Absolute Dance," in *Ecstasy and the Demon: Feminism and Nationalism in the Dances of Mary Wigman* (Berkeley: University of California Press, 1993), pp. 15–46.

10 Banes, *Terpsichore in Sneakers*, p. 44.

11 See Banes, "The 1960s: Breakaway Post-Modern Dance," in *Terpsichore in Sneakers*: "The early post-modern choreographers saw as their task the purging and melioration of historical modern dance, which had made certain promises in respect to the use of the body and the social and artistic function of dance that had not been fulfilled" (p. xv). Although Banes does not clarify what these promises were, I would assume they relate to radical social relevance. As such, these promises were clearly unfulfilled by the early 1950s.

12 See *Aesthetics and Politics*, ed. Ronald Taylor (London: Verso, 1980).

13 See Mark Franko, "Bodies of Radical Will," in *Dancing Modernism / Performing Politics*, pp. 25–33.

14 See Yvonne Rainer, "A Quasi Survey of Some 'Minimalist' Tendencies in the Quantitatively Minimal Dance Activity midst the Plethora, or an Analysis of *Trio A*," published in *Minimal Art: A Critical Anthology*, ed. Gregory Battcock (New York, 1968); reprinted in Yvonne Rainer, *Work, 1961–73* (New York: New York University Press, 1974), pp. 63–69. This collection of Rainer's writings relative to her choreography and her first films will be referred to hereafter as *Work*.

15 Rainer, *Work*, p. 63.

16 Banes, *Terpsichore in Sneakers*, p. 44. See also, Clement Greenberg, "Avant-Garde and Kitsch," *Partisan Review* 6 (Fall 1939), pp. 34–49, "Towards a Newer Laocoön," *Partisan Review* 7 (July–August 1940), pp. 296–310, and "The New Sculpture," both reprinted in *Arrogant Purpose, 1945–1949*, pp. 313–19.

17 Robert Morris, "Notes on Sculpture," in *Artforum* 4, no. 6 (February 1966), p. 44.

18 Banes, *Terpsichore in Sneakers*, p. 54.

19 Michael Fried, "Art and Objecthood," in *Minimal Art: A Critical Anthology*, ed. Gregory Battcock (New York: Dutton, 1968), p. 145.

20 Ibid., p. 146.

21 Robert Morris, "Notes on Sculpture Part II," in *Artforum* 5, no. 2 (October 1966), p. 23.

22 On the relationship of poststructuralist thought to [illegible] "[illegible]mique," in *Bodies of the Text: Dance as Theory, Literature as Dance* (New Brunswick: Rutgers University Press, 1995), pp. 205–16.

23 Fried, "Art and Objecthood," p. 145.

24 Ibid., pp. 139, 125. The sort of time that appears is not the "presence" of the I/eye in the cogito's seat, but one of "human" time in which things are experienced with constant differences, precisely because of time's interference. If this notion of difference as a literalist practice encapsulates Jacques Derrida's critique of Western metaphysics, it is ground for recognizing Derrida's humanism.

25 Fredric Jameson, *Postmodernism, or, The Cultural Logic of Late Capitalism* (Durham: Duke University Press, 1991), p. 154.

26 "Reduce dancing to doing, reduce creating to carpentry. A box is no more 'essential' than a Rodin sculpture. Picking up a box is no more 'pure' than picking up Giselle (or Clytemnestra)." Letter from Yvonne Rainer to the author, 7 February 1995.

27 Rainer, *Work*, p. 180.

28 Ibid., p. 187.
29 Ibid., p. 238.
30 Ibid.
31 Rainer, *Work*, p. 238.
32 Yvonne Rainer, "Looking Myself in the Mouth. Sliding Out of Narrative and Lurching Back In, Not Once but . . . Is the 'New Talkie' Something to Chirp About? From Fiction to Theory (Kicking and Screaming) Death of the Maiden, I Mean Author, I Mean Artist . . . No, I Mean Character. A Revisionist Narrativization of/with Myself as Subject (Still Kicking) via John Cage's Ample Back," *October* 17 (Summer 1981), p. 68.
33 Ibid., p. 72.
34 Or, at least, as the possibility of bridging their false divide. In 1973 she asked: "Is 'objectification' through 'lists, sequences, repetitive images and actions' truly antithetical to psychological and social content? And need the emergence of such context automatically 'dematerialize' an event and 'exceed its formal structure?'" My point, however, is that this question and the opening of the position it implies was only available to Rainer from the vantage point of film. See Yvonne Rainer, "Letter," in *Artforum* 12, no. 1 (September 1973), p. 10.
35 Nan Piene's letter to Yvonne Rainer, reproduced in *Work*, p. 239.
36 Ibid., p. 240.
37 The following reading is based on the 1978 film and a more recent revival for the stage. I do not broach the complex issues of the work's evolution, its original incarnation as a trio, the question of whether it is a movement phrase or a dance, the multitude of contexts in which it has been inserted—in sum, its identity problem.
38 Rainer, *Work*, p. 67.
39 Ibid., p. 66. Annette Michelson defines the task as "movement whose quality is determined by its specifically operational character." *Trio A*, she notes, radicalizes the notion of task performance because objects usually operated upon become the movement itself. This implies that movement is treated objectively but not reduced, almost in a phenomenological sense, to its essence. See her "Yvonne Rainer, Part One: The Dancer and the Dance," *Artforum* 12 (January 1974), p. 58.
40 Rainer, *Work*, p. 71.
41 Ibid., p. 46. This remark is excerpted from her discussion of *Terrain* (1963).
42 Ibid., p. 67.
43 Jill Johnston, "The New American Modern Dance," *Salmagundi* 33–34 (1976), p. 184.
44 Susan Foster, *Reading Dancing: Bodies and Subjects in Contemporary American Dance* (Berkeley: University of California Press, 1986), pp. 175–76.
45 Maurice Berger, *Labyrinths: Robert Morris, Minimalism, and the 1960s* (New York: Harper and Row, 1989), pp. 84–85.
46 Ibid., p. 63.
47 Rainer, *Work*, p. 51.
48 Ibid., p. 71.
49 Rainer, *Work*, p. 238.
50 Rainer's program note to the premier of *The Mind Is a Muscle* stated: "My connection to the world-in-crisis remains tenuous and remote." "My body," she added, "remains the enduring reality." Ibid., p. 71.
51 T. J. Clark, "Clement Greenberg's Theory of Art," *Critical Inquiry* 19, no. 1 (September 1982), p. 149.

52 Rainer seems to have become critically conscious of this with respect to her *Continuous Project—Altered Daily* (1970) when she wrote: "I am talking mostly about behavior rather than execution of movement. It is not because I value one over the other, but because the behavior aspects of this enterprise are so new and startling and miraculous to me." Yvonne Rainer, *Work*, p. 149.

53 Ibid., p. 65.

54 Ibid., p. 67.

55 See Franko, "The Politics of Expression," in *Dancing Modernism / Performing Politics*, pp. ix–xiv.

56 I make this case in my *Dance as Text: Ideologies of the Baroque Body* (Cambridge: Cambridge University Press, 1993).

I am dressed as a lecturer holding myself dancing in my hand

16 HOMOGENIZED BALLERINAS

Marianne Goldberg

Prologue, 1997: A miniature city of ballerinas, pressed (against her heart) onto acid free paper, dancing, for posterity, for academia, for syllabi and alibi, amidst columns and mutating paragraphs. So as not to turn invisible by staking visible form, or, so as not to interrupt the gorgeous historical flow of text and illustration, the ballerinas are dancing, so as to continue to insist on their existence, ephemerally, through the centuries, so as not to expire within discourse, however unwinged, so as not to turn, invisibly, in perpetual pirouette . . .

In 1987, dressed as a lecturer, holding myself dancing in my hand, I wrote: "Images of gender in traditional physicality are petrified in an opposition of so-called 'masculine' and 'feminine' movement choices which are social and artistic conventions rather than physical or physiological fact. The body is constructed through discourse, inscribed through patterns of social gesture, through the training systems of choreographed dance, as well as through the ways that words or visual images chart conceptions of physicality. The body is constructed through a sequence of identifications, which are political, historical, and economic. The ways the body travels through space, wields force, or expends energy are culturally established, as are the ways that male and female bodies interact: who has access to touching whose body where, who supports the weight of another's body, who accommodates. Physical language reveals no more about what is essentially female or male than does verbal language or subconscious imagery. The body accumulates and sheds meanings through social practice; it can lie as easily as the word.

Body	Body
Woman	*Man and Woman*

Nature	Culture
Unconscious	*Conscious*
Outside History	Within History
Outside Discourse	*Constituted by Discourse*
Primitive	Civilized
Organic	*Arbitrary*

The Sleeping Beauty. Choreographer Marius Petipa. Classic Ballet in three acts, with prologue. First presented at the Maryinsky Theater, St. Petersburg, Russia, 15 January 1890. First performed in Western Europe, 1921, in London, with additional choreography by Bronislava Nijinska.

Sleeping Beauty lies dormant—her coming of age cursed by enforced passivity, dependent on the desire of an unknown prince who will awaken her. The town she inhabits lies suspended in time—waiting. Unconscious, she remains in limbo until rescued by her hero as he crosses the boundary of surrounding forest to discover her female space. The prince's vision of her, his gaze, his kiss, brings her to life.

'Feminine'
  Anonym
Antonym
  Access
Sleeping Beauty
  Cold Cream

Swan Lake. Choreographed 1895. When Prince Siegfried comes of age, on the other hand, he goes hunting. Like Sleeping Beauty's prince, he actively journeys to the female terrain. He happens upon a field of white swans. One of them—the swan maiden Odette—emerges from the anonymity of the landscape of the corps de ballet and transforms into a beautiful girl. Corps: body: core: substance: corpse: corpuscle. She is cursed to remain a swan until a man promises to love her and remain faithful. The only woman in the story who enters a male landscape is Odile, the daughter of the evil Von Rothbart, the man who keeps Odette under his spell. Odile travels to Prince Siegfried's court, where she aggressively seduces him. Traditionally, she is crass and selfish, an interloper costumed in black. Odette and Odile are counterparts—the same ballerina plays both roles. As White Swan and Black Swan, like virgin and whore, these two fairytale ballerinas occupy the opposite poles of conventional gender roles for women. The *good* ballerina serves as a liminal space, a landscape, between nature and culture which the prince colonizes, thereby becoming a hero.[1]

AT SEVEN YEARS I PERFORMED THE PRINCE TO MY SISTER'S PRINCESS

History, nature, the body: inherited definitions. I danced the part of the sleeping princess at the Maryinsky in 1890. I slept for a hundred years until a prince lifted me effortlessly. In the early 1900s, Isadora taught me that underneath my corsets I had a free unfettered woman's body to be discovered. I believed Martha Graham when she told me that my body does not lie: my body as magical access to authenticity/originality/newness/raw material. In 1931 I danced her *Primitive Mysteries* and knew that amidst all-female performers, the stage could become a mythical realm where a goddess in white could materialize. I dreamt I performed Yvonne Rainer's 1966 *Trio A*, turning my gaze away from the audience to break the movement phrasing that historically identified woman as object of display. Watching Rainer dance the piece on film, I felt an intensely suppressed eroticism that held great sex appeal, despite or perhaps because of her efforts.

SHE WAS OVERCOME WITH A HEAVY SLEEP. WHO GAVE HER THE SLEEPING TABLETS?

Princes and princesses are manufactured from the ways male and female bodies interact in physical terms. Support, initiation, strength, adaptability, delicacy, directness—all occupy their niches on the continuum of gender identity. Without the polarities of masculine and feminine movements, the conventional dance narratives could not progress. To maintain these narratives, the woman's body serves as a spectacle, arranged and displayed frontally in open, vulnerable positions. Her body is often fragmented so that part comes to stand for whole. A fetishized arabesque, like Marlene Dietrich's gesture of her legs, becomes the metonym for the ballerina, breaking her power. The way the ballerina is framed by her male partner within the proscenium establishes certain display mechanisms that build the way she is to be looked at into the spectacle.[2] Rather than accept this as mere convention, the ballerina who is centerstage, presented and often manually sculpted by the male dancer, might ask whether she is necessarily at the center of the action.

How do we read against the grain of the patriarchal body? How does the fledgling ballerina vomiting in the school bathroom refuse her anorexia and recognize that the unattainable White Swan she is looking for in the mirror is an imaginary, fictional Woman?[3] To what extent do the representations on the dance stage become enacted in daily life? What are the boundaries of masquerade? At what point does the female spectator become the ballerina, or the performer her role? In what ways do these images of passivity affect the identity of the

M. Goldberg lectures on Dance History
Elaine Fifield in *Swan Lake*
Nijinska in costume for *Sleeping Beauty*
Isadora Duncan

Bronislava Nijinska directs rehearsal of *Les Noces*
Martha Graham in *Primitive Mysteries*
Yvonne Rainer in *Trio A*

female choreographer? (Bronislava Nijinska, one of the greatest twentieth-century choreographers, transformed balletic pointe work into thrusting movements of the legs. In her version of a wedding dance, Les Noces, *her female dancers pounded out syncopated rhythms and pierced through space with their toe shoes. Despite the importance of her own choreography, she devoted her published memoirs almost entirely to a description of the significance of her brother's choreography. She also has been left out of most of the history books.)*

GENDERED BODY: MASQUERADE

I want to reexamine the conventions and ideologies of the dance stage and the ways in which they determine expectations about gender, to insert a different female body into representation, to bend the rules of the frame of the theater to shift the way the woman's image is received by the spectator, to jar the stage until the discourse of the body shifts the meaning of:

1. The accepted range of motion for the female body
2. Partnering conventions
3. Narrative structures
4. Visual gaze and display mechanisms
5. The spectator-performer relationship
6. The performance space: proscenium, loft, environment
7. Gendered aspects of costuming
8. The sequencing/contexting of movements
9. The juxtapositions of motion and sound/language/visual image
10. The marketing of the performance

A shift in any one of these codes can impinge on the others. A word, for instance, could be wedged underneath a leg or arm, the untamed word freeing the tamed body. Language re-creates the body/or the body re-creates narrative/or narrative re-creates partnering conventions. This requires disassembling and rebuilding.

MY BODY FOLDED UNDER THE WEIGHT OF MY MIND . . .

Years of theoretical thinking left dancing to the crevices of experience. Sorting through the significance of a physical impulse while immersed in doing a gesture, I understand it one way. Watching a gesture, another. Immersed in what a choreographer tells me about her gesture, another. Thinking over the ramifications of a gesture, turning it around in my mind even many years later, still another. A memory of motion as it recedes into the past accumulates new meanings like a snowball rolling away from me. Many choreographers do not have the skills or desires to think theoretically about movement. Most thinkers don't spend time really getting to know their bodies. For years I have encouraged dancers to write about their own work rather than forfeit that right to critics. Educational institutions separate physical and intellectual pursuits, yet the theoretical and literal bodies are really one body. The way we think about our hands, nose, hips, breasts defines them. So much feminist writing points to the theoretical or metaphorical reclaiming of the body without considering the material, experienced body.

BODY: NATURE

Is there a body outside the idea of the body, and if so, how do we discover it? Through Martha Graham's breath rhythm (the simulation of which actually requires stopping the breath at times)? Through Isadora Duncan's impulse from the solar plexus (which she believed in over impulses from other parts of her body)? Through a search for the subjective desires of the body as a form of kinesthetic honesty (which assumes that there is a naive body waiting to be discovered beneath civilization)? Standing behind every Woman is an Unspoken Parenthesis. It was Graham's psychologist's father who told her the body does not lie.

BODY: HISTORY

So many of the women who established dance companies in the 1970s focused on the body as form. Not a sexual form, but a geometrical or architectural one. Cancellations of sexuality meant the articulation of the limbs deflecting focus from a sexy circle of the hips, with the intellect newly claimed as the most important resource for female physicality. Choreographers like Trisha Brown, Lucinda Childs, or Laura Dean short-circuited the notion that the woman's body represents nature, constructing elaborate grids that told them where to place their bodies in space, rather than glorifying female intuition in physical terms. What differentiates these gridlike forms from the geometrization of the twenty-four swan maidens who appear as a landscape in *Swan Lake*, flocking in triangles or rectangles? Is it that they avoid the frontal organization of the female body in relation to the proscenium frame, or that they break the static arrangement of the female body along a perspective grid that since the Renaissance has equated woman and displayed object, spectator and consumer? Is it that, for the most part, roles are not distributed along gender lines, and with the gaze of the male dancer no longer claiming the female dancer within the stage space, the gaze of the spectator-as-consumer is consequently deactivated as well?

PRINCE: 'IT'S GREAT TO BE SO FAR FROM CIVILIZATION.'
PRINCESS: 'I HOPE YOU BROUGHT YOUR CREDIT CARDS.'

Is a *pas de deux* only a love story when a man initiates and the woman responds? Without gender polarities, can the same story go on? If there were no princes and princesses, but instead two lovers whose differences are not based on gender but on their own specific yet shifting identities, what kind of story would they tell? And how would the spectators understand the story? Stay tuned for further details.

Tension in my body working upward from toes to head. Three dimensionality: I am a series of round, linear cylinders: foot / leg / torso / arms / neck smooth cylinders. All sides are equally humming. Searching for a place of balance where I feel in line with a gravitational pull. My rib cage realigns itself backward so I feel at home. Turning to the left each surface of my body participates sequentially: all rotations are spirals, and: all rotations are desires. Do these experiences, in which my body seems a sensuous organism, have anything to do with gender?

Motion: time, space, energy, form. The icon is not raw material mediated into meaning, language, or narrative. The syntax of iconicity or physical sensation is not less culturally formed than linguistic structures, not more 'natural.' There is no body underneath: sexuality is exterior, history interior. There is no prehistoric virgin forest to return to.

Vessel
    Vestal Virgin
Vestibule
    Pathway
Landscape
    Sphinx
Construction Worker
    Construction

One option: to return to an instinctive body. The extreme contradiction: goddesses created by patriarchal myths. The Sphinx as landscape in the male journey.[4] Women as circles, internal, softly undulating. Men as the equivalent of industrial machinery. Another option: to refuse the representation of the female body as image. The extreme contradiction: a refusal of the female body altogether. Eradicate sex, avert the eyes, abstract the body. A third option: to explore the contradictions, to locate a source of pleasure that sets the female body in motion, to remake the meaning of the image from a position of pleasure. (And I do not mean the kind of visual 'pleasure' that works against woman.) A pleasure in moving, breathing, changing, improvising.

BODY: DISCOURSE

Lying on my back, sensing the inside of my skull and jaw.
A disjunction between head and neck that is alarming.
I feel frozen but I am not sleeping.
I cannot find the effort to move my lips to make a sound.
People around me are crying.
Their pain is my body and it is paralyzing me.
I want to feel the release of sleep along the surfaces of my face.
Somewhere inside this fear is a still marginal physicality with not-
yet coalesced perceptions that I know must emerge for my body to
rearrange itself.

If gestures are broken down into small units, how minuscule must they become before they lose gender definition? Is the relation of gesture to its gendered meaning as distant or as arbitrary as the relation between a word and a meaning? (Wide stance = male / delicate articulation = female) Is it possible to suppress the defined meaning of even the smallest units long enough to discover a unit of movement that has the requisite ambiguity to shift meaning in multiple directions / to disrupt conventional movement phrasing / to assert gender nonsequiturs that might allow different meanings to arise? Would this kind of movement then be (A) neutral in terms of gender or (B) a composite of all the known capabilities of both genders or (C) new movement not yet discovered within the established gendered options or (D) movement which evades sexuality or evades difference or (E) NONE OF THE ABOVE.

I place myself at the middle of meaning—at the point of contradiction where meanings are formed in the body. I am not a sculptured landscape, a surface for projected meanings. At the middle point: intense changes of perception redefining my body, strands of information, desire for motion. My body is: a vessel of psychological memory or emotional elation or trauma / an imprint of verbal language or visual image / an antenna to outside surroundings or internal physiological needs. Are there any purely kinetic experiences? Are meanings grafted onto physical sensations or are they intermeshed in the body's tissues? If I find my way to a conventional balletic arabesque, I may not perceive it as an arabesque but as something other. My new perception might collide with the usual meaning of the movement: arabesque: and lend it an alternative meaning, layer a new meaning onto the old.

"Speaking"

'Masculine'
    Motorcar
Masterful
    Mutilated:
That kind of gaze
is not
striking my face
or your face:
obliterating
the binary
the bridling of
both male and female

I circle my pelvis in shifting directions, suspending conventional associations to discover what else it might mean. If I perform this movement on stage (or on the page) how quickly does it become sexual display and nothing else—its difference disappearing into the equivalent of bump and grind? How soon does 'sexual display' turn my body into the cliché of an object, activating the consuming gaze of the spectator ('YOU'). Consumed, eaten, spent, consummated, confiscated. What must I do to cancel the expected meaning if I intend to communicate something different? Corral you? Disbar you as my spectator? Seduce you from a different angle of vision? Bargain with you? Trust that you know what I mean? In repeated cancellations of conventional sexual meanings, what kinds of pleasure must I forfeit and what do I gain?

Can the frame of the stage be redefined to support an altered gender content so that attention is riveted not on the spectacle of an athletic but still objectified female body but on what that body is communicating by inscribing itself in time and space? The stage re-framed as a context in which the female dancer can be viewed differently. Traces of the ballerina icon no longer so ingrained in the very form of the dance spectacle that it is impossible to see anything else. Circumventing the way the person moving has been framed/glorified/immortalized/defiled.

Metonym
    Pseudonym
Figure of Speech
    Accommodating
Speaking

I spent years in the studio of choreographer-filmmaker Elaine Summers, who built an intricate technique for retraining physicality: passing balls under the body to articulate motion at the points of contact with rotating baseballs, tennis balls, beach balls. Transformation: coming of age, waking up. To trade one alternative for two or more, to cajole meanings. The body perches between the formed and the unformed. This is either an impasse or a way to pass through.

At all-girl parties I passed oranges chin to chin. On my birthday I went early to watch Mickey Mantle warm up: passing balls, powering balls into the grandstand, catching balls mid-leap. I played basketball with my high-school buddies. At Passover holidays, I passed my grandmother's matzo balls while listening to my grandfather lead the litany of forefathers. They told me to ask, 'What is different about this night than all others?' Difference, diffidence, deterrence. I bypassed my thirteenth birthday. Coming of age I balked at debutante balls but rarely bawled myself out before bowling with twenty female adolescents on my boisterous birthday. I keep a photo of my grandmother with her 1910 women's softball team dressed in bloomers and ties. Begging the Question, Blowing my Trumpets, Bill of Rights, Bird of Freedom, Breaking the Ice, Breaking to Smithereens, Breaking Ground, Breaking into a Smile.

IN CASE YOU WERE WONDERING ABOUT A MALE LANDSCAPE OR A FEMALE HERO . . . AND I DO NOT MEAN A MEATBALL SANDWICH . . .

If the body is to become subversive in gender terms, it must exceed the representational frame of the patriarchal stage. The insistence on binary physical differences—male/female—can give way to a fluid spectrum of oppositions that have meaning other than 'masculine' and 'feminine.' The body redefines itself in relation to others: those others, whether male or female, need to allow shifts in the potential meanings of touch/initiation/response/strength/subtlety. The male body moves beyond the 'masculine' as patriarchally defined, just as the female body is not limited by the 'feminine.'

NAVIGATING . . . CONVERGING . . . BURGEONING

Meanings continually form and re-form over the surfaces of the body. The body is stage which must reinvent itself: wings, curtains, action, space, bones, muscles, and flights of fantasy. If a woman is to make the meaning of her own image, her body must surpass itself through the very discourse in which it is embedded. Bedding, Budding, Butting. With the jolt of adrenaline that comes with the anticipation that desires can become reality, the sleeping princess awakens as she reconstructs her body in the friction between image and flesh."

Epilogue, forever: Four inches tall, the ballerinas on the birthday cakes of four-year-old girls are perching on pointed toes, their pink plastic skin glistening, their inner thighs turning in the wide yearning that travels along the cool surfaces of their legs.[5] Carrying their own weight, excited to move, a place of great luxuriousness and pleasure . . .

AFTERWORD

This essay was first presented in lecture form, next as a lecture-performance, in radically altered form, with text spoken at a podium, accompanied by gestures. Still later I danced it as a performance with lecture material inserted into it. For its original publication, titled "Ballerinas and Ball Passing," I invented a genre I call the "performance piece for print," composed of text and photographed gestures. In this genre I conceive the printed page as a kind of stage, and reading as a theatrical act. In *Ballerinas* images of myself as a lecturer and as dancer-choreographer are interspersed with images of choreography by other artists, both historical and contemporary. Gestures are choreographed in counterpoint with text, then printed on a two-dimensional surface. The resultant work is intended to be held in the hands of the spectator-reader, first alone, and later potentially in discussion with others.

Experimental scholarly writing, which rarely fits into what we already know how to read, evokes questions about the articulation of dance in relation to the printed word. Due to the particular mechanics and forms of reproduction of intellectual discourse, experimental writing often remains invisible, unprintable, never making it to publication. The traditional format for constructing and reproducing theoretical insight erodes changes on a piece like *Ballerinas and Ball Passing*, which intentionally and ironically plays with conventional structures for text, illustration, punctuation, kinetic image, caption, or footnote.

The standardized visual format of a scholarly anthology, which presents a seamless, homogenized flow of text with occasional kinetic images available only as illustrations, actually makes it impossible to reproduce a piece such as the original *Ballerinas.* This new version stands in relationship to its predecessor as a filmscript stands in relation to a film, missing as it does its graphic layer, as well as its entire visual structure for experience. Because of this, for publication here I change its title to *Homogenized Ballerinas*, recognizing that a work in such a different context is no longer the "original" and is in fact a substantially altered piece, a permutation on the previous form that now works intertextually with it in intriguing ways.

In publishing this text in a book such as *Meaning in Motion*, my intention is to work referentially within scholarly discourse and to point—through jarring juxtapositions of modes of address or of experiential and theoretical language—to frames unconsciously placed around explorations of dance. To rework the deconstruction that is *Ballerinas*, I take that essay apart by trying to put it together into a text-only form that will fit the visual requirement of a traditional anthology. A commentary emerges about what we as scholars, writers, and editors believe must be included or occluded to constitute erudite discourse. *Homogenized Ballerinas*, which for the most part consists of the word minus its partnered body, is available to the reader to consider alongside the version of "Ballerinas and Ball Passing" printed in *Women & Performance* journal in 1987, and alongside the live performance versions choreographed and rechoreographed for various theatrical and theoretical formats. The shifts in medium might serve as bridges between experiential realms.

Photo Credits

Photographs of myself in the "lecturer" costume of a suit are by Babette Mangolte.
Photographs of myself in dance costume are by Helma Klooss.
Elaine Fifield in *Swan Lake*, Sadler's Wells Theater Ballet; Nijinska in costume for *Sleeping Beauty*, circa 1921; Isadora Duncan; Martha Graham in *Primitive Mysteries*: all photos courtesy of The Dance Collection, New York Public Library for the Performing Arts, Astor, Lenox, and Tilden Foundations.
Nijinska directs rehearsal of *Les Noces*, photo courtesy of Nijinska Archives. Yvonne Rainer in *Trio A*, photo by Jack Mitchell.

Notes

I dedicate the publication of "Ballerinas" in this anthology to Judy Rosenthal, who was inspirational in its adaptation for this new context.

Material from this essay was first published as "Ballerinas and Ball Passing" in *Women & Performance: A Journal of Feminist Theory* 3, no. 2.6 (1987/1988), pp. 7–31. I greatly appreciate the encouragement of the editorial collective of *Women & Performance* in developing my "performance pieces for print," which explore relationships between dancing, writing, and graphic forms.

1 Teresa de Lauretis, in her book *Alice Doesn't: Feminism, Semiotics, Cinema* (Bloomington: Indiana University Press, 1984) develops the idea that narrative itself positions the male hero as traveler and the female as obstacle or landscape in his travels.

2 Here I refer obliquely to Jacque Lacan's "mirror stage," in which the child's identity is established by gazing in a mirror. I do not agree with Lacan that preceding the child's entry to verbal language she exists in the "Imaginary"—a realm of unmediated drives. I suggest that in the time period before language, a child's movements become structured within a symbolic order—a nonverbal, iconic, kinesthetic one—replete with gendered identifications. See Kaja Silverman's *The Subject of Semiotics* (New York: Oxford University Press, 1983), pp. 157–62, for an analysis of Lacan congruent with my point of view. Lacan sees women as lacking a position as speaking subjects of discourse. My article is a round rejection of the

definition of woman as anonym of the male. Silverman states: "Once we deny this primordial lack, we are free to understand all ideal representations as culturally manufactured and to relocate the mirror stage inside the boundaries of the symbolic" (p. 192).

3 Laura Mulvey, in her essay "Visual Pleasure and Narrative Cinema," *Screen* 16 (Autumn 1975), pp. 6–18, takes apart the nature of cinematic gaze and display mechanisms. In my artile, through the content of words and their juxtaposition with photographs, I explore the display apparatus of both the dance stage and the printed page.

4 De Lauretis uses the example of the Sphinx, who never tells her own story but serves as a symbolic boundary between nature and culture as a signpost in the male story. See her chapter "Desire in Narrative," especially p. 109, in *Alice Doesn't: Feminism, Semiotics, Cinema.*

5 The image of ballerinas on birthday cakes is inspired by my current improvisational work with dancer Christianne Brown.

17 DANCE ETHNOGRAPHY AND THE LIMITS OF REPRESENTATION

Randy Martin

The distance between representation and object has engaged the intellectual energies of those writing on dance as a kind of bricolage where the dance event appears to occasion writerly structure. These energies have been occupied in writing on other objects by a theory that simulates the complexity of the object in the writing itself. The traces of participation, the work an audience does to create a sense of the object as it is presented to them, are nowhere to be found in the standard means of representation and documentation and, as such, are absent from the ways in which history is conventionally conceived.

Reception of dance, especially of the kinds of Western concert dance that will provide the focus for this essay, is realized only in the particular performance event. The dancers constitute themselves in anticipation of performance. This anticipation bears the anxiety of uncertainty, of something that can be completed only through its communication. The performance is the execution of an idea by dancers whose work proceeds in expectation of an audience that is itself only constituted through performance. The audience has no identity as audience prior to and apart from the performative agency that has occasioned it. As such, the audience is intrinsically "unstable," both in terms of its own presence and in its ability to occasion and then disrupt the very anxiety of performance. At the same time, it is the work that the audience does, the participation that it lends to performance to make the latter possible, that is irrecuperable to representation. It is, like the dance activity itself, an untranslatable object. But unlike dancing, forms of representation rarely make an effort to recognize audience participation, which springs from this disruptive potential, itself an indeterminacy of representation internal to the performance. So if writing and documentation cannot recuperate the traces of participation found in performance, minimally they can recognize the disruptive effects of the work of participation lost to representation.

The shift in perspective to participation rather than representation as suggested by the conceptual challenges posed by dance, here understood as the particularization of the performer-audience relation, has an import beyond dance writing. This perspective simulates a relation of performer and audience where the activity of performers (the artistic object of performance) puts into operation the notion of "agency," and where the audience suggests a mobilized critical presence such as that implicit in radical notions of "history."[1]

This distinction points to a conception of history which joins historical project—as the formation of an identity—and historical possibility—as the capacity for continued mobilization; and as such focuses on the moment of reception in relation to the object. The full appreciation of the place of reception, of the unstable audience, has the potential to extend an understanding of the political.

I claim that the procedure most appropriate to exploring the relation of agency and history simulated in performance is ethnographic. Ethnography is an appropriate method for appreciating the disruptive presence that divides representation and its object in that it conveys through language that the ethnographic procedure is radically different from what it looks at. Ethnography is an activity of textual appropriation of difference that rests upon a prior cultural appropriation through colonial contact. Hence, while ethnography results in representation, with sufficient methodological reflection, it points to what is lost to representation just as does the performer-audience relation in dance.

A revisionist ethnography has appeared in the last ten years that, in the face of what it sees as the loss of the exotic, seeks to locate its activity wholly within representation as a rhetorical reflection of writing.[2] Without doubt, scrutinizing the authority of representation, calling into question the distance of the cultural object, and asserting the partiality of truth as both "committed and incomplete" all render ethnographic practice more fully reflexive.

Yet this consciousness of self can come at the expense of a comprehension of what that self appropriates and what lies beyond that appropriation. My concern is that the unruly engagement with difference which currently marks Western culture must be recognized if what reconstituted colonial energies now do to the world is to be kept alive to analysis.[3] The self-awareness gained by revisionist ethnography over the objectivistic conventions of its forebears threatens to be recuperated wholly within the politics of writing per se.

I would instead privilege a strategy made intelligible through an analysis of dance that would reaffirm and relocate the exotic within ethnographic representation, precisely that of the unstable audience. The ethnography of this strategy consists in writing that fully displays the disruptive potential of that which it represents in analysis. Here the ethnographic field is neither the undifferentiated space of the Other visited by the ethnographer or the seamless space of representation in which an ethnographer writes. It is, rather, like dance performance, a relation of forces joined in tension yet fundamentally unlike one another. By identifying such tensions, fieldwork becomes more problematic, more contingent, and more susceptible to contention and reformation, because fieldwork is constituted by difference rather than merely reflecting difference.

In this regard, ethnographic writing identifies politics where there was thought to be none. This is not to say that one should expect to hear more from a given audience at a dance concert; clearly that would take some other event, tied to a sustained mobilization. But if analysis is to understand what keeps any audience coming back for more, if it is to grasp what sustains any mobilization irrespective of its duration, analysis had better attend closely to the dynamics of performance.

Difference hitherto relegated to some exotic Other elsewhere now lies within the account of the object as destabilized and destabilizing. Context here is not what lies beyond the object but what the object cannot grasp and what thus appears as a momentary assertion. If traditional ethnography had asserted the (colonial) context unproblematically as beyond the cultural object, and revisionary ethnography lost context to its own representation, this dance-based ethnographic prospect insinuates context in the midst of the object without being absorbed by that object. The Other, grounded in practical terms as the mobilized presence of the unstable audience, provides momentary context to the agency of the object itself, now the writing of spatial inscriptions or dancing, or of ethnographic texts.

Such a conception of ethnography could be applied to any number of situations, from television watchers to soldiers in battle, from movements of capital to those against it. But to develop its terms of analysis, it should logically begin with the highly particularized relations of dance where the participation of audience refuses to be subsumed by the representation of performance.

In what follows, I would like to privilege four texts that illustrate many of the issues raised thus far, and in so doing, contribute to the development of a performance ethnography. Three are studies of dance and one is an investigation of theater that presents a view of the "unstable audience." While Deborah Jowitt's *Time and the Dancing Image*[4] is an essentially descriptive dance history and Susan Foster's *Reading Dancing: Bodies and Subjects in Contemporary American Dance*[5] is a uniquely rigorous application of contemporary theory to dance analysis, both provide ethnographic models for the study of dance. *Democracy's Body*,[6] Sally Banes's account of experimental dance at Judson Church in the

1960s, suggests the possibility of dance as an analytic frame and the limits to the autonomy of that frame. Finally, Herbert Blau's *The Audience*[7] is included to extend the analysis beyond that of the performers.[8]

Representing the Object of Performance: The Anxiety to Capture and Chronicle

A kind of formalism has reigned in dance criticism under the rubric of the review. Indeed, a review presents itself as a document of the dance rather than as an evaluation of it. Evaluation is eschewed for "description" conceived of as a representation of specific activity, without appeal to context and where selection is made to appear self-evident. While reviews in other media are seldom reflexive, it is not uncommon for them to join description of the object with some explicit problem for representation, be it a struggle over context that suggests controversy, or a question regarding the work's sources or conditions of reception. Yet the dance review's presentation of its material as a simulation of the performance suggests a relation of universal powers of appropriation to a particular event, with critical attitude being tied not to evaluation but a somehow objective orientation to the object. The reviewer's authority to represent is translated into any viewer's capacity to relate experience of the object ("I was there. Let me tell you how it was"). Given the instability of the traces left by dance performance, such claims become all the more tenuous.

For twenty years Deborah Jowitt, lead dance critic for the *Village Voice*, has been most strongly associated with this nonevaluative, documentary trend in dance criticism. Undoubtedly, when documentation as a simulation of performance becomes a critical trope, one is tempted to overlook the critic's own dispositions. In return for this loss, each dance is given an originary status, a freshness in performance that gives the critic's review the mark of discovery, and the performance that of thing-in-itself. Jowitt voices her concern among those who practice her craft "that in our anxiety to capture and chronicle a notoriously ephemeral art we do it an inadvertent disservice: we focus so intently on it that we sever it from the culture that spawned it and which it serves."[9] It is no small irony then that she produces a representational strategy that extends precisely the model of formalist dance criticism she has helped develop to a culturally informed account of the history of dance.

Despite her professed sensitivity to context, she produces nothing to offset the context, denying "anxiety to capture and chronicle" (a phrase that could have been lifted right from Columbus's diaries), which she takes as the reviewer's burden. She speaks of her book's method as an extension of writing criticism to writing history, where her ability to deny her own cultural links to what she observes enables her to account for the cultural relations that generated Western concert dancing:

> A dance critic, attending performances night after night, devises strategies for keeping eye and mind fresh. Some years ago, no doubt influenced by a long-standing addiction to *National Geographic*, I began to find it useful, on occasion, to blot out all expectations based on knowledge of styles or techniques. Instead I imagined myself an anthropologist skulking in ambush, observing the activities of members of a hitherto undiscovered tribe—trying to discern their customs and social hierarchy before I stepped out of the bushes and made myself known to them.
>
> The game, idly begun, eventually generated this book. The approach turned out to have variants that were applicable to the study of the past.[10]

Her gesture to anthropology has, as she sees it, tremendous meaning for the method and orientation of her book, *Time and the Dancing Image*. Not only does the span of time it covers fit that of the history of anthropology (dating from the middle of the nineteenth century), it presents the history of dance as a persistent reaching for the Other at the moment that it dissolves exotically over the horizon just beyond the march of Western capitalist society. Jowitt is explicit about this relation to and by the Other—which she identifies as "Orientalism"—as constituting the history of dance. But in her refusal to theorize it in terms that can show the necessity of such a representation within, say, an episteme, she places it ambiguously against her own critical disposition as something others chose.

The play of desire and power is central to the Orientalist thematic in dance, and Jowitt attempts to name some of its aspects. Yet without the aid of theory she seems to redouble some of these relations in her historical account. The very devices of proscenium presentation construct a spectacle of a world distant in time and space that is made intimate through a special mode of visual conquest where the virtuosic efforts of a female dancer are offered for the private pleasures of a male consort.

Embedded in the colonization offered by Romantic ballets such as *La Sylphide*, of Bournonville or Taglioni, and Coralli and Perrot's *Giselle*, are relations of gender, race, and class made innocent and unencumbered by worldly power through amorous trysts and metaphysical interventions. Each of these categories, however, are paradoxical within the Romantic ballet. The ethereal sylph typically occupies more real time on stage than the male "hero" who pursues her and to whom she is invariably appropriated: and she occupies more real space than her role in narrative seemed to entail: presumably because she was, Jowitt says, to be "substantial enough to play a shadow."[11] The prima ballerina as sylph is the presence of an absence, against which the concreteness of the drama of gender is played out by the male. This probably refigured an Occidental ideal of domesticity in the opposition of merely physical presence and the real, motivated presence of the male signified by the sylph's occupation of space and time. He is spatial and temporal while she is only *in* space and time.

Yet for the ballet corps, the women of generally working-class origin who typically compose the social body or ensemble of the mis-en-scène, the suggested gender relations of the ballet are played out with male patrons from the audience. Jowitt sees this rather complex form of sex-work as inscribing its own fantasy of class mobility onto a terrain reserved for the upper crust. Ironically, those women of the corps who married their patrons found the power of their desire shifted from the public site in which consciousness was possible, even if only as fantasy, to a private situation where even fantasy could be dangerous.

The prospect of women exercising the power of their desire, either as spectators or dancers, seems to be denied by the way in which Jowitt frames the subject of the Orientalist ballet: "The dreamed-up Oriental woman, fired by passion, was apparently capable of a daring beyond that of the proper European lady, and certainly beyond that of the real sultana, whiling away the long hours of her indolent and restricted life."[12] What Jowitt here calls the "courage and initiative that these Orientalist ballerinas display,"[13] both as agents of their own desire and defiers of those who wield power over them (as in the heroine's resistance to a "tyrannical government figure" in Taglioni's *Brahma, le dieu et la bayadere*), is instead clearly restricted within the male gaze that founds that courage and initiative, as the latter's conditions. The ballerina in her circumscribed space is too easily made exceptional to the sexless Occidental woman or the lazy "real sultana" of the East, not to mention the possibility that Jowitt herself is intrigued by the Orientalist vision.

If nineteenth-century ballet tended to displace women's labor onstage onto the prior image of an exotic Other that could not carry the weight of intention and hence could not work, the women who inaugurated modern dance could restore this relation of act and meaning. The work of Loie Fuller, Isadora Duncan, Ruth St. Denis, and Maud Allan provides an image of agency that had previously been denied women on the stage. Yet this very celebration in Jowitt's hands relies on an appropriation of the exotic Other as the source for dance that she had identified with the Romantic ballets of the nineteenth century. Like the figure of the Orientalist ballerina, the modern dancer Isadora

Duncan is represented by Jowitt as an originality, a singularity without history. While Jowitt wants to contextualize Duncan's contribution to dance, she instead appeals to Duncan's essence as a performer to account for the emergent character of the dancer's work. Her contemporaries, the sources "who were actually there" upon whom Jowitt relies, were thus moved to present their "responses" to Duncan, rather than "writing about what she actually did,"[14] suggesting an opposition between a rationalist mode of science and an intuitive mode of human and cosmological nature. Jowitt applies this opposition to her own historiography. "She evoked an idyllic 'nature,' even as developments in science and industry were shrinking the countryside, finally stripping poverty of its last veil, picturesqueness."[15] In her own work, Duncan denies having been subject to any influence, suggesting her own experience as her only inspiration.

Yet, as Jowitt notes, Duncan had studied the movement systems of Delsarte, which he claimed represented a fully scientific approach to the body. The problematic character of any interpretation of Duncan lies in an opposition of nature and science, conceived of as an obligation of analysis that divides dance's essential sources from the activity of dancing. Thus the motion of veiling and unveiling, culture/science and nature, is inscribed not merely outside as Jowitt might suggest, but also on Duncan's body as a body. That is, it both reveals and is an act hinting at a desire to reveal. The imagery of the veil receives attention in Jowitt's chapters on Duncan and St. Denis. In the latter case, the modernist impulse is connected to the more "universal" Orientalist roots of Western dance:

> Perhaps the most potent image lingering from St. Denis's early-twentieth-century American Orientalism is that of this idealized self. But to the modernists who were her pupils, her legacy was not veils and exotic disguises. These they discarded. What they seized on was her conception of a dance as a vehicle for showing change, rather than for displaying the status quo, her idea that one didn't end quite as one began. They did not need the Orient as a pretext. In 1906, seeking a form of personal expression beyond the parts she was offered in plays and the traditional show-off roles then open to the dancer, St. Denis had found the East to be a store-house of guises. These, in their mystery, beauty, theatricality, "otherness," facilitated the transmission of ideas that, as Ruth St. Denis, she would not have known how to convey on stage. Asia was her better self.[16]

In the spectacles of nineteenth-century ballet, the Orient is appropriated in the service of a single colonizing gaze that disciplines gender, race, and class in the ballerina's romantic loyalty to the heroic male figure who authorizes her labor. Modernism psychologizes this appropriation as an interior division of the self into consciousness and the unconscious. Jowitt writes a myth of modernist creation where Orientalist content is replaced by an aestheticized self-appropriation. The external "real" or concrete veil and its hint at a nature beneath is replaced by an internal territorialization of self, one part of which is populated by the exotic Other as the labor of the creative process.

Jowitt goes on to write the history of American concert dance (a field that retains its apparent modernism in the persistent figuration of individual auteurs as sources of diverse dance styles) through this optic. For example, in the work of Martha Graham, "Eastern theater" was a source for dances such as *Cave of the Heart* and *Clytemnestra*, but more profoundly, "Orientalisms . . . resided in Graham's muscles."[17] Former Graham dancer Merce Cunningham's use of chance techniques is interpreted by Jowitt as an affirmation of "the philosophers of the ancient East."[18] Similarly, the experimentalists of the 1960s, "when American interest in Eastern art, philosophy, and culture was escalating along with the war in Vietnam,"[19] were drawn to an image of the Orient absolutely distracted from the conjunctural significance of that image in United States culture and politics of the Vietnam era.

The point here is not to question Jowitt's assertion of the presence of an Orientalism within the history of Western concert dance, but to scrutinize the place of the Orientalist imagination in the service of criticism. It is one thing to configure creativity by an appeal to the exotic which is also an appeal to a particularity, the irrational (or the primitive), and quite another to construct a mythological place called the East as a preserve for these qualities. It elevates the artist to the status of an eccentric being among Westerners who is uniquely capable of appropriating the Other as labor power in such a way that it appears without history and therefore as an executant of a more essential agency. At the same time, precisely what the artist is in this mastery of the world through the appropriation of this labor is unclear. The seemingly unnoticed irony of interest in Eastern thought escalating while Vietnam was being destroyed by war is symptomatic of a persistent refusal to confront the relation between art and power as that of creativity of thought and the labor of manifesting thought. Jowitt's peculiar anthropological vision, one with certain parallels to standard ethnography, denies events their context by deriving the latter from the autonomy of criticism itself.

Rather than seeking tensions between dance and its world that might shed light on the world, Jowitt treats the history of modernity as an evening at the theater. Continuity and context deny the critic her moment of absolute judgment. To avoid that, dancing is reduced by Jowitt to a moment of essence that the critic discovers night after night ("This is not to say that *dancing* gets better, only that the technical ante has been upped").[20] In its Oriental fullness, dance becomes a refuge for the human from the technological world gone wild with instrumentalism. "Not only does it sometimes propose the human as alternative to, and rival of, the computer, it can suggest a hope that human virtues will survive in a universe at the edge of destruction."[21] Clearly there is in this last remark an enormous appeal to the fear of being victim to others' decisions. Perhaps if one turns to the East in order to, among other things, see the effects of the West's destructiveness, then the alternatives and hopes that dance proposes might foreground critical aspects of our own culture. For this to occur, criticism must begin within history and not against it. Then it can exchange the false innocence of an originary experience for a self-critical approach to its own recurrent criteria.

The Structural Autonomy of Dance Practices

A very different sort of dance writing, more visibly self-critical and more comfortable with the contemporary theory of representation than any other, refers to ethnography, but in a way that attempts to foreground the subject. Citing Barthes's study of Japan, in which he selects features of a "faraway" world to construct "a system of signification exemplified by a few well-chosen social customs and artifacts," to locate an "epistemic foundation utterly foreign to the West," Susan Foster turns once again to the absolute difference signified by the Orient. This time the Orient is invoked not as a series of motifs or as an essential impulse for appropriation, but to identify a series of tropes that will illuminate the historicizing foundations for dance hitherto unappreciated by dance analysis. In *Reading Dancing* Foster remarks, "I am attempting to accomplish a similar kind of 'ethnography' by isolating and then comparing choreographic projects as discrete cultural systems, systems created from a combination of what the choreographers have written and said, what has been written about them, and my own observations and experiences watching their dances and studying in their traditions."[22] Here an ethnographic procedure in search of previously unrecognizable epistemic foundations is used to "'denaturalize' our notions of the self and our assumptions about the body" in order to show "how the body and the subject are formed—how they come into being—through participation in a given discourse."[23]

Jowitt's ethnographic gaze brackets its theory of appropriation to make strange each occasion of dance such that each paradoxically becomes an instance of the same (the originary status of the Oriental). Foster's strategy accomplishes just the opposite. Her theory of dance representation produces different modes of reading autonomous dance practices. Hence, each particular instance is normalized and made familiar through an explicit theoretical procedure that accepts four tropes or figures of speech derived from literary theory—metaphor, metonymy, synecdoche, and irony—as embodying the fundamental relations between all things in the world (including dance).[24] Hence the elusiveness of the ways in which dances produce meaning is rendered into a set of structural categories that are evident in any set of human practices. This procedure is stated in extensive footnotes apart from her main text; they can be read in their entirety as methodological appendices. It is this text, really a commentary about dance commentary, that I want to treat here.

Foster is not aiming to identify the essence of dance history so much as to present "outlines of paradigmatic approaches to making and viewing dances."[25] In this she is concerned with emphasizing those apparatuses by which dance is appropriated in writing rather than in reading, in order to feature the self-constitution of the production and reception of dance in dance commentary. This entails providing categories for distinguishing between dance work that yields "a sustained, humorous, critical and communal practice," as in the work of the improvisationally based dance experimentalists of the 1970s, such as Grand Union or Meredith Monk, on the one hand, and reflexive dance practice "that reinforces conservative values even as it leads to a profound sense of alienation,"[26] as evident in Twyla Tharp's choreography.

At the same time, she retains a sensitivity to the historical. Her embrace of Foucauldian taxonomy for the representation of historically constituted forms of discursive practice suggests a solution to essentialist historiography that is not without its own complications. "Instead of advocating a single aesthetic project by showing its resilience over time or its development through various stages, the arrangement of historical dance forms side by side supports and encourages a diversity of choreographic pursuits."[27] Yet while she appears to have avoided a periodization that relies on finality, teleology, she presents the autonomous periods of "distinct cultures or strata" where these distinctions depend on an absolute chronology ("1400 to 1650, 1650 to 1800, and 1800 to some time in the early twentieth century"). What she is able to avoid in denying finality, she yields to in subjecting periods to an abstract and historicizing standard.

Her efforts to project an isomorphism between the tropes of choreography and those of historiography relies on Hayden White's discussion of tropes in *Metahistory*. "Following White, I assume that the mode of representation—the tropological equation that allows art to represent life—offers the primary entry point into each period's epistemological organization."[28] However, White's study of major historiographers of the nineteenth century was intended to identify the relationship of their selection of tropes to their politics. Foster avoids political assessments in all but the reflexive episteme of the 1960s and 1970s, in order to discriminate between the "conservative" choreography of Twyla Tharp and the "critical" work of Meredith Monk and Grand Union.

Within each discursive episteme of metaphor, metonymy, synecdoche, and irony, the primary mode of representation identifies both the signifying chain of a dance form (from conception through performance to interpretation) and its relation to history.

> The nature of that relationship may be more precisely expressed as follows: [Deborah] Hay maintains a metaphorical relation with the Renaissance dances by *resembling* them. [George] Balanchine's relation to the eighteenth century is metonymic, or *imitative.* [Martha] Graham, as emblematic of expressionist dance [1890–1950] stands in synecdochic relationship to it. And [Merce] Cunningham retains an ironic distance from his objectivist descendants.[29]

The isomorphism Foster attributes to literary trope, choreographic mode of representation, and contemporary and historical choreographic examples begs the question of politics in favor of an idealization of epistemes. In the environment of difference which comprises the aesthetic Foster wants to champion, the principle of communal practices she sees as responsible for a resistive form of dance-making and viewing cannot be accounted for historically. The tension between the aesthetic autonomy among the different tropes and the engagement of difference necessary to produce community is lost in Foster's framework. There is no sense of historical contexts or problems that choreographers, dancers, and audiences might respond to and emerge within as a condition for their work. Rather, the structural characteristic of a period marks the structure of a given dance work. The very analytic procedure that frees Foster to theorize the construction of meaning in a particular work occludes access to the interference between conflicting choreographic or social principles that could give dance its historical quality.

Such a procedure does distance itself from the judgmentalist attitude toward works that Foster justifiably seeks to avoid, and it allows her to refrain from the essentialism of asserting boundaries among works. But it does so at the expense of historical context and the social principles with which works are animated. In effect, by beginning with the autonomy of a given artist's discursive practice, the emergent character of the work and hence its historical character is left unaccounted for. She evades the relationship of the work to the broader interdiscursive field within which all choreographic projects collide. As Foster acknowledges in her discussion of Tharp, on the one hand, and

Monk and Grand Union, on the other, not all the play of difference yields collectivity. Foster wisely avoids any reference to the reflection by dance of "its" time. Instead, she imputes a structural identity to dance and history that does not specify conditions of production. The autonomy of epistemes achieved through a radical refamiliarization of a given aesthetic project (her "ethnographic" procedure) appears to segregate accounts of the arts from accounts of society, agency, and history.

Alternative Public Sphere and the Agency of Performance

In certain respects, the historiographical problems raised by Jowitt's and Foster's studies are familiar to those engaged in a critique of representation. Taken together, they show that at least one limit to a strategy of defamiliarization and refamiliarization lies in its ability to account for what cannot be represented. The special problems dance presents for representation, insofar as it is an object that leaves traces only in a highly particularized and therefore unstable audience, did not, at least in the case of the two texts examined here, produce unique approaches to analysis. If dance provides a special challenge to the conventions of representation but does so in a way that does not make its challenge clear, a critical strategy that takes the problem of the disruption of dance representation and object is in order.

Rather than consider how representational strategies account for dance, one might examine how dance can be used methodologically to account for worldly problems. A close examination of dance works might reveal methodological insights into the tensions between agency and the representation of history lost to other analytic maneuvers. While the claims to closeness are problematic in their own right, a text that purports to account for a particular dance activity might make an effort to situate a reader within the apparently eccentric experience of dance-making by orienting the analysis toward more familiar activity. This is what seems to be ventured in Sally Banes's account of the conjuncture of an alternative public sphere and experimentation with social space in the works presented at the Judson Church in the 1960s.

Banes's study concentrates on sixteen dance concerts given by a small group of performers between 6 July 1962 and 29 April 1964 at the Greenwich Village church.

> Perhaps even more important than the individual dances given at Judson concerts was the attitude that anything might be called a dance and looked at as dance; the work of a visual artist, a filmmaker, a musician

> might be considered a dance, just as activities done by a dancer, although not recognizable as theatrical dance, might be reexamined and "made strange" because they were framed as art.[30]

Taken as suggestive of a general methodological attitude rather than simply as site for a specific dance activity, Judson becomes a "frame" within which any sort of activity can be examined. Unlike either the exoticization of dance or its overparticularization as a separable discourse, here there is a world to be defamiliarized through the writing of dance. This world is indicated by the book's title, *Democracy's Body*, which suggests both the virtual social space that could constitute democracy and the form of agency required to construct that virtuality.

While Judson dance itself can be considered a framing device that makes uncritically accepted activities strange by subjecting them to the perceptual attention that defines art, Banes attempts to account for how that frame was constructed. In this regard, her study is relevant to ethnographic activity that is self-critical about how it identifies and appropriates its field. The participants in Judson Church were assembled through a choreography workshop given by Robert Dunn, a composer and accompanist at Merce Cunningham's studio in the fall of 1960. The course that established Judson was given by a nondancer at the request of the composer John Cage, whose work with chance compositional techniques provided the basis for the activity of the workshop. Judson was initiated without any appeal to a dance essence. Instead, appeal was made to an engagement with already written material, an idea that could be said to have anticipated poststructuralism. As Banes explains, "The *writing* of dances—the "-graphy" in choreography—was crucial to the composition process Dunn outlined for his students, not necessarily in the sense of permanently recording what the dance was, but in order to objectify the composition process, both by creating nonintuitive choices and by viewing the total range of possibilities for the dance."[31]

The writing procedure facilitated the appropriation of materials formerly considered as outside of the scope of dance, thereby creating a distance that led to an estranging objectivization of materials against the putative experience of the choreographer as "author." The "author's" task was to reach into the historical vocabulary of dance but not to compose in the sense of regulating the performance activity. Musical scoring techniques were then brought into the dance in order to permit a variable range of materials to be written as choreography, thereby providing authority for executing the material in performance. The scores allowed the scarcity of dance space to be a resource rather than a constraint, since the choreography could be actualized in any space whatsoever, including a space occupied by a single individual. Like the Dunn workshops, this virtual space resisted any imputation of essence to the performance of an underlying "dance," since performances were enabled but not dictated by the choreography. Judson, Banes informs us, was founded on a goal of community service, and a principle of not "proselytizing in a community that was primarily Italian Catholic." Its mandate for theater under Minister Al Carmines was "One, not to do religious drama. Two, no censorship after acceptance."[32]

That the church was so actively affiliated with the labor movement of the 1930s and the civil rights movement of the 1950s and 1960s indicates that it stood as a site of opposition. Its refusal to stamp its religious "content" on the poetry, visual art, theater, and dance presented there permitted a range of artistic possibilities. The Judson dancers took their name from an activity of writing or inscription in a virtual space. That space was actualized, although only briefly, by bringing dance to a place already defined as oppositional by other, nonartistic activities. The possibility for democracy came by situating a generative principle for dance activity within the particular framing provided by the church that had as its project the constitution of a public aesthetic space.

Banes's appropriation of available critical terms in dance commentary has apparently occurred without evidence of any assimilation of the theoretical discussions associated with those terms. Yet without theorizing them as such, Banes's study of Judson indicates what may be some of the more familiar aspects of postmodern art, though in unfamiliar manifestations.[33] Pastiche is evident in the parody of schools of dance presented in the course of an evening's concert. The leveling of high and popular culture is apparent in the framing of pedestrian movement as dance; it is complicated, however, by Judson's maintenance of an avant-gardism and its dancers' links with the canons of modern dance and ballet through their technical training and professional work. Finally, the fragmenting of authorial integrity, identified with the 1960s' attack on bourgeois individualism and the myth of the self, was displayed in Judson's collaborative process only to reveal something of the fragility of that critique.

The premise of Judson was to couple a nonhierarchical and participatory principle, a body politic, with a nonauthoritative compositional process. These dimensions comprised the democracy that Banes's title imagines as the ultimate project of Judson Church. The chronicle of its breakup displays the outer boundary of the analytic frame that dance provides and points to the conceptions of democracy it claims emerge from avant-garde art. The Judson dance group grew out of a workshop and remained together for two years. Banes's account of its demise resonates with other experiences:

> Individuals were emerging from the group whose needs were no longer satisfied by the collective concerts; an influx of new younger participants made the content of the workshop sessions redundant for the original group; the somewhat utopian community that had developed over several years was rent by the conflicts over the out-of-town concerts and, ultimately, over the identity of the group.[34]

Conflicts over the out-of-town concerts both preceded the formation of the group and were a product of its success. Half a dozen of the Judson dancers were in Merce Cunningham's company, and their employment with him influenced the autonomy of Judson in the same way that any market setting influences, or mediates, the autonomy of the avant-garde. When group participants went to Ann Arbor in February 1964 to perform in the Once Festival, a certain amount of estrangement among the artists was generated by the question of how to divide the payment of nine hundred dollars, the tensions over who would travel and who would remain in New York, and the problem of Judson without the specificity of the "Church" as a site. Was this a sacrifice of democracy to the market?

Judson's breakup represents a contradiction of participatory process and participation. If the democracy produced by Judson yielded to "an influx of younger participants," or if the presence of Robert Rauschenberg in some of the later concerts introduced hierarchy, or if accessibility of Judson's work to those outside the New York community produced conflicts over where and when to perform, it was at the very least a highly exclusive and troubled democracy. In her closing words, Banes seems to accept this account of the movement of innovation in art with a kind of evolutionary confidence. "And the expansion of dance as an art, so much of which had taken place at the Judson Dance Theater workshops and concerts, proliferated."[35] Proliferation, expansion, growth—but of something that no longer showed even the traces of the democracy that had been, according to Banes, its original project. This too is resonant of other experiences. Yet it would be unwise not to exercise caution in drawing conclusions in order to avoid confusing an analytic frame that may make democratic impulses and processes available with an expected autonomy of art from its social context. Otherwise, democracy appears altogether unsustainable, in life as in art.

Beyond Representation: The Public in History

Judson gave focus to the democratic project implicit in the production and collective appropriation of activity; but it gave equal focus to the context of mediations that inevitably compromised that project and opened the possibility of nondemocratic alternatives in art. No avant-garde controls the context that conditions its production and none can be assumed to provide a basis for mobilization beyond its particular audience. The democratic project could only be sustained if the critique of representation in regard to dance were to be incorporated into performance itself, and if the agency of performance were to be expansively extended to include its public, a public that could then be identified with respect to other sites and activities.

These two elements of democratization define the problematic of Herbert Blau's study *The Audience*. Blau's work is fully suffused with theory—and all the accompanying challenges to reading such theory implies—and often adopts in writing the very instability he attributes to audience, without, however, always recuperating the gains of that strategy. Blau conceives of audience as a kind of social movement precipitated by and further constituted in theater. This implies that the audience's presence simulates that of the figure of history occasioned by the agency or execution of idea within the performance itself. That is, in both cases there is the trace of a presence of something absent. Thus, the audience is a social body that appropriates by its gaze a subject that, in turn, marks its own tendency to disappear. The audience simulates the presence mobilized in history, but within the vulnerable and elusive constitution of the contemporary public sphere. The performance is, for its audience, momentarily contained. The audience is, for performance, thoroughly mediated by a different context; it is, therefore, relative to performance, indeterminate—or, in Blau's terms, unstable.

Because they do not theorize this indeterminacy of a public as an implication of performance, the accounts of dance examined above can be said to have slipped into representing (1) the performance as a thing-in-itself, for itself, (2) the audience as the mirror of a semiosis of performance, a receiver, and (3) the audience as contained by the performative agency onstage, the dance's "intention." These analyses must be extended if the project of democracy, that is, of fully realized participation in history, is to inform it. This entails a conception of public that goes beyond the audience ideally defined as merely "in" the theater; and it involves an appeal to contemporary theories of representation and the production of culture that have not been sustained among dance commentaries. Blau's theater commentary on the audience is thus helpful in conceptually bridging and extending the discussion of dance.

Banes construed the performative activity as in the service of a broader methodological procedure of writing. This allowed dance to be seen as revealing more general epistemological operations. But this was at the cost of fixing the frame and assuming that it operated autonomously, and therefore elided the historical aspect of the dance in relation to its production and the political context of its reception. Banes, like Jowitt and Foster, is vulnerable to presenting an apology for artistic production whose appropriations appear self-generating and auto-consuming, leaving the territory that they colonize, even if in the name of an oppositional sphere, unavailable to those in whose name they perform.

Such is the predicament of an ethnographic procedure that seeks to contain rather than display the disruptive potential of that which it represents in analysis. In this regard ethnography, whether in the traditional variant suggested by Jowitt's work or Foster's affinity with the revisionist versions, is situated within rather than against the larger historical context of colonialism. While clearly the colonization of a performance space does not invoke the same political forces and effects as other territorial appropriations, the effectiveness of the methodology developed through dance analysis hinges on the degree to which it makes available a representational strategy that grasps its own relation to colonization irrespective of the object. If performance activity is useful in featuring the resistance to colonization as it represents it, then ethnography that engages other domains may benefit from an analytic incorporation of the performative.

Blau's study can be seen as contributing to an ethnographic procedure that highlights the disruptive effects of the exotic Other it "captures and chronicles" (in Jowitt's terms) through representation. The audience figures in his account precisely, and paradoxically, as the indeterminacy of a specific representation internal to performance and therefore to its reception, as if the audience were both a simulation and a protective membrane of the autonomous theater, history being something that is added after the fact. Hence, Blau states, "the audience will serve as a heuristic principle for what is not altogether a secondary purpose of this book: a reflection upon recent cultural history in relation to performance as an activity of cognition."[36]

At issue therefore is not whether theater embodies a significant agency for the twentieth century. Blau is alert to the limits of its role and claims that "at its most expansive it is a minor art."[37] The issue is how theater displays the problematic of representation, agency, and participation as fragile terms of a dialectic. In this regard the mystique of an absolute horizon for the relation of audience and performance, of democratic participation, has failed in the theater as it has in history.

Beyond the specificity of theater, Blau sees the relation of history and performance as featuring what may be missed at a time when global circuits of cultural commodities approach a hegemonic culture that eclipses not only theater per se but the forms of immediate community suggested by relations of live performance. Blau goes on to explain the possible gain of such an enterprise in the light of the otherwise uncritical assessment of the way performance fits into, or even appropriates, its "multinational world,"

> which has given us as a by-product a random-access society. So random is the access that even in the remotest bush unity is disrupted and no otherness is protected. While radical economic differences exist as ever, even widening, the lines are narrowing on the grid of power, where undeveloped countries are drawn with all their impoverishment into the porousness of the media. It may not be what we mean by collective, but here we have another constituency—instantly accessed wherever aerials are—the incalculable presence of a spongy mass.[38]

Even under conditions of a globally mediated culture, the unstable audience may be said to stand for desire within the narrative of gathering and collectivity, which is to say, the desire for self and therefore history. This means that the audience as desire must not be confused with consumers as receptacles for images—and that theater is not adequately modeled by an economics of commodities. This is not to say that there is no politics of reception or socialization of communicative means associated with mass media. On the contrary, the "presence of a spongy mass" indicates more activity and collectivity than is suggested by consumer demand as the end point of a commodified image. When the audience is seen as consumers, they are being viewed from the perspective of an individuating process of circulation that only requires from them the promise of future demand without any reflection on what the conditions of demand had been. The consumer is therefore without history (lacking it and outside it). Commodification as an account of theatrical production refers to the self-consumption of the event, the "artifact." "As the real in its realest forms is conflated with image, the theater's appetite is a problem, like the universal wolf, whose appetite is insatiable, so that along with other commodities that it consumes—though it apparently consumes more than commodities—it at last eats itself up."[39] When, on the other hand, audience is viewed as a mobilized presence, it is what constitutes history and therefore enlarges a conception of what a politics—in the face of a commodified field such as that presented by corporate media—might be.

The space colonized by performance, which appropriates audience without recognizing it as anything but the consumption of product, simulates larger relations of colonization. Such simulation occurs whether or not colonization is thematized directly and emerges with the commodification of theater itself, as in Shakespeare's *The Tempest.* Yet as in any colonizing effort, appropriation is not without resistance, as Cuban critic Roberto Fernandez Retamar has made clear in his figuration of Caliban as the unruly response of the Other.[40] What performance can share with history is the sense of an otherness against which self-identity asserts itself. Without adequate historical reflection, however, this relation of self and Other can be conceptualized as one of a third world that reconfigures the colonial self and that self's utopian sense of a sweeping modernity.

At the same time, performance can stand as the converse of audience, namely, the desire to place limits on the randomness enforced by corporate culture's global reach. This is an opposition of performance to audience within the prefigured unstable audience. When people of what Blau terms the "undeveloped countries" (a phrase that only becomes meaningful when applied as an effect of global relations of exchange, and not, as Blau seems to imply, as sites for particular kinds of populations) are taken as the concrete manifestation in geopolitics of the exotica caught and tamed as the context for Western scenic arts, then more is at stake in his analysis than understanding theater. At the scene of capture, people are aware of what escapes, and those spectacles of appropriation translate themselves into the site of an "incalculable presence," an unrepresentable actuality in a world that determines historical judgment.

Such linkages have not been lost on those who emerged from the popular theater in Latin America, like Augusto Boal, whose "invisible theater" insinuates provocateurs or "jokers" in everyday sites where the contingency of the relations of authority can be staged. In Nicaragua, Alan Bolt has attempted to efface the boundaries of representation between art and life by joining theater with rural renewal.[41] In either case the particularized participation that dissolves in, say, the audience of a dance performance is reinserted by and into broader social mobilizations.

The sense in which that participation can be recuperated beyond those settings rests with the possibility of theorizing it as more than simply attendance at an event. For the work an audience does in performance to have a political efficacy beyond merely asserting a capacity as a public to mobilize productive energies without their being wholly reabsorbed by institutional apparatuses, there must be articulated what struggles there are over the context and configuration of a public sphere. But when questions arise as to whether the desire exists for such mobilizations, appreciating this capacity as a resource for politics is itself not politically insignificant.

More concretely, performance, like any other means of gathering a collectivity, cannot exist outside of the social regulation of public space that directly or indirectly invokes the state. The history of contemporary political performance, from the Soviet director Meyerhold to the Living Theater of the 1960s, is the history of boundaries for participation established as a particular conjuncture of civil society in the state.[42] The point, however, is that if performance is an agency that occasions participation, it also limits the scope, if not the persistence, of participation. The agency of performance is distinct from the one that transforms state or civil society as such, but in either case such an agency elicits a desire for further participation.

Blau's critique resonates with the promise that theater will remain a "minor art" apart from the technological question of its dissemination. If representation produces a simulacrum of consumption, it also reproduces the desire of the audience and therefore the impossibility of audience as consumer. Blau's own dilemma, however, is that he must historicize theater's problem without eliminating its place in history. If theater recurs because representation cannot be avoided, is there any way to refigure the relationship between representation and history without making that relationship a self-absorbing one? Blau grants theater the obligation of manifesting historical possibility through the dramatization of desire. To accomplish this, performance must paradoxically maintain its distance from the impulse to merge with the audience. As Blau concludes, performance must avoid absorbing audience through a unifying field of participation: "What I have been suggesting through this book, however, is that whatever the virtues of participation, the virtue of theater remains in the activity of perception, where participation is kept at a distance and—though it has come to be thought a vice—representation has its rites."[43]

The uneasy distance between performers and audience seems intended to prevent either of the two from being colonized for total appropriation as the exotic Other. Here the exotic makes its presence felt where representation and agency part company. Yet what accounts for relations in theater seems less fruitful than Blau assumes as a perspective for history. The "crisis in the history of a form" bears traces of a postmodern nostalgia but without the release postmodernism usually grants in irony or parody. The exchange of participation for representation may generate a new theater, but it would be one denied the disruptiveness of the historical effects of an agency that stands in opposition to the autoconsumption implicit in historical representation that is merely historicist.

Certainly Blau may be correct in recognizing the limits of theater and history as the point at which the two part company. Yet the point at which they remain joined, even for Blau, poses issues both methodological and conceptual, and perhaps with sufficient complexity that it is not possible to ascertain the point of disjuncture. If this is true, then it would be necessary to act as if history and performance are in fact the twins of a certain perception—one that includes participation as the recognition of the work done by any public to occupy an oppositional sphere. Otherwise one risks both aestheticism and historicism, both at the expense of the subjectivity, agency, that each purports to conserve.

Certainly, Blau's reading of the commodification scheme trades on the quotidian for its production of distance and estrangement necessary for agency and history. Here the normalization of the exotic, which is illustrated by the accounts of dance that I have discussed, helps sustain the virtue of agency and history in the face of the "vice" of representation. If the ubiquitous commodification, in which Blau places theater, makes theater as well as all performance depend on representation for its own capacity to reappear (its virtuality), the refusal by Jowitt, Foster, and Banes to acknowledge that dependence nevertheless has an analytic benefit. It allows dancing to appear as an agency which familiarizes the strangeness of the commodified world, making the latter yet more acceptable by being, as it were, the butt of jokes.

If these writings on dance acknowledged their own resistance to theory and had attempted to theorize that resistance, they would have provided precisely the context of self-denial that has been so fruitfully engaged by contemporary critical theories of representation: the denial of history always ends by being, and revealing, history. Here a critical dance ethnography would make its intervention. The analytic frame that a reflection on performance provides for theorizing history in terms of agency depends both on the distancing of the familiar that makes the problem of representation unavoidable, and the recovery of that unruly familiar otherness for a world that, from the heights of its imperial achievements, will always insist that the incessant disruptiveness of history is merely momentary and exotic.

Notes

I would like to thank Michael E. Brown, George Yudice, and the rest of the *Social Text* editorial board for helpful comments on earlier drafts of this essay.

1 This radical notion of history has by now been articulated in many ways. It could be traced initially to E. P. Thompson's idea of the prepolitical, but certainly was developed by the reception of such diverse figures as Gramsci, Williams, Foucault, and Bakhtin in this country. A useful discussion of how these literatures have come together can be found in Michael E. Brown, *The Production of Society* (Totowa, N.J.: Rowman and Littlefield, 1986).

2 For a programmatic statement see James Clifford's introduction to the volume he edited with George E. Marcus, *Writing Culture: The Poetics and Politics of Ethnography* (Berkeley: University of California Press, 1986), pp. 1–26.

3 This concern is shared by other critiques of this revisionist ethnography. See, for example, Lila Abu Lughod, "Can There Be a Feminist Ethnography?" *Women and Performance* 9 (1990), pp. 7–27, and is developed with respect to representation more broadly by Gayatri Chakravorty Spivak in *In Other Worlds* (New York: Routledge, 1988).

4 Deborah Jowitt, *Time and the Dancing Image* (Berkeley: University of California Press, 1988).

5 Susan Foster, *Reading Dancing: Bodies and Subjects in Contemporary American Dance* (Berkeley: University of California Press, 1986).

6 Sally Banes, *Democracy's Body* (Ann Arbor, Mich.: UNI Research Press, 1983).

7 Herbert Blau, *The Audience* (Baltimore, Md.: Johns Hopkins University Press, 1990).

8 These are rather eccentric choices within the field of performance studies and are selected for their particular affinity to this project. Jowitt's book distinguishes itself from the standard dance histories with its use of ethnographic language. Anya Peterson Royce's *The Anthropology of Dance* (Bloomington: Indiana University Press, 1977) and Paul Spencer, ed., *Society and the Dance: The Social Anthropology of Process and Performance* (Cambridge: Cambridge University Press, 1985) are good overviews of existing approaches that do not, however, utilize dance as an object of theory or methodological reformulations. Similarly, Judith Lynne Hanna, who has written a number of well-researched dance studies, relies on rather standard applications of survey analysis to evaluate attitudinal responses to dance in *The Performer-Audience Connection: Emotion to Metaphor in Dance and Society* (Austin: University of Texas Press, 1983). For a dance ethnography that is alive to many of the issues in this essay and that seeks to develop dance as an analytic frame for the construction of gender, see Jane K. Cowan, *Dance and the Body Politic in Greece* (Princeton: Princeton University Press, 1990). For an ethnographic study that focuses on the contemporary United States, see Cynthia Novack, *Sharing the Dance: Contact Improvisation and American Culture* (Madison: University of Wisconsin Press, 1990).

9 Jowitt, *Time and the Dancing Image,* p. 7.

10 Ibid.

11 Ibid., p. 47.

12 Ibid., p. 56.

13 Ibid., p. 55.

14 Ibid., p. 69.

15 Ibid., p. 70.

16 Ibid., p. 147.

17 Ibid., p. 226.

18 Ibid., p. 288.

19 Ibid., pp. 325–26.

20 Ibid., p. 369.

21 Ibid., p. 373.

22 Foster, *Reading Dancing*, p. 236.

23 Ibid., p. 237.

24 Ibid., p. 234.

25 Ibid., p. 259.

26 Ibid., p. 260.

27 Ibid., p. 100.

28 Ibid., p. 248.

29 Ibid., p. 247.

30 Banes, *Democracy's Body*, p. xviii.

31 Ibid., p. 7.

32 Ibid., pp. 36, 37.

33 In discussions of dance, Judson Church is seen as having inaugurated the postmodern moment in dance. Sally Banes's previous work, *Terpsichore in Sneakers*, 2nd ed. (Middletown, Conn.: Wesleyan University Press, 1987) is the first full-length study of that moment. Both

the discussion and the formulation of postmodernism in dance are distinct from those typical for other media. The definitions tend to be based on describable aspects of dance per se, rather than any consideration of the relations of dance production, reception, or aesthetics within a larger cultural conjuncture.

Postmodernism can be applied generationally, as to those, like the Judsonites, who came "after" modern dance masters like Martha Graham, Alwin Nikolais, Merce Cunningham, or Paul Taylor, despite the fact that they were, and, with the exception of the late Martha Graham, remain contemporaries. The term can also be applied to a putative collapse between twentieth-century ballet and modern dance, despite the fact that the tension between these styles never represented anything like an opposition between "high" and "popular," or avant-garde and kitsch (see for example, Susan Manning, "Modernist Dogma and Postmodern Rhetoric: A Response to Sally Banes's *Terpsichore in Sneakers*," *Drama Review* 32 (1988). The discussion seems quite consistent with a modernist critical vocabulary that emphasizes the primacy of innovation for the evaluation of art, of the autonomy of the aesthetic dimension, and ultimately of the artist's monologic representation of truth.

34 Banes, *Democracy's Body*, p. 209.

35 Ibid., p. 213.

36 Blau, *The Audience*, p. 28.

37 Ibid., p. 379.

38 Ibid., p. 29.

39 Ibid., p. 323.

40 Retamar's essay has appeared in English as *Caliban and Other Essays* (Minneapolis: University of Minnesota Press, 1989). The politics of Shakespearean drama and performance have been explored in different ways by Stephen Greenblatt, in *Shakespearean Negotiations* (Berkeley: University of California Press, 1988), and Walter Cohen, *Drama of a Nation* (Ithaca: Cornell University Press, 1986).

41 After his forced exile from Brazilian theater, Boal engaged in training "jokers" at centers in Africa, Europe, Latin America, and the United States before returning to Brazil. His methods are discussed in *Theater of the Oppressed* (New York: Urizen, 1979). Bolt's cultural movement emerged as a critical articulation within the Sandinista front and, as with popular culture in general, suffered with their electoral defeat. His theatrical project as a feature of the broader Nicaraguan context is discussed in Randy Martin, *Socialist Ensembles: Theater and State in Cuba and Nicaragua* (Minneapolis: University of Minnesota Press, 1994), pp. 45–77.

42 I have discussed the insertion of these theaters into their social context in *Performance as Political Act* (New York: Bergin and Garvey, 1990).

43 Blau, *The Audience*, p. 381.

18 VODOU, NATIONALISM, AND PERFORMANCE: THE STAGING OF FOLKLORE IN MID-TWENTIETH-CENTURY HAITI

Kate Ramsey

The peasant is the nobility of the earth, and the folklore, the soul of generations. To revive the traditions that were their *raison d'être* and their honor, the State itself would recover its personal dignity.—René Georges Aubrun, quoted in Michel Lamartinière Honorat's *Les danses folkloriques haïtiennes* (1955)[1]

This essay focuses on the performed representations of Vodou ritual dance that were mounted in Port-au-Prince during the 1940s and 1950s in the intersecting realms of ethnology, tourism, and state nationalism. In approaching this subject, I am interested in understanding why the "staging" of folklore[2] emerged as a major idiom of Haitian national identity construction during this moment, particularly in light of the 1915–34 U.S. Marine occupation of Haiti, and political and cultural interactions with the United States thereafter. This inquiry centers on the Haitian Bureau d'Ethnologie's creation of an archive of folklore constructions during the immediate post-occupation period that consistently privileged performance. It traces how this emphasis carried over into the realm of nationalist display during the late 1940s and early 1950s, when reconstructed indigenous forms became ciphers for official Haitian culture and identity. In examining the interconnection between ethnology and nationalism in post-occupation Haiti, this study also probes the complex relation between Haitian official nationalist thought and Euro-American imperial rhetorics about Haiti, and the ways in which constructions of Afro-Haitian performance figured prominently in both discourses at this time. A significant dimension of this history, I will argue, is that the "staging" of folklore transgressed the ethnographic and official domains that attempted both to produce and contain it. Thus this study examines the simultaneous proliferation of "unofficial" staged folklore performance during these years and the overlapping and uneasy relationship among ethnologic, touristic, and state constructions of folk heritage. Finally, this has led me to think about the interplay between the Vodou religion and the history of its representation, which in this century parallels that of its control.

The "folkloricization" of national identity through performance is, of course, by no means unique to Haiti but has played a part in twentieth-century nationalisms more generally.[3] Yet such formations have often been overlooked or trivialized in scholarship on nationalism, despite or perhaps because of their ubiquity. "A folk dance performance may seem a comparatively insignificant event to place at the center of an examination of a 'world-historical' force such as nationalism," Richard Handler observes at the outset of his *Nationalism and the Politics of Culture in Quebec*,[4] before proceeding to argue otherwise. My study begins with the contention that "staged folklore" was, precisely, *central* to political self-definition in post-occupation Haiti, often to the point of "summarizing" national "difference" once it became officially formulated. More broadly, I would argue that the staging of folklore represents a critical focus for scholarly research and analysis on nationalism as a site in which, as Benedict Anderson puts it, the tension between "the formal universality of nationality as a socio-cultural concept" and "the irremediable particularity of its concrete manifestations" has often been played out.[5] This paradoxical, contradictory dynamic is sharpened and complicated in the case of anticolonial/imperial nationalist movements—a point that has frequently been misunderstood in Western analyses of these struggles.[6]

In his *Nationalist Thought and the Colonial World: A Derivative Discourse* and *The Nation and Its Fragments: Colonial and Postcolonial Histories*, political philosopher Partha Chatterjee examines what has been the tendency of Western political theory to analyze "third world" nationalisms formulaically, as imitations of a few standardized or, in Anderson's terms "modular," Euro-American models adapted to local circumstances.[7] Questioning the historical grounds for, as much as the political implications of such readings, Chatterjee counters that the "most powerful as well as the most creative results of the nationalist imagination in Asia and Africa are posited not on an identity but rather on a difference with the 'modular' forms of the national society propagated by the modern West."[8] While it must be emphasized that Chatterjee's analysis of the history of Indian anticolonial nationalism cannot be simply or immediately applied to the case of Haiti, his critique of the discourse of "modularity" and his refocusing on the nationalist production and performance of particularity resonate with what I understand of ethno-official investment in staged folklore in mid-twentieth-century Haiti, and represent an opening for the way I would like to approach this history. If one chooses to look for or emphasize modularity, it is there to be found—certainly, as Chatterjee proposes, in the realm of institutions that deploy the "grammar" of Western political and social systems to signal their modernity in the face of colonial discourses imputing atavism and backwardness. Yet given the contradictoriness and ambivalence of nationalism in any context, and the political stakes of anticolonial/imperial nationalisms in particular, it seems crucial to resist the universalizing readings that, as Chatterjee puts it, tend to "reduc[e] the experience of anticolonial nationalism to a caricature of itself."[9] To efface deliberately constructed "difference," ignore its complexity, or make it part of a formula seems both cynical and ultimately less interesting than engaging with the articulation of particularity itself.

My interest in this essay is thus not with "proving the rule" but with understanding the exception and the specificity of this particular instance of "cultural objectification"[10]—which by no means forecloses the possibility of comparative study. To refocus my earlier questions about the history of Haitian folklore performance in the post-occupation period, I am specifically interested in the fact that, in this context, the category of the "folk" encompassed the ritual cultures of Vodou, which, in Haiti, have been the locus of subaltern resistance for over two centuries and, in the West, have been a site of sensationalist and primitivist imaginings for almost as long. What did it mean for first literary intellectuals and then successive Haitian states to found an inviolable national ideal on constructions of this "all powerful trope," as Joan Dayan has described the discursive field of Vodou?[11] This study focuses primarily on official representations of Haitian national identity and Vodou and their interplay with shifting Euro-American discourses of Haiti and "voodoo" in the wake of the nearly twenty year U.S. Marine occupation. What the folkloricization of Haitian national identity during this period meant for the status of the Vodou religion, as practiced in syncretic conjunction with Catholicism by over two-thirds of Haiti's population, is a crucial issue that the essay raises but only begins to address. Yet even thus circumscribed, this history is embedded with implications, if not answers, for that question. As much as first intellectual and then officially nationalist discourses of Haitian "difference" were being based, in effect, on the cultures of Vodou, its autonomous and heterogeneous existence, popular political power, and primitivism in Western eyes remained sources of great anxiety for ruling classes. I will suggest that once the post-occupation state had appropriated and constructed "folklore" as its own central signifier, the stakes for controlling the representation as well as the practice of Vodou became higher.

Occupation and Indigénisme

It is necessary to draw the substance of our works sometimes from this immense reservoir of folklore in which the motives for our decisions are compressed after centuries, in which the elements of our sensibility are elaborated, in which the fabric of our popular character, our national mind, is structured.—Jean Price-Mars[12]

In his *Notes on a Return to the Native Land*, Aimé Césaire refers to Haiti as the place where "*négritude* first stood up," no doubt alluding to then-St. Domingue's slave revolution and self-deliverance from French colonialism at the turn of the nineteenth century. Yet writing his *Cahier* in 1938, Césaire may well also have had in mind a more recent Haitian movement, and one a good deal closer to a conception of *négritude*. Perhaps he was also thinking of the cultural nationalism that swept through Haiti's intellectual and literary classes after July 1915, when U.S. Marines landed in Port-au-Prince to stay for nearly twenty years.

While the U.S. invasion of Haiti was seemingly precipitated by President Vilbrun Guillaume Sam's murder of 167 political prisoners and his own subsequent death at the hands of an elite-led mob on 28 July 1915, historical consensus has it that the Wilson administration had been planning Haiti's takeover for at least a year before these circumstantially precipitous events took place.[13] Under the pretext of protecting foreign nationals and establishing law and order, U.S. officials dissolved the Haitian legislature, installed a client-president, and took over the customhouses, the national bank, and most branches of the state administration. In 1918 Franklin Delano Roosevelt, then assistant secretary of the navy, drafted a new constitution which reversed the ban on foreign property ownership explicitly in place since the revolution. Article 5 now read: "The right to own real estate shall be given to foreigners residing in Haiti and to the societies organized by foreigners for purposes of residence, and agricultural, commercial, industrial, or educational enterprises."[14] Perhaps most residually damaging of all, the Marines dismantled the army that descended more-or-less directly from the revolutionary forces that overthrew France, training and arming in its stead a *gendarmerie*, not to defend Haitians but to internally police them.[15]

In the countryside, Marines revived the colonial *corvée*, a system of obligatory, unpaid labor in which peasants were roped together and forced, sometimes at gunpoint, to build roads for military transport from Port-au-Prince to Cap Haïtien. Heightening obvious analogies with the pre-independence slave regime, the *corvée* provoked widespread protest, which in 1918 mounted into a full-scale rural rebellion under the leadership of Charlemagne Péralte, a landowner and former soldier in the disbanded Haitian army. Harnessing the nationalist fervor of the pre-occupation *caco* movement, Péralte mobilized a peasant force numbering several thousand, and some historians claim as high as fifteen thousand.[16] Breaking the *caco* resistance became an immediate goal of the U.S. occupation (and specifically of the creation of the Haitian *gendarmerie*) and one linked to more fundamental objectives. Admiral William B. Caperton telegrammed the secretary of the navy early in the intervention: " 'Stable government not possible in Haiti until *cacos* are disbanded and power broken. Such action now imperative in Port-au-Prince if United States desires to negotiate treaty for financial control of Haiti.' "[17]

By 1920 the Marines had effectively suppressed armed resistance in the countryside. Yet the *caco* uprisings were not the only justificatory grounds for their repression of peasant communities. The Vodou religion was a particular target of and sometimes alibi for this "civilizing" mission that promised on "moral" grounds, as Colonel Eli K. Cole put it during the 1921–22 U.S. Senate hearings on the intervention, to " 'clean that place up and establish decency down there, because it does not exist.' "[18] Occupation officials banned Vodou, and throughout the intervention Marines repeatedly turned their campaigns against communities of worshippers. Raiding ceremonies, confiscating ritual vessels and drums, persecuting *ougan* (male priests) and *manbo* (female priests), they forced peasant practice of Vodou underground. Choreographer/anthropologist Katherine Dunham, who first traveled to Haiti during the early post-occupation period to research Afro-Haitian ritual dance, reported that when she "arrived in Haiti, not long after the exodus of the Marines, there were still baptized drums hidden in hollow tree trunks and behind waterfalls."[19]

Haitian writers from the 1920s to the present day have discussed the military occupation in terms of recolonization and, in this context, ranked its imprint, its ongoing pressure on the course of Haitian history and politics as second only to the legacy of the Haitian Revolution itself. Benedict Anderson has written of temporal "ruptures" that engender the "need for a narrative of 'identity,' "[20] perhaps illuminating how the "shock"[21] of U.S. military takeover and Marine racism became a coming-to-consciousness among many Haitian intellectuals that inspired an explosion of oppositional literary and artistic practice. The encompassing movement was termed *indigénisme*,[22] implying value in *native* roots, and its matrix was the Haitian peasantry whose resistance to the occupation stood in contrast to conservative elite collaboration. Long subject to a play of romantic idealization and violent repression on the part of ruling classes, peasant culture was turned to by these intellectuals as the discursive locus for a new liberatory poetics and politics. C. L. R. James notes in his essay "From Toussaint L'Ouverture to Fidel Castro," "In 1913 [*sic*] the ceaseless battering from foreign pens was reenforced by the bayonets of American Marines. Haiti had to find a national rallying point. They looked for it where it can only be found, at home, more precisely, in their own backyard. They discovered what is known today as Negritude."[23]

The mood of ideological opposition and literary experimentation that infused the young Haitian literary community during the mid-1920s resulted in a flourishing of new publications. None of these mostly short-lived journals and newspapers were as influential as *La revue indigène*, first published in July 1927 by a group of young writers—among them Carl Brouard, Emile Roumer, Normil Sylvain, Philippe Thoby-Marcelin, and Jacques Roumain—dedicated to the "indigenization" of Haitian poetics and "systematic use" of neglected folkloric, national, and popular themes. Challenging the nineteenth-century elite's thesis that Haiti was France's cultural province, the *indigénistes* (mostly themselves from the urban elite) refocused on the country's African patrimony, as exemplified by the beliefs and practices of isolated rural communities, repository for the nation's authentic cultural and revolutionary heritages and proper source and subject for the building of a national literature.[24] Thus revisioning Haitian national identity, the *indigénistes* began to inventory popular traditions, not merely as practices to be preserved but as forces that could propel the development of new revolutionary political, intellectual, and artistic cultures.

In his seminal 1928 reevaluation of Haitian culture, *Ainsi parla l'oncle* (So Spoke the Uncle), pioneer ethnologist Jean Price-Mars defined folklore as "the fundamental beliefs upon which have been grafted or superimposed other more recently acquired beliefs."[25] Michel Lamartinière Honorat, student of Price-Mars, conceptualized it similarly in his *Les danses folkloriques haïtiennes* as "that which [the human psychology] knows immediately, . . . that which it understands without great reflection, because it is an integral part of oneself."[26] To paraphrase Anderson on nationality, folklore, in these terms, is an unchosen inheritance, not only national but natural.[27] Born into and of a crisis in sovereignty, Haitian folklore studies were immediately infused with nationalist content, the destiny of the republic linked to the study and careful custodianship of popular cultures. This discourse intensified after the Marines were withdrawn in 1934, when folklore became increasingly implicated in and invoked by state claims to political legitimacy and programs of official nationalism.[28] Alongside literary/"print culture" productions, the performance of folklore came to occupy an increasingly privileged status in ethnographic and official representations of national culture, emerging as a primary site in which Haitian particularity was scientifically and creatively "imagined" into existence during the post-occupation years.

Ethnology and Superstition

"We, Elie Lescot, President of the Republic, personally recommend to the favorable consideration of the civil and military authorities of the Republic the Reverend Father C. Ed. Peters, missionary of the Company of Mary, and we approve entirely the mission which the Reverend Father Peters has undertaken to combat fetishism and superstition. . . . Without any violence being used against those who exercise fetish practices and superstitions, we demand of the civil and military authorities to give their most complete assistance to the Reverend Father Ed. Peters."—Presidential authorization by Elie Lescot, 23 June 1941[29]

The perspective of the French Catholic clergy on Vodou was never complicated by the ambivalence so defining of other dominant sectors of Haitian society. From the signing of the Concordat in 1860 on, the church enforced its unequivocal stance through intermittent episodes of violence against the spirituality that most Haitians considered inextricable from Catholicism itself. It was precisely this syncretism, the so-called "monstrous mixture," that obsessed the clergy and motivated their periodic attacks, in 1896, 1913, and none so damaging as the *campagne anti-superstitieuse* that traumatized peasant society from 1939 to 1942, reaching a brutal peak with state support in its penultimate year. In 1941, at the request of the church, President Elie Lescot (1941–46) directed the Haitian army and police to enforce what had become a zealous witch hunt on the part of many curés, who stormed sanctuaries, destroyed sacred sites and ritual objects, and drove *ougan* and *manbo* from their communities. In Haiti at the time, Swiss field ethnologist Alfred Métraux recalled "seeing in the back-yards of presbyteries vast pyramids of drums, painted bowls, necklaces, talismans—all waiting for the day fixed for the joyous blaze which was to symbolize the victory of the Church over Satan."[30]

There is no question that the "anti-superstition" campaign wrought a devastating effect on Vodou communities during these years, particularly coming on the heels of Marine repression during the occupation.[31] Patrick Leigh Fermor relates the violent fanaticism of one obsessed curé who, in the late 1940s, described his own participation in the attacks:

> "We began by cutting down trees which were said to be inhabited by their gods. . . . We demolished any numbers of trees and caves and 'sacred' rocks, and even cut down the centre poles of Voodoo temples, and made bonfires of the drums and instruments of the cult." He showed us photographs of these curious conflagrations. . . . Several were pictures of himself, or one of his party, with an axe raised, about to deliver the first blow to an inhabited tree.[32]

Yet the resilience of Vodou worship in the countryside and the fact that, in driving the religion further underground, curés were still ultimately, in the words of one of Métraux's informants, being hoodwinked into syncretically serving the *lwa* (Vodou spirits) summarizes the campaign's futility.[33] Métraux recounts that many of those victimized by clerical and military repression in the region of Marbial Valley told him that the attacks had by no means driven the *lwa* away. With characteristic adaptability, when their enclosing pot or tree was smashed, burned, axed, etc., they had simply found others. Some pragmatic *lwa* even suggested that their servants "recant and take communion in the Church . . . as this would make no difference to their relationship."[34]

Yet, on an artifactual level the "anti-superstition" campaign represented nothing short of catastrophe. As Michel-Philippe Lerebours has written recently, "It brought about the almost total disappearance, at least in the accessible regions of the country, of the artistic treasures of popular, religious and secular art accumulated for generations, going back as far as the Colonial and pre-Columbian eras."[35] Significantly, it was at the height of "anti-superstition" zealotry, while his army and police were placed in the service of clerical violence, that President Lescot sponsored Marxist writer Jacques Roumain's institutionalization of Haitian folklore studies. When Roumain founded the Haitian Bureau d'Ethnologie as a state research agency in October 1941, he had just returned from touring the countryside with Métraux, on a mission to save what they could from church fires. Roumain was an outspoken public critic of the *campagne anti-superstitieuse*, and in framing the bureau's mandate pointedly emphasized the conservation of ethnographic artifacts and protection of archaeological sites among the agency's other missions.[36] Of Roumain's commitment in founding the bureau, J. Michael Dash has suggested that he "saw in this institution the possibility of breaking down traditional prejudices against Haiti's indigenous culture, not by impassioned rhetoric this time, but by making Haitian ethnology a respectable, scientific discipline."[37] Lescot's investment in the institutionalization of folklore study, on the other hand, cannot be understood outside of his simultaneous support of the most violent attack on the Vodou religion to date. Susan Stewart has discussed how a rhetoric of ethnographic salvage almost always implies the "disappearance" of the folk referent—an extinction that is presented as the rationale for ethnographic representation, when in fact it often seems more like its condition.[38] If the belief, ritual, and revolutionary counter-history of Vodou as practiced by the majority of the Haitian population were threatening to state powers, the pots, flags, and drums removed from ritual practice and exorcised of that content, like *mapou* trees in the countryside, could become ciphers for official projections of national heritage and identity.

While the Bureau d'Ethnologie may have been primarily a repository for artifacts, Haiti's premier folklore stage performer, Jean-Léon Destiné (who emerges as a pivotal figure for a study of staged folklore in its several contexts), was a student at the Institut d'Ethnologie (founded by Jean Price-Mars in 1941) during its early years and remembers that performance was central to ethnological pedagogy:

> That's how we learned. You see they used to go to the countryside to pick up peasants . . . and bring them back to the Institute, and then, as they danced in front of us, we would . . . analyze the steps, trying to see what they meant, trying to see the background, and the interpenetration of the songs and rhythms. Naturally we also learned from books, but we got to associate what we read with what we saw.[39]

At a time when North American anthropology still often resisted studying ritual dance on the grounds that it raised problems for methodological conventions,[40] the orientation of Haitian ethnology toward performance is particularly notable. Photographs of demonstrations from classes at the bureau in the mid-1940s illustrate Institut d'Ethnologie graduate Michel Lamartinière Honorat's monograph, *Les dances folkloriques haïtiennes.*[41] They show a small gallery, masks, a ritual flag, and plaques covering the walls, with statues, bowls and other artifacts displayed on stands cordoned off around this perimeter. Some of these photographs also inadvertently suggest a gendering of ethno-official investment in folklore as a preserve of national culture and identity at this time: an audience of men in suits and ties sits focused on the room's center, where women in peasant attire demonstrate dances of Vodou ritual. As a teenager, Jean-Léon Destiné had been on the other side of this scrutiny, demonstrating ritual songs and dances for Jean Price-Mars's ethnological lectures at the Lycée Petion and other Port au Prince institutions. During his own tutelage at the Institut d'Ethnologie, Destiné recalled that students would watch such demonstrations to analyze how "the Yanvalou was the dance of the snake, the violent movements of the Petwo represented revolt, the Kongo is a dance of love, how the Ibo reflects resentment against the tyranny of the slave masters." Honorat's text reads like such a movement analysis, connecting mimetic form to ritual and historical "function"—dances such as the Petwo and Ibo considered to have revolutionary origin and utility.

Eventually, the Bureau d'Ethnologie organized a group of these performers into its own in-house folklore dance troupe which staged demonstrations at ethnological lectures and festivals throughout the 1940s. Honorat shared his impressions of one of these public ethnological performances, held, significantly, not at the bureau itself, but on the stage of one of Port-au-Prince's main concert halls:

> It is very dear to me, the memory of the great demonstration organized at the Rex Theater by the Association of Students of the Institut d'Ethnologie on October 18, 1947. . . . But that which struck me personally the most that day . . . was the behavior of the audience at the exhibitions of the Macaya Folkloric Troupe, which for the first time, showed itself. The performance was truly moving and consoling. The thunder of the applause which greeted each dance with the rise and fall of the curtain expressed the perfect communion of the soul of the spectators, of the artists, and of the interpretation. The joy—I would say nearly delirious—of the multi-colored multitude, where children, men, and women were intermingling in an excited mass, like the sea, made me observe and analyze how the human psychology wakes when it finds itself in the presence of that which it knows immediately, of that which it understands without great reflection, because it is an integral part of oneself.[42]

As Honorat's memory highlights, performance extracted from Vodou ritual was being figured as a constitutive element of Haitian cultural heritage during these early years of Haitian folklore studies—an emphasis that also positioned dance as a primary idiom of folkloric nationalism. This focus on performance derived, in part, from ethnological recognition of the primacy of dance in African and African diasporic cultures and, specifically, its centrality in Vodou ritual. Ethnologist Emmanuel C. Paul proposed that "the dance is perhaps with the song the most precious cultural baggage that the black transported to the Americas."[43] Given the orientation of Haitian ethnology toward performance and the built-in opportunity for spectacle, it is unsurprising that heritage dance troupes became accessory to official programs of identity production in the post-occupation period—almost as programs of applied anthropology.

Independent folklore choreographers in Haiti generally cite 1941 as staged folklore's originary moment. This was less for Lescot's institutionalization of ethnological studies than for his support of Lina Fussman-Mathon, a Port-au-Prince choir teacher, who assembled the first folklore troupe for the concert stage. Significantly, Fussman-Mathon's development of a folk repertory for her youth choir began with an early tourist encounter, when a group of German visitors attending one of her performances asked if the group could perform songs in Kreyòl. Working up a set of harmonized Haitian folk songs for subsequent concerts, Fussman-Mathon came to the attention of Lescot as he deliberated over how to represent Haiti at the 1941 National Folk Festival in Washington, D.C.[44] The former minister of Haiti to the United States, Lescot had diplomatic connections in Washington and, according to Destiné, a member of Fussman-Mathon's group, he "wanted to maybe show off a little bit. He said, we have to have Haiti represented [and told Madame Fussman-Mathon] that she was going to represent Haiti with her group. Could you imagine—something in Haiti they were looking down on, and then suddenly you hear the president of Haiti tell you you are going to Washington, D.C.?"[45] Lescot specifically wanted to send a dance troupe. To that end, Fussman-Mathon, Destiné, and the other members of her young choir made several trips into the countryside to learn traditional dances from native informants, then translated them for the proscenium stage, performing over a three-day engagement at Constitution Hall to popular and critical acclaim.[46] A 1942 U.S. State Department memorandum noted that the group's success had been widely reported in the Haitian press and suggested that this might have been "partially responsible" for what the legation in Port-au-Prince observed as "the awakening of Haitian interest in their folklore" at this time.[47]

Between peasants being brought to the Bureau d'Ethnologie for ethnological presentations and Fussman-Mathon's group visiting rural communities in preparation for these performances, the staging of folklore during the early to mid-1940s occasioned a significant degree of circulation between the capital and outlying areas. Consider, as well, the cooperative education program initiated by Lescot's minister of education Maurice Dartigue, designed to teach peasants to avoid soil erosion, drain swamps, create irrigation canals, and construct baskets and furniture. "Most unusual of all," remarked Edith Efron, a North American journalist living in Haiti at the time, "they were encouraged to sing their own folksongs, dance their own folk dances, use their own Creole language in the schools. A children's orchestra, emphasizing drum music, was even created."[48] The seeming redundancy of this cultural dimension of Dartigue's rural curriculum points to what I would suggest was its acculturative end—a sort of regulation in the name of encouragement. State intervention in indigenous practice in Haiti had long connected with efforts to control Vodou, which extend back to colonial times. Beyond the well-documented prohibition against slave gatherings in colonial St.-Domingue, Michel S. Laguerre notes that colonial authorities established a distinction between *dance* and *ritual*: "Colonists tolerated all the noisy dances of the slaves, but they feared Voodoo ceremonies. They were apprehensive of this cult for its mysterious allure and realized that it might be a strong element of cohesion for the slaves."[49] Long after the revolution (which was itself born during one of these ceremonies), state efforts to discourage and control Vodou practice upheld this distinction, based, at least partly, on the fear of ritual as a locus of peasant resistance. Selden

Rodman, writing in the mid-1950s, noted that, "the present method of controlling Vodou is to charge a fee of $30 for any ceremony involving religious sacrifice (cocks, goats, pigs, bulls and the like) but *considerably less for ceremonial dances alone.*"[50]

Throughout the nineteenth and early twentieth centuries, elite intellectuals generally either denied the existence of Vodou, condemned it, or sanitized their recognition of it according to Western conceptions of the "civilized." For example, in a 1904 address to the Société de Législation, Léon Audain, a distinguished medical doctor and writer, portrayed Vodou as a form of entertainment during which music and dance led to a communal feast. While acknowledging that animal sacrifice and possession did sometimes take place during these "amusements," he asserted that those elements were peripheral to the true purpose of the events, thereby concluding that they could be removed to purify Vodou into " 'a simple popular dance, joyful and decent.' "[51] Such a redemptive desire seemed to pervade official investment in folklore study and performance in the context of what J. Michael Dash has described as the "very elitist 'nationalism' " of the Lescot presidency.[52] In this respect, rather than contradictory policy, there was paradoxical complementarity in Lescot's simultaneous support of the church's "anti-superstition" campaign and his minister of education's performance-oriented rural curriculum. Lescot's annexation of indigenous dance culture as the official signifier of Haitian national heritage and identity did not imply increased tolerance or, much less, protection for the worship of Vodou—which was still officially considered a retrogressive and potentially volatile force in Haitian society. As Haitian popular culture became the matrix for official versions of national identity in the post-occupation period, the imperative to regulate the representation as well as the practice of Vodou became heightened.

Ethnology, Tourism, and State Nationalism

Resolves: That each country intensify the studies of its folklore by means of public and private institutes within the universities or in specialized organizations, or that such institutes be created if they do not exist. . . . That the Diplomatic Missions aid the development of artistic programs in state theaters, when the interpretive groups are an example of the finest folk expression of the country they represent.[53]—From the Final Act of the First Conference of Ministers and Directors of Education of the American Republics, Panama, 1943

The "Authentic Revolution" of 1946,[54] which saw the overthrow of Elie Lescot's consolidation of elite *mulâtre* power in the presidency and the installation of Dumarsais Estimé (1946–50), a moderate *noir* politician from the middle class, inaugurated an era that many urban Haitians still remember nostalgically. As a period when folkloric representation became the principal currency of programs of official nationalism and tourist development (themselves interlocking enterprises), the late 1940s emerge as the pivotal moment for this study. They are also years that underscore, again, how intricately linked the history of Haitian folklore is to the republic's twentieth-century political, economic, and cultural relations with the United States: if Marine invasion and the experience of occupation had provided an impetus for the emergence of folklore as an academic field, the advent of North American tourism catalyzed its commercialization, and, in both cases, the staging of folklore was permeated by nationalist significance. During these years, national culture became more implicated in the claim to political legitimacy and the right to rule, and the performance of folklore, increasingly central to its construction. While the arena may have shifted from the ethnological institute to the national stage, Haitian ethnologists were no less involved in the formulation of official culture and identity after 1946; in fact, many were more immediately implicated, as they now held government posts themselves.

Estimé's popularity and far-reaching political mandate at the start of his term grew out of the groundswell of public opposition that had risen against Lescot's color favoritism, retrogressive social policies, and assaults on national culture (most notably his government's support of the "anti-superstition" campaign and expropriation of peasant lands for U.S. wartime rubber production). Folklore performer/director Emerante de Pradines links the artistic and political efflorescence that accompanied the "Revolution of '46" to the ongoing legacies of Marine invasion and cultural reevaluation: "People were really hurt by the occupation, really very hurt. Then there had been a series of *mulâtres* in power, and all of a sudden, a *noir* became President and things began to open." She cites this as the moment when as a young artist, she "dropped the French *chansonnettes*" from her repertory and began to sing in Kreyòl.[55] Folklore study and performance held a privileged status under Estimé, a long-term supporter of the ethnology movement whose official investment in the field was informed by the revisionism of *indigénisme*, and, in particular, the connection Jean Price-Mars and others had drawn between elite contempt for Haitian popular culture and loss of political sovereignty in 1915.[56] In the wake of U.S. occupation and widespread public demoralization under Lescot, the Estimé state figured folklore as a space not merely for political self-definition but also, crucially, for the restoration of national self-determination and cultural dignity. Yet while the assaults on Vodou communities that marked the Lescot era were not repeated under Estimé, the slippage between official concern for "national culture" and ambivalence toward its "living" referent persisted during his presidency.[57] Such displacements even became more visible as official "uses" of folklore increased between 1946 and 1950—in the service of programs of state nationalism and in the development of an international tourist industry.

Haiti's tourist ministry was established in 1928 during the Marine occupation. Thereafter, for nearly three decades, Washington played a key role in developing the Haitian tourist economy, both as a source of foreign exchange for the island nation (which in regaining its sovereignty in 1934 in the midst of a global depression was saddled with debt to the United States), as well as a way to link Haiti more closely to North American corporate capitalism. Arthur Millspaugh, occupation official and historian, describes U.S. efforts to stimulate North American tourist interest in Haiti during the late 1920s:

> A well developed tourist trade might have brought noticeable economic returns. Information regarding the country was published; the Citadel of Christophe was renovated; and a good road built from Cap-Haïtien by way of Sans Souci to the Citadel. Haiti needed at least one modern hotel, and this need was not satisfied. Visitors to Haiti, though increasing, were never numerous enough to contribute appreciably to the invisible exports of the country.[58]

The initial failure of this project might well have been anticipated in light of the fact that Haiti was, at this point, still under military occupation and had suffered years of negative stereotyping—some of it orchestrated by the State Department itself. While the goals of military occupation and tourist development from Washington's point of view were quite similar—in both cases, solidifying U.S. political and economic hegemony in the region—the image of Haiti cultivated to justify U.S. imperialism was not one on which a tourist culture could also be based.

Since the late eighteenth century, Haiti had been constructed in the West as an imaginative space signifying atavistic magic, savagery, and sensuality, to which, after 1915, U.S. military officials added barbarism and incompetence. During the occupation, a spate of sensationalist adventure tracts and travelogues (titles such as *A Puritan in Voodoo-Land* and *Cannibal Cousins*) luridly backed up Washington's contention that civilization could only come to Haiti through U.S. military intervention. As the occupation dragged on, however, the subterfuge of such justifications was thrown increasingly into relief, without diminishing the aura of exoticism that still surrounded W. B. Seabrook's "Magic Island." James Weldon Johnson, Walter White, W. E. B. Du Bois, Rayford Logan, and Langston Hughes undertook fact-finding missions to

Haiti, denouncing the invasion and continued U.S. military presence in *Opportunity*, *The Crisis*, and *The Nation*.[59] The mainstream U.S. press eventually voiced opposition as well, particularly after student strikes, general uprisings, and the massacre of a group of peasants at Aux Cayes in late 1929 drew international attention to Marine repression.[60] By the time U.S. forces were recalled in 1934, two years short of their anticipated term of intervention, the occupation had become a national embarrassment, and the sign of "Haiti" in U.S. popular imagination was already on its way to being redefined. FDR's "Good Neighbor" Policy may have set the tone for this to some extent, but there were other revisionary currents in the air, most of them not directly orchestrated by Washington, that would redeem the image of Haiti and its "folklore" for North American tourism during the 1950s.[61]

One of these sites of rehabilitation was North American anthropology, as, by the early post-occupation period, Haiti had become a major field research site for anthropologists and folklorists, such as Melville J. Herskovits and Harold Courlander, interested in tracing Africanisms in the Americas.[62] Other important revisionary arenas included New York theater and Hollywood film, where Haitian material was frequently thematized during the twenties and thirties—the historical legend of Haiti's post-revolutionary King Henri Christophe alone inspiring interpretations by Eugene O'Neill, W. E. B. Du Bois, and Orson Welles. In the late 1930s, choreographer/anthropologist Katherine Dunham united these frames, developing a modernist concert dance idiom based on Afro-Haitian and Caribbean forms (figure 1) that not only contributed to widespread interest in and travel to Haiti in the 1940s and 1950s but also ensured that elements of African diasporic performance came to permeate North American concert dance. As Dunham noted in an interview, "'We really nourished Broadway and Hollywood for a long time, and I'm not the least embarrassed to say it.'"[63] Dunham's performances were more hybrid than documentary,[64] but, as souvenir programs and reviews from her cross-country and international tours reflect, much was made of her extended period of field research in Haiti during the mid-1930s. Through Dunham's experiments in a dance modernism built on African American and Caribbean forms, Haitian influence on North American concert dance would also lead quite directly to North American influence on Haitian folkloric dance—particularly as two of Dunham's former dancers, Jean-Léon Destiné and Lavinia Williams, went on to become principal exponents of that tradition. While the U.S. occupation had been a formative moment in the historical development and efficacy of Euro-American popular mythologies about Haiti—productively divided, as J. Michael Dash has noted, between "apologists for the Occupation and defenders of negro primitivism,"[65]—revisionary shifts were taking place in

1. Katherine Dunham and Lenwood Morris performing "Congo Paillette—Haitian Corn Sorting Ritual" at the Apollo Theater, 1942. Photo: M. Smith. Courtesy of the Morgan and Marvin Smith Collection, Photographs and Prints Division, Schomburg Center for Research in Black Culture, the New York Public Library for the Performing Arts, Astor, Lenox and Tilden Foundations.

this colonial imaginary by the forties and fifties, as "voodoo" came to be recast more in terms of creative power in North American popular discourses.

Beyond economic incentives, the development of an international tourist industry in Haiti was an extension of the Estimé government's efforts, as Jean-Léon Destiné puts it, to "change the picture of Haiti" both at home and abroad. In 1949, as nightclubs and hotels built around casinos, pools, and garden restaurants were being constructed in the hills above Port-au-Prince, the Estimé government mounted a major international exposition commemorating the bicentennial of the capital city's founding. A reporter for *Life* observed: "For years the Republic of Haiti . . . has hypnotized tourists as a fragrant land of black magic and black majesty, but for want of accommodations and salesmanship has been able to hypnotize only a few thousand of them a year. . . . The exposition . . . is only one of many signs that Haiti is awakening from a long sleep."[66] On a similar note, Katherine Dunham wrote that the exposition was intended to bring Haiti "to the attention of South America, North America, and Europe as its first positive achievement on an international level in over a century."[67] As an opportunity to recast the republic's maligned image internationally and continue the project of redefining cultural identity at home, this "little world's fair" was conceived as an antidote to Haiti's "inferiority complex"—the malaise theorized in ethnological writing of this period to have debilitated the Haitian nation for over a century, culminating in loss of sovereignty. Thus, if primarily a project of tourist development, the bicentennial was also part of the Estimé government's program for national regeneration, and its cultural focus served both ends. While local criticism of the exposition focused on its cost (reported to be $8 million[68]), public opinion toward the project, particularly among urban middle classes, tended to be positive.[69] This points to the wider significance of the *indigéniste* revisioning of Haitian national culture and identity outside of strictly literary, ethnological, and state realms, and the sense in which the 1949 exposition represented a kind of official legacy of that earlier movement. As Michel-Rolph Trouillot notes more generally of the Estimé years, "a majority of the population in the cities and towns was supportive of any attempt to restore national and cultural dignity, especially since the U.S. Marines had displayed to the Haitians, in their own country, the crassest dimensions of international racism."[70]

The site chosen for construction of the Cité de l'Exposition complex, including the state-of-the-art open-air Théâtre de Verdure, was a sixty-acre slum on the south end of town, which was razed and its occupants displaced.[71] Fourteen countries erected pavilions and a traditional midway was set up, operated by an amusement company from the United States. *Life* marveled over Estimé's transformation of this "expanse of slummy, malarial waterfront on Port-au-Prince Bay" into "a garden of palm trees, statuary . . . and modernistic buildings clothed with eloquent murals,"[72] and framed the visitor's experience thus:

> In this opulent setting the tourist may wander through pavilions of foreign countries, inspect latest works of Haitian primitive painters, watch native dances, attend cockfights and gamble in a trim little government-sponsored casino or gambling ship nearby. At night he may sip rum punches, dance the *meringue* and watch the moon peeking through the palm fronds at the Simbie, an open-air nightclub. Or he may stroll the midway, a bedlam of carrousels, kootch dancers and carney pitchmen from the U.S. county-fair circuit. And when he goes to sleep, in one of Port-au-Prince's old or new hotels, he may hear the faint beating of voodoo drums.[73]

Given that the exposition was mounted to present Haitian popular culture as the embodiment of the newly renovated national ideal, the Estimé government exerted considerable control over how that identity was represented. In preparation for the opening of the bicentennial, an ordinance requiring peasants to wear shoes when journeying to Port-au-Prince was revived and enforced by local authorities. *Time* reported that "sound trucks blared the order: 'Wear shoes when you come to town, put on clean clothes, look tidy and decent. It is a shame to go walking around barefoot in your country's capital.' "[74]

But beyond attempting to regulate the appearance of the indigenous "folk" community, the Estimé state conceived of the exposition as an opportunity to present a more precise construction of Haiti's renovated national heritage to local and foreign audiences. While the by then internationally recognized Haitian "primitive" painting movement provided cultural content toward this, Estimé persuaded Haiti's premier dancer (and former ethnology student) Jean-Léon Destiné, at that time in New York working at the Museum of Natural History, to return home to form and direct a national folklore dance company. Estimé's choice of a *dance* troupe can be understood both in terms of the Haitian ethnological orientation I noted earlier toward performance in general and dance in particular, as well as the precedent set by Lina Fussman-Mathon's group.[75] Upon returning to Haiti, Destiné held auditions for this polyglot company in every Haitian department with the assistance of the Ministry of Tourism. Announced in advance, these competitions generated an unexpected degree of local interest across the country: Destiné remembers that those who came to audition were often outnumbered by the audiences who attended to watch. Assisted by his long-time dance partner Jeanne Ramon, Destiné chose dancers who "specialized" in particular regional traditions that could be performed as solos in the troupe's repertory. Permission to represent certain of these dances outside of ritual contexts was required by local *ougan* and the state paid fees for these rights—an ironic reversal of the usual direction such charges were exacted.[76] Destiné completed the audition circuit in Port-au-Prince, selecting the majority of the company's twenty-five members from the ranks of the small folklore groups that had formed throughout the 1940s to perform Afro-Haitian dance and ritual forms at ethnological lectures and festivals.[77] The regional scope of this audition process was designed to ensure that the company would be nationally representative and that each performer could, as Emerante de Pradines notes, "dance his or her own dances."[78] "I had mostly native dancers and they couldn't follow difficult choreography," Destiné explains. "I had to make it simple enough but let them express themselves fully in their own way. Instead of giving them steps of my own, I let them do their own steps, and I staged it." Drawing not only on his own considerable knowledge of Haitian popular performance but also on the professional guidance of ethnologists and the expertise of his performers, Destiné created a repertory of dances that married indigenous tradition and ethnographic construction with Western production values. A typical program of short selections by the Troupe Folklorique Nationale (accompanied by the "Jazz des Jeunes" orchestra) included stylized sacred dances from the Rada, Kongo, and Petwo rites of Vodou; a carnival dance; a dance of the peasant work crew or *konbit*; a *contredanse*; Destiné's own liberatory "Dance of the Slave" (figure 2); and a comic skit of peasant life, often, it seems, a scene of flirtation ending in a *bamboche* or party.[79] *U.S. News and World Report* observed that the performances of the company were the "high spot of the exposition for both Americans and Haitians."[80]

Western theatrical constraints of time, space, and spectacle necessitated considerable adjustment in translating these indigenous performance traditions to the national stage. As Destiné noted: "We could not possibly present what the peasants do under the *tonnèl* on stage. Those ceremonies go on for hours and hours. The audience would be bored to death." So these dances were performed as ethnographic fragments, programmed into a theatrically coherent whole. While they seem to have been performed quite "faithfully" with respect to steps, they were also often spatially choreographed according to Western dance figures and patterns. Audience expectation of virtuosity created a special irony, as, in Vodou, brilliant performance is considered the province of the gods during possession, not of "unmounted" human per-

2. Jean-Léon Destiné performing his "Dance of the Slave" during the Haitian International Exposition, Port-au-Prince, Haiti, 1950. Credit: Gordon Parks/*LIFE Magazine* © TIME Inc.
3. Lavinia Williams performing the role of the "Maiden in the Community" in Katherine Dunham's "Rites de Passage," 1942. Courtesy of Diana Dunbar and Vera Jacobs.

formers. Destiné anticipated this problem and arrived at an inspired solution: during his field research he concentrated on watching possessed dancers because he found their movements (or rather those of the *lwa* who "danced" them) more immediately translatable for the stage.[81]

In terms of the dances adopted from Vodou, another major point of departure was the role of drumming. Whereas in ritual master drummers structure the event of possession through their rhythms, drummers for these staged rites followed rhythmic configurations established in advance and were discouraged from improvisation or otherwise deviating from a set score. A specific example of the altered relationship between drummer and dancer in staged performance was the nature of the folkloric *kase*. In ritual contexts, the *kase* is a dramatic rhythmic break, dictated by the master drummer, that often induces (or builds to) possession, while in staged folklore the choreographer established in advance precisely when such "breaks" should occur. As drummed and danced, the folkloric *kase* became a stage convention and, importantly as well, a means of structuring and linking different sections of choreography. The codified movement sequences that signified the danced *kase* in staged folklore often served as a bridge between different dances, just as, in ritual, possession is the hinge between the progression of rites. In the sense that the folkloric *kase* represented a moment of choreographic *transition*, it maintained a vestige of its originary liminality.[82]

These were several of the more obvious and inevitable accommodations that the Troupe Folklorique Nationale made in translating popular traditions for the stage. But as much as Western theatrics, the pressure of ethnographic accuracy guided these performances of national heritage, and Haitian ethnologists participated quite assertively in coining a set repertoire of dances and skits. Destiné recalls that ethnologists would attend performances to audit his representations:

> There was a group of ethnologists that had a newspaper called *Le réveil* and they were very upset because they were not hired as consultants. I told them "this is not voodoo, this is not ethnology, we are doing theater as the national troupe. We want the work to be done close to the traditional, but we don't want the real, authentic thing on stage. We want it to be theatrical and therefore, do not need ethnologists." So they were watching me every night and I had to be very careful. One evening I did a number showing Spanish and French influence on Haitian dance. . . . The costume was blue, white and red, like the French flag, which was appropriate, but I felt like I needed a decoration, so I had a big hat, and instead of keeping it on top of my head, I pushed it back behind.[83]

In a subsequent issue of the publication Destiné was attacked for allowing a "Mexican" motif to enter the national repertory encoded in the positioning of this hat. Such academic and statist pressure combined with the inevitable routinization of a nightly performance schedule assured that certain indices of authenticity became canonized for the Troupe Folklorique Nationale's performance of national heritage at this time, and thus for the larger repository of Haitian ethnology. For ethnologists such as those self-appointed to critique Destiné's representations, any departure from these authorized markers not only distorted the Haitian folk tradition but also potentially threatened the national ideal, as more and more folklore performance was being circumscribed as an official domain of Haitian identity. Uncomfortable with the constraints held over him by state and ethnographic authorities in Port-au-Prince, Destiné returned to New York at the close of his six-month contract and built an international choreographic and teaching career that continues to the present day.[84]

While Estimé's exposition drew only about nine thousand visitors to Haiti in 1949,[85] the event generated a great deal of promotion in the United States—with reports in the *New York Times*, *Holiday*, *U.S. News and World Report*, and *Time*, and a color photographic spread and article in *Life*. By the early 1950s, such publicity had stimulated a thriving tourist culture. Noel Coward, Paulette Goddard, Truman Capote, and Irving Berlin were among visitors of note during this period, which Michel-Rolph Trouillot describes as "the decade of government display, of picture-postcard projects."[86] Estimé was overthrown in May 1950 by Colonel Paul Magloire, who continued the tradition of grandiose official display, one-upping his predecessor's exposition by reenacting the final battle of the Haitian Revolution on its sesquicentennial anniversary in 1954.[87] North American tourism peaked under Magloire's rule and Haiti became the "in" destination of the hip international traveler.[88] Herbert Gold, among their numbers in the early fifties, described them as "a sub-category of the bohemian floaters—the international students, anthropologists, askew Francophiles or wanderers in Africa and the Caribbean, artistic seekers who had answered the rumor that here was a place like none other."[89] Back in New York, Destiné headlined the April 1951 "Haiti Week" sponsored by the Haitian government, culminating in a gala performance by the Troupe Folklorique Nationale at the Ziegfeld Theater. That year nearly eighteen thousand tourists traveled to Haiti; by 1956, that figure had more than tripled.[90]

One of the performers participating in New York's "Haiti Week" was Lavinia Williams, a former Dunham dancer and dance educator, who had worked as well in Europe and on Broadway. Observed giving a class at the Haiti festival by a committee of visiting artists, Williams was subsequently invited by the Haitian government to give physical culture and body conditioning courses to members of the national troupe. Arriving in Port-au-Prince in April 1953, Williams was to have a profound effect on the development of staged folklore in Haiti, and she is widely credited with being the first to formulate a technique for its study. Among those continuing this diverse tradition in Port-au-Prince today, she is frequently cited as a crucial influence, and in several cases, mentor (figure 3). As her colleague Emerante de Pradines notes, "Lavinia made a really good impression on the people here. She was right at home and stayed." Hired to train Destiné's original company according to principles of Western theater dance, Williams grew familiar with the troupe's repertory as she drilled them in technique and attended their tri-weekly performances. She became concerned about the likelihood of misunderstanding during these tourist spectacles, after, as she writes, "I heard someone in the audience say that the troupe was dancing the 'Mahi', when I knew it was the 'Petro,' " so she offered her services as English narrator for the performances, becoming mistress of ceremonies at the Théâtre de Verdure.[91] Assembling a small dance troupe herself, "The Haitian Voudoo Dancers," comprised of Vodou initiates and drummers from nearby *houfò*, plus her own students, Williams began to perform at the available venues—mostly hotels. As she writes in her 1959 book *Haiti-Dance*: "We were a smash hit. Other hotels saw the value of presenting native shows to their guests, and after a few months of rehearsals, my troupe had auditioned for the Ibo Lélé Hotel, to dance around its swimming pool. We signed a contract and when the Shango Night Club opened there, we were the featured attraction for years."[92] Staged folklore in Haiti thus entered a new chapter. While the Troupe Folklorique Nationale continued to perform under the auspices of the state and under the scrutiny of the Bureau d'Ethnologie, smaller groups proliferated outside the domain of official culture and became featured attractions at hotels, resorts, and nightclubs frequented by tourists. Developing her tourist productions in the spirit of cross-cultural understanding, Williams reported encouraging her dancers: "We can make a respected art form out of the Vodoun letting it be our source of inspiration."[93]

Alfred Métraux was conducting fieldwork in Haiti during the years that Port-au-Prince debuted as the new hub of North American tourism in the Caribbean. Charging that this industry posed a far graver threat to the integrity of Vodou than church or state ever had, he singled out staged ritual for special condemnation:

> Although neither Church nor State has succeeded in breaking the hold of Voodooism, tourism, on the other hand, in its most commercial forms is having a rapidly destructive effect. For several years now, thanks

> to the efforts of the government, Port-au-Prince has been turning into a vast tourist centre. Every American who disembarks there has but one word on his lips—"Voodoo"; and one wish—to see ceremonies which he imagines to be orgiastic and cruel. . . . Some enterprising *hungan* have even put on Voodoo "shows" which are repeated weekly and designed purely for tourists. . . . Sanctuaries have become neon-lighted theatres.[94]

The response of Haitian ethnologists to the commercialization of folkloric performance was, on the whole, similarly censorious. However, the alliance of ethnology and tourism in the service of state nationalism during the 1940s and 1950s made their relationship to commercial folklore more complex. Emmanuel C. Paul wrote that international interest in Haitian folklore after 1949 had, in fact, provided an incentive for his ongoing efforts to inventory tradition: "The flight taken by tourism since the International Exposition of Port-au-Prince's Bicentenary in 1949 provoked so much interest in the subject, that I have found there a certain encouragement not to renounce the project."[95]

But the uneasy reciprocity between ethnological and commercial folklore at this time is probably best captured in Michel Lamartinière Honorat's aforementioned 1955 *Les danses folkloriques haïtiennes*, which reflects the anxiety that for many ethnologists accompanied the popularization of folklore performance outside of the Bureau d'Ethnologie. As an ethnography, Honorat's monograph is fascinating in that it often seems to be based not on traditional field research but on observation of staged demonstrations at the Bureau d'Ethnologie and the Théâtre de Verdure, where he gathered much of his information on regional and particularly northern Haitian dance traditions during performances by the national company.[96] As a result of this, his text sometimes reads (and, with illustrative photographs of demonstrations at the bureau, looks) more like a study of the staged folklore tradition of the forties and early fifties than of Haiti's indigenous dance cultures. Yet Honorat begins his monograph with an indictment of the commercial elements of the *mouvement folklorique*, including its state-sponsored realm, writing: "Even the official sphere, where a good tourism policy ought to be staked on a good usage of our rich folklore, permits itself to be advised by people who do not know our dances . . . not even their names."[97] In his introduction he warns that through the increasing "stylization" of native dances for tourist consumption, "exploitative motifs" were entering the stage repertory at the hands of unskilled artists, who "disorient the choreography of our dances" with an "unimaginable off-handedness."[98] Honorat was sufficiently alarmed by this trend to offer up his monograph itself as a kind of textual "preserve" for vernacular traditions endangered by the corruptions of the representational tourist economy. He writes,

> In order to protect [our dances] against the contingencies of the Haitian *milieu* and the vicissitudes of this superficial layer of occidental civilization covering our social body, "in order to avoid the slow death of our traditions, in order to give them strength and vigor again," as the author of *Les Danses du Limousin* [Roger Blanchard] has put it, I present the results of my inquiries on the folkloric dances of Haiti.[99]

While Alfred Métraux's denunciation of "voodoo tourism" seems to have been motivated by his conviction that the religion was itself being harmed (a concern that bears its own authenticating logic and desire), Honorat seems more focused on form and interpretation—that folklore choreographers and performers participating in tourist productions were departing from authorized ethnological models, thereby corrupting Haiti's traditional dances, as distinguished from Vodou. His worries seem significantly less about the impact of tourist performance on subaltern cultural practices than about the distortion of the Bureau d'Ethnologie's constructions, codified and canonized through ethnological study and staging. In attributing tourist folklore's degradation of these ethnographic models to what he calls "the inferiority complex that is manifesting itself everywhere and in everything throughout this country," Honorat foregrounds what seems to have been, for many ethnologists at this time, the central issue. Ultimately, the reason he and others were distressed by the popularization of "voodoo tourism" was precisely because folklore performance had become an official domain and preserve of Haitian national culture and identity during the post-occupation period. Honorat's apprehension that, as he put it, "improvising artists" were irresponsibly transforming and misinterpreting traditional folkloric forms resonates with his colleague Emmanuel C. Paul's warning about the necessity of specialized translation for such material: "To describe the facts of popular culture without interpreting and explaining them too often gives rise to misinterpretations or errors of judgment that, among the young and the uninformed public, are likely to maintain an inferiority complex that is dangerous for our collective behavior."[100]

The specter of the Haitian "inferiority complex" haunts ethnological writing from this period. Theorized by the *indigénistes* to have resulted from the elite's nineteenth-century repression of African cultural patrimony, this ruling-class malaise was held to account for the disintegration of the Haitian nation that culminated, in 1915, in the loss of sovereignty. As invoked by Honorat and Paul in their anxiety over the potential distortions of extra-official folkloric representation, it throws into relief the precariousness of the original redemptive inversion on which Haitian folklore studies were founded. *Indigénisme* made peasant culture the matrix for a renovated Haitian nationalism. Peasant culture was inseparable from the Vodou religion; and Vodou was the object of great ruling-class ambivalence and Western fascination and malign. When one understands that the integrity of the nation was in some sense being based on the reclamation and re-presentation of a culture which had been a primary locus of subaltern resistance since before the revolution and which, constructed as "voodoo" beyond national borders, still often subsumed Haiti in sensationalism and stereotype, it becomes more clear why the ethnological and official stakes for controlling folklore representation in these post-occupation years were so high.

There is a way in which "voodoo tourism" of the type Métraux excoriates above may have been most distressing and threatening of all. This was the genre where, as he describes, "the *humfo* threw wide their doors to the tourists; link-ups were made between hotel porters and *hungan*, to such good effect that on Saturday evenings long files of cars may be seen in some wretched back-street near a sanctuary."[101] In constructing folk culture as the national ideal, the ethno-official project mandated increased surveillance of the *practice* of Vodou, control of representation extending to control of communities. It therefore seems unsurprising that the rural education curriculum Estimé implemented upon his elecion in 1946, yet more ambitious than that of Lescot, was, as Edith Efron describes, "inevitably cultural as well":

> Again scientists and "folklorists" found themselves united. Peasant adults and children, in these communities, were encouraged to compose and produce small plays based on peasant life. There was also a Friday-afternoon recreational program, in which adults and children of the school community told folk tales, sang folk songs, and danced folk dances.[102]

Allied with the project of codifying and canonizing folklore forms for nationalist heritage performances, these model "schools of orientation" as they were called (their acculturative dimension thus foregrounded) were an applied counterpart to the project of identity construction that was taking place concurrently at the Bureau d'Ethnologie and on the national stage. As had been the case under Lescot, the educational project of incorporating rural populations into a "national" community was pursued through cultural means; and again, I would suggest, it was predicated in part on the detachment of "folklore" from Vodou ritual. Addressing the Union Nationale des Instituteurs Haïtiens (UNIH) in 1955, ethnologist Emmanuel C. Paul made the possibility of such a separation central to his advocacy for the integration of folklore material into public instruction:

> We agree that there are elements in folklore that it is desirable to see disappear. . . . The best thing for the educator is to get to know it first of all, and to exploit it cleverly. If in the course of school festivals one has the students perform a song or a dance on the stage, one ruins the belief that they have a magical significance. In utilizing them for recreational ends they lose, in this frame, their sacred character, while taking on a new content that has no relation whatsoever with the belief in a god. This is certainly preferable and more efficacious than sermons on their diabolic character.[103]

In some sense, Paul's argument echoes Léon Audain's aforementioned vision of converting Vodou into a "simple popular dance, joyful and decent." Yet the possibility of such a reinterpretation, in which, as Paul notes, "staging" has a potentially important role to play, took on, I would argue, a particular political priority in the context of official nationalist programs in the post-occupation era. The reclamation of the "popular" as grounds for nationalist identity is always, to some degree, a sanitizing, normalizing project. In the case of Haitian post-occupation folkloric nationalism, the implications of this ubiquitous project of "normalization," were, as I see them, twofold, in both cases turning on the fact that Vodou was at the center of the discursive field. On the one hand, there was the pervasive sociopolitical power and plurality of this religion; on the other, there was the history of "voodoo" as a Western construct. For official nationalists in the 1940s and 1950s, this amounted to a kind of double jeopardy, encouraging greater scrutiny over all "extra-official" representations of Vodou, including those of indigenous practice. Thus these years saw a marked increase in state intrusion into peasant society. While the Catholic Church's "anti-superstition" campaign belongs in a different category of intervention than do Elie Lescot's and Dumarsais Estimé's music and dance education curricula, there was a certain continuity in logic and goals, if not in means.

In his regret over the fate of early nationalist imaginings of community in colonial India, Partha Chatterjee emphasizes the original "autonomy" of these formulations, eventually "swamped by the history of the postcolonial state."[104] I have traced a similar genealogy with regard to *indigénisme* in Haiti, but see the issue of "autonomy" as engendering another sort of crisis. In the case of Haitian nationalism, the constitution of post-occupation identity in distinction not only to "Westernness" but also to Western imaginings about "Haitianness" made for a kind of representational instability that put official formulation of Haitian identity at risk even as its autonomous existence was being asserted. The staging of folklore was central to the Haitian state's articulation of political self-definition during the post-occupation period, but in neither theatrical nor, certainly, indigenous realms were such performances officially containable. This was the complexity of official claims to national particularity in the post-occupation moment. The (re)visionary imaginative project of *indigénisme* necessarily infused the official construction of national culture in Haiti during these years, but what had started as an oppositional discourse of "difference" came to be assimilated by the state as a conservative fixing of identity—one which the performance of folklore, in any context, would always exceed.

Notes

I am deeply grateful for the generosity and guidance of the artists who shared these histories with me: Willfred Brignole, Suzette Carter-Saulnier, Jean-Léon Destiné, Katherine Dunham, Vivian Gauthier (with Hervé Martin), Eileen Herzog-Bazin, François Fritz Jolicoeur, Lina Mathon-Blanchet, Emerante de Pradines, and Lavinia Williams. I owe a special debt of gratitude to Antoine and Claude Jean-Charles and their family. I would also like to thank Cynthia J. Cohen Bull, Erik Davis, Jane Desmond, Amitav Ghosh, Barbara Kirshenblatt-Gimblett, John F. Szwed, Michael Taussig, Tim Watson, and Joe Wood for their invaluable contributions to this essay. I wish to acknowledge the support of the Tinker Foundation and the Columbia University-New York University Consortium in Latin American and Caribbean Studies, which made possible my research in Haiti during the summer of 1991. An earlier version of this essay appeared in *Women & Performance: A Journal of Feminist Theory* 14–15 (1995), pp. 187–216.

1 Quoted in Michel Lamartinière Honorat, *Les danses folkloriques haïtiennes* (Port-au-Prince, Haiti: Imprimerie de l'État, 1955), p. 16. All quotations from this text are my translation.

2 I am indebted to Lois E. Wilcken's *Music Folklore among Haitians in New York: Staged Representations and the Negotiation of Identity* (Ph.D. diss., Columbia University, 1991), for this formulation.

3 See, for example, Barbara Kirshenblatt-Gimblett, "Objects of Ethnography," in *Exhibiting Cultures: The Poetics and Politics of Museum Display*, ed. Ivan Karp and Steven D. Lavine (Washington, D.C.: Smithsonian Institution Press, 1991), pp. 386–443; Yvonne Daniel, *Rumba: Dance and Social Change in Contemporary Cuba* (Bloomington: Indiana University Press, 1995); Richard Handler, *Nationalism and the Politics of Culture in Quebec* (Madison, Wis.: University of Wisconsin Press, 1988); and Jean Decock, "Pré-Théâtre et Rituel: National Folk Troupe of Mali," *African Arts* 1, no. 3 (1967), pp. 31–37. See also Sterling Stuckey's work on the ring shout in *Slave Culture: Nationalist Theory and the Foundations of Black America* (New York: Oxford University Press, 1987).

4 Handler, *Nationalism and the Politics of Culture in Quebec*, p. 13.

5 Benedict Anderson, *Imagined Communities: Reflections on the Origin and Spread of Nationalism* (1983; London: Verso, 1991), p. 5.

6 In his discussion of the "problematic of state and nation" in the case of Haiti, Michel-

Rolph Trouillot makes the crucial point that while "all states derive the right to dominate their people in part from global recognition within the interstate system. . . . economic dependency does not imply that third world rulers blindly follow the dictates of their industrialized patrons. Further, the peripheral state, as the European state before, can claim to dominate a nation only to the extent that it lays claim to some 'national unity' based on culture and history. . . . It cannot avoid recognizing the existence of the nation, because in so doing it would undermine its own legitimacy." Michel-Rolph Trouillot, *Haiti: State against Nation* (New York: Monthly Review Press, 1990), p. 29.

7 Chatterjee focuses his critique, in part, on Anderson's contention in *Imagined Communities* that eighteenth- and nineteenth-century nationalist experience in the "New World" colonies, western Europe, and Russia gave rise to "modular" formations of nation and nationness that twentieth-century anticolonial nationalisms then imitated. See Partha Chatterjee, *Nationalist Thought and the Colonial World: A Derivative Discourse* (Minneapolis: University of Minnesota Press, 1986), and his *The Nation and Its Fragments: Colonial and Post-Colonial Histories* (Princeton: Princeton University Press, 1993).

8 Chatterjee, *The Nation and Its Fragments*, p. 5.

9 Ibid.

10 I take this term from Richard Handler, who uses it to convey the notion "of seeing culture as a thing: a natural object or entity made up of objects and entities ('traits')." *Nationalism and the Politics of Culture in Quebec*, p. 14.

11 Joan Dayan, "Vodoun, or the Voice of the Gods," *Raritan* 10, no. 3 (1991), p. 35.

12 Jean Price-Mars, *So Spoke the Uncle*, trans. Magdaline W. Shannon (1928; Washington, D.C.: Three Continents Press, 1983), p. 178.

13 Following the Spanish-American War of 1898, the United States undertook repeated military interventions and corporate land takeovers in the Caribbean under the pretexts of promoting order and peace, protecting U.S. interests, preventing revolution, and establishing prosperity. All told, thirty-three invasions took place before Teddy Roosevelt's "gunboat diplomacy" was succeeded by the "Good Neighbor" policy of his nephew. In the case of the invasion and occupation of Haiti, the primary objectives seemed to have been ensuring the island republic's subservience to North American interests during World War I and stabilizing its politics and economy for U.S. investment thereafter.

14 Arthur C. Millspaugh, *Haiti under American Control: 1915–1930* (Boston: World Peace Foundation, 1931), p. 222.

15 See Trouillot, *Haiti: State against Nation*, p. 106. The role of the Haitian *garde* recalls that of colonial militaries, which as Benedict Anderson notes, were "ideologically conceived as an internal police force." Anderson, *Imagined Communities*, p. 151.

16 Kethly Millet, *Les Paysans haïtiens et l'occupation américaine, 1915–1930* (La Salle, Canada: Collectif Paroles, 1978), p. 95.

17 Quoted in Millspaugh, *Haiti under American Control*, p. 205.

18 Quoted in David F. Healy, *Gunboat Diplomacy in the Wilson Era: The U.S. Navy in Haiti, 1915–1916* (Madison: University of Wisconsin Press, 1976), p. 213.

19 Katherine Dunham, *Island Possessed* (Garden City, N.Y.: Doubleday, 1969), p. 1.

20 Anderson, *Imagined Communities*, p. 205.

21 Michel-Philippe Lerebours writes: "We have largely insisted on the 'shock' provoked by the American occupation of Haiti and on the flow of ideas which, contrary to all expectations, has come out of it, because it is difficult, if we forget these facts and ideas, to

understand the subsequent evolution of aesthetic thought (all of the generations to follow would consciously or unconsciously claim to be Indigenists)." "The Indigenist Revolt: Haitian Art, 1927–1944," *Callaloo* 15, no. 3 (Summer 1992), p. 711.

22 This coincided with the emergence of *indigenismo* across Latin America—literary and artistic movements also focused on the reclamation of "folk" cultures.

23 C. L. R. James, *The Black Jacobins: Toussaint L'Ouverture and the San Domingo Revolution* (1963; New York: Vintage Books, 1989), p. 394.

24 Although, as Michel-Philippe Lerebours notes, "the manifesto of *La Revue Indigène*, if it asked to come closer to popular sources and to be inspired by them, did not care about breaking with the aesthetic tradition of French literature. Despite the advice of Dr. [Jean] Price-Mars, works written in Creole were rather rare." See Lerebours, "The Indigenist Revolt," p. 712.

25 Price-Mars, *So Spoke the Uncle*, p. 13.

26 Honorat, *Les danses folkloriques haïtiennes*, p. 9.

27 "As we have seen earlier, in everything 'natural' there is always something unchosen. In this way, nation-ness is assimilated to skin-colour, gender, parentage and birth-era—all those things one can not help" (Anderson, *Imagined Communities*, p. 143).

28 Sidney W. Mintz has suggested that the post-occupation "pressing" of anthropology into a political mold in Haiti anticipated "similar developments in other 'colonial' countries." See his *Caribbean Transformations* (1974; New York: Columbia University Press, 1989), p. 289.

29 Quoted in *Le matin*, 22 March 1942; enclosed with memorandum of J. C. White to the Secretary of State, 25 March 1942, U.S. Department of State, Decimal File 838.404/71, National Archives.

30 Alfred Métraux, *Voodoo in Haiti* (1959; New York: Schocken Books, 1972), p. 343.

31 These went on until early 1942, when President Lescot withdrew police and military support, alarmed by peasant resistance, general public opposition to the attacks, and the riddling of a Catholic church with gunfire as the priests inside celebrated an anti-Vodou mass.

32 Patrick Leigh Fermor, *The Traveller's Tree: A Journey through the Caribbean Islands* (London: Penguin Books, 1950), pp. 248–49.

33 Métraux reports in *Voodoo in Haiti*: "For many Voodooists the 'renunciation' became a genuine dilemma of conscience which some solved in a rather subtle way. One of these was Sylvestre who, having sworn never to serve the *loa* again, identified them 'in spirit' with the saints, whose pictures he had retained. He no longer went to the *hungan*, but he did say mass which 'in spirit' was always addressed to the *loa*. He put tasty dishes near the pictures of the saints to round the ceremony off. Cynically he admitted: 'That's how we fix things, so the *curé* serves the *loa*' " (p. 351).

34 As the *ougan*/artist Andre Pierre put it more recently: "If they cut down a tree sacred to our *loa*, we will worship the roots" (quoted in Joan Dayan, "The Crisis of the Gods: Haiti after Duvalier," *Yale Review* 77, no. 3 [1988], p. 325).

35 Lerebours, "The Indigenist Revolt," p. 721.

36 Honorat, *Les danses folkloriques haïtiennes*, p. 7.

37 J. Michael Dash, *Literature and Ideology in Haiti, 1915–1961* (London: Macmillan, 1981), p. 140.

38 See Susan Stewart, *Crimes of Writing: Problems in the Containment of Representation* (Durham: Duke University Press, 1994), particularly chapter 4, "Scandals of the Ballad."

39 Jean-Léon Destiné, interview with author, New York City, 21 January 1992. All subsequent references are from this same interview unless otherwise noted.

40 As when Melville J. Herskovits laments in his *The Myth of the Negro Past* (1941; Boston: Beacon Hill, 1958), p. 269 that "no method has as yet been evolved to permit objective study of the dance."

41 See note 1.

42 Honorat, *Les danses folkloriques haïtiennes*, p. 9.

43 Emmanuel C. Paul, *Panorama du folklore Haïtien (presence Africaine en Haïti)* (Port-au-Prince, Haiti: Imprimerie de l'État, 1962), p. 51. All quotations from this text are my translation.

44 Lavinia Williams Yarborough, *Haiti-Dance* (Frankfurt: Bronners Druckerie, 1959), p. 3.

45 Quoted in Wilcken, *Music Folklore among Haitians in New York*, p. 152.

46 Lina Mathon-Blanchet, interview with author, Port-au-Prince, Haiti, 25 June 1991. All subsequent references are from this same interview. The troupe's engagement at Constitution Hall took place, notably, two years after Marian Anderson had been denied use of the hall on racial grounds.

47 J. C. White to the Secretary of State, 24 September 1942, U.S. Department of State, Decimal File 838.404/85, National Archives.

48 See Edith Efron, "The 'New Movement' in Haiti," *Caribbean Quarterly* 4, no. 1 (1955), p. 27.

49 Michel S. Laguerre, "The Place of Voodoo in the Social Structure of Haiti," *Caribbean Quarterly* 19, no. 3 (1973), p. 44.

50 Selden Rodman, *Haiti: The Black Republic* (1954; Old Greenwich, Conn.: Devin-Adair Co., 1980), p. 68, my emphasis.

51 Quoted in Nicholls, *From Dessalines to Duvalier: Race, Colour, and National Independence in Haiti* (Cambridge: Cambridge University Press, 1979), p. 133.

52 Dash, *Literature and Ideology in Haiti*, p. 161.

53 Resolutions approved by the First Conference of Ministers and Directors of Education of the American Republics, Panama, 27 September to 4 October 1943, Congress and Conference Series No. 45 (Washington, D.C.: Pan American Union, 1943), pp. 11–12.

54 Articulating their right to rule as foremost, an issue of legitimacy, the so-called "Generation of '46" reasoned that, given the predominance of Haiti's black population and African cultural heritage, *noirs* were the only group capable of recovering the nation's dignity and identity, lost with Haitian sovereignty during the U.S. military occupation (Trouillot, *Haiti: State against Nation*, pp. 132–34).

55 Emerante de Pradines, interview with author, Port-au-Prince, Haiti, 25 June 1991. All subsequent references are to this same interview.

56 Trouillot, *Haiti: State against Nation*, p. 131.

57 Wistful for the days when the government backed the church in its crusade against "superstition," members of the French Catholic clergy publicly attacked the Estimé government's patronage of the folklore movement on the grounds that ethnologists-turned-statesmen were attempting to establish Vodou as a "national religion." See Nicholls, *From Dessalines to Duvalier*, p. 197. Yet Estimé's own outlook on Vodou as a religious *practice* was a good deal more equivocal than clerical uproar over his ideological promotion of "superstition" would seem to suggest. Katherine Dunham, who knew Estimé during her first period of field research in Haiti in the mid-1930s, recalled that he disapproved of her visits to the Vodou *houfò* almost as much as her interactions with elites: "Estimé . . . hated the *vaudun*, or I should say held it in ridicule, feeling that the worship of African

gods tied the people to ignorance, diverting them from recognition of their immediate and real problems." See Dunham, *Island Possessed*, p. 26.

58 Millspaugh, *Haiti under American Control*, pp. 145–46.

59 J. Michael Dash, *Haiti and the United States: National Stereotypes and the Literary Imagination* (London: Macmillan, 1988), p. 51.

60 Hans Schmidt, *The United States Occupation of Haiti 1915–1934* (1971; New Brunswick: Rutgers University Press, 1995), pp. 204–5.

61 See Brenda Gayle Plummer's *Haiti and the United States: The Psychological Moment* (Athens: University of Georgia Press, 1992), particularly chapter 7, "Le Vogue Nègre," which examines the rise of tourism to Haiti during the post-occupation years.

62 Melville J. Herskovits, *Life in a Haitian Valley* (1937); Harold Courlander, *Haiti Singing* (1939).

63 Quoted in Ruth Beckford, *Katherine Dunham: A Biography* (New York: Marcel Dekker, 1979), p. 117.

64 As Joyce Aschenbrenner and Vèvè A. Clark have discussed, critical disapproval of Dunham's work often focused on the liberties she took with ethnographic representation without understanding, as Clark writes, "that Caribbean dance has been stylized and transformed throughout its history" (p. 191). See Joyce Aschenbrenner, *Katherine Dunham: Reflections on the Social and Political Contexts of Afro-American Dance* (New York: Congress on Research in Dance, 1981), and VèVè A. Clark, "Performing the Memory of Difference in Afro-Caribbean Dance: Katherine Dunham's Choreography, 1938–87," in *History and Memory in African-American Culture*, ed. Geneviève Fabre and Robert O'Meally (New York: Oxford University Press, 1994), pp. 188–204.

65 Dash, *Haiti and the United States*, p. 25.

66 "Caribbean Carnival: 'Little World's Fair' is Haiti's Big Bid for Tourists," *Life*, 13 March 1950, p. 98.

67 Dunham, *Island Possessed*, p. 44.

68 *Life* put the cost of the exposition at closer to $9 million and noted that this figure was the "equivalent of three-quarters of the government's entire annual budget" (13 March 1950, p. 105).

69 Jean-Léon Destiné, interview with author, New York City, 2 April 1996.

70 Trouillot, *Haiti: State against Nation*, p. 133.

71 Plummer, *Haiti and the United States,* p. 134.

72 The construction itself was directed by a North American, August F. Schmiedigen, who had worked on the 1937 Paris International Exposition.

73 *Life*, 13 March 1950, p. 98.

74 "Shod by Order," *Time*, 2 February 1948, p. 26. There may have been a more medically compelling rationale for the revival of this ordinance. Katherine Dunham notes that even in the mid-1930s Estimé spoke of controlling "diseases and intestinal parasites and yaws and elephantiasis . . . by enforcing a law that existed but had been forgotten: all people of all classes should wear shoes at least in the capital, even if they were sandals of the cheapest manufacture" (Dunham, *Island Possessed*, pp. 45–46).

75 Yarborough, *Haiti-Dance*, p. 6.

76 Destiné, interview with author, New York City, 2 April 1996.

77 de Pradines, interview. In her *Haiti-Dance* (p. 7), Lavinia Williams Yarborough lists some of these small groups as the Damballa Dance Troupe, the Lecocia Dancers, the Aida Troupe, the Erzulie Dancers, the Dantor Dancers, and the Macaya Folk Group.

78 de Pradines, interview, 25 June 1991. See Barbara Kirshenblatt-Gimblett's discussion of instances "when people themselves are the medium of ethnographic representation, when they perform themselves, whether at home to tourists or at world's fairs, homeland entertainments, or folklife festivals—when they become living signs of themselves." Kirshenblatt-Gimblett, "Objects of Ethnography," p. 388.

79 Yarborough, *Haiti-Dance*, p. 7.

80 "Haitians Build a Big Exposition along Avenue Harry S. Truman in a Drive to Win Tourists and Influence International Trade," *U.S. News and World Report*, 17 March 1950, p. 38.

81 Destiné explains, "Sometimes when they are possessed they do fantastic things that they cannot repeat because they don't control themselves. So I am there, like a camera, watching. When I go home I start to practice them right away and they always come back, sooner or later."

82 See Vèvè A. Clark, *Fieldhands to Stagehands in Haiti: The Measure of Tradition in Haitian Popular Theatre* (Ph.D. diss., University of California, Berkeley, 1983); Wilcken, *Music Folklore among Haitians in New York*; and Joan Hamby Burroughs, *Haitian Ceremonial Dance on the Concert Stage: The Contextual Transference and Transformation of Yanvalou* (Ph.D. diss., New York University, 1995), for further discussion of the history, process, and implications of staging Vodou ritual forms.

83 Destiné, interview, 21 January 1992.

84 Edith Efron wrote of the foreign appreciation that was building for the national troupe at this time: "The variety and charm of these folk arts were such that Haitian folklore was the unquestioned triumph of the Exposition, winning international plaudits, publicity . . . and producing foreign engagements for Destiné, the native dancers and drummers" ("The 'New Movement' in Haiti," p. 18).

85 Alan Bruce Goldberg, *Commercial Folklore and Voodoo in Haiti: International Tourism and the Sale of Culture* (Ph.D. diss., Indiana University, 1981), p. 144.

86 Trouillot, *Haiti: State against Nation*, pp. 140–41.

87 James Ferguson, *Papa Doc, Baby Doc: Haiti and the Duvaliers* (Oxford: Basil Blackwell, 1987), p. 35.

88 Plummer, *Haiti and the United States*, p. 131

89 Herbert Gold, *Best Nightmare on Earth: A Life in Haiti* (New York: Touchstone, 1991), p. 32.

90 Goldberg, *Commercial Folklore and Voodoo in Haiti*, p. 144.

91 Yarborough, *Haiti-Dance*, p. 3.

92 Ibid.

93 Wilcken, *Music Folklore among Haitians in New York*, p. 158.

94 Métraux, *Voodoo in Haiti*, pp. 56–57.

95 Paul, *Panorama du folklore Haïtien*, p. 3.

96 Given that Jean-Léon Destiné had recruited dancers from every Haitian department to create Haiti's national troupe, Honorat's inclination to conduct at least part of his research at these displays is understandable: in comparison, the demonstrations at the ethnological museum were less "representative"—most of the dancers assembled from communities just outside the capital.

97 Honorat, *Les danses folkloriques haïtiennes*, p. 10.

98 Ibid.

99 Ibid.

100 Paul, *Panorama du folklore Haïtien*, p. 4.

101 Métraux, *Voodoo in Haiti*, pp. 56–57.

102 Efron, "The 'New Movement' in Haiti," p. 28.

103 Emmanuel C. Paul, "Folklore et Education," *Bulletin du Bureau d'Ethnologie*, ser. 2, no. 13 (1956), p. 30.

104 "Here lies the root of our postcolonial misery: not in our inability to think out new forms of the modern community but in our surrender to the old forms of the modern state" (Chatterjee, *The Nation and Its Fragments*, p. 11).

NOTES ON CONTRIBUTORS

ANN COOPER ALBRIGHT is both a performer and feminist scholar. Currently associate professor in the dance and theater program at Oberlin College, she teaches a variety of dance, performance studies, and women's studies courses which seek to engage students in both the practice and theory of the body. She received a 1993 Ohio Arts Council Individual Artist Award in Dance Criticism, and is currently writing a book entitled *Choreographing Difference: The Body and Identity in Contemporary Dance.* Albright holds a B.A. in philosophy from Bryn Mawr College, an M.F.A. in dance from Temple University, and a Ph.D. in performance studies from New York University.

EVAN ALDERSON is Dean of the Faculty of Arts at Simon Fraser University in British Columbia, where he also teaches interdisciplinary art history and theory in the School for the Contemporary Arts. He has published and presented numerous essays on dance, with a focus on theoretical approaches to performance and reception. He holds a Ph.D. from the University of California–Berkeley.

NORMAN BRYSON is Professor of Fine Arts at Harvard University and author and editor of numerous books, including *Vision and Painting: The Logic of the Gaze* (1986), and *Looking at the Overlooked: Four Essays on Still Life Painting* (1990). He is also the editor, with Michael Ann Holly and Keith Moxey, of two collections: *Visual Theory: Painting and Interpretation* (1990) and *Visual Culture: Images and Interpretations* (1994).

CYNTHIA JEAN COHEN BULL was Associate Professor of Dance at Wesleyan University, where she taught the cultural and historical study of dance, dance composition, improvisation, and technique. A dancer and a scholar, she held a Ph.D. in cultural anthropology from Columbia University. Her book, *Sharing the Dance: Contact Improvisation and American Culture* (1990) is in its second printing, and her articles have appeared in *The Drama Review*, *Women and Performance*, *Blurring Genres (Studies in Cultural Practice)*, and in a number of anthologies of writings about dance. At the time of her death in 1996, she was collaborating with Richard Bull and others on a book about choreography and improvisation. Most of her previous works have appeared under the name Cynthia Novack. Her untimely death has robbed the dance world of one of its leading dancer/scholars.

ANN DALY is Associate Professor of Dance History/Criticism at the University of Texas at Austin. She has written on dance, gender, and culture for journals and anthologies including *The Drama Review*, *American Studies*, *Ballett International*, *Dance Research Journal*, *High Performance*, *Women and Performance*, *DanceView*, and *Gender in Performance* (1992). Daly is contributing editor and co-editor of book reviews for *The Drama Review.* Her book *"Done into Dance": Isadora Duncan in America* was published in 1995.

JANE C. DESMOND is Associate Professor of American Studies and Women's Studies at the University of Iowa and a member of the graduate faculty. Formerly on the dance faculties of Cornell University and Duke University, she has worked as a professional modern dancer and choreographer, and in film. She is the co-producer of the award-winning PBS film *Chuck Davis: Dancing through West Africa* and the co-designer of movement for Volker Schlondorff's film *The Handmaid's Tale.* Her articles on visual representation and bodily display in dance, experimental film, and popular culture have appeared in *Cultural Studies*, *Signs*, and *Cultural Critique*, among others. Her book *Physical Evidence: Bodies / Identity / Performance* is under contract with the University of Chicago Press. She holds a Ph.D. in American studies from Yale University.

SUSAN LEIGH FOSTER is Professor of Dance and Chair of the Dance Department at the University of California–Riverside, which has recently instituted the first Ph.D. program in the United States in dance history and theory. She is the author of numerous articles and of *Reading Dancing: Bodies and Subjects in Contemporary American Dance* (1986). She is the editor of *Choreographing History* (1995), among other works. As a performer and choreographer she has toured her own work throughout the United States and Europe. She holds a Ph.D. from the History of Consciousness Program at the University of California–Santa Cruz.

MARK FRANKO is Associate Professor of Dance and Performance Studies at the University of California at Santa Cruz and was recently a scholar in residence at the Getty Center for the History of Art and the Humanities. He is author of *Dancing Modernism / Performing Politics* (1995), *Dance as Text: Ideologies of the Baroque Body* (1993), and *The Dancing Body in Renaissance Choreography* (1986), as well as of articles that have appeared in *Res*, *Discourse*, *Degres*, *Theatre Journal*, *The Drama Review*, *PMLA*, and elsewhere. He is also a dancer/choreographer and founder of the company Novantiqua, which has appeared in the United States and Europe since 1985. His current scholarly work focuses on the performance of radicalism in the 1930s.

MARIANNE GOLDBERG is a scholar, choreographer, and performer based in New York City. She is a contributing editor to *Women and Performance: A Journal of Feminist Theory* and editor of a special issue of that journal, "The Body as Discourse" (vol. 3, no. 2.6, 1987–88). Her work on dance, gender, and visual display has appeared in journals and art magazines. She holds a Ph.D. in performance studies from New York University.

BRENDA DIXON GOTTSCHILD is Professor of Dance at Temple University and teaches performance history, theory, and criticism. She is the Philadelphia critic for *Dancemagazine* and has written articles for *The Drama Review*, *Dance Research Journal*, *Design for Arts in Education*, and *The Black American Literature Forum*, as well as dance, film, and book reviews for numerous other publications. She is co-author of the third and most recent edition of *The History of Dance in Art and Education* (1991) and contributed the final chapter on contemporary dance for the revised edition of *Black Dance from 1619 to Today* (1988). She is the author of *Digging the Africanist Presence in American Performance: Dance and Other Contexts* (1996). Gottschild holds a Ph.D. in performance studies from New York University.

AMY KORITZ is Associate Professor of English at Tulane University. She writes about dramatic literature, dance, and theater, and has published articles on Yeats, T. S. Eliot, Oscar Wilde, and the London Music Hall. She is the author of *Gendering Bodies / Performing Art: Dance and Literature in Early Twentieth Century British Culture* (1995).

SUSAN KOZEL received a Ph.D. in philosophy from the University of Essex and holds a Foundation Lectureship at the Department of Dance Studies, University of Surrey, England. Her research focuses on phenomenology, French feminism, and new technologies. Her articles and performances include "Choreographing Cyberspace," *Dance Theatre Journal* (Summer 1994), and "Telematic Dreaming," a 1994 collaborative media-performance piece for the *I and Other* exhibition in Amsterdam. Her current project is called "An Aesthetics of Virtual Reality" and involves both theoretical and choreographic investigations.

SUSAN MANNING is an Associate Professor of English and Theater and an affiliate of the interdisciplinary Ph.D. program in Theater and Drama at Northwestern University. Her first book, *Ecstasy and the Demon: Feminism and Nationalism in the Dances of Mary Wigman*, won the 1994 de la Torre Bueno Prize, given annually by the Dance Perspectives Foundation to the year's most important contribution to dance studies. Her current research centers on the formation of a national identity for American dance from 1930 to 1965.

RANDY MARTIN, Associate Professor of Sociology at Pratt Institute in Brooklyn, is the author of *Performance as Political Act: The Embodied Self* (1990) and *Socialist Ensembles: Theater and State in Cuba and Nicaragua* (1994) and co-editor of *New Studies in the Politics and Culture of U.S. Communism* (1993). He is also an editor of the journals *Social Text* and *Socialism and Democracy*.

ANGELA McROBBIE is Reader in Sociology at Loughborough University in Leicester, England. She is the author of several books, including *Postmodernism and Popular Culture* (1994).

KATE RAMSEY is a doctoral candidate in anthropology at Columbia University and holds a master's degree in performance studies from New York University. She was associate director of the multidisciplinary arts collective Pepatián from 1992 to 1996. Her work has appeared in *Women and Performance: A Journal of Feminist Theory*, the *Village Voice*, and the *Movement Research Performance Journal*, among other publications. She is currently working on a study of Afro-Haitian performance and the history and politics of its representation following the U.S. occupation of Haiti.

ANNA BEATRICE SCOTT is a graduate student in the Department of Performance Studies at Northwestern University, where she holds a Ford Foundation pre-doctoral fellowship. Her research on black carnival performance has been supported by grants from the Committee for Institutional Cooperation (of the "big ten" universities) and the Center for International Studies at Northwestern. She describes her work as that of a scholar/producer/vibe groover/conceptual artist working mainly in "dance/memory" mode. Preferring guerrilla performance over the proscenium, she hopes to liberate hips and minds everywhere with the power of polyrhythm. One of her most recent performance works is an adaptation of Randall Kenan's short story "Let the Dead Bury Their Dead."

JANET WOLFF was born in Manchester, England. After working as a secretary and studying modern dance, she taught at the University of Leeds, where she was Reader in the Sociology of Culture and the founding director of the Centre for Cultural Studies. She is now resident in the United States, where she is Professor of Art History and Director of the Graduate Program in Visual and Cultural Studies at the University of Rochester. She is the author of several books, including *The Social Production of Art* (1981, 1993); *Aesthetics and the Sociology of Art* (1983, 1993); *Feminine Sentences: Essays on Women and Culture* (1990); and *Resident Alien: Feminist Cultural Criticism* (1995).

PERMISSIONS

Permission to reprint the following articles is greatly appreciated.

Alderson, Evan, "Ballet as Ideology: *Giselle*, Act II," *Dance Chronicle* 10.3 (1987), pp. 290–304.

Daly, Ann. "Classical Ballet: A Discourse of Difference," *Women and Performance: A Journal of Feminist Theory* 3, no. 2 (1987–88), pp. 57–66.

Desmond, Jane. "Embodying Difference: Issues in Dance and Cultural Studies," *Cultural Critique*, no. 26 (Winter 1993–94), pp. 33–63.

Foster, Susan Leigh. "Dancing Bodies." In *Incorporations*, ed. Jonathan Crary and Sanford Kwinter. New York: Zone Books, 1992, pp. 480–95.

Koritz, Amy. "Dancing the Orient for England: Maud Allan's 'The Vision of Salome,'" *Theatre Journal* 46 (1994), pp. 63–78.

Martin, Randy. "Dance Ethnography and the Limits of Representation," *Social Text* 33 (1992), pp. 103–23.

McRobbie, Angela. "Dance Narratives and Fantasies of Achievement." Chapter 7 in her *Feminism and Youth Culture: From "Jackie" to "Just Seventeen."* Boston: Unwin Hyman, 1991, pp. 189–219. The assistance of Macmillan Press, London, and Routledge, New York, in granting reprint rights is appreciated.

Ramsey, Kate. Portions of "Vodou, Nationalism, and Performance: The Staging of Folklore in Mid-Twentieth-Century Haiti" previously appeared in *Women and Performance: A Journal of Feminist Theory* 14–15 (1995), pp. 187–216.

Wolff, Janet. "Reinstating Corporeality: Feminism and Body Politics." Chapter 8 of her *Feminine Sentences: Essays on Women and Culture.* Berkeley: University of California Press, 1990, pp. 120–41.

INDEX

Library of Congress Cataloging-in-Publication Data

Meaning in motion : new cultural studies of dance / edited by Jane C. Desmond.
p. cm. — (Post-contemporary interventions)
Includes index.
ISBN 0-8223-1936-5 (cloth : alk. paper). — ISBN 0-8223-1942-X (alk. paper)
1. Dance—Sociological aspects. 2. Dance—Anthropological aspects. 3. Dance—theoretical and cultural aspects. 4. Human beings—Attitude and movement. 5. Human locomotion.
I. Desmond, Jane. II. Series.
GV1588.6.M43 1997
306.4'84—dc20 96-43776 CIP